D0889840

Suicide
and the
Unconscious

Suicide
and the
Unconscious

Edited by

Antoon A. Leenaars, Ph.D., C. Psych.

and

David Lester, Ph.D.

JASON ARONSON INC.
Northvale, New Jersey
London

This book is set in 10-point Baskerville by TechType of Upper Saddle River, New Jersey, and printed and bound by Book-mart of North Bergen, New Jersey.

Chapter 16 was originally published in *Specialized Techniques for Specific Clinical Problems in Psychotherapy*, edited by T. B. Karasu and L. Bellak, copyright © 1980 by the editors and reprinted in softcover in 1994 by Jason Aronson Inc.

10 9 8 7 6 5 4 3 2 1

Library of Congress Cataloging-in-Publication Data

Suicide and the unconscious / edited by Antoon Leenaars and David
    Lester.
        p.   cm.
    Includes bibliographical references and index.
    ISBN 1-56821-724-2 (alk. paper)
    1. Suicidal behavior—Psychological aspects.   2. Subconsciousness.
I. Leenaars, Antoon A., 1951-   .   II. Lester, David, 1942-   .
    [DNLM: 1. Suicide—psychology.   2. Unconscious (Psychology).
3. Psychotherapy.   HV 6545 S94848 1996]
RC569.S9335   1996
616.85'8445'0019—dc20
DNLM/DLC
for Library of Congress   95-30948

Manufactured in the United States of America. Jason Aronson Inc. offers books and cassettes. For information and catalog write to Jason Aronson Inc., 230 Livingston Street, Northvale, New Jersey 07647.

To Susanne Wenckstern
and
Bijou Yang

CONTENTS

PREFACE

The unconscious is an important concept in understanding the human mind because it helps explain a wide range of phenomena, from dreams to slips of the tongue, to the writing of suicide notes.

Following earlier thinkers, Freud realized that, for the pain of many of his patients, there were no physical determinants and no conscious reasons. The person, for example, suffering from hysterical blindness had not decided to be blind. Freud's patients could describe essential, conscious details about the blindness, but they were unaware of critical aspects.

Thus, Freud in *The Unconscious* (1915) wrote:

> The assumption of the existence of something mental that is unconscious is necessary and legitimate. It is necessary because the data of conscious have a very large number of gaps in them; both in healthy and in sick people, psychical acts often occur which can be explained only be presupposing other acts, of which, nevertheless, consciousness affords no evidence. At any given moment consciousness includes only a small content, so that the greater part of what we call conscious knowledge must be for very considerable periods of time, in a state of latency, that is to say, of being psychically unconscious. The assumption of an unconscious is, moreover, a perfectly legitimate one, inasmuch as postulating it, we are not departing a single step from our customary and generally accepted mode of thinking. [p. 166]

What one knows about one's behavior provides only a fragmentary aspect of the total of the human mind. To understand human acts, including suicide, one must be conversant with the concept of the unconscious. Suicidology would be overly barren without it. Suicidologists, we believe, can learn much about suicide by focusing on both conscious and unconscious processes of the suicidal mind.

Today there is a wealth of experience in the study of suicide from many diverse perspectives, including anthropology, criminology, epidemiology, medicine, psychiatry, psychology, and sociology. Yet, the research and theory have failed to provide us with an adequate understanding of each particular suicide, and statistical rarity of suicide makes simple explanations insufficient. Why, for example, did George Eastman, the founder of the Eastman-Kodak Company, or Marilyn Monroe, or Sigmund Freud choose to commit suicide? Freud was indeed suffering from the advanced stages of cancer when he asked his personal physician to inject him with a lethal dose of morphine. However, the vast majority of cancer patients choose to die from their cancer and do not commit suicide. Findings from epidemiological studies (suicide is more common in patients with cancer) or psychiatric studies (suicide is more common in depressed persons) fail to pinpoint the reasons for this particular suicide. It is here that the concept of the unconscious, rarely studied empirically, is not only legitimate but necessary.

This is why (consciously) we decided to produce this book—to further our understanding of the suicidal person as a unique individual (an idiographic approach) rather than only as an example of a broader general phenomenon (the nomothetic approach). Both approaches are embraced by the chapters in this volume, and it is likely that both approaches, even with the unconscious, will be needed to explicate why individuals kill themselves.

The chapters in this book come from experts in the field of suicidology, from a variety of countries, and with a variety of perspectives. We have asked psychotherapists and researchers to reflect on the role of the unconscious, many of whom have addressed the role of the unconscious, only in passing or not at all.

This book represents the breadth of knowledge about suicide, conscious and unconscious. The significance is not only that it represents the first synthesis of the topic in the literature since Freud's own writings, but also that it reviews the achievements in the area of suicide and the unconscious to date. We report this knowledge and define problems and methods for future study in this area of suicidology. In this sense, we aspire to follow the processes of science.

Antoon Leenaars and David Lester

REFERENCE

Freud, S. (1915). The unconscious. *Standard Edition* 14:15–215.

CONTRIBUTORS

Frank Auld, Ph.D., is professor emeritus of psychology at the University of Windsor, Windsor, Ontario, Canada. He is co-author of three books, *Steps in Psychotherapy, Scoring Human Motives*, and *Resolution of Inner Conflict: An Introduction to Psychoanalytic Therapy*. He is active in promoting the research-clinical model for clinical psychology and continues in private practice.

John Benjafield, Ph.D., is professor of psychology at Brock University, St. Catharines, Ontario, Canada, and a fellow of both the Canadian Psychological Association and the American Psychological Society. In addition to publishing numerous articles in a variety of subject areas, he has recently authored three books: *Cognition, Thinking Critically about Research Methods*, and *History of Psychology*.

Douglas Berger, M.D., is an assistant professor of psychiatry at Albert Einstein Medical College, Bronx, New York, and a visiting researcher at the Tokyo Institute of Psychiatry, Tokyo, Japan. He is currently studying suicide in Japan.

Edward A. Connors, Ph.D., C. Psych., is a consulting psychologist and is located at the Rama Health Centre in Rama, Ontario, Canada. He is vice president of the Canadian Association for Suicide Prevention and he consults with Aboriginal organizations throughout Canada. He is of Mohawk and Irish ancestry and is a band member of Kahnawake First Nation. Dr. Connors is active in the prevention of suicide with Aboriginal people on Turtle Island.

Elmar Etzersdorfer, M.D., is a psychiatrist at the Universitatsklinik für Tiefenpsychologie und Psychotherapie at the University of Vienna and in private practice, Vienna, Austria. He is secretary of the Austrian Association of Suicide Prevention and is active in epidemiological and psychodynamic studies of suicide.

James R. Eyman, Ph.D., is a licensed psychologist in private practice in Topeka, Kansas. His numerous publications are in the area of suicide, psychological testing, psychotherapy, and hospital treatment. He is currently a consultant to the Menninger Clinic, Topeka, Kansas, and a faculty member of the Karl Menninger School of Psychiatry and Mental Health Sciences. He has been active in the study of transference and countertransference when treating suicidal patients.

Benigna Gerisch, M.A., is a psychotherapist and researcher at the Centre for Therapy and Research of Suicidal Behavior, University Hospital of Hamburg, Eppendorf, Germany. She practices crisis intervention and psychodynamic short-term therapy. Dr. Gerisch has published on the gender differences in suicidal behavior and has been active in addressing gender issues in the prevention of suicide.

Herbert Hendin, M.D., is professor of psychiatry at New York Medical College, New York. He is executive director of the American Suicide Foundation and was its first president. His books include *Suicide and Scandinavia, Black Suicide, The Age of Sensation, Wounds of War*, and *Suicide in America*. Dr. Hendin has recently been active in the study of assisted suicide and euthanasia in America.

David A. Jobes, Ph.D., is associate professor of psychology at Catholic University of America in Washington, D.C. He is treasurer of the American Association of Suicidology. He has published numerous papers in clinical suicidology, is co-author of *Adolescent Suicide: Assessment and Intervention*, and is co-editor of *Youth Suicide: Issues, Assessment, and Intervention*. Dr. Jobes has recently been active in examining the implications for psychotherapists of suicide in their patients.

Edward A. Johnson, Ph.D., C. Psych., is assistant professor of psychology at the University of Manitoba, Winnipeg, Manitoba, Canada. His research examines the influence of nonconscious components of self-representation on adjustment.

Mary Pat Karmel, M.A., is currently working on her Ph.D. in clinical psychology at Illinois Institute of Technology, Chicago, Illinois. Her research and interests are in clinical suicidology.

Michael J. Kral, Ph.D., C. Psych., is assistant professor of psychology at the University of Windsor, Windsor, Ontario, Canada, and adjunct professor in the Department of Psychology, Lakehead University, Thunder Bay, Ontario. He is a past vice president of the Canadian Association for Suicide Prevention, is on the board of directors of the American Association of Suicidology, and is co-editing a forthcoming book, *Suicide in Canada*.

Eric Kulick, M.D., is a psychoanalyst and psychiatrist in private practice in Prairie Village, Kansas. He is a faculty member of the Topeka Institute for Psychoanalysis, National Institute for the Psychotherapies, and the Colorado Center for Psychoanalytic Studies, and a former staff member of the Menninger Clinic, Topeka, Kansas.

Antoon A. Leenaars, Ph.D., C. Psych., is in private practice in Windsor, Ontario, Canada, and a faculty member of the Faculty of Social Sciences, Department of Clinical and Health Psychology, University of Leiden, the Netherlands. He is the first past president of the Canadian Association for Suicide Prevention, and president of the American Association of Suicidology. Dr. Leenaars is editor in chief of *Archives of Suicide Research*, the official journal of the International Academy for Suicide Research and is author/editor/co-editor of numerous books including *Suicidology: Essays in Honor of Edwin Shneidman* and *Treatment of Suicidal People*.

David Lester, Ph.D., is executive director of the Center for the Study of Suicide in Blackwood, New Jersey. He is a past president of the International Association for Suicide Prevention. Dr. Lester is a prolific researcher and is author of the reference book *Why People Kill Themselves* (now in its third edition). He has recently completed studies on gun control, serial murder, and homicide-suicide. His most recent book in suicidology is *Women and Suicidal Behavior*.

Charles N. Lewis, Ph.D., is a psychologist at the Edith Nourse Rogers Memorial Veterans Hospital, Bedford, Massachusetts. He sees suicidal patients in psychotherapy, and he has published numerous articles on the assessment of unconscious influences revealed in psychological testing, art works, and during the ongoing course of therapy. He has also published studies in homicide.

Brenda McLister, Ph.D., C. Psych., is a psychologist at the Grey-Bruce Regional Health Centre, Owen Sound, Ontario, Canada. Her Ph.D.

dissertation involved the analysis of unconscious processes in suicide notes.

Joseph Richman, Ph.D., is in private practice in New York City, and is professor emeritus at Albert Einstein College of Medicine, Bronx, New York. He is a prominent scholar in gerontological suicidology and the author of *Family Therapy for Suicidal People* and *Preventing Elderly Suicide: Overcoming Personal Bias, Professional Neglect and Social Bias*. He has been active in the discussion of assisted suicide and euthanasia.

Edwin S. Shneidman, Ph.D., is professor of thanatology emeritus at the University of California at Los Angeles School of Medicine. In the 1950s he was a cofounder and codirector of the Los Angeles Suicide Prevention Center and was the founder, in 1968, and the first past president of the American Association of Suicidology. He is the author of numerous books, including *Definition of Suicide*, *Suicide as Psychache*, and *The Suicidal Mind*.

Gernot Sonneck, M.D., is professor and head of the Institute of Medical Psychology at the University of Vienna and medical head of the crisis intervention center, Vienna, Austria. He is past general secretary of the International Association for Suicide Prevention and, with the close collaboration of Dr. Erwin Ringel, has published numerous papers on the suicide of schizophrenic patients, the presuicidal syndrome, and vital instability.

Yoshitomo Takahashi, M.D., is vice-councillor of research, Department of Psychopathology, Tokyo Institute of Psychiatry, Tokyo, Japan. Between 1987 and 1988, he was given an opportunity by the Fulbright Commission to study suicidology under Professor Edwin Shneidman at the University of California at Los Angeles. In October 1994, he organized and chaired the first national conference of suicide in Japan, hosted by the Tokyo Institute of Psychiatry. He has published numerous papers on cultural aspects of suicide in Japan.

Susanne Wenckstern, M.A., C. Psych. Assoc., is a psychological associate at the Windsor Board of Education, Windsor, Ontario, Canada. She is secretary of the Canadian Association for Suicide Prevention, co-editor of *Suicide Prevention in Schools*, and is co-editing a book, *Suicide in Canada*.

Part I
A HISTORICAL
INTRODUCTION

Although suicide is a multidimensional malaise, the psychological dimensions of suicide, to use an arboreal image, form the trunk of suicide. At the core of every conscious decision to end one's life are causes and motivations rooted in the personal history of the individual. Some of these are accessible to that individual and form the basis of his or her conscious decision. Yet, there are others of which the individual remains unaware or only partially aware; these are often the more powerful processes. Part I examines the various meanings of the word *unconscious*, and illustrates that it is very difficult to give a precise definition to these powerful unconscious causes.

1: THE UNCONSCIOUS: A HISTORICAL VIEW

John Benjafield

Rather than attempt to summarize material that is reviewed in histories of the concept of the unconscious (e.g., Ellenberger 1970), I base my approach on an analysis of the various meanings of the word *unconscious*. It is very difficult to give a precise definition of *unconscious* because it has meant many different things to different people at different times. I will examine the history of the meaning of *unconscious* in the way that Natsoulas (1978) analyzed the concept of *consciousness* — using the *Oxford English Dictionary* (OED) as a guide to the various meanings.

The *Oxford English Dictionary* is organized historically, with each entry tracing the historical development of the various senses of a word. In the entry for *unconscious* the OED provides four basic senses of the word:

1. "Not conscious or knowing within oneself; unaware, regardless, heedless."
2. "Not characterized by, or endowed with, the faculty or presence of consciousness."
3. "Not realized or known as existing in oneself."
4. "Not attended by, or present to, consciousness; performed . . . without conscious action."

At first these various senses of the word may seem very similar, and indeed they do shade into one another. However, in what follows we will see that the various ways in which *unconscious* has been used involve very different psychological assumptions that have far-reaching consequences for both theory and practice.

MEANING 1

Not conscious or knowing within oneself; unaware, regardless, heedless.

The simplest use of *unconscious* is to refer to those beings that lack conscious-ness entirely. Thus, it might be supposed that inanimate matter is totally devoid of consciousness. However, drawing the line between those things that are conscious and those things that are not conscious (i.e., *unconscious*) has never been easy. A more interesting way of using the word *unconscious* is to refer to beings that are capable of consciousness, but who are not aware of some particular event or class of events. A good example of this sense of the word is the quotation, given by the OED, describing an "unconscious model, i.e., one taken unawares with a detective camera." Another illustration from the OED is the case of animals who "never having been disturbed, . . . were unconscious of danger." This meaning of *unconscious*, while covering a great many cases, may appear to be psychologically uninteresting, because it involves no activity on the part of the subject. However, a moment's reflection demonstrates the psychological importance of this category. People can be enormously influenced by events of which they not only are not aware, but cannot be aware. In the preceding examples, the subject does not know, and cannot know, about something that may affect him or her profoundly. Psychologists have not considered this kind of unconsciousness in any detail, because it refers to events that leave no psychological trace in the person, but that may still have serious consequences for them. Notice that this form of unconsciousness is more or less impervious to psychological investigation, because patients cannot inform us in any way about some of the events that may profoundly influence their lives. No form of interrogation, however subtle, will reveal these particular events to the investigator. It is always wise to remember that many things happen that we cannot know about, and that what we don't know can hurt us.

MEANING 2

Not characterized by, or endowed with, the faculty or presence of conscious-ness.

This sense of *unconscious* is more complex, and closer to the way in which psychologists have traditionally used the word. Notice the negative forms of all the definitions of *unconscious*. Unconsciousness is typically regarded as something we are not. The OED quotes William James (1890, I, p. 199) as he refers to "sleep, fainting, coma, epilepsy, and other 'unconscious' conditions." "Temporarily devoid of consciousness" is an important variant of this sense of the word. According to this reading of the word's meaning, we may be unconscious for a while, but return to consciousness later, as in some of the cases described by James. No doubt such lapses of consciousness have been of interest to psychologists, as when, for example, they explore the psychological consequences of loss of consciousness due to head injury. However, this particular sense of the word has never excited the curiosity of psychologists as much as the following, which the OED lists as another variant of the second sense of the word. However, this meaning is so important to psychologists as to almost merit a category of its own.

MEANING 2A

Applied to mental or psychic processes of which a person is not aware but which have a powerful effect on his [or her] attitudes and behavior, . . . processes activated by desires, fears, or memories which are unacceptable to the conscious mind and so repressed; also designating that part of the mind or psyche in which such processes operate.

The OED labels this meaning as peculiarly psychological, and associates it specifically with "Freud's psychoanalytic theory." To illustrate this meaning of the word, the OED cites Freud (1912, p. 25): "The term unconscious, which was used in the purely descriptive sense before, now comes to imply something more. It designates not only latent ideas in general, but especially ideas with a certain dynamic character, ideas keeping apart from consciousness in spite of their intensity and activity." This quotation is from a paper Freud wrote in English for the Society for Psychical Research, in which he introduces this particular meaning of *unconscious* because it seems to him to be required by the phenomena of hypnosis, in particular posthypnotic suggestion. Freud described one case as follows:

While he was in a hypnotic state, under the influence of a physician, he was ordered to execute a certain action at a certain fixed moment after his awakening, say half an hour later. He awakes, and seems fully conscious and in his ordinary condition; he has no recollection of his hypnotic state, and yet at the pre-arranged moment there rushes into his mind the impulse to do such and such a thing, and he does it consciously, though not knowing why. [p. 23]

In fact, there is an intimate relationship between Freud's meaning of *unconscious* and the history of hypnosis:

A widely held oversimplification of the history of hypnotism has been that the concept of "animal magnetism," a quasi-electrical fluid responsible for certain interesting phenomena, was displaced in the second half of the nineteenth century by the concept of "hypnosis," which was in turn closely linked to newly emerging notions about the unconscious mind. But in fact ideas about the unconscious mind, or dissociated or relatively independent streams of consciousness, initially emerged in the context of animal magnetism . . . and were well advanced long before hypnotists took them over. [Gauld 1992, p. 159]

This quotation treats the unconscious mind and dissociated streams of consciousness as equivalent, but Freud (1912) was clear about the fact that this is not what he meant by the term. He argued that "we have no right to extend the meaning of this word so as to make it include a consciousness of which its owner is himself not aware" (pp. 25–26), and ridiculed the idea of an "unconscious conscious," presumably because it was an oxymoron. Nevertheless, it has not always been easy to disentangle "hidden streams of consciousness" (Gauld 1992, p. 395) from what is meant by the unconscious.

There was yet another meaning of *unconscious* from which Freud (1912) distanced himself. He argued that his conception of the unconscious differed from the notion that "every latent idea was so because it was weak and that it grew conscious as soon as it became strong" (p. 25). Latent ideas that present themselves to consciousness as they gain strength were to be called preconscious to distinguish them from truly unconscious ideas.

Freud (1920) regarded suicide as the outcome of an "unconscious death-wish" to punish someone else: "Probably no one finds the mental energy required to kill himself unless, in the first place, he is in doing this at the same time killing an object with whom he has identified himself, and in the second place, is turning against himself a death-wish which had been directed against someone else" (p. 220).

Freud's usage of *unconscious* was in many ways unique, and to be distinguished from one of the other psychological meanings of *unconscious* that is usually traced back to Herbart (1891), whose theory of the unconscious was intimately associated with the concept of a threshold. Events below the threshold of consciousness were "unconscious," and, under the right circumstances, could become conscious. Herbart's usage of *unconscious* is similar to the way Freud used the word *preconscious*. Although different from Freud's, Herbart's view of the unconscious is still consistent with the broader definition of *unconscious* with which we are now dealing, and is historically of sufficient importance to warrant our considering it in some detail.

Herbart's (1891) psychology rests on the assumption that all mental life is the "result of the action and interaction of elementary ideas" (Ward 1910). By elementary ideas, Herbart meant "entirely simple concepts or sensations — e.g., red, blue, sour, sweet, etc." (p. 395). Herbart suggested that ideas may be opposed to one another, and act like forces upon each other. Such inconsistent ideas will tend to reduce the intensity with which each one is experienced. For example, as I am writing this, all my thoughts tend to be connected to Herbart's psychology. Any other thoughts, such as whether the Boston Red Sox will ever win a World Series again, tend to be suppressed by my preoccupation with Herbart.

Herbart argued that one idea can never push another completely out of awareness, and ideas above the threshold of awareness never reach a state of complete balance, or equilibrium (Ward 1910). However, there are usually a great many ideas active at the same time, and Herbart suggested that two or more ideas acting together could drive another idea below the threshold of consciousness. Thus, consciousness would tend to consist of those ideas that mutually facilitate each other, while inconsistent ideas would tend to be below threshold. Any one idea may be kept outside of awareness if "the field of consciousness is occupied by a long-formed and well-consolidated 'mass' of presentations — as, e.g., one's business or garden, the theater, etc., which properly inhibit the isolated presentation if incongruent, and unite it to themselves if not" (Ward 1910, p. 337). Herbart used the term *apperceptive mass* to refer to that set of ideas that assimilates ideas consistent with it, and rejects ideas inconsistent with it. The concept of apperception originated with Leibniz (1646–1716), who used it to refer to the process whereby the mind becomes fully aware of ideas.

Herbart (1891) believed that it was a fundamental feature of ideas that they "strive against suppression, and certainly submit to no more of it than is absolutely necessary" (p. 397). This striving for expression in consciousness is the source of the emotions. "So far as it represents or conceives, the soul is called mind; so far as it feels and desires, it is called the heart. . . . The disposition of the heart, however, has its source in the mind" (p. 408). An unpleasant feeling will result if an idea is pressing to enter consciousness, but is resisted. If, however, an idea pressing for expression finds several allied ideas, and consequently a welcome in consciousness, then this process is experienced as pleasant. "Here is the source of the cheerful disposition, especially of joy in successful activity. Here belong various movements, instigated from without, which . . . favor one another as in the case of dancing and music" (p. 411). Herbart's psychology is very dynamic, with the contents of consciousness in constant flux, and ideas passing back and forth across the threshold of consciousness.

Herbart's psychology was an applied psychology that profoundly influenced nineteenth century educational practice. According to Meyer (1975), Herbart believed that

> education's primary mission is to instill in the young the values held dear by the custodians of established social order, to believe, in short, in all things that law-abiding citizens of Christendom believe in, from truth and justice to service, duty, good works, and a healthy body and mind. Not knowledge, but character and social morality, should be the end of education. [pp. 236–237]

These goals of education could be achieved through the application of Herbart's psychological theory to the pedagogical process.

One can easily imagine the Herbartian educational psychology, with its emphasis on preparing the student to apperceive only those things that "law abiding citizens of Christendom believe in," and minimizing the chance of acquiring "undesirable" ideas. To the postmodern ear, this may sound quaint, but it did provide young people with a well-organized belief system that could guide them through the hazards of everyday life. Our educational system is part of a more fluid cultural context that may lead to an easier flow of ideas back and forth across the threshold of consciousness, so that less and less remains unconscious, and more and more may become conscious. What the young person gains in flexibility s/he may lose in stability. One may wonder how much this uncertainty contributes to suicide in young people.

MEANING 3

Not realized or known as existing in oneself.

Here we have a different approach to the nature of unconsciousness, which blends together some of the former meanings of the word. Unlike the first sense of the term, this sense suggests that what is unconscious is psychologically real. However, unlike the second sense, this sense suggests that what is now unconscious may never have been conscious. Thus, the unconscious contains what has yet to become conscious. This includes unrealized potentialities of both a positive and a negative character. This sense of the unconscious sounds most like what Jung (1933) meant by the term:

> The unconscious is not a demonic monster but a thing of nature that is perfectly neutral as far as moral sense, aesthetic taste, and intellectual judgment go. It is dangerous only when our conscious attitude towards it becomes hopelessly false. And this danger grows in the measure that we practice repressions. [p. 19]

Jung has noted the ubiquitous power of the unconscious, and the interdependence of its constructive and destructive aspects: The unconscious has a double-edged potential. Hillman developed this Jungian meaning of the unconscious in relation to suicide. Becoming aware of the double-edged potential existing within oneself can be a dangerous thing:

> As individuality grows so does the possibility of suicide. . . . Where man is law unto himself, responsible to himself for his own actions (as in the culture of cities, in the unloved child, in Protestant areas, in creative people), the choice of death becomes a more frequent alternative. In this choice of death, of course, the opposite lies concealed. Until we can choose death, we cannot choose life. Until we can say no to life, we have not really said yes to it. . . . To continue life knowing what a horror one is, takes indeed courage. And not a few suicides may arise from an overwhelming experience of one's own evil, an insight coming more readily to the creatively gifted, the psychologically sensitive and the schizoid. [p. 64]

MEANING 4

Not attended by, or present to, consciousness; performed, employed, etc., without conscious action.

This meaning of *unconscious* was perhaps best captured by Angell (1906) in his famous presidential address to the American Psychological Association. In that address, he defined conscious as "accommodatory activity" (p. 87), and argued that "consciousness [is] substantially synonymous with adaptive reactions to novel situations," and "no real organic accommodation to the novel ever occurs, save in the form that involves consciousness" (pp. 89–90). This makes of consciousness the "primary accommodative process" (p. 101). This way of conceiving of consciousness leads directly to a conception of unconscious processes as responsible for regulating our behavior in familiar situations: "Consciousness is constantly at work building up habits out of coordinations imperfectly under control; . . . as speedily as control is gained the mental direction tends to subside and give way to a condition approximating physiological automatism" (p. 89). Although not usually associated with Angell, his distinction between controlled (conscious) and automatic (unconscious) processes has become a staple of contemporary psychology (e.g., Shiffrin and Schneider 1977).

Baumeister (1984, Baumeister et al. 1985) has drawn out some of the social implications of the distinction between controlled and automatic processing. Drawing on the work of Schlenker and Leary (1982), Baumeister discusses the ways in which self-consciousness may create problems for us in situations in which it might be better to behave unconsciously. Here is a situation of the sort Baumeister (1984, Baumeister and Steinhilber 1984) has analyzed, in which paying attention to a well-practiced skill has negative consequences.

Imagine that you are a hockey player. It is the last minute of a championship game in which your team is down by one goal. Suddenly you find yourself on a breakaway, alone in front of the goaltender. This is a situation you have practiced over and over, and you automatically make exactly the right moves to fake the goaltender out of position. The empty net opens in front of you. However, at that point you suddenly become aware of what you are doing. You realize that all you have to do is slide the puck into the net. But as you try to slip the puck along the ice, it rolls off the end of your stick, and glides past the net, harmlessly into the corner of the rink. The game ends. How could you miss such an easy chance? You feel horrible. You have let everyone down.

Such incidents illustrate in microcosm an important process whereby we may become too conscious of ourselves, with potentially devastating consequences. A process best left to unconscious regulation has become one to which we inappropriately pay attention. One might say that in such situations we are not unconscious enough. Baumeister (1991) argues that painful self-consciousness is an important component of the suicidal process. "The period before a suicide attempt is indeed one of high and unpleasant self-awareness" in which "suicidal people find themselves wanting" (pp. 97–98). We would do well to remember that a little unconsciousness can be a good thing, just as too much consciousness can be a bad thing!

CONCLUSION

When we look over the variety of possible meanings of *unconscious*, it may seem like a hopelessly tangled thicket, through which one may never find one's way. Fortunately, however, there are expert guides available, many of whom have written chapters for this volume. In the chapters that follow you will find sound advice concerning the best ways to make use of this complex but rich concept.

REFERENCES

Angell, J. R. (1906). The province of a functional psychology. In *American Psychology in Historical Perspective*, ed. E. R. Hilgard, pp. 81–104. Washington, DC: American Psychological Association, 1978.

Baumeister, R. F. (1984). Choking under pressure: self consciousness and paradoxical effects of incentives on skillful performance. *Journal of Personality and Social Psychology* 46:610–620.

Baumeister, R. F., Hamilton, J. C., and Tice, D. M. (1985). Public versus private expectation of success: confidence booster or performance pressure? *Journal of Personality and Social Psychology* 48:1447–1457.

Baumeister, R. F., and Steinhilber, A. (1984). Paradoxical effects of supportive audiences on performance under pressure: the home field disadvantage in sports championships. *Journal of Personality and Social Psychology* 47:85–93.

Ellenberger, H. F. (1970). *The Discovery of the Unconscious*. New York: Basic Books.

Freud, S. (1912). The unconscious in psychoanalysis. In *Collected Papers*, vol. 4, pp. 22–29. New York: Basic Books, 1959.

———— (1920). The psychogenesis of a case of homosexuality in a woman. In *Collected Papers*, vol. 2, pp. 202–231. New York: Basic Books, 1959.

Gauld, A. (1992). *A History of Hypnotism*. Cambridge, UK: Cambridge University Press.

Herbart, J. F. (1891). A textbook in psychology. In *The Classical Psychologists*, trans. M. K. Smith, ed. B. Rand, pp. 395–415. Gloucester, MA: Peter Smith, 1966.

Hillman, J. (1964). *Suicide and the Soul*. New York: Harper & Row.

James, W. (1890). *Principles of Psychology*. New York: Holt.

Jung, C. G. (1933). *Modern Man in Search of a Soul*. New York: Harcourt Brace.

Meyer, A. E. (1975). *Grandmasters of Educational Thought*. New York: McGraw-Hill.

Natsoulas, T. (1978). Consciousness. *American Psychologist* 33:906–914.

Schlenker, B. R., and Leary, M. R. (1982). Social anxiety and self-presentation: a conceptualization and model. *Psychological Bulletin* 92:641–669.

Shiffrin, R. M., and Schneider, W. (1977). Controlled and automatic human information processing: II. Perceptual learning, automatic attending, and a general theory. *Psychological Review* 84:155–171.

Ward, J. (1910). Herbart, Johann Friedrich. In *Encyclopaedia Britannica*, 11th ed., vol. 13, pp. 335–338. New York: Encyclopaedia Britannica Company.

Part II
THEORETICAL PERSPECTIVES
ON SUICIDE AND THE UNCONSCIOUS

Theories of psychology can help us to begin to make sense of the unconscious. They allow us to understand suicide, an act and a choice that often seems bereft of logic and sense. Understanding what is known of the unconscious is valuable and critical, not only for praxis but for knowledge itself. Although Sigmund Freud's psychoanalytic perspective on the unconscious is best known, there are several theoretical perspectives. All of these perspectives on the unconscious aim to make sense of suicide. Part II consists of four chapters: two chapters on different views of Freud's perspective; an outline of Jung's perspective, the most articulated alternative view; and an examination of a cognitive view.

2: THE PSYCHODYNAMICS OF SUICIDE*

Herbert Hendin

Patients with depression, alcoholism, and schizophrenia have been shown to have a high risk for suicide (Barraclough et al. 1974, Dorpat and Ripley 1960, Robins 1959, Robins et al. 1981); more recently panic disorder has been linked to a high frequency of attempted suicide (Weissman et al. 1989). The vast majority of patients in any one of these categories, however, are not suicidal. Nor does suicide seem to be simply a symptom of an underlying diagnostic condition that goes away if the condition responds to treatment. The current revival of interest in the psychodynamics of suicide derives in part from the increasing realization that assigning a patient a diagnosis that has a high risk for suicide is not in itself an explanation for suicide.

As a consequence, attention has focused on differentiating those factors within any diagnosis that distinguish patients who are suicidal from those who are not (Beck et al. 1985, Drake et al. 1984, 1985, Roose et al. 1983, Weissman et al. 1973), and on the lethal factors that cross traditional diagnostic boundaries. Contemporary biological research into suicide moves largely from this starting point (Brown et al. 1982, van Praag 1983) as does contemporary psychodynamic interest (Hendin 1986).

As used in contemporary psychiatry, psychodynamics deals with the quality of interpersonal relations, recurrent conflict patterns, and ultimately the meaning of actions and experiences (Malan 1976, Perry et al. 1987). Such meaning is refined by the psychosocial context in which suicide occurs, but it is also understood by observing both its affective and cognitive components.

---

*This chapter is adapted from articles in *American Journal of Psychiatry* and *International Review of Psychiatry*.

AFFECTIVE STATE

It is helpful to begin by understanding the affective (emotional) state or states in which the patient commits suicide, partly because the affective state usually clarifies and structures the cognitive (perceptual) one. Although suicide is often described imprecisely as an escape, it is usually an escape from an intolerable affective state. Hopelessness, despair, rage, and guilt are some of the emotions that have been shown to predominate in suicidal patients. The nature and intensity of these emotions help us to distinguish patients who are suicidal from those who are not (Beck et al. 1985, Hendin 1969a,b, Hendin and Haas 1991, Maltsberger 1981, Murphy et al. 1979).

Rage

Clinical study of seriously suicidal young urban African-Americans indicated that, among this population, the problems of suicide, rage, and violence were related (Baker 1989, Frederick 1984, Gibbs 1988, Hendin 1969a,b, Seiden 1970). Suicide was usually the outgrowth of a devastating struggle to deal with conscious rage and conscious murderous impulses originating in early personal exposure to violence.

One young man who eventually killed himself had been trapped as a boy in a room with his father who was engaged in a shootout with the police. The police had been called because he had been beating his wife. The father, although wounded, continued to fire with a small arsenal until he was killed. As a teenager this young man came to admire Hitler's ability to kill millions. He was arrested for violent fights and wrestled with the idea of knifing his mother and brother before attempting suicide. What he found most disturbing about his violent behavior was the loss of control that he experienced when enraged; he thought he might enjoy killing if he could do it in a cool, controlled, detached manner.

The origin of youthful rage in a violent family situation that produced identification with a parent or parental surrogate who was violent, self-destructive, or both, is typical of young African-American suicides of both sexes. What they find most disturbing is the feeling of being overwhelmed by the loss of control over angry homicidal impulses, and what they describe seems to be a fear of ego disintegration. Their concern is less with the consequences of their violence than with the feeling that they could not predict or control their impulsive rage and that it threatens their capacity to function. Suicide can be a form of control exercised by people who feel torn apart by rage and violence (Hendin 1969a,b).

The interrelation of rage, violence, and suicide is not limited to African-Americans. Individuals who have killed others have a suicide rate several hundred times greater than those who have not (Hendin 1986,

Wolfgang 1958). That rate is largely the result of murder followed quickly by suicide — more frequent among whites than among the African-American population (Wolfgang 1958). A recent review of studies of the relationship between suicide and violence estimates that about 30 percent of violent individuals have a history of self-destructive behavior, while about 10 to 20 percent of suicidal persons have a history of violent behavior (Plutchik and van Praag 1990). Psychological autopsies of young suicide victims indicated that just under one-half of them had histories of aggressive and antisocial behavior, a much higher rate than that of older age groups, while only one-quarter had histories of major depressive disorder, a much lower rate than has been found in older populations (Gould et al. 1990). With nonviolent patients as well, the open expression of hostility and rage distinguishes depressed patients who are suicidal from those who are not (Weissman et al. 1973).

Hopelessness, Despair, and Desperation

Beck and his colleagues (1985) found that the seriousness of suicidal intent correlates less with the degree of depression than with one particular aspect of depression — hopelessness about the future. They observed high suicidal intent in some patients who showed minimal depression but whose expectations for the future were also minimal.

Eighty-nine of 207 patients, hospitalized because they were contemplating suicide, rated high on a measure of hopelessness. In the subsequent five years, 14 of the 207 patients committed suicide; 13 of them were from the group of 89 who rated high on the measure of hopelessness. A variety of diagnoses were given the patients who ranked high on hopelessness, but half were diagnosed as having some form of depression.

Despair rather than *hopelessness* has been used to convey the emotional state distinguishing suicidal patients from those who are depressed but not suicidal. Despair has been described as developing from aloneness, murderous hate, and self-contempt (Maltsberger 1981) or, more generally as resulting from any state that leads to the individual's "inability to maintain or envision any human connections of significance" (Lifton 1989).

Experience, however, with patients seen a few days prior to their suicide suggests an affective state closer to *desperation* than to hopelessness or despair. Many patients who feel despair or are hopeless about the future are resigned to their situation. Desperation implies not only a sense of hopelessness about change, but also that life is impossible without such change. Anxiety and urgency are an integral part of this desperation. The importance of these affective elements is confirmed by the recent study by Fawcett and his co-workers (1989) of patients with major affective disorder; they demonstrated that among those patients, anxiety is a stronger predictor of short-term risk for suicide than is hopelessness.

Guilt

In a recently completed study of suicide and posttraumatic stress disorder (PTSD) in Vietnam veterans (Hendin and Haas 1991), of 100 veterans with PTSD, 19 had made suicide attempts and 15 more were preoccupied with suicide. Guilt over actions committed in combat, usually involving the killing of civilians, and most often while feeling out of control, was the variable best able to explain their suicidal behavior. Although these actions took place on average fifteen years before these men were seen in our study, their guilt persisted and fueled their suicide attempts and actual suicides. Their nightmares were often filled with images in which they were punished in ways that reflected their actions in Vietnam.

In the vast majority of suicidal cases, the actions committed understandably led to post-service guilt, self-hatred, and nightmares of punishment.

Typical was the experience of a forward artillery spotter who, after seeing friends killed in combat, called for artillery fire on a village he knew to be friendly. Through his binoculars he saw an old woman with betel-nut stains on her teeth blown up by a shell while running toward the fire as though trying to stop it. At the time he laughed, but later he could not believe he had become so callous. In his most repetitive nightmare, he is captured, tied to a pole and spat on by the villagers, led by the old woman with the stained teeth.

In a few cases, however, the combat actions were equivocal and some were combined with guilt over surviving when close friends had not.

One veteran shot and killed a woman who advanced toward his patrol and did not heed his order to stop. She turned out to be wired with explosives, but the veteran ruminated over whether he could have stopped her by firing a warning shot or wounding her in the legs. Subsequently, his closest friend, who had extended his tour in Vietnam so they could come home together, was killed. The veteran's suicide attempts were related to dreams that linked his guilt over both deaths.

When things go well at work or in personal relations, such veterans tended to feel they have no right to be enjoying what their friends who had died could never enjoy, and they act in ways that sabotage their success.

The guilt seen in Vietnam veterans was usually conscious, but at times was only suspected from their behavior and became evident when they discussed their dreams, fantasies, and associations. Consciously expressed, excessive or inappropriate guilt is considered to be one of the cardinal symptoms of a major depressive episode. Such guilt may be elaborated in a delusional way, focused on ideas of sin or worthlessness. Depressed patients who are delusional have been shown to be far more likely to kill themselves than those who are not; yet the delusions were not found to be the outgrowth of a greater degree of depression (Roose et al. 1983).

COGNITION AND MEANING

The cognitive component of the meaning of suicide helps clarify the affective aspects of the suicidal act. For example, the guilt of veterans over their combat actions complements their view of suicide as a punishment they deserve. Kernberg (1987) aptly points out that in clinical practice the question is not the patient's general feeling of hopelessness, but what the patient is feeling hopeless about.

Cognition generally refers to conscious ideation, while *meaning* includes both conscious and unconscious affects and perceptions. The meanings of suicide can be usefully organized around the conscious and unconscious meanings given to death by the suicidal patient.

Evidence to determine any such meaning should not be limited to information the patient volunteers or to his responses to questions. The meanings of suicide are often unconscious, and then best elicited by free associations and dreams. Serious suicide attempts usually stimulate dreams: two-thirds of the suicidal patients in a study by Raphling (1970) remembered dreams from the period prior to their attempt; patients who do not recall such dreams will often do so under hypnosis (Hendin 1963). Those who have studied the dreams of patients shortly before or after suicide attempts have found that the dreams were invariably helpful in understanding their motive for suicide (Gutheil 1940, Hendin 1963, Litman 1980, Raphling 1970). Eliciting the dreams of suicidal patients is an important part of a psychiatric evaluation, much as it is in cases of PTSD. The dreams of acutely suicidal patients are similar to those of patients with PTSD in the minimal extent to which unconscious material is disguised (Hendin 1991).

We have learned that suicidal patients give a special meaning to death, using death in their adaptation to life. Critical is their actual or fantasized use of their own death in an effort to control others or to maintain an illusory control over their own lives.

Some of the common meanings given to death described in suicidal patients are death as reunion, death as rebirth, death as a retaliatory abandonment, death as revenge, and death as self-punishment or atonement.

REBIRTH AND REUNION

Some suicidal patients cherish fantasies of effecting a rebirth or a reunion with a lost object through suicide. Death is attractive to these patients as more than simply an escape from crises.

An intelligent woman in her twenties, well educated and successful in her work, was seen after she jumped under a train and lost both legs. Her suicide attempt was precipitated by the end of one of her many unhappy and complicated love relationships and by the vacation of her therapist, both of which she related to an earlier abandonment by her father.

When she was 9 years old, her father, whom she idealized, deserted the family, and she never again saw or heard from him. Her mother, overwhelmed, had been unable to function as head of the family. The patient had been fascinated by death and dying all through adolescence and could recall in detail the death scenes in many novels, vividly recalling the scene in *Anna Karenina* where Anna kills herself by jumping in front of a train. Her relationships with men had been painful recapitulations of the earlier rejection by her father, and one previous unhappy love affair had been followed by a suicide attempt.

She had the following dream about her suicide attempt: She was in a long, narrow tunnel and could see a light at the end of it. She walked toward the light and there she saw a man and woman standing over a manger. In her associations to the dream the tunnel suggested to her the subway from which she jumped and the way in which the train came out of the tunnel and into the lighted platform area. Moving from the darkness of the tunnel and into light brought to her mind the process of birth. The man and woman she saw as her father and mother. The child in the manger was both the Christ child and herself. (She particularly identified with the sense that death united Christ with his father.) She saw her life as set on a course in which gratification of her fantasies was only possible through her death. One can see how much she accomplished in her death fantasy. She is reborn into an intact family, is reunited with her father, and finally, she is omnipotent. For a patient with such fantasies, the thought of dying has become more tolerable (Hendin 1963).

Early in this century Ernest Jones and Carl Jung recognized the importance of rebirth and reunion fantasies in suicidal patients. Jones suggested that such fantasies had as their prototype the wish to return to the mother's womb, while Jung and his followers emphasized the unconscious need for spiritual rebirth. This dynamic was reemphasized in the 1930s by Zilboorg (1938), who wrote that "the drive towards death, always with the flag of immortality in hand, carried with it the fantasy of joining the dead or dying or being joined in death" (p. 197).

Pollack (1989), writing several decades later, emphasizes the suicide's regression to a state where there is little differentiation of self and object. The suicidal victim gives himself up to an undifferentiated blissful state of reunion. This state of narcissistic fusion or symbiotic union with a powerful figure is said to overcome the dread of death and accounts for the patient's fantasies of grandiosity and immortality.

Pollack believes that what may look like identification of the suicide with someone dead is simply apt to be "reflective of the wish to reunite with the one from whom the separation occurred" (p. 178). His view is somewhat different from that of Hendrick (1940), who described the suicide in depression as the consequence of identification with a lost object in contrast to those suicides, usually in schizoid or schizophrenic individuals, where identification with someone dead is the purpose of dying and represents fulfillment of the identification.

RETALIATORY ABANDONMENT

A college student who had been failing in school was seen following a serious suicide attempt with 60 barbiturates, which he barely survived. His attempt was precipitated by his rejection by a male friend without whom he felt life was intolerable. Although he had never mentioned to the boy his sexual interest in him, the friend apparently became alarmed at the intensity of the patient's feelings and broke off the relationship.

Shortly after his suicide attempt, the patient had a dream in which he was working for the United Nations where he had an office comprising the entire first floor of the U.N. building. He was interviewing one of his friends who was applying for a position, and was reviewing his qualifications. Finally he told his friend that he did not qualify for the job.

The patient here accomplishes the same goal in the dream and in the suicide attempt: through rejection, he gains an illusory control over an interpersonal relationship. In the dream, if there has to be a rejection, he is going to do it; similarly by committing suicide, he becomes the one who leaves and rejects (Hendin 1963).

His holding an important U.N. position and large office in his dream strongly suggest that he also experiences a feeling of omnipotent mastery through death. Suicide attempts and the possibility of suicide give some people the illusion that they have mastery over a situation through their control over their living or dying. That is probably why some of them keep the means for suicide readily available, whether or not they ever attempt to kill themselves.

REVENGE

Freud's (1917) view of suicide derived from his observation that depression was an attempt to regain through introjection a lost object that is both loved and hated. In depression, the hate originally directed toward the object becomes displaced onto the internalized representation of the object. The hated person, now identified with the self, can be destroyed by destroying the self. In Freud's formulation, suicide expressed a repressed wish to kill an ambivalently regarded lost love object, and thus it was ultimately an act of revenge.

A 44-year-old woman made a suicide attempt with over thirty sleeping pills about a year after the breakup of her marriage. The husband had been unfaithful during the twenty years they had been together and finally left to live with another woman.

While under the influence of the sleeping pills taken in her suicide attempt, she had the following dream: She saw a cap belonging to her husband's father floating on the sea and realized he had drowned. Her husband's father had been a sea captain and closely resembled her husband in being extremely domineering. She related the dream to her desire to strike back at her husband. She spoke vindictively of the problems that the children, a boy 19 and a girl 15, would cause him after her death. Her suicide attempt appeared to be the product of her impotent rage toward her husband and was an indirect attempt at revenge similar to that described by Freud (1917).

The mechanism in such cases is seen as primarily unconscious. Although the depressed Viennese patients described by Freud were not violent, hostility is often strikingly conscious when young people use suicide as an expression of revenge toward their parents. Such youngsters usually feel overwhelmed by murderous feelings toward their parents and are even fearful that they may act on them. These feelings may be conscious, as well as expressed in dreams. The suicide may be precipitated by some immediate frustration followed by an impulsive response, but there is invariably a history of a youngster who, even if still functioning seemingly well, is increasingly unable to cope with murderous rage toward his or her parents.

A middle-class girl of 15, who was doing well in school, was well liked by her many friends, and was said by her parents to have shown no evidence of problems, shot herself in the head with a gun belonging to her father after a fight with her parents over their refusal to allow her and a friend to go to an amusement park some distance from their home. Sessions with the parents after her death revealed that there were long-standing problems between the girl and her mother. After the suicide, her grandmother told the parents that the young woman had indicated her anger toward her mother in telling the grandmother a day or two before the suicide that she dreamed she had killed her mother; shortly before killing herself she told a friend that suicide would be a way of getting back at her parents (Hendin 1991).

SELF-PUNISHMENT OR ATONEMENT

In the early psychodynamic formulation of suicide as the product of unconscious hostility toward an introjected lost love object, guilt over hatred of the object was seen as underlying the need for self-punishment. In destroying himself *and* the object, the individual accomplishes atonement as well as revenge.

In a classic paper on suicide Kilpatrick (1948) wrote, "When we understand narcissism not as love of the self, but as love of the idealized image of the self, we become aware of the quantity of self-hate and alienation which must be present" (p. 19). She pointed out that the unconscious idealized self-image is often accompanied by its counterpart, a despised self-image. Contemporary object relations theory, with its emphasis on the importance of splitting as a mechanism of defense, has increasingly seen suicide as an attempt by the superego, with which the good self is identified, to eliminate the bad self.

After Bibring (1953) focused attention on depression as an independent primary affect, "the emotional correlate of a partial or complete collapse of the self-esteem of the ego, since it feels unable to live up to its aspirations" (p. 26), greater attention was paid to suicide as a form of punishment or atonement for such failure. Haim (1974) noted the "peculiarities" in the organization of the ego ideal in adolescents who are prone to suicide, describing an "archaic megalomaniacal ego ideal" with a "demand for the absolute" and "absence or inadequacy of reshaping when put to the test of reality." Mack (1981), in his description of Vivienne, an adolescent female suicide, sees her suicide largely as the result of an inability to live with an ego ideal affected by early damage and low self-esteem and the impossibility of fulfilling her mother's need to realize, through Vivienne, her own needs for perfection.

Although suicide has been mentioned as a self-inflicted punishment in Vietnam veterans guilty over actions in combat, comparable dynamics are seen in civilian life, perhaps with less frequency today than heretofore, in those people who, having been raised in fundamentalist religious families, are in anguish over their failure to fulfill moral expectations. They tend to see their drinking, fighting, or other antisocial behavior as sins, and suicide as a form of expiation. Their dreams in connection with suicide attempts often contain images of hell, fire, and brimstone (Hendin 1964). In psychotic individuals these ideas are expressed as delusions of sin.

Common in psychiatric practice today are individuals who feel they have failed to meet their own and their families' academic, vocational, and social aspirations, and fall short of matching the achievements of their siblings and peers. Their lives are filled with a sense of failure and humiliation, their dreams frequently center on "having missed the boat" (Hendin 1964), and their suicide is often an expression of self-hatred and a need for punishment.

Typical was a patient who committed suicide after he recorded this dream in his diary: "I was back at high school and saw familiar faces. I felt embarrassed and humiliated. They were going on with life. I tried to be incognito but was spotted." In a similar vein he wrote, "When I think of myself as a recovering patient, I am more patient with myself and more willing to change things. When I compare myself to my potential, I mourn" (Hendin 1991, p. 1154).

DISCUSSION

Although these dynamic themes have different significance in different patients, they are not mutually exclusive. The dependent and aggressive aspects of suicide can both be active in some patients, as Klein (1964) recognized long ago when she wrote, "In some cases the fantasies underlying suicide aim at preserving the internalized good objects and that part of the ego which is identified with good objects, and also at destroying the other part of the ego which is identified with the bad objects" (p. 296). At times the self-punishment resulting from self-hatred seems to have become an end in itself, but there is usually evidence in suicide (Asch 1980) of "a double aim of first cleansing the self, and then uniting (actually reuniting) with an omnipotent love object" (p. 52). Whether the aim is to cleanse or to rid oneself of the "bad part," purification achieved by either exorcism or self-punishment is seen as enabling the individual to hope that he can be loved by a significant object once again.

A theme that may run through the varying psychodynamic meanings of suicide is the perception of suicidal patients, experienced unconsciously and/or consciously, that they are already dead. Dreams of death, dying, coffins, and burial are frequent (Hendin 1963, Litman 1980, Raphling 1970) in suicidal individuals who experience emotional death in their attempts to bury their rage and despair. The preoccupation of some with death is often the climax of having felt emotionally dead for a lifetime (Hendin 1975a, b).

All of the psychodynamic meanings given to death by suicidal patients can be conceptualized as responses to loss, separation, or abandonment. Rebirth and reunion fantasies may be seen as attempts to undo or deny such a loss. Becoming the one who leaves is one way to avoid the feeling of having been left. Feelings of rage that are repressed, suppressed, or expressed may derive from the experience of loss. Self-punishment may express guilt at having been responsible for a loss and the fantasy of rapprochement through atonement. Even numbness or deadness and the insistence that one is already psychologically dead may reflect determination not to live without the lost object (Hendin 1986, 1987). Although suicidal patients may have in common their use of their own death to deal with their loss, the various meanings they give to their death accounts for the variety in the psychodynamics of suicide.

For most suicidal patients, a rejection of life usually includes a rejection of the parents from whom it originated (Hendin 1986, 1987, Menninger 1938). Anyone so doing is likely to feel in a deep way that he or she was abandoned first. In that sense, Freud's insight into the relationship of abandonment, loss, and suicide has perhaps the most meaning and has stood the test of time.

Life and growth inevitably mean emotional separation from parents; for the potentially suicidal, separation, loss, and death are often equated, are intolerable, and leave the individuals feeling desperately out of control of their lives. Suicide can be used to control others or to maintain the sense of control over one's own life. To obtain such control, seriously suicidal individuals often make their living conditional: "I won't live unless I can get this particular position," ". . . unless this person will care for me," and so on (Hendin 1987).

THERAPEUTIC CONSIDERATIONS

The need to use one's death to express desperation, rage, or guilt reflects, among other things, difficulty in utilizing less-extreme forms of communication. Understanding and conveying to the patient what it is that he is hoping to communicate by dying can provide crucial relief to the patient and can reduce the short-term risk of suicide.

The affective states and their accompanying death fantasies are often activated by trauma and seem in part an attempt to resolve an intolerable emotional state through use of a fantasized or inappropriate object tie. The patient's own unique psychodynamic constellation of affect, cognition, and meaning is most dramatically prominent immediately before or after a suicide attempt, during what is referred to as a suicidal crisis or episode (Mintz 1971, Pfeffer 1985). The same combination of psychodynamic factors is present in suicidal patients during the chronic phases of their illness, and is a central element of the individual's psychic life. For example, grandiose fantasies revolving around conquering or controlling death, immortality, identification with Christ, Hitler, or a U.N. dignitary are common among suicidal patients. Kohut (1971a,b) Kernberg (1985), and others have emphasized that such grandiosity usually reflects disturbances in self-esteem and identity formation occurring early in childhood. The fears of disintegration or identity diffusion that often derive from such developmental disturbances are frequent in borderline or schizophrenic patients who become suicidal, in suicidal veterans with posttraumatic stress disorder, and in enraged suicidal patients regardless of their diagnoses. Although the acute threat of disintegration remits as the suicidal crisis is resolved, the underlying identity problems remain, as does the fantasy of resolving them through suicide.

It is the patient's use of the possibility of ending his life to deal with both internal conflict and relations with other people that is unique to the suicidal patient, colors the transference and countertransference, and presents special problems in treatment.

Studies of therapeutic interactions in patients who killed themselves while in treatment find that rejection by the therapist is a precipitating factor in many of these cases. Such rejection most often results from the therapist's countertransference anger or hatred, which is often unconscious, and often a response to patients' angry criticisms or demands (Bloom 1967, Wheat 1960). The threat of the patient's death, if his demands are not met, may lead a therapist to bury awareness of his own anger, to feel coerced into obeying such demands, or conversely into reacting punitively to them. Maltsberger and Buie (1974) have pointed out that the most vulnerable therapists are those whose need to see themselves as able to save any patient renders the possible suicide of a patient narcissistically devastating. Suicidal patients understand the fear they can produce through their death threats and use it in ways that often lead to temporary control over, but eventual rejection by, their therapists as well as others.

Since the suicidal patient uses his or her possible death as a way of relating to and controlling the therapist as well as other people, the psychodynamics underlying their suicidal feelings can be seen in the transference.

One woman, seen following a serious suicide attempt, had persuaded her therapist to call her every morning at 7 A.M., threatening that otherwise she would kill herself. Her therapist's anxiety had led him to permit her to act out her fantasy of exercising power over him and over life and death in this manner. Nonetheless, his calling did not prevent an almost fatal suicide attempt.

Early recognition of the role in which the patient is attempting to cast the therapist is critical for progress in treatment.

A young man who survived shooting himself in the chest came into therapy saying he would give the therapist six months to make him feel better or else he would be dead. The first months of treatment were spent understanding his need to establish a relationship that made the therapist responsible for whether he lived or died (Hendin 1981).

Therapists may be cast in, or may be tempted to play, the role of saviors; just as often they are cast in the role of executioners (Asch 1980). They may be incorporated into patients' rebirth or reunion fantasies, and they often become the targets of those suicides motivated by revenge. The therapist of the patient, mentioned earlier, who jumped in front of a train had tried to be available to her in ways that her father was not. Afterward he realized that she had been determined to perceive him as responsible for her death. Both before and after her attempt she made an effort to see to it that her therapist would be blamed. By splitting her feelings toward her father, she could perceive her therapist as the destroying father making it easier to preserve her fantasy of salvation through reunion with her natural father, whom she could idealize as loving.

Early Experiences

Recent work has questioned the observation by Zilboorg (1936) more than a half century ago that the loss through death of a parent during the patient's childhood was a significant factor in suicide. Barraclough (1987) found parental loss in childhood to be no more frequent in his suicide sample than it was in his control group. He did find, however, that the recent death of a parent or spouse occurred significantly more frequently among the suicides.

In adolescents the factors of parental death and recent object loss tend to merge, since a parent's death is likely to have been a recent event. In any case, what Zilboorg was observing was the impact of such deaths on his patients, an impact he attributed to the patient's identification with the dead parent. It is possible that in suicidal patients, even if the frequency of parental death is not extraordinary, its impact is greater, perhaps because of such identification.

Maltsberger and Buie (1989) have provided us with a broader explanation of the suicidal patient's vulnerability to loss. They build on Kohut's (1971a,b) postulate that the experience of an empathic, nurturing mother is a prerequisite for the individual's developing soothing introjects and the ability to comfort himself in times of loss. Individuals who lack this ability tend to form relationships in which the other person is not viewed independently but is seen instead as an extension of the self. When these patients lose an object they feel a narcissistic insult that can lead to depression or anxiety over disintegration, anxiety that Kohut (1984) saw as the deepest anxiety anyone can experience. Some patients can turn to others for comfort, but Maltsberger and Buie point out that suicidal patients have difficulty in doing this. Instead, they are isolated in a paralyzing sense of aloneness — a state of vacant cold isolation accompanied by varying degrees of terror — that Maltsberger and Buie liken to the infant's experience of separation anxiety.

A developmental explanation is given by object relations theory for the self-punitive elements seen in suicide. Early intrapsychic conflicts are seen as producing a susceptibility to splitting in the patient's self-representation in times of stress. The suicide may then involve the patient's identifying with the good self and punishing the bad self (Kernberg 1970).

The question remains as to why some individuals feel that death is the only way to control their sense of fragmentation or express their need for punishment. Studies of the family relationships of suicidal youngsters may provide some clarification. Retrospective studies conducted in the 1960s and

1970s consistently found the suicidal youngsters were alienated from their families in early childhood by parental attitudes of resentment, hostility, and rejection (Dorpat et al. 1965, Greer 1964, Hendin 1975a,b, Jacobs and Teicher 1967, Sabbath 1969, Teicher and Jacobs 1966). A more recent psychological autopsy study of young suicides confirmed that significantly more frequent parental abuse or rejection had been experienced by the suicidal youngsters than by the control group.

Whether these parental responses were reactions to the child's behavior or purely the product of the parents' pathology, the recollections of suicidal youngsters repeatedly invoke parental figures who were frustrating, rejecting, or controlling. Some young people may express their distress through such reckless behavior with cars, motorcycles, or drugs that their parents are forced to acknowledge their self-destructiveness. In some cases the child becomes such a disturbance in the family that the parents indicate they wish the youngster were out of the family (Sabbath 1969).

In other families the parents seem to want the child's presence, but they do not want to be emotionally involved with the child (Hendin 1975a, b, 1982). They want the child to be there and not be there at the same time—to be under their control and to gratify their demands, but not to have an independent character or wishes. The youngster may incorporate parental expectations in a mechanical manner but they derive little pleasure or satisfaction from fulfilling them. At the same time they do not feel free to act in ways that would separate them from their parents. Such youngsters often make no emotional demands but instead become withdrawn, depressed, and quietly preoccupied with death and suicide.

This formulation is confirmed by an English study of adolescents who were treated psychoanalytically after a serious suicide attempt; it found that the suicide attempts were triggered by the adolescents' experience of failure in the attempt to separate from the mother. The failure, which was the outgrowth of a long-standing disturbed parent–child relationship, led to an intensification of maternal ties and to displacement of the experience of rejection and anger from the mother to an external object. Displacement of anger away from the mother diminished the guilt that inhibited action, permitting the anger to be expressed in suicide (Novick 1984).

Reconstructions of early family experiences of adults have severe limitations, and most of the retrospective studies of the families of suicidal youngsters are not controlled studies. Retrospective accounts cannot tell us if family pathology produced the vulnerability to suicide, or if the family problems developed in response to an already disturbed child. Although the opportunity to observe directly the families of young patients may strengthen the validity of family formulations, the patient's own response to separation may also have biological or genetic roots.

FUTURE DIRECTIONS

There is much we do not know. Recent work on the relation of panic disorder and anxiety to attempted suicide and suicide is likely to focus our attention on the role of anxiety as an important affect in suicidal patients regardless of their diagnosis (Fawcett et al. 1989, Weissman et al. 1989). Evidence suggests that the level of anxiety may distinguish borderline (Perry 1989) and schizophrenic patients (Drake et al. 1984, 1985) who are suicidal from those who are not. As indicated earlier, there is now more definitive evidence that this is true for patients with major depressive disorders (Fawcett et al. 1989).

The capacity to bear hopelessness, rage, anxiety, and other unpleasant affects without collapse or regression (Zetzel, 1970a,b) has attracted little attention from either biological or psychodynamic investigators. This should change. The capacity or incapacity to self-regulate mood states may derive from biogenetic endowment as well as from struggles over the introjection of ameliorative or destructive objects.

Although suicide often appears to be a form of affect regulation in individuals whose lives feel out of control, in some cases the dysregulation and the suicide attempt appear to be expressed in an impulsivity akin to that seen in violent behavior (Apter et al. 1990, Peterson et al. 1985). The possibility of measuring the use of particular defense mechanisms to differentiate the relative risk for suicidal or violent behavior is attracting investigators. Pfeffer and colleagues (1987) found introjection and splitting to be fundamental defenses in suicidal children, while compensation, projection, and displacement were correlated with assaultive behavior. Apter and colleagues (1990) found that repression was correlated with risk for suicide, and projection and denial were correlated with risk for violence, while denial was negatively correlated with risk for suicide. It will be interesting to see what patterns of defense mechanisms emerge in patients who are both suicidal and violent.

In the past decade, specific psychodynamic conflicts seen in suicidal patients have begun to be linked to particular diagnoses. In addition to the rage toward a lost love object seen in depression, other such linkages are conflicts over separation and abandonment in borderline personalities (Perry 1989), fear of disintegration in schizophrenics (Drake et al. 1984, 1985), guilt over combat action in veterans with PTSD (Hendin and Haas 1991), and grief over recent loss in alcoholics (Murphy et al. 1979). It would not be surprising if further evidence of such linkages were found.

Understanding what is known of the psychodynamics of suicide is valuable and critical in treating suicidal patients. There has long been concern over suicidal patients who did not receive appropriate psychotropic medication or were not hospitalized when necessary. Today an equally common concern involves suicidal patients, in or out of hospitals, who are receiving appropriate medication, but inadequate psychotherapy. The example of the patient who kills himself after his depression has lifted in response to medication serves as a reminder that more than depression is involved in suicide. The best treatment today focuses on the interactive role that diagnosis, medication, and psychotherapy play in the treatment of those who are suicidal (Dulit and Michaels 1990). If the psychotherapy of such patients is to be effective, it must be guided by a knowledge of the psychodynamics of suicide.

REFERENCES

Apter, A., Plutchik, R., Sevy, S., et al. (1989). Defense mechanisms in risk of suicide and risk of violence. *American Journal of Psychiatry* 146:1027–1031.

Apter, A., Van Praag, H. M., Plutchik, R., et al. (1990). Interrelationships among anxiety, aggression, impulsivity, and mood: a serotoninergically linked cluster? *Psychiatry Research* 32:191–199.

Asch, S. (1980). Suicide and the hidden executioner. *International Review of Psychoanalysis* 7:51–60.

Baker, F. M. (1989). Black youth suicide. Literature review with a focus on prevention. *Report of the Secretary's Task Force on Youth Suicide*, vol. 3, pp. 177–191. Washington, DC: U.S. Dept. of Health and Human Services.

Barraclough, B. (1987). *Suicide: Clinical and Epidemiological Studies*. Chichester, England: Croom Helm.

Barraclough, B., Bunch, J., Nelson, B., and Sainsbury, P. (1974). A hundred cases of suicide: clinical aspects. *British Journal of Psychiatry* 125:355–373.

Beck, A. T., Steer, R. A., Kovacs, M., and Garrison, B. (1985). Hopelessness and eventual suicide: a 10 year prospective study of patients hospitalized with suicidal ideation. *American Journal of Psychiatry* 142:559–563.

Bibring, E. (1953). The mechanisms of depressions. In *Affective disorders*, ed. P. Greenacre, pp. 13–48. New York: International Universities Press.

Bloom, V. (1967). An analysis of suicide at a training center. *American Journal of Psychiatry* 123:918–925.

Brown, G. I., Ebert, M. H., Goyer, P. F., et al. (1982). Aggression, suicide, and serotonin: relationship to CSF amine metabolites. *American Journal of Psychiatry* 139:741–746.

Dorpat, T., Jackson, J., and Ripley, H. (1965). Broken homes and attempted and completed suicide. *Archives of General Psychiatry* 12:213–216.

Dorpat, T. L., and Ripley, H. S. (1960). A study of suicide in the Seattle area. *Comprehensive Psychiatry* 1:349–356.

Drake, R. E., Gates, C., Cotton, P., and Whitaker, A. (1984). Suicide among schizophrenics: who is at risk? *Journal of Nervous and Mental Disease* 172:613–617.

Drake, R. E., Gates, C., Whitaker, A., and Cotton, P. G. (1985). Suicide among schizophrenics: a review. *Comprehensive Psychiatry* 26:90–100.

Dulit, R. A., and Michaels, R. (1990). Psychodynamics and suicide. In *Suicide and Clinical Practice*, ed. D. Jacobs, pp. 43–53. Washington, DC: American Psychiatric Press.

Fawcett, J., Scheftner, W. A., Fogg, L., et al. (1989). Time-related predictors of suicide in major affective disorder. *American Journal of Psychiatry* 147:1189–1194.

Frederick, C. J. (1984). Suicide in young minority group persons. In *Suicide in the Young*, ed. H. S. Sudak, A. Ford, and N. Rushforth, pp. 31–44. Boston: John Wright.

Freud, S. (1917). Mourning and melancholia. In *Complete Psychological Works*, vol. 2, ed. S. Cannard, pp. 152–170. London: Hogarth Press, 1957.

Gibbs, J. T. (1988). Conceptual methodological and sociocultural issues in black suicide. *Suicide and Life-Threatening Behavior* 18:73-89.

Gould, M., Shaffer, D., and Davies, M. (1990). Truncated pathways from childhood to adulthood: attrition in follow-up studies due to death. In *Straight and Devious Pathways to Adulthood*, ed. I. M. Robins, and M. R. Rutter, pp. 3-9. Cambridge: Cambridge University Press.

Greer, S. (1964). The relationship between parental loss and attempted suicide: a control study. *British Journal of Psychiatry* 100:698-705.

Gutheil, E. A. (1940). Dreams and suicide. *American Journal of Psychotherapy* 2:283-294.

Haim, A. (1974). *Adolescent Suicide*. New York: International Universities Press.

Hendin, H. (1963). The psychodynamics of suicide. *Journal of Nervous and Mental Disease* 136:236-244.

———— (1964). *Suicide and Scandinavia*. New York: Grune & Stratten.

———— (1969a). Black suicide. *Archives of General Psychiatry* 21:407-422.

———— (1969b). *Black Suicide*. New York: Basic Books.

———— (1975a). *The Age of Sensation*. New York: Norton.

———— (1975b). Growing up dead: student suicide. *American Journal of Psychotherapy* 29:327-338.

———— (1981). Psychotherapy and suicide. *American Journal of Psychotherapy* 35:469-480.

———— (1982). *Suicide in America*. New York: Norton.

———— (1986). Suicide: a review of new directions in research. *Hospital and Community Psychiatry* 37:148-154.

———— (1987). Youth suicide: psychosocial perspectives. *Suicide and Life Threatening Behavior* 17:151-165.

———— (1991). The psychodynamics of suicide with particular reference to the young. *American Journal of Psychiatry* 148:1150-1158.

Hendin, H., and Haas, A. P. (1991). Suicide and guilt as manifestations of post-traumatic stress disorder in Vietnam veterans. *American Journal of Psychiatry* 148:586-591.

Hendrick, I. (1940). Suicide as wish fulfilment. *Psychiatric Quarterly* 14:30-42.

Jacobs, J., and Teicher, J. (1967). Broken homes and social isolation in attempted suicides of adolescents. *International Journal of Social Psychiatry* 13:139-149.

Jones, E. (1911). On "dying together" with special reference to Heinrich Von Kleist's suicide. In *Essays on Applied Psychoanalysis*, vol. 1, pp. 9-15. New York: International Universities Press.

Jung, C. G. (1959). The soul and death. In *The Meaning of Death*, ed. H. Feifel, pp. 3-15. New York: McGraw-Hill.

Kernberg, O. (1970). A psychoanalytic classification of character pathology. *Journal of the American Psychoanalytic Association* 18:800-822.

———— (1985). *Borderline Conditions and Pathological Narcissism*. New York: Jason Aronson.

———— (1987). *Diagnosis and Clinical Management of Suicidal Potential in Borderline Patients: The Borderline Patient*, vol. 2. Hillsdale, NJ: Analytic Press.

Kilpatrick, E. (1948). A psychoanalytic understanding of suicide. *American Journal of Psychoanalysis* 8:13-23.

Klein, M. (1964). A contribution to the psychogenesis of manic depressive states. In *Contributions to Psychoanalysis, 1921-1945*, pp. 282-310. New York: McGraw-Hill.

Kohut, H. (1971a). *The Analysis of the Self*. New York: International Universities Press.

———— (1971b). *The Restoration of the Self*. New York: International Universities Press.

———— (1984). *How does Analysis Cure?* Chicago: University of Chicago Press.

Lifton, R. (1989). Suicide. In *Suicide: Understanding and Responding*, ed. D. Jacobs, and H. Brown, pp. 459-469. Madison, CT: International Universities Press.

Litman, R. E. (1980). The dream in the suicidal situation. In *The Dream in Clinical Practice*, ed. J. Natterson, pp. 283-299. New York: Jason Aronson.

Mack, J. (1981). *Vivienne: The Life and Suicide of an Adolescent Girl.* Boston: Little, Brown.

Malan, D. H. (1976). *Frontiers of Brief Psychotherapy.* New York: Plenum.

Maltsberger, J. T. (1981). *Suicide Risk: The Formulation of Clinical Judgment.* New York: New York University Press.

Maltsberger, J. T., and Buie, D. H. (1974). Countertransference hate in the treatment of suicidal patients. *Archives of General Psychiatry* 30:625–633.

———— (1980). The devices of suicide: revenge, riddance, and rebirth. *International Review of Psychoanalysis* 7:61–72.

———— (1989). The psychological vulnerability to suicide. In *Suicide: Understanding and Responding,* ed. D. Jacobs, and H. Brown, pp. 59–71. Madison, CT: International University Press.

Menninger, K. (1938). *Man Against Himself.* New York: Harcourt, Brace & World.

Mintz, R. (1971). Basic considerations in the psychotherapy of the depressed suicidal patient. *American Journal of Psychotherapy* 25:56–73.

Murphy, G., Armstrong, J., Hemele, S., et al. (1979). Suicide and alcoholism. *Archives of General Psychiatry* 36:65–69.

Novick, J. (1984). Attempted suicide in adolescence: the suicide sequence. In *Suicide in the Young,* ed. N. Sudak, A. Ford, and M. Rushforth, pp. 115–137. Boston: Wright.

Perry, J. C. (1989). Personality disorders, suicide and self destructive behavior. In *Suicide: Understanding and Responding,* ed. D. Jacobs, and H. N. Brown, pp. 157–169. Madison, CT: International Universities Press.

Perry, S., Cooper, A. M., and Michaels, R. (1987). The psychodynamic formulation: its purpose, structure, and clinical application. *American Journal of Psychiatry* 144:545–550.

Peterson, L. G., Peterson, M., O'Shanick, G. J., and Swann, A. (1985). Self-inflicted gunshot wounds: lethality of method versus intent. *American Journal of Psychiatry* 148:228–231.

Pfeffer, C. (1985). *The Suicidal Child.* New York: Guilford.

Pfeffer, C., Plutchik, R., Mizruchi, M. S., and Lipkins, R. (1987). Assaultive behavior in child psychiatric inpatients, outpatients, and non-patients. *Journal of the American Academy of Child and Adolescent Psychiatry* 26:256–261.

Plutchik, R., and van Praag, H. M. (1990). Psychosocial correlates of suicide and violence risk. In *Violence and Suicidality: Perspectives in Clinical and Psychological Research,* ed. H. M. van Praag, R. Plutchik, and A. Apter, pp. 37–65. New York: Brunner/Mazel.

Pollack, G. H. (1989). Manifestations of abnormal mourning: homicide and suicide following the death of another. In *The Mourning-Liberation Process,* vol. 1, pp. 155–180. Madison, CT: International Universities Press.

Raphling, D. (1970). Dreams and suicide attempts. *Journal of Nervous and Mental Disease* 15:404–410.

Robins, E. (1981). *The Final Months: A Study of the Lives of 134 Persons who Committed Suicide.* New York: Oxford University Press.

Robins, E., Murphy, G., Wilkinson, R., et al. (1959). Some clinical considerations in the prevention of suicide based on a study of 134 successful suicides. *American Journal of Public Health* 49:888–889.

Roose, S. P., Glassman, A., Walsh, B. T., et al. (1983). Depression, delusions, and suicide. *American Journal of Psychiatry* 140:1159–1162.

Sabbath, J. C. (1969). The suicidal adolescent: The expendable child. *Journal of the American Academy of Child Psychiatry* 8:272–289.

Seiden, R. H. (1970). We're driving young blacks to suicide. *Psychology Today* 4(3):24–28.

Shafii, M., Carrigan, C., Whittinghill, J. R., and Derrick, A. (1985). Psychological autopsy of completed suicide in children and adolescents. *American Journal of Psychiatry* 142:1061–1064.

Teicher, J., and Jacobs, J. (1966). Adolescents who attempt suicide: preliminary findings. *American Journal of Psychiatry* 122:1248–1257.

van Praag, H. M. (1983). CSF 5-HIAA and suicide in nondepressed schizophrenics. *Lancet* 2:977–978.

Weissman, M., Fox, K., and Klerman, G. L. (1973). Hostility and depression associated with suicide attempts. *American Journal of Psychiatry* 130:450–455.

Weissman, M., Klerman, G., Markowitz, J., and Ouellette, R. (1989). Suicide ideation and suicide attempts in panic disorder and attacks. *New England Journal of Medicine* 321:1209–1214.

Wheat, W. (1960). Motivational aspects of suicide in patients during and after psychiatric treatment. *Southern Medical Journal* 53:273–278.

Wolfgang, M. (1958). An analysis of homicide-suicide. *Journal of Clinical and Experimental Psychopathology* 19:208–218.

Zetzel, E. R. (1970a). On the incapacity to bear depression. In *The Capacity for Emotional Growth*, ed. E. R. Zetzel, pp. 82–114. London: Hogarth.

_____ (1970b). Anxiety and the capacity to bear it. In *The Capacity for Emotional Growth*, ed. E. R. Zetzel, pp. 33–52. London: Hogarth.

Zilboorg, G. (1936). Considerations on suicide with particular reference to the young. *American Journal of Orthopsychiatry* 7:15–31.

_____ (1938). The sense of immortality. *Psychoanalytic Quarterly* 7:171–199.

3: AN INTERPRETATION OF FREUD'S IDEAS ABOUT SUICIDE

James R. Eyman and Eric Kulick

Suicide was not a central preoccupation of Freud's work. Although comments about suicide are scattered throughout case examples and theoretical papers, he did not devote one full article to the problem of suicide. Even in *Mourning and Melancholia* (1917), his single most important work on the problem of depression and suicide, he addressed only one paragraph specifically to understanding the motivation for suicide. Despite the lack of any systematic focus on the problem of suicide, Freud's contributions to the understanding of psychopathology in general, and to the understanding of depression and suicide specifically, form a fundamental basis for the modern psychological understanding of suicide and for psychotherapeutic intervention. For example, the concept that symptoms have a psychological meaning, that there is a relationship between childhood experiences of loss and the subsequent development of depression in adulthood, and the recognition that the majority of mental phenomena are unconscious are all an outgrowth of Freud's work.

In this chapter we trace the development of Freud's understanding of how an individual can take his or her own life. To fully understand Freud's contributions to the theory of suicide, we will also need to discuss his understanding of the development of the mind, including his changing conceptions of the unconscious and instinctual life.

TOPOGRAPHIC MODEL

From the time of the *Studies of Hysteria* in 1895 to the publication of *Beyond the Pleasure Principle* in 1920 and *The Ego and the Id* in 1923, Freud's paradigmatic model of the mind was his topographic theory. This theory divided the mind into three systems: the conscious, the preconscious, and the unconscious.

Consciousness includes whatever an individual is aware of at the moment. The preconscious includes areas of which the individual is not aware but could easily become aware with a minor effort of will. The unconscious involves thoughts, ideas, and fantasies that are hidden from awareness and are separated from consciousness by what Freud termed a *repressive barrier*. Only through an unusual effort can one overcome the repressive barrier so that the material becomes available to awareness. The variation in difficulty of bringing to awareness something from the preconscious or the unconscious is one of relative difference in the degree of energy used to ward off the material, with the preconscious having a less-intense barrier.

Freud distinguished what he termed the *descriptive unconscious* from the *dynamic unconscious*. The descriptive unconscious refers to the experience of contrast between that which is conscious and in awareness, and that which is part of the individual's experience but is not consciously known at the moment. The descriptive unconscious includes the unconscious and the preconscious systems. The dynamic unconscious includes only that which is beyond the barrier of repression, which Freud often referred to as "the repressed," and includes only the unconscious system. Freud's early psychoanalytic investigations focused on the barrier between the preconscious and unconscious systems. His first model of intrapsychic conflict posited the locus of tension between the repressed unconscious material and the repressive barrier in the preconscious.

The content of the repressed material was the libidinal drive, or the sexual instinct. At this point, Freud postulated two basic drives: the species-preservative drive he called libido or the sexual instinct, and the ego instinct, which refers to the drive to preserve the life of the individual. Thus, Freud felt that human nature was basically motivated by drives to promote life at both the individual and the group levels. From this vantage point, suicide remained an enigma because it went against his understanding of human nature's fundamental goal of self-preservation and, therefore, seemed to Freud to be anti-instinctual. This conceptual conflict remained a fundamental dilemma that Freud was unable to solve until the publication of *Beyond the Pleasure Principle* and the introduction of the dual-drive theory of the life and death instincts, which will be discussed later.

FREUD'S EARLY COMMENTS
ON THE PROBLEM OF SUICIDE

In 1901, *The Psychopathology of Everyday Life* was published and within this document Freud included a section titled "Bungled Actions." He discussed a number of "accidental events" that had an unconscious motivation of self-destruction.

I have now learned and can prove from convincing examples that many apparently accidental injuries that happened to such patients are really instances of self-injury. What happens is that an impulse to self-punishment, which is constantly on the watch and which normally finds expression in self-reproach or contributes to the formation of a symptom, takes ingenious advantage of an external situation that chance happens to offer, or lends assistance to that situation until the desired injurious effect is brought about. [pp. 178–179]

Two examples in *The Psychopathology of Everyday Life* poignantly convey the unconscious intentionality behind apparent accidents.

"A young married woman broke her leg below the knee in a carriage accident, so that she was bedridden for weeks" (p. 179). The young woman was married to a very jealous husband. One evening, while with a number of relatives, she danced the cancan, "which was received with hearty applause by her relatives but with scanty satisfaction by her husband" (p. 179). The husband remarked, "carrying on like a tart again" (p. 179). The young woman spent a restless night, and the next morning decided to take a ride in a carriage. Her younger sister asked to take her baby and her nurse along for the ride. The patient vigorously refused this request. During the ride, the patient became increasingly nervous about the behavior of the horses, and at one point she jumped out of the carriage in fright and broke her leg. Those who remained in the carriage were unharmed. Freud commented, "We cannot fail to admire the skill which forced chance to mete out a punishment that fitted the crime so well. For it had now been made impossible for her to dance the cancan for quite a long time" (p. 180).

Another example of an unconscious wish toward self-destruction that actually ended in death was the case of Fraulein Z. She was a 34-year-old woman whose fiancé had died in World War I. After again becoming engaged, she was ambivalent toward her second fiancé and was noted to be quite moody. She was run over by a horse-drawn cab on a street that she had walked many times. Her second fiancé commented, "We had crossed at that point hundreds of times before; Fraulein Z. was exceedingly careful, and very often prevented me from being rash; on this morning there was almost no traffic whatever, the trams, omnibuses, etc. were on strike. Just about that time there was almost absolute quiet; even if she did not see the cab she must at all events heard it" (Freud 1901, p. 187). Her fiancé regarded the event as a suicide with the unconscious purpose disguised as a chance mishap, to which Freud concurred. It was felt that "the whole thing" was "an effect of the loss of her former fiancé, whom in her eyes, nothing could replace" (p. 187).

These early examples illustrate the role of unconscious conflict, guilt, and loss in the development of self-destructive behavior. A further example of the role of conflict and guilt comes from Freud's analysis of the Rat Man, which was published as *Notes Upon a Case of Obsessional Neurosis* in 1909. In this case study Freud made the connection between suicidal feelings and both murderous feelings toward another and the need to punish the self.

Among the Rat Man's many obsessions were recurrent thoughts of slitting his throat. One example of the occurrence of these suicidal feelings in the analysis was a recollection of suicidal feelings occurring at the time when his girlfriend (his cousin) was visiting her sick grandmother. First the Rat Man became aware of a command to cut his throat with a razor. Then he thought, "No, it's not so simple as that. You must go and kill the old woman [his girlfriend's grandmother]" (p. 187). Freud and he were able to reconstruct that, out of anger at his girlfriend's absence, he thought, "Oh, I should like to go and kill that old woman for robbing me of my love" (p. 188). Subsequently, the Rat Man experienced a command, "Kill yourself, as a punishment for these savage and murderous passions" (p. 188). Freud commented that these thoughts reached consciousness in reverse order; the command to kill himself came first followed by the murderous impulse that caused the guilt and necessitated the punitive command.

In 1910, the Vienna Psychoanalytic Society held a discussion regarding suicide with particular reference to adolescence. The presenters were Alfred Adler, Josef Friedjung, Karl Molitor, David Oppenheim, Rudolph Reitler, J. Isidor Sadger, and Wilhelm Stekel. At the end of the conference, Freud commented on psychoanalytic theory's inability to resolve the mystery of suicide. In his concluding remarks he stated, "Gentlemen, I have an impression that, in spite of all the valuable material that has been brought before us in this discussion, we have not reached a decision on the problem that interests us. We were anxious above all to know how it becomes possible for the extraordinarily powerful life instinct to be overcome: whether this can only come about with the help of a disappointed libido or whether the ego can renounce its self-preservation for its own egoistic motives" (Freud 1910, p. 232). He then suggested the way to answer this psychological question was by "taking as our starting-point the condition of melancholia, which is so familiar to us clinically, and a comparison between it and the affect of mourning" (p. 232). Freud then took up his own suggestion and published *Mourning and Melancholia* in 1917.

Mourning and Melancholia

Mourning and Melancholia is of seminal importance in Freud's writings. It was a ground-breaking paper in many respects beyond its contribution to the understanding of suicide, representing a transition from the early topographic model to the beginnings of a structural model, and from the libido theory to the dual-drive instinctual theory. It also may represent the birth of object relations theory. As described below, Freud recognized that the melancholic person was engaged in an internal dialogue between the self and the representation of another (the object). In *Mourning and Melancholia*, Freud began to recognize the central importance of aggression and its vicissitudes in human functioning that later necessitated the elevation of aggression to independent drive status. He also recognized that one portion of the ego, which he referred to as the "critical agency," sets itself up as a critical judge against another portion of the ego resulting in the formation of guilt. The critical agency discussed in *Mourning and Melancholia* later developed into the superego in *The Ego and the Id* in 1923. In a precursor to object relations theory, Freud recognized the importance of identification with a lost person, and came to understand that the melancholic person's self-reproaches are actually an internal dialogue between the internal representation of the lost object (person) and the critical agency (later to become the superego).

In *Mourning and Melancholia* Freud detailed his theoretical understanding of suicide. His approach was to compare normal mourning and grieving with the pathological state of melancholia (pathological mourning). He found that symptomatically there is a great overlap, with both a person in mourning and the melancholic person showing painful dejection, cessation of interests, inability to love, and a generalized inhibition. The one thing that distinguishes melancholia from mourning is the "loss of the self-regard." Freud, struck by the self-reproaches of the melancholic person, examined this process and found it notable that there was a shameless aspect to the person's self-condemnation. The melancholic person appeared to be anxious to announce personal failings to the entire world. One would expect the person to want to hide these shortcomings. In attempting to understand this contradiction, Freud discovered that unconsciously these reproaches were not directed against the self but rather against the lost love object. He believed that the melancholic's self-accusations are not applicable to the patient but to someone the melancholic "loves or has loved or should love." Freud concluded that this is "the key to the clinical picture: we perceive that the self-reproaches are reproaches against a loved object which have been shifted away from it onto the patient's own ego" (p. 248).

Through identification with the lost love object, the critical agency can attack and torment the portion of the ego identified with the lost object. Freud writes, "The shadow of the object fell upon the ego. . . . In this way an object loss was transformed into an ego loss and the conflict between the ego and loved person into a cleavage between the critical activity of the ego and the ego as altered by identification" (p. 249).

It is the sadism that is heaped upon the ego by the critical agency that is the key to Freud's understanding of suicide. Thus Freud asserts that the unconscious fantasy of the suicidal patient is that what is being killed is the abandoning or rejecting love object. The loss may be either that of a previously idealized person or of a cherished ideal or value. The precondition for this melancholic state and its possible culmination in suicide involves the object or ideal being "ambivalently held," meaning that the object is both simultaneously loved and hated.

In addition, Freud believed that a narcissistic object or more primitive type of object relations was essential.

> We have long known, it is true, that no neurotic harbors thoughts of suicide which he has not turned back upon himself from murderous impulses against others, but we have never been able to explain what interplay of forces can carry such a purpose through to execution. The analysis of melancholia now shows that the ego can kill itself only if, owing to return of the object-cathexis, it can treat itself as an object — if it is able to direct against itself the hostility which relates to an object and which represents the ego's original reaction to objects in the external world. [p. 252]

THE STRUCTURAL MODEL

In 1923, Freud published the *Ego and the Id*, which ushered in the second psychoanalytic paradigm — that of the structural model of the mind, which now replaced and subsumed the earlier topographic model. This shift was necessitated by the weight of clinical data, which increasingly strained the heuristic and explanatory power of the topographic model. Essentially the topographic model could no longer account for the nature of intrapsychic conflict as clinical psychoanalytic data accumulated. In the topographic model, the locus of conflict is between the system preconscious and the system unconscious. The system unconscious contains the instincts or drives, while the repressing force would be located in the system preconscious. However, Freud found that not only were the drives unconscious, but the defense mechanisms arrayed against the drives were also unconscious and could be made conscious only through psychoanalytic work. Additionally, Freud noted that there was a third unexpected element in the unconscious — a moral agency associated with guilt. Thus the topographic theory could not account for the existence of unconscious defense mechanisms and unconscious guilt. In the *Ego and the Id*, Freud reformulated his paradigm of the mind, suggesting now that there were three essential structures: (1) the id — the locus of the sexual and aggressive drives; (2) the ego — containing the conscious, experiencing self, a set of functions (intellect, judgment, secondary process thought, reality testing, etc.), and the defense mechanisms; and (3) the superego — involving a critical agency and the locus of guilt. Henceforth, the topographic model would be used only descriptively, and it was recognized that the id, the ego, and the superego each contained conscious and unconscious elements. The site of intrapsychic conflict is now between the ego and the id.

The Death Instinct

Although Freud had developed a psychological understanding of how a human being can commit suicide based on the unconscious fantasy that he or she is killing someone else, he was still faced with the dilemma of how the life-preservative instinct could be overcome. With the publication of *Beyond the Pleasure Principle* in 1920, Freud answered this question with the reorganization of his drive theory and the creation of the death instinct. In this monograph, Freud now subsumed both the libidinal and ego instincts as part of a general life instinct. The goal of this instinct is to promote the individual's and the species' life and to help man grow, develop, and achieve greater organization.

Freud introduced the idea of another set of instincts of a more conservative nature, which he termed the *death instinct*. This is an instinct to return to a prior set of conditions. As organic matter has always evolved from inorganic matter, this instinct is ultimately a death instinct that impels us back to the inorganic state. In *An Outline of Psychoanalysis* (Freud 1940) he stated,

> The aim of the first of these basic instincts (the life instinct) is to establish ever greater unities and to preserve them thus — in short, to bind together; the aim of the second (the death instinct), on the contrary, to undo connections and so to destroy things. In the case of the destructive instinct we may suppose that its final aim is to lead what is living into an inorganic state. For this reason we also call it the death instinct. [p. 148]

Freud had now postulated what overcomes the life-preserving instincts in suicide. In *The Ego and the Id*, Freud introduced the tripartite structural theory dividing the mind into the id, the ego, and the superego. We can now modify Freud's insights found in *Mourning and Melancholia* with these theoretical advancements made in 1920 and 1923. Freud now stated that the "critical agency" that attacks the ego is a permanent psychological structure whose purpose is to monitor and criticize the individual's behavior against an ideal (ego-ideal). The energy that empowers this superego is derived from the death instinct. Freud stated in *The Ego and the Id* (1923):

> If we turn to melancholia first, we find that the excessively strong superego which has obtained a hold upon consciousness rages against the ego with merciless violence, as if it had taken possession of the whole of sadism available in the person concerned. Following our view of sadism we should say that the destructive component had entrenched itself in the superego and turned it against the ego. What is now holding sway in the superego is, as it were, a pure culture of the death instinct, and in fact it often enough succeeds in driving ego into death. [p. 53]

Freud suggested that the death instinct may be dealt with in a variety of ways. It is often rendered harmless when fused with erotic components, and it may be deflected from the self by being diverted toward the external world in the form of aggression; however, to a significant extent it continues its internal self-destructive work silently. Paradoxically for Freud, the more one directs aggression outward, the less vulnerable one is to directing aggression internally.

In *Civilization and Its Discontents*, published in 1930, Freud spoke of the self-destructive potential of the interplay between the life and death instincts as a salient dilemma within civilization as a whole. Freud viewed civilization as a process occurring in the service of eros, the life instinct. The ultimate purpose of eros is "to combine single human individuals, and after that families, then races, peoples in nations into one great unity, the unity of mankind" (Freud 1930, p. 122). Opposed to this is the destructive impulse, "the hostility of each against all and of all against each" which opposes the "program of civilization" (p. 122).

> And now, I think, the meaning of the evolution of civilization is no longer obscured to us. It must present the struggle between eros and death, between the instinct of life and the instinct of destruction, as it works itself out in the human species. This struggle is what all life essentially consists of, and the evolution of civilization may therefore be simply described as the struggle for life of the human species. [p. 122].

FREUD'S CONTRIBUTIONS TO THE THEORETICAL UNDERSTANDING OF SUICIDE

Freud made several significant contributions to the understanding of the psychology of the suicidal individual. He recognized the role of pathological relationships and how they become internalized within the individual's psyche. He recognized that relationships involving more primitive need fulfillment were the most likely to be involved in the predisposition to suicide. The more ambivalent feelings one had toward the person, the more problematic the process of mourning becomes and the greater the chance of mourning becoming depression. He recognized that the very act of suicide always involved the unconscious fantasy of not the self being killed but this ambivalently regarded person or ideal being destroyed. The death instinct was a unique contribution, albeit a controversial one, as the anergic force that fuels the compulsion to suicide. A critical superego that torments and tortures the ego is an essential component of someone being vulnerable to suicide. Freud also discussed the failure in suicide of more adaptive and appropriate ways of managing the death instinct. Finally, he recognized the role of "accidents" in self-destructive behavior.

KARL MENNINGER'S PLACEMENT OF SUICIDAL MOTIVATIONS IN THE STRUCTURAL MODEL

Freud did not integrate his ideas about suicide with his structural model. The most significant attempt to do so was made by Karl Menninger, who in 1938 published *Man Against Himself*, a pivotal book in the field of suicide and other self-destructive behavior. Menninger's contribution will be discussed to illustrate the value of Freud's structural theory in understanding suicide. Toward the beginning of the book, Menninger stated that the popular notion that suicide is an escape from an intolerable life situation does not capture the complex psychological motivations that are brought to bear when an individual ends his or her own life. He posited three components to the suicidal act—the wish to kill, the wish to be killed, and the wish to die—that derive from the ego, superego, and id, respectively.

The wish to kill relates to Freud's description in *Mourning and Melancholia* of the suicidal individual wishing to murder an "ambivalently held person" and turning that anger inward to destroy the psychological representation of that ambivalently held individual. Menninger described many examples of this process—for example, a young boy, who had been scolded by his father for some minor dereliction, hanging himself in the barn a few hours later.

> It must have been his father whom he really wished to kill. We know that some boys do kill their fathers under just such circumstances but evidently this boy couldn't do that; perhaps he loved his father too much to kill him; perhaps he feared him too much; perhaps he feared the consequences; at any rate, he couldn't do it. What he could do was to kill the father that existed within himself, technically, the introjected father. [p. 32]

Menninger then asked why the individual does not attack the real object of hate and kill the person. He elaborates on several reasons such as fear of the consequences, difficulty killing someone who is loved (albeit ambivalently so), and guilt, which he elaborated on under the context of another motivation.

Menninger explained the transmutation of the wish to kill into suicide as

> arising from primitive destructiveness, invested with weak neutralization in one or several objects whose sudden removal or faithlessness dislodges the attachment, defuses the elements of the emotional bond and allows the murderous impulse, now freed, to expend itself upon the person of its origin as a substitute object, thus accomplishing a displaced murder. [p. 45]

The wish to kill is then an aggressive derivative of the death instinct that for many suicidal individuals entails a partial or complete erotization of cruel and sadistic urges. Turning the wish to kill into action against the self originates in the ego, the area of the psyche felt to contain the individual's identification with the ambivalently held object.

With the idea of the wish to be killed, Menninger highlights the central role of masochism in a suicidal individual, that is, the enjoyment of submission, pain, defeat, ultimately an embracing of death. The wish to be killed stems from unconscious guilt so that suicide becomes the "death penalty" for murderous wishes. Thus this motivation for suicide not only gratifies the individual's need for punishment but also increases pleasure in masochistically succumbing to pain and death. The superego contains the harsh and critical directives against the murderous impulses toward another.

The wish to die originates in the id, driven by the death instinct. Menninger acknowledges the controversial aspect of the death instinct and therefore the wish to die, but nevertheless postulates a mechanism for the interplay between the life and death instinct in suicide.

> In a person who commits suicide, on the other hand, it [the death instinct] suddenly bursts its bonds, springs into power and puts an immediate end to the existence of the individual. Such a turn of affairs must be regarded as exceptional, accomplished only in the face of some relative weakness of the life instinct, i.e., some deficiency in the capacity for developing love, since it is the function of love [the erotic instinct] to convert destructive impulses into measures of self-defense and socially useful adaptations, or into conscience. Gradually, to be sure, all these devices fail and death wins; but sometimes it threatens to win prematurely, aided often by incomplete or inefficient functioning of the neutralizing devices of love. [p. 70]

In one of our cases, a 34-year-old Caucasian professional woman came to psychotherapy because of a long history of severe depression and suicidal behavior. At the beginning of treatment, the patient had no understanding about her motivations for suicide nor the precipitants of her depression. Gradually, through psychodynamically oriented psychotherapy, the motivations for her suicidal behavior became clear. The patient began to recognize that she felt the most depressed and despondent when she perceived herself as being slighted or abandoned by someone. As she began to explore these situations, she also recognized her intense angry and rageful reactions toward the individuals she believed were involved in abandoning her. She felt very distressed by her growing awareness of her anger, which for a time, led her to become even more suicidal. Eventually, she recognized that the discomfort with her anger was due to experiencing herself as being like her father who had seriously abused her in fits of unpredictable angry rage.

From Menninger's elaboration of Freud's theory about suicide, the dynamics and motivations for the patient's suicidal urges can be clearly understood. The series of perceived abandonments and slights reawakened in the patient earlier parental experiences of deprivation and abandonment. She reacted to these current situations as she did as a child, with anger and rage. The experience of rage led to an identification of herself with her father. This experience of rage and anger led her to become suicidal, which could be understood as the wish to kill her self, as the self was identified with the father. Thus we see one piece of Menninger's triad, the wish to kill the father, by killing herself and therefore killing the internal psychological representation of her father. The patient also felt extremely guilty about her anger. She felt her angry wishes made her an even more bad and unacceptable person. Thus, another aspect of her suicidal motivation was a wish to punish herself for her unacceptable angry feelings and to alleviate her unconscious guilt. Therefore, a second component of the triad—the wish to be killed as punishment—can be seen. During her suicidal crisis, the patient talked extensively about the overwhelming pain and suffering. She spoke about wanting to alleviate this painful turmoil, and how, at moments of desperation, it felt like the only way to do so would be to die. This exemplifies the third component—the wish to die—in that the patient was looking for a cessation of psychological turmoil and freedom through the peace of death.

CLINICAL IMPLICATIONS OF FREUD'S
THEORY OF SUICIDE

The clinical implications of Freud's theory of suicide are numerous. Although current psychodynamic treatment of suicidal patients would include advances in ego psychology, object relations theory, and self psychology, a number of Freud's insights remain pertinent and indeed may still be fundamental. Freud alerted us to a number of factors that the clinician must keep in mind when treating suicidal people: directing anger against the self, the role of loss, the harsh and persecutory superego, the death instinct, and unconscious motivations.

There is a need to help the patient identify and integrate aggression, and learn how to appropriately express and channel anger.

A borderline woman in her early 20s, a victim of sexual abuse as a child at the hands of her uncle, recently encountered him again. She became suicidal and with much embarrassment reported to her therapist that she had wet her bed the previous night. She described to the therapist her rage and hatred toward her uncle. The therapist wondered if she had wanted to urinate on her uncle instead of on herself. The patient responded that indeed, before going to sleep the previous night, she had a fantasy that when her uncle died she would urinate on his grave. The patient entered the session feeling suicidal, depressed, and ashamed, but after becoming more aware of her anger toward her uncle, she felt better about herself, more in control, and was more overtly rageful toward her uncle. Here we see the utility of Freud's conceptualization of depression involving rage turned inward against the ego and how the task of therapy is to help the patient redirect the anger to its original source.

Freud's theoretical contributions have led to the recognition of the need to help the patient consciously recognize what has been lost and the impact of that loss on his or her functioning. The loss may relate to a person or to a cherished ideal. For Freud, the loss results in identifying with, internalizing, and then attacking the lost object. For example, it is a common experience in psychotherapy for patients whose self-esteem is vulnerable to experience any separation or loss from the psychotherapist as leading to a diminution of their self-esteem. This narcissistic injury often results in depressive or suicidal feelings. The clinical task is one of helping these patients examine why the separation so adversely affects their self-esteem and of helping them reconstruct the childhood antecedents of that experience.

A 40-year-old married Caucasian male social worker engaged in twice weekly psychotherapy for treatment of low self-esteem, work inhibition, and marital problems. He came to a session prior to the therapist's absence with a copy of an obituary page he had found in an old newspaper, bearing the last name of the therapist. He said, "I thought you'd be interested in this." He proceeded to talk about feeling quite depressed and not knowing why. He acknowledged being irritable and overreactive with his wife. He then said he didn't imagine that his depression had anything to do with the upcoming interruption due to the therapist's absence. At that point, the therapist pointed out to him that he had started the session off by delivering the therapist's obituary. The patient laughed and said, "Is that what you think it is?" The therapist pointed out to the patient that his giving him the obituary suggested both that he experienced the upcoming absence as a death, and might also imply some anger toward the therapist for leaving him.

At that point the patient remembered that over the previous several sessions he had reported a series of dreams that depicted his rage toward the therapist. He acknowledged that indeed he had left the last session quite touched by an intervention the therapist had made and was tearful about feeling understood and validated. He remembered feeling bad that his dreams seemed to depict so much anger toward the therapist. After acknowledging his feelings of loss, guilt, anger, and the centrality of the relationship with the therapist in his life, the patient became more animated and lively, and reported a lessening of his depression by the end of the session.

Here we see a situation in which the patient's revelation of rageful feelings toward the therapist was followed by his learning of an interruption and the temporary loss of his therapist, and his unconsciously linking the rage in his dreams with the reason for the therapist going away.

Freud also said that in depression the loss could involve a cherished ideal. Although Freud did not explicate this mechanism, we can infer that, when a cherished ideal is lost, there is also the loss of a corresponding idealized self-image. That a formerly idealized self-image can then be treated as an object of attack is exemplified by the following suicide note:

"This is Mary. I have said before that I don't know her any more. I have disappointed everyone and I have disappointed you. I hope I have the strength to do this one last thing. I used to be very strong but I have no strength. I'm very disappointed with myself. I guess that's the biggest disappointment of all, to be disappointed with yourself. It leaves you nothing. I don't know Mary anymore. I thought I did. I had ideals for her. I wanted to go to New Orleans to work for the poor. It was my only desire. My dreams and hopes were about that, now my dreams are no more, they are all over. I can't wish anymore for that. I am too disappointed in myself, I have no more. I have nothing, it's hopeless. I have disappointed myself so much. I have not lived up to my ideals in life. So when one has no more meaning to life, then there's no more meaning to live it."

Another clinical implication deriving from Freud's theory is the recognition of the role of the severe, persecutory superego in suicide. The therapeutic task is to help the patient identify the manifestations of the severe, persecutory superego and to ameliorate the harmful consequences and subsequent lowering of self-esteem. Much of this work can be done through the analysis of transference in which the severely critical superego is projected onto the therapist and the therapist is seen as a persecutory and critical figure. Again, the working through of this transference and the subsequent internalization of the therapist as a more benign and loving person is curative. In fact, Strachey (1934) suggested that this is the central component of the therapeutic interaction.

A 25-year-old unmarried African-American female nurse was hospitalized at a long-term facility because of severe chronic depression, multiple suicide attempts, repeated episodes of self-mutilation, and an increasing inability to function. Among the patient's many problems was a most unusual symptom. The patient pretended to be blind, even to the extent of using a cane and dark glasses. But she also made it quite obvious to those around her that she wasn't blind. Thus, for example, while using her dark glasses and cane, she would walk up to people and comment on the color of their tie or the nature of their dress. She also made it quite clear, when she walked, that she would avoid obstacles before her cane had in any way touched the obstacle.

She reported that she had been a paratrooper during the Vietnam war, and that after six months she was thrown out because they realized she was blind — after having made numerous dangerous jumps in enemy territory. The fact that there were no female paratroopers at the time, or that this story was inconsistent with other stories she had told about the same time period, only tended to confirm her presentation of herself as a liar. We came to understand this unusual behavior as representative of a factitious disorder, that the patient could see, and consciously knew she could see. However, what was unconscious was the motivation for pretending not to see.

Initially, the patient's relationship with peers, staff, and even her psychotherapist was one in which she continually provoked people into experiencing her as a liar. Thus her therapy sessions, participation in team meetings, and relationships with other patients were a relentless series of prosecutorial attacks on her. People would repeatedly bring up all the evidence that she was lying, both with regard to her blindness, or with regard to her "tall stories." The patient would react by becoming quite hysterical. She would cry and complain that no one believed her and no one understood her. At a point where she felt condemned universally, she made a very serious suicide attempt, attempting to hang herself. At this point, her therapist recognized that a pathological transference–countertransference paradigm had become entrenched. The patient experienced her therapist as hating, attacking, persecuting, and humiliating her. The patient's therapist and the rest of the staff, in the countertransference, indeed felt provoked, angry, and wanted to accuse the patient of being a malingerer.

It became apparent that this paradigm represented the externalization of the patient's inner world. She had projected her severe persecutory superego onto her therapist, the staff, and indeed on all her relationships in the hospital. When the therapist and the staff were able to recognize this circumstance, in the wake of the serious suicide attempt, a change in approach to the patient took place. The therapist no longer challenged the patient's blindness, but instead empathized with her plight of feeling that she was in terrible distress, and no one understood or cared.

This shift in attitude led to a change in the nature of the patient's relationship with her therapist. From that point on the patient herself began to express her own doubts about her blindness, and revealed a history of sexual and physical abuse at the hands of her father. It turned out that the patient's experience of incest had been accompanied with a directive from her father after it was over, "This never happened." Thus the patient revealed that she subsequently never knew what was real and what was not. It turned out that her experience of herself as a liar, and her presenting herself that way, had to do with her confusion about whether or not her incest memories were indeed true. They also involved the wish that indeed she was a liar, and that her father was not guilty of incestuous abuse. The staff's persecution of the patient served to affirm her badness and absolve her father of guilt.

With the shift in the staff's attitude, and the patient's increasing ability to own the conflict within herself, the severity of her depression and relentless self-destructive behavior lessened. Over time, she was able to acknowledge that indeed she wasn't blind, and she was able to go to an ophthalmologist and obtain prescription glasses for myopia. She ceased her relentless self-destructive behavior, and was able to interact with others in a less provocative and more warm and mutual way. Her relations with her self correspondingly improved, as her self-esteem improved, and we saw the gradual diminution of the severity and persecutory nature of her superego.

At a higher level of abstraction, Freud ultimately saw the problem of depression and suicide as a manifestation of thanatos or the death instinct. For Freud there were two great forces operating within each person. Eros was the force of life, of love whose characteristic is that of bringing things together through integration — integration within the person, and integration of the person within the family, the community, the nation, and the world. Therefore, the main function of eros is to maintain life, maintain society and civilization, and maintain relationships. Juxtaposed against eros is the force of thanatos or the death drive. The death drive involves fragmentation, entropy, things coming apart, and a drive toward death. Thanatos characterized what Freud called the *nirvana principle*, the tendency of all living things to seek a state of zero stimulation.

For Freud, the death drive is a fundamental, bedrock phenomenon, which cannot be analyzed away. The psychotherapist can only help patients to turn away from the attraction to self-destruction, and help them to maintain their focus on eros — on life and love. How can one use such a concept clinically? In Freudian terms, the psychotherapist has to help the patient to simply turn away from the attraction to self-destruction, and to invigorate that part of the person that is dedicated to life. The psychotherapist can assume that as long as a person is still alive there must be some strength to eros, and one can seek to enhance it. Thus for Freud, when dealing with the suicidal person for whom the death instinct is at its height, the fact that that person is still alive is a sign of the suicidal person's ambivalence. The source of ambivalence around suicide is the struggle between eros and thanatos, and the fact that the person is still alive is a sign of the continued presence, even if weak, of eros.

With the addition of the American and English schools of object-relations theory, as well as Kohut's psychology of the self, what Freud called the death instinct is viewed from a different perspective. No longer an immutable and fundamental drive, the destructive potential of the death instinct can be resolved. From the relational perspectives of object relations theory and self psychology, the healing power of the therapeutic relationship itself is paramount. Thus it is the relationship with the therapist that can heal the tendencies toward self-destruction and suicide.

From a self-psychological perspective, what Freud called the death drive would be viewed as a breakdown or disintegration product of a fragmenting self. In the context of a psychotherapeutic relationship, suicidal urges and the fragmenting of the self would be viewed as a sign of a lapse in the integrity of the therapist–patient bond. An intact therapist–patient bond expresses the patient's sense of unity and cohesion. When there is a serious disruption in the integrity of the relationship between patient and therapist, what Kohut refers to as a *disintegration phenomenon* occurs. The disintegration phenomena involve experiences of depression, self-destructive ideation and behavior, withdrawal from people, and a fragmentation of the self. Thus fragmentation phenomena refer to things coming apart, both within the person and between the person and the rest of the world — it is the phenomenon of Freud's death drive.

From an object relations perspective, the self-destructive drive is related to the emergence of more severe persecutory ideas (bad internalized objects). These bad objects are critical, demanding, sadistic, and dangerous internal psychological representations and bad experiences with important care-taking figures, which may also incorporate the patient's fantasied elaborations of the real relationship. Thus the bad internalized objects and their persecution of and danger to the patient may go well beyond what actually occurred in the person's life. For example, even in situations where the patient experienced real psychological, physical, and/or sexual abuse, the internal representation of those experiences is an amalgam of both the reality and the patient's fantasies of the experience.

In a suicidal crisis, the patient's bad internal objects become more and more paramount, eventually threatening to overwhelm whatever good, soothing, and comforting internal objects are available. From this object relations perspective, the benign, understanding, and containing aspects of the therapeutic relationship can be used to reestablish the integrity of the therapeutic relationship, and help activate the patient's good internalized objects. Through the process of internalization of the positive and comforting aspects of the therapist, the patient becomes more adept at soothing and comforting himself or herself under periods of psychological stress or trauma. Therefore, from an object relations point of view, what Freud called the death instinct would involve the activation of the bad persecutory internal objects within the person. Eros could be viewed as the evocation and establishment of the good, soothing, and life-supporting internalized-other representations.

In the literature on suicide, one often finds the term *management of suicidal urges and behaviors* being used synonymously with treatment. The focus tends to be on keeping the patient safe and the reduction of depressive symptoms. In this era of managed care and cost containment, the emphasis is increasingly on brief, symptom-oriented management of depressive symptomatology and suicidal crisis. Although the management of these depressive and suicidal symptoms is important, Freud's insights into the nature of depression and suicide teaches us that unless attention is paid to resolving the underlying dynamics, the patient remains vulnerable to entering again into a suicidal crisis. In addition to the use of medication and protective measures, when a patient is in the midst of a suicidal crisis, Freud's delineation of the unconscious dynamics related to loss and aggression point to the necessity of dynamic psychotherapy to ultimately resolve the vulnerability to suicide.

REFERENCES

Freud, S. (1901). Psychopathology of everyday life. *Standard Edition* 6: 162–190.

_____ (1909). Notes upon a case of obsessional neurosis. *Standard Edition* 10:153–249.

_____ (1910). Contributions to a discussion on suicide. *Standard Edition* 11:231–232.

_____ (1917). Mourning and melancholia. *Standard Edition* 14:237–258.

_____ (1920). Beyond the pleasure principle. *Standard Edition* 18:1–64.

_____ (1923). The ego and the id. *Standard Edition* 19:12–59.

_____ (1930). Civilization and its discontents. *Standard Edition* 21:64–145.

_____ (1940). An outline of psychoanalysis. *Standard Edition* 23:144–207.

Freud, S., and Breuer, J. (1895). Studies in hysteria. *Standard Edition* 2:1–241.

Menninger, K. A. (1938). *Man Against Himself*. New York: Harcourt, Brace.

Strachey, J. (1934). The nature of the therapeutic action of psychoanalysis. *International Journal of Psycho-Analysis* 15:127–159.

4: JUNGIAN PERSPECTIVES ON THE UNCONSCIOUS AND SUICIDE

David Lester

Although Freud's psychoanalytic perspective on the unconscious is the most well known, later psychodynamic theorists have also included the concept of the unconscious in their theories. The best articulated of these alternative propositions comes from Carl Jung, whose ideas about the structure of the mind differed greatly from Freud's in the concepts proposed to account for psychological phenomena. However, perhaps more importantly, the Jungian conception of the unconscious is far more positive than Freudian conception, and this too affects the way in which the theory deals with the issue of suicide. It is useful first to review the basic elements of Jung's theory of the mind.

JUNG'S THEORY OF THE MIND

The Jungian Unconscious

Jung accepted Freud's descriptions of the conscious mind and the unconscious mind. The Freudian unconscious contains wishes that often stem from childhood and that, therefore, are often primitive, unorganized, and nonspecific. These wishes are often concerned with oral needs, dependency needs, cleanliness and dirtiness, struggles with authority figures, and sexual desires—wishes that have their origin in the early psychosexual stages described by Freud (the oral, anal, and phallic stages). The unconscious set of wishes also contains wishes that the person once was consciously aware of but that were punished by the parents and other authority figures and, as a result, were repressed or counter-cathected. Jung called this set of wishes the *personal unconscious*.

However, Jung felt that the conscious and the personal unconscious described only a part of the mind of the individual. In addition to the personal unconscious, Jung believed there was a large part of the mind that he called the *collective unconscious*. This part of the mind was called "collective" because Jung believed that all of us had similar elements in our collective unconsciouses.

Jung, a holistic theorist, called the mind as a whole the *psyche*, and he believed that the mind was composed of various *complexes*, autonomous partial systems of organized psychic contents. In the collective unconscious, the complexes, or subsystems, are the *archetypes*. An example of a possible archetype present in our collective unconscious is the hero. In this archetype there is usually a miraculous and humble birth. Early in life he shows superhuman strength, and often he has a tutelary figure who aids him. There is a rapid rise to power and fame as he battles the forces of evil, followed by a fall from power due to his pride (hubris) or a betrayal. He dies in a heroic sacrifice. Examples include Achilles and Cheiron, Perseus and Athena, Theseus and Poseidon, King Arthur and Merlin, as well as such figures as Jesus Christ and Superman.

Jung believed that the archetypes were inherited. The reason a particular theme appears in religion, fiction, paintings, or dreams in people in different parts of the world and in different eras is because we inherit similar archetypes. Most modern psychologists have rejected this idea, preferring to explain the coincidences described by Jung as the result of the cultural diffusion of ideas. However, it is possible to reformulate Jung's ideas so that they might be more acceptable to modern psychologists.

First, Progoff (1973) has proposed that, rather than inheriting the archetypes directly, we inherit the psychic structures that enable us to generate the archetypes as our mind develops. We have similar collective unconsciouses because we inherit similar psychic structures. To take an analogy, we do not inherit castration anxiety. Rather we inherit an anatomical structure that is external to the body, and later, perhaps as a result of observing injury to other parts of our body, we develop a fear that we might injure or lose by amputation this particular anatomical structure.

A better analogy might be drawn with Chomsky's (1972) theory of language development. Chomsky argued that it was highly unlikely that we developed the ability to generate complex linguistic utterances simply by being reinforced for speaking as the behaviorists would have us believe. He suggested that we inherit the cognitive structures that permit us to generate a universal grammar. Once we learn a language, with its own particular version of this grammar, the universal grammar enables us to generate sentences and compositions that we have never heard before and for which we were never reinforced.

It can be seen that Chomsky's inherited cognitive structures, which permit the mind to generate a universal grammar, are similar to Progoff's inherited psychic structures, which enable us to generate the archetypes. Despite this similarity, Chomsky's ideas have been received with greater acceptance than Jung's concept of the collective unconscious.

Jung viewed the collective unconscious as a source of knowledge. If we could tap into the collective unconscious, we would be able to tap directly the wisdom that has shaped the religions, philosophies, and art of the world. For example, dreams, which can be stimulated by the archetypes, are sometimes unintelligible to us, not because we would be stricken with anxiety if we were to be aware of the unconscious elements motivating the dream, but because the archetypes stimulating the dream do not use the particular language that we use in thought and speech. The archetypes use universal symbols. Thus, the task in interpreting such dreams is not one of uncovering the hidden wishes that are really motivating the dream, but rather one of interpretation — translating the archetypal symbols into the symbols we use in our language.

Complexes

Jung identified several complexes in the conscious. The *ego* refers to the complete set of conscious contents and includes percepts, memories, thoughts, desires, and feelings. The *persona* is a subsystem within the ego and is the self that we present to others, the mask we wear in daily interaction with others. It consists of the roles we play in our lives. Since we have several roles, it may make more sense to speak of the various components of the persona.

Each complex in the ego has a parallel complex in the unconscious. The *shadow* consists of psychic elements in the personal, and, to a lesser extent, the collective, unconscious that are in opposition to the ego. The shadow is less developed and less differentiated than the contents of the ego, but its presence is made apparent to the ego whenever the boundaries between the systems break down and contents from the shadow intrude into the ego.

In addition, the subsystem in the collective unconscious that is in opposition to the persona is called the *anima* in men and the *animus* in women. Jung was writing almost a century ago, and it is natural that he fell into sexist thinking here. He identified the sexes with the stereotypic qualities and, as a result, he attributed sexist qualities to the anima and animus. For example, women were "feminine," that is, irrational and emotional, and so the animus was described as rational and discriminating. If Jung were formulating his ideas today, it is unlikely that he would have adopted such a sexist description. He would have noted that whatever qualities the persona has, the "animum" would have contrasting properties.

The *self* is the part of the psyche that eventually becomes the synthesized whole, an integrated combination of the opposed complexes, in the second half of our life.

Psychic Function and Attitudes

Jung suggested that the psyche responds to stimuli (internally or externally generated) by sensing them, interpreting them, evaluating them, and sometimes having an immediate awareness and understanding of them. He called these functions sensing, thinking, feeling, and intuiting, respectively. Jung proposed that functions develop to a different extent in people, thereby providing a basis for typing people. He conceptualized them in pairs: sensing versus intuiting, and thinking versus feeling. The ego typically develops one of the functions in each pair more fully than the other. The opposed function of the dyad then becomes the dominating function of the shadow.

Jung also distinguished two *attitudes* of the psyche. The attitude of extroversion orients the person toward external stimuli, while the attitude of introversion orients the person toward internal stimuli. If the conscious part of the psyche (the ego) adopts one attitude, then the personal unconscious (the shadow) will have the other attitude.

Although many psychologists credit Jung with being one of the first psychologists to draw attention to the dimension of extroversion-introversion, it should be remembered that his definition of this term differs from the definitions offered by modern personality theorists.

Abnormal Behavior

Abnormal behavior can result from several causes. The goal of the psyche is to unite into a complete whole, a process called *individuation*. In order to unite, the psyche first has to split into various subsystems (complexes) as we explore the various facets of our experience. Abnormal behavior can result when one subsystem becomes dominant over another or when one subsystem takes over the system of which it is but one part. For example, in some people the persona takes over the ego. The person who was presenting himself as a teacher to only his students now becomes a "teacher" toward everyone he meets.

Neurosis was for Jung a term that described the condition in which a group of psychic contents (a complex) moves from the unconscious and disturbs the conscious. It occurs whenever any particular subsystem (or complex) has become overdifferentiated from the others. The goal of the unconscious is to restore the balance in the psyche whenever the conscious psychic contents begin to dominate the psyche. The more the conscious systems become autonomous, the more the unconscious systems will become autonomous, leading to an inner cleavage in the psyche. Thus, neurosis is a state of being at war with oneself, a dissociation of the personality. To cure a neurosis, the contending systems (and their system principles) must be fused into a new identity greater than either alone, which will then be the "self."

A psychosis is differentiated from a neurosis only by the degree of control exerted by the conscious part of the psyche over the unconscious complexes. In a psychosis, elements of the unconscious intrude into the conscious ego. If the intrusion is partial, the ego may simply continue to exist with these unassimilated elements. If the intrusive elements are integrated into the ego, the ego may identify with them and accept them as ego-derived elements. In a neurosis the conscious elements of the ego remain in control of the psyche; in a psychosis the unconscious elements are in control.

Symptoms for the neurotic will stress the weakest activity. For example, if the ego has most fully developed the thinking function, the neurotic symptoms will involve feeling functions. The symptom therefore describes what the ego is *not* doing and so establishes an agenda, pointing to the direction that the psyche must take.

The basic goal of the psyche then is individuation (integration). Individuation involves the balancing and harmonizing of the psyche. Jung's concepts typically involve opposed systems, processes, functions, and attitudes, and so synthesis of these opposites makes an obvious end state for the psyche to attain. This feature of Jung's theory is sometimes called the "principle of opposites."

JUNGIAN APPROACHES TO SUICIDE

James Hillman (1964) has presented a Jungian approach to the study of suicide rather than a Jungian theory of suicide. For Hillman, suicide is one of the many human possibilities, and the critical question for the psychologist concerns the individual meaning of suicide. This meaning is not social (Douglas 1967), that is, provided by the social context in which the suicide occurs, but rather has an internal meaning provided by the individual's psyche. We need to ascertain what mythic fantasy the person is enacting.

Suicide is an attempt at transformation, albeit a hasty transformation. Suicidal fantasies provide freedom from the actual and usual view of things. Suicide is certainly an attack on the body, but not necessary upon the soul, for we do not know if the soul dies. The impulse toward death is also an impulse toward meeting God. Rebirth is impossible without death.

The moment we are born, we are old enough to die. Because death is the only condition that *all* life must take into account, it is the only human *a priori*. Because living and dying imply each other, any act that holds off death prevents life. Suicide is a selfish act, a paradigm of our independence from others, but it also an affirmation of individuality.

To understand the meaning of the suicide of a person, we have first to understand his life. To understand the suicide, we must first understand the soul's history, that is, we must explore the archetypal meaning of the person's complexes rather than the traumatic history of the development of the complexes. The suicidal death, no less than death from an assassin's bullet or a viral infection, belongs within the mythic pattern of the person's fate. Myths govern our lives, good or bad. Some people must live life wrongly and then leave it wrongly.

These views of Hillman are similar to those of Progoff (1975). For Progoff also there is a pattern to our lives that we may never comprehend in intellectual terms. However, the pattern is there to discern at some level of consciousness if we permit ourselves to reflect on our life. In one of his intensive journal exercises, Progoff has participants sit quietly and list the important stepping stones of their lives in an effort to let their unconscious detect the pattern.

A person's death, therefore, should be consistent with his or her lifestyle, one of the possible criteria that Lester (1989) has suggested as making a death *appropriate*. For example, consider how you would like to die. What fantasies have you had about death? As an adolescent, in my daydreams I died in heroic sacrifices, killing a wild beast (and dying along with it) to save others. I fought and died in foreign wars (on the "good" side). I committed suicide and imagined the guilt of all those who had been unkind to me as they stood by my grave. Like many of us, I would like to die in old age, in my bed asleep. These fantasies and desires reflect our personality and our fears, but they also reflect our lifestyle. People often have deaths that fit their lifestyle. The passive individual may choose to die from disease or illness. An aggressive individual may choose to die in a brawl or in war. The person with a self-destructive lifestyle may commit suicide.

For example, consider the death of Ernest Hemingway (Lester 1988a). Hemingway had been seeking and risking death ever since he had been injured by a bomb exploding behind him during the First World War. The fear and anxiety caused by that experience led to a repetition compulsion to prove to himself that he could face death without fear. When he was old, seriously diseased, and showing signs of psychiatric disturbance, it was consistent with his lifestyle that he chose to shoot himself rather than die as a senile old man locked up in a psychiatric ward, with his memory shocked away by electroconvulsive therapy.

Examples of suicide committed so as to preserve a self-image or a lifestyle were recently presented by Litman (1989). He described a psychiatrist who was in treatment for a manic-depressive disorder but refused to be hospitalized. He said that hospitalization would destroy his image of himself as a practicing psychiatrist. When his therapist was away on vacation, he shot himself. Litman commented that preserving his image was more important than preserving his life.

Litman presented another case, a man whose financial empire was in ruins, who killed himself with carbon monoxide. He left a forty-minute tape recording of his last thoughts, which included an admission that it would be easy for him to slip out of the country and never be found. But he said emphatically that he could not do that. It simply was not his way. He would commit suicide because that was his way. Litman commented that the act of suicide confirmed his identity. If his life could not be lived in a particular way, it would be *no* way.

Although Jung referred to the problem of suicide in his writings, he never developed a theory about suicide. However, Leenaars (1988) identified the passages where Jung addressed suicide, and he summarized Jung's views in ten protocol sentences, which are listed in Table 4-1. Leenaars had judges rate genuine suicide notes for the presence or absence of these ten components, and four of the protocol sentences—protocols 1, 2, 3, and 6—were identified in at least two-thirds of the genuine notes.

Lester (1991) took Leenaars's analysis of Jung's theory of suicide and applied it to the lives of thirty suicides sufficiently famous or interesting to warrant a full-length biography. Each of the ten protocol sentences was judged as appropriate for each suicidal life. Four protocol sentences were identified as being quite common in the lives of these suicides (that is, characteristic in two-thirds of the lives or more)—protocols 1, 2, 6, and 7. Three of these protocol sentences are identical with those found to be common in Leenaars's study of genuine suicide notes.

The suicide most congruent with Jung's theory of suicide (as articulated by Leenaars) in Lester's study was that of the American poet Sylvia Plath. Let us then examine the life and death of Sylvia Plath to illustrate Jung's theory of suicide. Plath died at the age of 30 in 1963 in England by putting her head in the gas oven. For the details of her life, I have relied on the biography by Butscher (1976).

THE LIFE OF SYLVIA PLATH

Sylvia's father, Otto Plath, was born in 1885 in Germany. He emigrated to the United States when he was 15 to join his father. After college, he pursued his interest in entomology, going to Harvard for his doctorate. He began teaching at Boston University where he met and married a student named Aurelia Schober, twenty-one years his junior, born in Boston to Roman Catholic parents who were from Austria.

Sylvia was born on October 27, 1932. She was blond and somewhat frail because of a sinus condition that plagued her for the rest of her life. Two and a half years later, her brother Warren was born. Sylvia's early years were uneventful. She apparently was quite bright and used her intelligence to please her father, as many firstborns do. She learned the Latin names for insects, and Otto would show off her skill to visitors. From the beginning, she earned straight A's in school, impressing teachers with her intelligence and dedication.

TABLE 4-1

LEENAARS'S PROTOCOL SENTENCES

1. A "complex" is evident, that is, something discordant, unassimilated, and antagonistic exists (e.g., symptoms, ideas), perhaps as an obstacle, pointing to unresolved problems in the individual.
2. Unresolved problems in the individual are evident, where he has suffered defeat, at least for the time being, and where there is something he cannot evade or overcome. His weak spots are evident.
3. A clash is evident between a demand of adaptation and the individual's constitutional inability to meet the challenge.
4. Suppressions of infantile and primitive demands for cultural reasons are evident.
5. At least symbolically, there is a distance, a lack of balance, a lack of harmony between the conscious and unconscious attitudes, impulses, and so on, resulting in a conflict and the individual's destructive character.
6. The person communicates the existence of a traumatic event (e.g., an unmet love, a failing marriage, disgust with one's work) that results in a deep hurt, being desperate, and, ultimately, the suicide itself.
7. It appears that a wave of depression and desperation snaps the individual's link with his relation to the world, resulting in fantasies ("a new undreamt-of world of stars") that for the individual is far beyond the grievous earth.
8. There is an open conflict between the physical (material) and the spiritual aspects of the individual.
9. If written by a male, there is evidence for the existence of feminine (anima) traits (e.g., sentimentality, emotional weakness). If the note is written by a female, there is evidence for the existence of masculine (animus) traits (e.g., argumentation, rationalization).
10. It appears that inherent reasonableness was prevented from being conscious; rather illogical and irrational characteristics are evident that are related to the self-destruction.

Otto was diabetic but neglected his condition. His leg became gangrenous and was amputated, but the complications of bronchopneumonia killed him on November 5, 1940, nine days after Sylvia's birthday. Aurelia left both children at home during the funeral, which was later one of Sylvia's grievances against her mother.

The family was now in financial difficulty. Aurelia took a teaching position at Boston University's school for secretarial studies and had her parents and brother move in with her to share expenses. Eventually, she decided to move to Wellesley where she could raise her children in an educated and middle-class community and help Sylvia's sinus condition and Warren's asthma. Thereafter, Aurelia strove to give her children high-achievement experiences. In addition to school, she provided extracurricular activities in scouting, sailing, piano and viola lessons, dancing, painting, and summer camps.

Sylvia's first poem appeared in the *Boston Sunday Herald* when she was 8, and she won a prize with a drawing in another contest. As she progressed through school, her work continued to be outstanding, receiving many awards. She quickly developed an interest in literature and in writing. At junior high school (for grades seven through nine) she received straight A's and a perfect record of punctuality. Her poems and drawings continued to win prizes. Her IQ was 160. Socially she was a bit of a loner, although she had many good friends. She did not date much and spent long hours studying, reading, and writing.

High school continued in the same vein. She took the advanced literature courses and edited the school magazine in her senior year. Her stories and poems appeared in *Seventeen* and the *Christian Science Monitor*. She was also active in the local Unitarian church and the community. She was admitted to Smith College and awarded a scholarship.

The only symptoms Butscher mentions in these early years are severe depressions whenever her sinuses or menstrual cramps bothered her. The frequency and severity of the depressions is unclear.

Smith College and the First Suicide Attempt

Sylvia's career at Smith was outstanding. From the first, she obtained A's, and her literary achievements grew steadily. She made many friends there, some staying close to her for the rest of her life. It was considered crucial at Smith to date the right kind of men. Since Sylvia had no relationships with appropriate men from her school days, she went on many blind dates, until a friend from high school days, the Buddy Willard of her novel *The Bell Jar*, took her to the Yale senior prom. Her relationship with Buddy was full of friction, and eventually other boyfriends would come along. But Butscher feels that Sylvia saw marriage as an inevitable and desirable goal and needed always to have a man in her life who could be viewed as a potential husband. Periods of unattachment were hard for her.

Buddy was admitted to Harvard Medical School but had to drop out because he contracted tuberculosis. Sylvia wrote to him and maintained the illusion that he was her boyfriend, but she gradually began to get involved with others.

Sylvia's stay at Smith was the first separation from her mother. Aurelia used to write to Sylvia every day, which suggests that the separation was harder on Aurelia than on Sylvia. In addition, the status of being a scholarship student did carry an inferior status in those days. But there were few other traumas for Sylvia. Sylvia decided that a successful college career involved extracurricular activities, and so she participated in all kinds, successfully building up a record of involvement.

In her junior year she officially broke up with Buddy, who had already been unofficially replaced by Myron Lotz. She broke her leg while skiing during the Christmas recess, but this did not impede her college work. The year ended with Sylvia winning a position as guest editor for *Mademoiselle* for June.

This was the summer of 1953, which is the focus of Sylvia's novel *The Bell Jar*, written mostly during 1961 and 1962. For this month, Sylvia worked for Cyrilly Abels, reading and judging manuscripts, and participating in all of the social activities planned for the group of guest editors. Abels noticed Sylvia's distancing and tried to break through and relate to the real Sylvia, but she failed to penetrate Sylvia's social mask.

Back in Wellesley, Sylvia was rejected for a course on creative writing at Harvard summer school, which left her with two months to fill. She fell into an increasingly severe depression. Aurelia eventually became concerned enough to take her to a local psychiatrist, the Dr. Gordon of the novel, who after a few sessions of psychotherapy recommended electroconvulsive therapy at his clinic. (We must also remember that, in the 1950s, effective antidepressant medications had not yet been developed.)

The idea of suicide grew. She contemplated using a razor blade and drowning. But eventually, on a Monday morning in August, she took forty-eight sleeping pills from where her mother had locked them up, went into the basement of the house, after leaving a note saying that she was going for a hike and would be back the next day, and crawled behind some wood that was stacked there. Her mother called the police that evening, and search parties were organized. But Sylvia was not found until Wednesday afternoon, when her grandmother went into the basement to do the laundry and heard Sylvia moaning.

After a week in the hospital, Sylvia was transferred to the locked psychiatric ward at Massachusetts General Hospital. Sylvia's patron at Smith College, Mrs. Prouty, paid for her to be transferred to McLean's Hospital. There Sylvia received insulin shock therapy at first and then electroconvulsive therapy again, but this was supplemented by psychotherapy from a female psychiatrist, the Dr. Jones of *The Bell Jar*. She was released just before Christmas 1953.

Sylvia spent another year and a half at Smith, graduating in June 1955. This period saw a more extroverted Sylvia, one who now also took pains to be beautiful and fashionably dressed, still the campus literary star and with a romantic aura from being an attempted suicide. Her virginity was lost (and she developed the reputation of being rather loose). There were minor upsets, such as rejection by Myron Lotz, whom Sylvia had seen as a potential husband. She continued to see Dr. Jones occasionally. Sylvia was awarded a Fulbright scholarship upon graduation in 1955 and decided to go to Cambridge University in England to study.

Cambridge University and Ted Hughes

Sylvia spent two years at Cambridge University, at Newnham College, where she eventually obtained her second bachelor's degree. Her stay there was filled with course work, writing, and dating. At Christmas, she visited France and a former lover who was now there. But in February 1956, she met Ted Hughes whom she would soon marry.

Ted, an aspiring poet and writer like Sylvia, had graduated from Cambridge University in 1954 and had worked in various odd jobs. He was now living in London. Sylvia planned to visit Germany in the spring where her current "potential husband" was living, but they argued and broke off their relationship. Sylvia also saw her ex-lover in France for the last time. On her return to England in April 1956, Sylvia and Ted became engaged. They married in June, with Sylvia's mother in attendance, and went to Spain for their honeymoon.

Their first year of marriage was made difficult by the fact that undergraduates could not marry without permission at Cambridge University. Eventually, Sylvia was pardoned and moved out from Newnham College into an apartment with Ted. Their income was from Sylvia's Fulbright award, which had been renewed, and Ted obtained a teaching job at a boys' secondary school.

Sylvia began to work with dedication on their literary careers, typing up and sending off submissions of both her work and Ted's. Their publications grew more and more numerous, and Ted had his first collection of poems accepted for publication in 1957.

They decided to move to the United States in 1957, and Sylvia got a teaching job at Smith College. Ted remained unemployed until 1958, when he got a teaching job at the University of Massachusetts. Sylvia found that an instructor's position teaching freshman English left little time for writing, and so she decided to quit teaching at the end of the year in 1958.

The marriage seemed quite happy. In these initial phases, Ted was the more successful poet. He soon had a second book of poems completed and a book of children's stories. His poems appeared in *The New Yorker*.

They decided to return to England, especially as Ted was not happy in the United States. But first they spent a year in Boston, supported by Sylvia working at odd jobs for a while and then by a Guggenheim fellowship won by Ted. They were trying to have children (although Sylvia was more motivated to have a family than was Ted) and sought medical advice when conception did not occur soon enough. They spent three months touring the United States during the summer of 1959, and during this trip Sylvia became pregnant.

After a stay at Yaddo, the artists' colony near Saratoga Springs in New York, Sylvia and Ted left for England in December 1959. Sylvia was 27, pregnant, and headed for permanent residence in a foreign country.

England and the End

They first rented an apartment in London. Sylvia gave birth to a daughter, Frieda, in April 1960 and, after a miscarriage in February 1961, to a son, Nicholas, in January 1962. Sylvia and Ted's literary careers continued to progress, and Sylvia had her first book of poems published in 1960. They won prize after prize and by 1961 were successful enough as writers that their finances were thereafter in good shape. In 1961, Sylvia was awarded a Saxton Foundation grant to work on *The Bell Jar*.

In 1961, they bought a house in Croton, Devon, with the help of loans from both of their families. Life was full and busy with writing, the children, and a new house to fix up. Butscher describes Sylvia in early 1962 as tense and tired and subject to fits of depression. Yet visitors saw no marital trouble and viewed the life there as idyllic.

Butscher says little about Ted. Perhaps Ted was not enthusiastic about having children? Perhaps after being the more successful writer in the family at first, he was threatened by Sylvia's growing ability and success? But he was instrumental in the decision to move back to England and to live in Devon. However, by the summer of 1962 another woman had entered his life. Butscher calls her Olga, married to a Canadian poet (after a failed first marriage). Olga seems to have pursued Ted, flirting with him even in his own home in Croton. But he too fell in love with her. The affair was in earnest by the summer of 1962.[1]

In August, Olga telephoned Ted, trying to disguise her voice. Sylvia ripped the telephone off the wall and fled to friends. She returned the next day and asked Ted to leave as soon as her mother had departed for

---

[1]Olga appears to have been quite unstable herself, later identifying with Sylvia and believing herself to be Sylvia's reincarnation. She later committed suicide with gas, killing her young daughter, too, possibly Ted's child, although Butscher is not explicit about this.

the United States. Sylvia kept hoping that Ted would come back to her. She came down with a severe bout of influenza, and Ted did come back to help out. In September, Sylvia thought she and Ted were to have a holiday together in Ireland, but Ted left her after one day to visit Olga in London.

Her thirtieth birthday came in October 1962, with Sylvia alone in Devon with two children, deserted by her husband, writing poems furiously every morning. Sylvia decided to find an apartment in London and rent the house in Devon to others. She moved in the middle of December.

Sylvia was secure financially, although, of course, she worried a lot about money. However, in London she found that many of "their" friends were now "his" friends. Both she and Ted also worked for the BBC, which was sometimes awkward. Sylvia was alone with the children that Christmas. Ted visited the children regularly, but these meetings were difficult for Sylvia.

The last few weeks of her life were full of stress. She had corrected the galley proofs for *The Bell Jar* and was awaiting publication and comment. She was working feverishly, smoking heavily, hardly sleeping, and eating little. She had lost twenty pounds since the summer. She had influenza, after which the children came down with it. The winter was one of the worst ever, with frozen plumbing, strikes by the electrical workers, and snow and ice everywhere. Sylvia endured a bathtub that would not empty and dripping pipes in the ceiling. The weather did not break until the end of January.

The reviews of her book appeared at the end of January, and they were lukewarm. (She had published it under a pseudonym, which meant that reviewers would be less likely to give the work close attention and less likely to praise the Sylvia Plath whom they knew.) Her recent poems were being rejected. Sylvia had plans for the future, though. The Devon house was to be rented to an Australian couple, and she was to return there in the summer. Nicholas needed medical treatment for his eye, and Frieda was enrolled in a nursery school.

In the last week of her life, from February 4, 1963, to February 11, Sylvia had a fever and wild fluctuations in her moods. She had lost her au pair girl, and the weather was still bad. Her physician recognized her depression and had arranged for Sylvia to see a therapist (whose letter to her was delivered to the wrong address). By Friday, February 8, he had tried to get three clinics to admit her, but all refused. He arranged for a nurse to come on Monday morning. Sylvia went away for the weekend to visit friends, returning on Sunday evening.

At 6 A.M. on Monday February 11, Sylvia took milk and bread up the children's rooms and went to the kitchen where she sealed the door.

She put her head in the gas oven and was found there later in the morning when the nurse finally broke in with the aid of some workmen.

Analysis

The loss of her father when she was 8 looms large as a factor in Sylvia's life, especially because of the way she wrote about him. However, after reading of her anger toward him in her novel and poems, it is a shock to find that he was a mild-mannered academic, the age of a grandfather more than a father, who died of natural causes (rather than deserting his family for another woman). His greatest fault seems to be that he spent too much time with his bees and his research.

Nonetheless, Sylvia was full of anger for his rejection of her, both while he was alive and in his death. Her poem *Daddy*, written in the months prior to her suicide, casts him as a devil, a concentration camp guard with her as a victim. She sees Ted as a father substitute. And yet she loves her father, too, and casts her suicide attempt years earlier as an attempt to be reunited with him. (Interestingly, her identification with him was strong. Sylvia eventually kept bees, as did her father, and she studied German, the language of her father.)

Although her depressions are not documented well at all, it is likely that she had an affective disorder. It led to her breakdown as an undergraduate, and she lived in fear that it would occur again. Might her suicide have been motivated in part also by a fear of becoming seriously depressed in the future?

We have the precipitant of a loss. Her husband, whom she loves and who provided her with the environment to flourish as a mother and author, rejects her for another. (Interestingly, Sylvia was upset in her marriage by the very close relationship between Ted and his sister Olwyn, which she calls incestuous. And in a memorable row when Sylvia was eight months pregnant with Nicholas, Olwyn told Sylvia how much she resented her. Ted did not take Sylvia's side at all in this, which hurt her deeply.)

In her novel about the breakdown in 1953, Sylvia shows a distrust of her own ability. She had worked hard to get good grades and to publish, but such people often fear that the success is temporary. They dread getting a grade of B and signs that their talent is dying. However, Sylvia was quite resilient in her writing, sending off poems and stories despite rejections, knowing that one has to keep submitting writing if one is going to be successful.

Butscher makes much of Sylvia's facade. She seems, more than the average person, to have suppressed the real Sylvia, assuming a mask that would get her approval from others. Good grades (reinforced by her father's admiration for her academic skills), desirable boyfriends (and eventually lovers), and awards and honors all served to bolster her self-esteem. But eventually one must come to like oneself for who one is, regardless of the reactions of others, and this perhaps comes in middle age, too late for Sylvia.

Sylvia Plath's Life and Jung's Theory

When we look at Sylvia Plath's life in relation to the ten protocol statements listed by Leenaars as characteristic of Jung's theory of suicide (Table 4-1), it is clear that Sylvia had discordant complexes (protocol 1). She had never come to terms with her father's death, and her life after his death was in part an attempt to find a replacement for him. She viewed her suicide as a chance to be reunited with him. Other complexes are evident, too, including her doubts as to her ability. Was she talented or was she a fraud?

Sylvia clearly had unresolved problems (protocol 2) from her childhood, and a resolution of her recent problems (the breakup of her marriage) was made more difficult by these earlier ones. The childhood desires for her father had to be suppressed and may never have been adequately dealt with in her later life despite her psychotherapy (protocol 4). This suggests a lack of harmony between her conscious and her unconscious attitudes (protocol 5). Furthermore, Sylvia was not able at the time of her suicide to adapt to the difficult situation facing her (protocol 3).

There is clear evidence of current trauma (protocol 6), which resulted in a deep hurt and depression, and Sylvia in her reunion fantasies seems to have lost a secure link to the real world (protocol 7), while her thinking appears to be illogical and irrational (protocol 10). I am uncertain whether there is clear evidence only for protocols 8 and 9 in Sylvia's life.

It can be seen then that Jung's theory of suicide as articulated by Leenaars applies to the life and death of Sylvia Plath quite well.

ARCHETYPES OF SUICIDE

As I noted at the beginning of this chapter, archetypes are themes in the collective unconscious that can be identified from their appearance in myth, legend, and fairy tale, as well as in ordinary imagery. Jungian psychologists have not considered the existence of archetypes that might incorporate suicidal themes, and so it is not possible to review their ideas. The themes identified here are intended to suggest possibilities for such archetypes and are presented to provoke readers into pursuing these ideas.

Just as Jung distinguished between the personal unconscious and the collective unconscious, the motivations for suicide may derive from both the personal and the collective unconscious. For example, in the Theban plays by Sophocles, when Oedipus discovers that he did indeed murder his father and marry his mother, his first thought is to take his sword and go in search of his mother. He crashes through the door to her bedroom ready to slay her, only to discover that she has hanged herself. He drops the sword and blinds himself using brooches from her dress. In a later play in the series, when Haemon finally persuades his father, Creon, to save Antigone from the death Creon has decreed for her, they break into the cave in which she was sealed only to find that she has hanged herself. Haemon tries to kill his father with his sword, but fails, whereupon he turns the sword on himself.

It is clear that Sophocles captures in these characters some of the Freudian thoughts about suicide, that suicide is a result of anger toward another (for Oedipus his mother and for Haemon his father) that is turned inward upon the self in self-destructive behavior. The question is whether Oedipus and Haemon represent an archetypal suicidal theme? I think not. Although Oedipus himself provides the label for a more powerful archetype (known to us as the oedipal complex), his self-blinding (or *focal suicide* to use Menninger's [1938] term) seems to result from processes in the personal unconscious.

Which suicides, then, might be representative of archetypes? Consider the kamikaze pilots of Japan in the Second World War. They aimed their planes at American ships or other targets and died in the crash. They committed suicide for a cause, a heroic self-sacrifice. During the Iran–Iraq war, young Iranian soldiers performed similar sacrificial acts. In fact, in any war, soldiers give their lives to save fellow soldiers or civilians, as do firefighters and others involved in rescues on a daily basis. Although Jesus' life may illustrate many archetypes, his refusal to act so as to prevent his own death sentence and execution can be seen as similar, for he died willingly to save others. This theme of suicide as self-sacrifice occurs in daydreams and stories, and perhaps reflects an archetype.

Romeo and Juliet also has potential as an archetype. In this story of a love that the society will not permit, the lovers are teenagers. (Would the story have as much power if the people were middle-aged?) Their parents will not let them meet, and certainly not become lovers, so they seek union in death. The same theme has been documented in real life in the young lovers jumping to their deaths into the volcano at Mount Mihara in Japan (Ellis and Allen 1961).

Suttee, the Hindu custom of widows committing suicide on the funeral pyre of their husbands, is reminiscent of the practice of the Chinese emperor's concubines committing suicide after his death during the Ming dynasty. A different theme, although similar, is the suicide of the elderly, particularly to avoid being a burden to their family, a custom well documented in the Arctic cultures and in rural Japan in the last century.

This type of suicide is also found among individuals today. While I was working at the suicide prevention center in Buffalo in 1970, an elderly couple went over Niagara Falls to their death because the husband believed he had cancer and the wife did not want to live without him. The suicide of Stefan Zweig, the Austrian writer, was unusual because his young, healthy wife decided to die along with him rather than live alone.

Similarly, it is not uncommon today for those who know that they are dying to commit suicide, at least in part to spare their family the expense of a lingering illness and emotional pain. Indeed, as the psychosocial problems of dying with AIDS have become increasingly clear in recent years, more and more thought has been given to suicide as a rational way of death for those with the disease (Lester 1988b).

Thus, personal decisions to commit suicide may be motivated not only by conscious desires and desires in the personal unconscious, but they may also reflect themes from the collective unconscious. Although I did not discuss the suicides of Ernest Hemingway and Marilyn Monroe in this section as illustrations of possible archetypal themes, I have wondered whether the fascination of the general public with both of them signifies that their deaths in some way touch upon archetypal themes in the society.

DISCUSSION

In this chapter, I have reviewed Jungian ideas on suicide and found that Jung's implicit theory of suicide, made a little more explicit by Leenaars, has value in explaining the lives and deaths of some suicides. I have shown that Hillman's philosophical attitude toward suicide makes at least some suicides appear to be less pathological in nature and suggests that suicide may be a reasonable development and extension of a person's life. I have proposed that suicide may be present in some archetypal themes, and I have suggested some possible themes.

This chapter then is more of a prolegomenon to a study of the unconscious in the suicidal process, as is this book as a whole. Despite the many thousands of sociological, psychological, and psychiatric studies into suicide, I have often felt that I do not truly understand why any particular individual commits suicide. Although it may be difficult to bring the unconscious into the range of convenience of scientific research, in doing so there is perhaps the possibility of greatly advancing our understanding of why people commit suicide.

REFERENCES

Butscher, E. (1976). *Sylvia Plath*. New York: Seabury.

Chomsky, N. (1972). *Language and Mind*. New York: Harcourt Brace Jovanovich.

Douglas, J. D. (1967). *The Social Meanings of Suicide*. Princeton, NJ: Princeton University Press.

Ellis, E. R., and Allen, G. N. (1961). *Traitor Within*. Garden City, NY: Doubleday.

Hillman, J. (1964). *Suicide and the Soul*. New York: Harper & Row.

Leenaars, A. A. (1988). *Suicide Notes*. New York: Human Sciences Press.

Lester, D. (1988a). *Suicide as a Learned Behavior*. Springfield, IL: Charles C Thomas.

———— (1988b). Suicide and AIDS. *Archives of the Foundation of Thanatology* 14(4):unpaged.

———— (1989). *Can We Prevent Suicide?* New York: AMS.

———— (1991). The study of suicidal lives. *Suicide and Life-Threatening Behavior* 21:164–173.

Litman, R. E. (1989). Suicides: What do they have in mind? In *Suicide: Understanding and Responding*, ed. D. Jacobs and H. N. Brown, pp. 143–154. Madison, CT: International Universities Press.

Menninger, K. (1938). *Man Against Himself*. New York: Harcourt Brace.

Progoff, I. (1973). *Jung's Psychology and its Social Meaning*. Garden City, NY: Anchor.

———— (1975). *At an Intensive Journal Workshop*. New York: Dialogue House.

5: SUICIDE, SELF-DECEPTION, AND THE COGNITIVE UNCONSCIOUS

Michael J. Kral and Edward A. Johnson

A return to theories of the mind is occurring within suicidology and other human sciences. The modern study of suicide was inspired by such a focus, in the meeting held in Freud's apartment in 1910 where Wilhelm Stekel proposed that suicide is a murderous wish turned toward the self (Shneidman 1969). A resurgence in the study of consciousness and the unconscious is now taking place in psychology, philosophy, and related disciplines (e.g., Bowers and Meichenbaum 1984, Davies and Humphreys 1993, Kihlstrom 1990, Searle 1992, Uleman and Bargh 1989). Epstein (1994) has recently described a new look outside of, but bridging with, the field of psychoanalysis, referred to as the *cognitive unconscious*. In this account of the mind, cognition outside of awareness is viewed as "a fundamentally adaptive system that automatically, effortlessly, and intuitively organizes experience and directs behavior. . . . [it] holds that most information processing occurs automatically and effortlessly outside of awareness because that is its natural mode of operation, a mode that is far more efficient than conscious, deliberative thinking" (p. 710).

The conceptual lens is now widening, and the publication of this book on the suicidal mind attests to this direction. Yet in spite of an increased awareness over the past few decades of many pieces to the puzzle of suicide, a puzzle it remains. In this chapter we examine the psychology of suicide through an emergent model in which suicide is viewed as a conscious decision that is part of a process outside of awareness, a process in which self-deception may, for some, play a prominent and ultimately lethal role. It is hoped that this contribution might suggest some additional directions within suicidology.

COMPLETED SUICIDE

Maris (1992) has recently called for a clearer definition of the various types of suicide. Importantly, suicidology needs to continue focusing on the differentiation of completed suicide from other self-harming behaviors in order to better identify the individual at risk for this final act. Although it was suggested several decades ago that completed and attempted suicide are different phenomena (Shneidman and Farberow 1961, Stengel 1964), we are only recently learning from research that this is an area worthy of further serious investigation. For example, those who have killed themselves have not tended to seek professional help in their lifetimes and are rarely in treatment at the time of their deaths (Clark and Horton-Deutsch 1992).

That people who ultimately kill themselves avoid the mental health system is borne out in other research. When compared with suicide attempters, completers have been found more likely to be male, particularly males from socially disrespected groups, socially isolated and alone, alcohol abusive, medically ill, hopeless, anxious, suffering from a major mood disorder, less likely to report being suicidal, less likely to report family problems, and less likely to have a history of attempts (Beck and Steer 1989, Dingman and McGlashan 1988, Fremouw et al. 1990, Klerman 1987, Maris 1981, Morgan and Priest 1984). It appears that while mental health workers are being reached by many people in crisis, including crises involving suicidal ideation and self-harming behavior, those who go on to kill themselves may often be missed not so much due to inadequate assessment methods but rather because they are less oriented toward seeking help. Although one could argue that many persons who seek and obtain treatment might otherwise have killed themselves (and for the vast majority of cases we will never really know if they would have done so), the suggestion that completed suicides are indeed different is, at this time, compelling. Shneidman (1985) has even suggested that the motivation for suicidal behavior is different for attempters than for completers. While attempters may seek communication, completers seek escape. It is to the motivation of escape that we turn.

ESCAPE THEORY

Psychological theories of suicide have as one core motivational theme the escape from unbearable consciousness or stress. Suicidal people do not wish to be dead so much as they wish to stop suffering, a central (and potentially life-saving) aspect of their ambivalence. By 1910 Freud had linked escape from humiliation with suicide (Litman 1970), and later Menninger (1938) highlighted escape as one of the motives behind the act. Shneidman (1985) has identified egression as a significant commonality across all suicides, and both Baechler (1975) and Maris (1992) have highlighted escape within their theoretical models of suicide. The most detailed escape theory of suicide, however, has been proposed by Baumeister (1990) in his view of suicide as escape from self.

Baumeister has identified self-destructive behavior in general as motivated by a need to escape from high self-awareness that is accompanied by negative emotions (see Baumeister and Scher 1988). He has suggested a stepwise causal model of suicidal behavior beginning with the experience of a setback/failure, whereby outcomes or circumstances fall below standards one has set for oneself. This is followed by negative self-attributions, a negative and aversive state of high self-awareness, more negative affect, and a temporary escape from this self-awareness into a "relatively numb state of cognitive deconstruction." The inevitable return to painful self-awareness only strengthens the resolve to escape. Finally, reduced inhibitions during this cognitive state result in suicidal behavior as an "escape from meaningful awareness of current life problems and their implications about the self" (Baumeister 1990, p. 91).

The strength of Baumeister's escape theory of suicide is his use of recent empirical research on the self, affect, cognition, and self-awareness, and avoidance of the common tautology of suicide caused by mental disorder. It is a strong argument about how suicide becomes a choice for a select few. As Baumeister (1990) notes, the vast majority of individuals who experience personal setbacks and the ensuing negative affect and self-awareness will not choose suicide as a means of coping. It is not clear, however, that when suicidal ideation and behavior is chosen in the face of intense personal distress, such a result is simply the product of the intrapsychic states identified by Baumeister. The idea of suicide as a means of escape encompasses much more.

Shneidman (1985) has suggested that suicide can be viewed as a function of two necessary, sufficient, but quite different conditions: perturbation and lethality. Perturbation is the degree of upset, agitation, pain, and ennui that a person can experience to the point of intolerance. He defined lethality as the degree of a person's deadliness, how "deathly suicidal" a person is, or the likelihood of a suicidal person having a "lethal outcome" (pp. 205, 230). Kral (1994) has suggested that, in suicide, perturbation be viewed primarily as *motivation*. When people reach a point at which they can no longer stand the perturbation, they are motivated to do something about it. What they do is open; unbearable perturbation is nondirectional and merely a motivator for action toward reducing the state of upset. The expression and tolerance/ intolerance of perturbation is subjective, has both stable and changing qualities for a person, and has constitutional and contextual determinants (see Harre 1986, Lewis and Haviland 1993). Escape theories of suicide, including Baumeister's, all center around escape from unbearable perturbation. As Shneidman has pointed out, however, perturbation alone never leads to suicide. And when most people reach their point of intolerance, suicide is not the escape route.

Extending Shneidman's concept of lethality, the term is conceptualized here as the *idea* of suicide as the means to escape unbearable perturbation

(Kral 1994). It is the idea that includes planning, decision, and action—lethality as the conative, directional *choice* regarding what to do given the motivation for action. The idea of suicide comes not from "within" the person but from the incorporation of socially available options, from cultural models (see, e.g., Markus and Kitayama 1991, Schwartz et al. 1992). Indeed, we are only beginning to discover how culture and context afford certain cognitive, behavioral, and affective (i.e., narrative/schematic) pathways of experience, expression, and coping while simultaneously constraining others. The notion of an "automatic, effortless, and intuitive" cognitive unconscious is quite compatible with a particular cognitive style or styles—for example, motivational schemas—developed within one's cultural context. D'Andrade (1992) has outlined how cultural schemas can have "directional force" for what is perceived to be intuitive and for providing logical connections between experience and action.

For example, regardless of one's perspective on the *actual* incidence and prevalence of multiple personality disorder/dissociative identity disorder, it is clear by any standard that, over the past decade or so, this particular way of configuring one's experience has been transformed from being a rare form of psychopathology to becoming a much more common means of exhibiting distress (Hacking 1986, 1992, Spanos 1994). Such a cultural psychological perspective suggests that suicide be viewed as a function of a person's experience of intolerable perturbation together with the selection of suicide as a choice of method to alleviate the pain from among forms of coping adopted from within the cultural and local context. Once formed, the idea of suicide will have been available in the mind for some time, has now become accessible from one's hierarchy of conscious and nonconscious options, and, given agitated cognition in the context of a depressed, alienated, hopeless state, is activated and may be perceived as the only choice that "makes sense" to the person (Kral and Dyck, in press). The seeming odd sensibility of this choice will be discussed in a later section.

Which people are more vulnerable to accept the idea of suicide, the motivational schema or action plan, into their concepts of self and choice? That some of the characteristics of those at risk for completed suicide include avoidance of potential help, less disclosure about their intent or about problems in general, and less parasuicidal behavior in their history suggests that the motivation to escape is indeed applicable to this group. Viewing suicide as escape, we need to examine those people for whom escape from negative self-awareness might be a *characteristic psychological style*, for whom the idea of suicide might "fit" with their more usual patterns of responding to this form of stress. We turn now to a detailed discussion of an escape-driven defensive style that may predispose some people, under certain conditions, to selecting suicide as an extreme yet logically compatible route.

REPRESSIVE COPING AS A PERSONALITY STYLE

Habitual avoidance or escape from aversive self-awareness and the notion of repression go back at least to Freud (Ellenberger 1970). Shevrin and Bond (1993) have defined repression as "*motivated* forgetting of some *ideational* content related to a conflictual unconscious wish," with the ideational content being "an idea, cognitive in character, rather than affect" (p. 312, original italics). Others, such as Singer (1990) and Erdelyi (1990), combine conflictual affect with cognition that together can evoke undesirable experiences, for which repressive forgetting and defense mechanisms such as isolation, dissociation, intellectualization, denial, and projection serve to protect the self from certain kinds of psychological pain. Singer (1990) has proposed repression as an umbrella term for mechanisms that prevent conscious awareness of negative self-relevant thoughts and emotions. Two highly related terms—*self-deception* and *repression*—are often used synonymously, however. Following Sackheim and Gur (1978) and Schafer (1992), we view self-deception theoretically as the broader, more inclusive category that simply denotes motivated nonawareness of conflicting beliefs or selves. Schafer (1992) provides a general definition of "self-deceiving actions" that allows for both adaptive and maladaptive outcomes:

> In times of apparent danger, and in order to be able to function less anxiously and in a less restricted or damaging manner, the subject . . . will aim to develop or restore subjective feelings of safety and confidence by employing forms and contents of thought whose nature it is to transform threatening conceptions of the current state of affairs and threatening courses of action, or both, into less threatening ones. [p. 41]

The first use of the term *unconscious* in this chapter is thus focused on *content*: nonawareness of negative self-relevant material. Yet how can negative psychological states exist if, according to this definition, one is not aware of them? What then "happens" to them?

One area of investigation demonstrates this seeming contradiction rather well. Researchers have found that significant discrepancies between various aspects of the self, such as between real versus ideal or public versus private aspects (e.g., Higgins 1987), are related to psychological vulnerability. More recently, a stylistic personality trait is being studied whereby under stressful conditions a contradiction exists between two modes of emotional expression: verbal report and physiological responding. This particular form of "repressive coping style" was originally identified by Weinberger and colleagues (1979) among people who scored low on a self-report measure of trait anxiety and high on a need-for-approval scale, yet whose autonomic (sympathetic) arousal was higher than that of people self-identified as highly anxious. The repressors' abnormally high level of autonomic arousal was present even under minimally threatening conditions. The threatening conditions causing high arousal had to do with the possibility of being viewed in a negative evaluative light by others and ultimately by the self. Unique to the repressors was that they evidenced the highest levels of autonomic arousal across low-anxious and high-anxious groups yet continued to deny the subjective experience of even minimal distress. Although somewhat recondite within even the Freudian notion of unconscious affect (see Tov-Ruach 1988), they seemed to be, in a sense, anxious without knowing it.

Whereas the subjective experience and verbal expression of emotion is very much a product of one's learning and conditioning history, of one's familial and social contexts (see Avrill 1986, Lutz and White 1986), there is some evidence that the autonomic expression of basic emotional states may be "hard-wired" across cultures (Frijda 1986, Levenson et al. 1992). Research and theory suggest that subjective awareness of, or experiential correspondence with, autonomic functioning aids in and is perhaps critical to its own regulation and homeostasis (Ader et al. 1988, Baars 1983, Mandler 1983, Melnechuk 1988, Schwartz 1986). Although verbal reports of one's physiological responses can be rather inaccurate, what appears to matter is that verbal self-reports and autonomic functioning exhibit some degree of correspondence (Asendorpf and Scherer 1983, Jorgensen et al. 1992, Mandler et al. 1961). The consequence of not being in synchrony with one's body—being disconnected from oneself, in a sense—may be of some consequence regarding one's physical and mental health.

A particular psychological style linked to some mental health risk has indeed been found for people with repressive coping styles. Reviewing the relevant research, Bonnano and Singer (1990), Schwartz (1990), and Weinberger (1990) have found that this style has been linked to depression; a preference for solitary activity; less willingness to disclose personal information; a denial of problems and being overly positive in self-presentation, even when signs of hopelessness and helplessness are present; effortful self-control; a rigidly maintained self-concept, including being less willing to entertain the possibility of changing something about oneself; poorer ability in making social inferences; problematic interpersonal relationships; a greater avoidance of negative memories and generally less recollection of early childhood memories; and a higher likelihood of using distancing, distraction, intellectualization, and recoding (neutralizing threatening content by interpreting it as unintentional or unimportant) as defense mechanisms. These reviews also found that this coping style may also compromise physical health, being related to higher resting levels of systolic blood pressure, greater change in blood pressure and slower general autonomic recovery to baseline following mentally stressing tasks, and lower levels of natural killer cell activity and earlier death in patients with malignant melanoma (see also Eysenck 1994). Greater diastolic blood pressure has also been found among repressors following stress (Jorgensen et al. 1991), and male repressors have been found to be a higher risk for atherosclerotic diseases (Niaura et al. 1992).

Others have found that, when compared to those who report richer emotional experiences, individuals with less emotional self-awareness process negative information more slowly (Turner 1978), spend less time attending to negative aspects of the self and more time on positive information (Franzoi and Brewer 1984), manifest less self-focused attention, report less extreme emotions, respond to and recall emotional information more slowly, and "actively attempt to inhibit ongoing thoughts, emotions, or behaviors" (Pennebaker 1989, p. 338). They appear to have a need for self-defense that is stronger than their need for self-knowledge (Franzoi et al. 1990). In several studies Davis and Franzoi (1987) found a strong relation between the habitual avoidance of attention to private, negative aspects of oneself, low self-disclosure, and less-satisfying interpersonal ties.

Thus, in addition to lack of awareness of negative content regarding the self, a second definition of the unconscious used here places an emphasis on a cognitive *process* or form of thought that is largely outside of awareness: habitual use of escape strategies or mechanisms in order to avoid or minimize confrontation with negative self-schemas. The picture that emerges from the literature cited above, then, is rather consistent in spite of the several different ways investigators have identified people as repressors. It is one of repressors manifesting verbal-autonomic discrepancies, being unaware of negative self-schemas, and being unaware of the process by which they typically avoid the potential activation of negative self-awareness. This apparent lack of awareness of a range of emotional experience appears to have adverse physical and mental health consequences. As a form of self-deception, one might ask whether one such consequence is increased risk for completed suicide.

An early scale of self-deception that has in fact rarely been used as such is the K scale of defensiveness on the Minnesota Multiphasic Personality Inventory (MMPI) (Meehl and Hathaway 1946). Some have linked high K scores to self-deception (Greene 1991, Meehl and Hathaway 1946, Monts et al. 1977), and K is highly correlated with scales that load most highly on a factor identified as self-deceptive responding (Paulhus 1986). Some earlier studies point to a relationship between persons who obtain high scores on K and the stylistic pattern of repressors described above. For example, people with elevations on K have been found to be more effortful in trying to maintain self-esteem and to block personal insights (Rogers and Walsh 1959), and among psychiatric patients are characterized as being more rigid and inflexible, with slower recovery and less likelihood of remission and release from hospital (Glassock 1955). Yet high K scores are also related to good self-management and control, personal effectiveness in a variety of situations (e.g., Berger 1953, 1955, Heilbrun 1961, Sweetland and Quay 1953, Weiner

1951), and consistency in self-presentation and personality organization over time (Fiske 1957, Gynther and Brilliant 1968, Reis 1966). Already here we have an early indication that there are two sides to self-deception: adaptive and maladaptive.

There has been very little but suggestive work on the K scale and suicide. In a study conducted at the Los Angeles Suicide Prevention Center, Jones (1969) gave the MMPI to suicidal patients presenting to the outpatient clinic and compared the response patterns of those who went on to complete suicide with those who did not. His data showed that while both groups demonstrated a classic "suicide risk" profile, the patients who killed themselves had higher K scores (both groups' K scores were above average) and appeared to be experiencing more anxiety at the time of testing. It may have been this anxious-depressive perturbation that brought them into the clinic in the first place, yet they had a higher-than-average level of self-deception. Kral (1992) reported two cases of completed suicide with similar MMPI profiles of high K and suicide risk. After being hospitalized for depression with suicidal ideation, both patients presented with a relatively quick tendency toward emotional self-control. Yet when pressed during interviews, they also demonstrated, but were quick to cover up, a painfully acute state of anxiety and hopelessness. One of these patients demonstrated particular difficulty around self-awareness when being asked about her current mood; she could not use the personal pronoun *I* when speaking about herself, but used only *you* or *one* (e.g., "One can be sad when . . ."). Although her eye contact was otherwise good, during this time she avoided looking at the examiner and her eyes darted nervously around the floor. Furthermore, she seemed unable to switch to the first person even when this was pointed out to her.

While at this time merely suggestive, a number of studies and clinical observations are suggesting an emergent pattern for those who complete suicide. It includes many of the repressive tendencies noted thus far in conjunction with a high level of perturbation. There is a strong suggestion that such people had struggled unsuccessfully with an unbearable psychological pain they could no longer keep out of awareness. Given the potentially vital link between this stylistic pattern and risk for completed suicide, in the next section we will explore theory and some recent findings on the psychology of self-deception before returning to suicide.

SELF-DECEPTION AND THE ILLUSION
OF INVULNERABILITY

Research has consistently shown that we employ self-serving cognitive heuristics and biases to the exclusion of otherwise important information in our perceptual worlds (Kahneman et al. 1982, Kuhn 1989, Nisbett and Ross 1980, Piattelli-Palmarini 1994). Clearly, there are adaptive benefits to sustaining illusions of invulnerability. Janoff-Bulman (1992) has argued that to function effectively in a world fraught with perils, including death, disaster, illness, and other misfortunes, some degree of reliance on illusions of invulnerability and the like is not only useful, but necessary. It would appear that, in order to proceed in life without being paralyzed by anxiety or despair, it is necessary to adopt various illusory beliefs about life and, when they are exposed as such, to deceive oneself into believing them all over again. Indeed, theorists have argued persuasively that positive illusions (Taylor 1989, Taylor and Brown 1988) and self-deception (Sackheim 1983) be viewed as not merely sustaining positive adjustment in times of crisis, for instance, but as bedrock constituents of positive mental health. In their review of research on the adaptive value of positive illusions, Taylor and Brown (1988) conclude that overly positive self-evaluations, along with illusions of control and exaggerated optimism, contribute to greater personal happiness, creativity, productivity, and an enhanced ability to care for others, all of which are important features of mental health (Jahoda 1958, Jourard and Landsman 1980).

These considerations pose a serious challenge to the model of repression as a risk factor for maladaptive psychological outcomes, particularly suicide. In the face of these contradictory research findings, a reconsideration of some elementary assumptions and the meanings of terms such as *self-deception* and *positive illusions* is in order.

Adaptive and Maladaptive Illusions

William James once remarked that in our credulity we are haunted by the need to believe. Here we find both an acknowledgment of the inescapable necessity of belief as well as a hint that the consequences of this necessity are not always positive. For James, the essential defining fact of persons is their beliefs. Accordingly, a meaningful existence seems to require having a core set of beliefs about the world, one's self, and the relation of the two that is viable and promotes adaptive functioning. It is here, in the requirement that such beliefs be connected to reality as well as promote adaptive responding, that we detect the tension between accuracy and adaptiveness. The notion that self-deception is inherently maladaptive rests on two apparently straightforward assumptions. First, it is generally supposed that one simply cannot sustain beliefs that are contradicted by the harsh facts of reality, or at least not for long. Second, it is assumed that, were one able to succeed in sustaining an inaccurate, self-deceptive belief in the face of overwhelming contradictory evidence, the cost of severing one's contact with reality to such an extent would far outweigh the advantages accrued from maintaining a particular belief. To summarize, the argument against self-deception asserts that self-deception cannot take you where you want to go, and where it takes you no one would wish to be.

How then should we define self-deception? Obviously, it is wrong to say that anyone who holds a false belief is self-deceived since the falsehood could have been the result of a lie or simple mistake. *Self-deception*, as the term suggests, must involve a process of actively deceiving oneself. Freud held that self-deception is an unconscious act, in that "a deception cannot succeed if it is known as a deception" (Schafer 1992, p. 48). As numerous commentators have pointed out, however, this requirement seems to involve a contradiction (Demos 1960). By lying to myself I come to believe what I know to be false. This paradox of self-deception is all the more tantalizing for appearing to be at once both true to experience yet logically impossible. Sartre (1943) formulated the paradox of self-deception thusly:

> The one to whom the lie is told and the one who lies are one and the same person, which means that I must know in my capacity as deceiver the truth which is hidden from me in my capacity as the one deceived. Better yet, I must know the truth very exactly in order to conceal it more carefully. [p. 49]

Whereas lying entails *knowing* that what one is communicating is false, as well as *intending* to induce a false belief in someone, the notion of being deceived is less restrictive and need not involve either knowledge or intent to occur (Mele 1983, Sackheim and Gur 1978). Thus, one may speak of having been unintentionally deceived, as for example by a visual illusion. All that is essential to the notion of deception is that a person comes to accept a false belief. As Fingarette (1969) argues, furthermore, self-deception consists of more than a mere inconsistency in one's beliefs, even if self-induced. Allowing that self-deception is not accidental does not entail that it be intentional and purposeful (Sackheim and Gur 1978). One's actions may be motivated yet fall short of being intentional. Accordingly, in their model of self-deception, Sackheim and Gur assert that self-deception consists of holding two contra-dictory beliefs, one of which is not subject to awareness, and it is this lack of awareness that is motivated.

This view of self-deception appears to satisfy a logical and semantic analysis of the notion of self-deception. Indeed, it offers a useful way of conceptualizing the mental processes and contents involved in cases of what may be dubbed "perceptual" self-deception in which an individual attempts to avoid perceiving something that would be unpleasant to conscious experience. For example, Gur and Sackheim (1979) found that people who misidentified their own voice on a tape recorder as another's evaluated that voice more positively than those who correctly identified their own voices. Yet a limitation of this approach to self-deception is that, while it provides a plausible account of what we may term *perceptual* forms of self-deception, it is much less adequate for *inferential* kinds of self-deception. The distinction between perceptual and inferential self-deception closely parallels the com-monly made distinction between denying a fact and denying the implication of that fact (cf. Lazarus 1983). If in perceptual self-deception the goal is to avoid consciously perceiving a certain perceptual fact, the goal of inferential self-deception is to avoid drawing reasonable, probable, but painful conclusions from the perception of a fact or set of facts; that is, in cases of inferential self-deception no attempt is made to dispute or disavow the existence of something that is painful or unpleasant. Rather, the goal is to draw a preferred interpretation of the facts, thereby preempting a more accurate but painful conclusion. For instance, one may grudgingly accept the fact of being fired from a job, but vigorously insist the fault was in everyone and everything but oneself.

These cases of inferential self-deception come much closer to our intuitions of what most people mean by self-deception. However, unlike the act of perception, which is rapid and relatively automatic and effortless, the act of drawing a conclusion from a set of facts can, depending on the amount and complexity of the circumstances, require considerable thought and effort to complete (Johnson-Laird 1983). Accordingly, we cannot assume, as may be reasonable in cases of perceptual self-deception, that the self-deceiver *knows* at some subterranean level the truth of the matter that he or she consciously disavows. What seems more probable is that in many cases individuals will receive bad news and simply choose not to unpack its implications, or, alternately, they may construct an explanation for them that if true would render them harmless or even advantageous. In this vein, Greenwald (1988) developed his "junk-mail" model to explain how the mind can expertly avoid information and conclusions without already knowing them in advance. Greenwald observes that most of us are familiar enough with the contents of junk mail solicitations that we no longer have to open such mail to "know" what is inside. In the same fashion, a self-deceiver upon receiving bad news (e.g., being fired from work) may decide not to think about the reason for the firing. When viewed from a "junk mail" perspective, we do not have to assume that this person already knows the reason and thus avoids it. Rather, the self-deceiver may know that whatever explanation is arrived at will be aversive and therefore simply avoids doing the thinking that would be necessary to develop one. The self-deceiver has "recoded" it.

WHEN SELF-DECEPTION FAILS

Sackheim and Gur (1979) found evidence that the tendency to self-deceive is a stable personality trait that can be reliably assessed. Individuals who exhibited self-deception on the voice-identification task referred to earlier obtained a high score on a questionnaire specifically designed to measure self-deception—the Self-Deception Questionnaire (SDQ). Many of the items on the SDQ concern thoughts and impulses that are thought to be universally true but embarrassing or shameful to admit, even to oneself (e.g., enjoying one's bowel movements). Studies examining the relationship between scores on the SDQ and various measures of psychopathology and adjustment appear to support the view of self-deception as adaptive. The SDQ has been found to be moderately negatively correlated with a variety of standard measures of psychopathology (Roth and Ingram 1985, Sackheim 1983, Sackheim and Gur 1979), and positively correlated with measures of adjustment that include self-esteem and ego-resiliency (Paulhus 1986).

This evidence provides support for the adaptiveness of self-deception but remains weak insofar as it relies on self-report evidence. Because the accuracy of self-deceivers' self-reports is by definition open to question, research employing objective performance measures is necessary to overcome the limitations inherent in self-report measures of outcome. In two recent studies, Johnson (in press) assessed the ability of high and low scorers on Paulhus's (1986) revised SDQ to solve word problems following a failure experience on a purported test of intelligence. In the first study, subjects were initially exposed to solvable or unsolvable concept-formation problems before attempting solvable anagrams. The anagram task required subjects to search for an underlying pattern in each of the anagrams that, if found, would allow them to solve them rapidly. As expected, those who initially received the unsolvable problems subsequently had more difficulty solving the anagrams and finding the underlying pattern than those who initially received solvable problems. However, the impact of prior exposure to success or failure had little to no impact on non–self-deceivers, but a considerable effect on self-deceivers. Indeed, contrary to predictions derived from the adaptiveness hypothesis, self-deceivers' performance was significantly *worse* following exposure to unsolvable problems. That is, while a self-deceptive coping style appeared to be of some advantage following a success experience, it was a clear disadvantage following failure.

In the second study, Johnson (in press) attempted to determine whether the poor performance of self-deceivers following failure might have been due to the clear and unambiguous nature of the negative feedback they received. It was hypothesized that if negative feedback were provided in a more ambiguous context, the opportunity for self-deception might be enhanced. Thus, in this study subjects were exposed to failure in either the standard unambiguous condition or in a new ambiguous condition. In the ambiguous condition subjects were provided with a potential excuse for poor performance. Subjects in this condition were told that the tasks they would be working on were designed to measure different aspects of intelligence. In short, the ambiguous condition was designed to provide subjects with an excuse that would allow them an opportunity to dismiss (i.e., recode) their poor performance on the earlier tasks and thereby approach the next tasks with greater confidence.

As expected, when initially exposed to unambiguous failure, self-deceivers did very poorly on subsequent problem-solving tasks. Once again, when confronted with *unambiguous failure experiences*, self-deceivers appear to be at a considerable disadvantage in coping relative to non–self-deceivers. However, when exposed to the same degree of failure in an ambiguous interpretive context the self-deceivers subsequently performed at the same near-ceiling level as non–self-deceivers at a demanding cognitive task.

A recent, well-designed study adds another risk factor to self-deceptive failure: the sensitivity to perceived negative and inescapable evaluation evinced by self-deceivers appears to be heightened especially when this perception is *threatened with public exposure*. Baumeister and Cairns (1992) found that the presence of an audience had a unique effect on self-deceivers. Unlike those low in self-deception, self-deceivers in the presence of others spend more time worrying about others' negative evaluations of them; when alone they spend less time attending to negative feedback about themselves. Self-deceivers were found to be particularly attentive to the evaluative tone of the situation, being more likely to tune in more strongly and have better recall of positive evaluations yet tune out and forget negative evaluations than people low in self-deception. The social context of interpretation appears to be highly salient for those who manifest the tendency toward self-deception.

Our suggestion is that people who rely on self-deception as a means of coping with life events have a radically different orientation toward success and failure than those who do not typically rely on self-deception. For those who employ self-deception, it appears that maintaining a highly positive view of themselves (and logically also believing that others hold similarly positive views of them) is an important goal that organizes much of their way of perceiving experience. One consequence of this is that such individuals are more likely to be attuned to subtle nuances in how evaluative information about themselves is or might be interpreted. Whenever the interpretive context permits it, self-deceivers are likely to (1) detect an opportunity to make a self-enhancing interpretation of evaluative feedback, and (2) use that opportunity to do so. They have a strong sensitivity and preparedness to act on the interpretive implications of evaluative information possibly to the exclusion of using or even developing alternative coping strategies. Escape from negative self-awareness, particularly in the public domain, is their first line of defense.

Persons with low self-esteem (e.g., depression) may be at particular risk if they rely stylistically on self-deceptive coping strategies. Those who are critical of claims for the adaptiveness of self-deception point to the fact that measures of self-deception and self-esteem are typically moderately positively correlated. This raises the possibility that any adaptive benefits associated with self-deception may actually be a result of self-esteem. We have argued that the unconscious mechanisms at work in self-deception are a denial of negative self-awareness together with habitual escape-related defensive processes to avoid and/or minimize such negative self-awareness. Theoretically, people with high self-esteem would not be worried about this. It is only those with a nonconscious negative self-regard who would be threatened with its exposure to the self and others.

In a recent study Johnson (1994) compared the explanatory power of scores on measures of self-deception, trait self-esteem, and state self-esteem. In a protocol similar to that described in one of the studies above, Johnson exposed people who were high or low in self-deception, as measured by the SDQ, to unsolvable problems prior to receiving solvable problems in either ambiguous or unambiguous conditions. The manipulation of ambiguity was unsuccessful, however, as subjects in both conditions tended to have equally poor levels of success in discovering the underlying solutions to the problems. Hierarchical multiple regressions were employed to compare the relative explanatory power of self-esteem against self-deception. Interestingly, self-deception was found to contribute significantly toward the explanation of variability in problem solving after accounting for the effects of self-esteem. However, the direction of the contribution was opposite for self-esteem and self-deception. Both trait and state self-esteem were found to be positively associated with performance measures, whereas self-deception had a negative association. This finding indicates that following unambiguous failure, greater self-esteem is associated with enhanced problem-solving ability, whereas greater self-deception is associated with impaired problem-solving ability. Self-esteem and self-deception are positively correlated, yet have opposite effects on cognitive enhancement versus disruption following unambiguous failure.

Although we do not yet fully understand the reasons for this divergence in the relationship of self-esteem and self-deception to performance, one possible explanation is that when failure is encountered in an unambiguous context, attempts at self-deception are not only ineffective, they may be counterproductive. If under these circumstances one has the capacity to accept a negative result calmly and to engage in other forms of coping such as reminding oneself of one's other areas of strength, a successful outcome is possible. It is interesting to note in this regard that Paulhus and Reid (1991) have recently argued for a distinction between two types of self-deceptive responding: the endorsement of positive, self-enhancing self-statements, and the rejection of negative and critical self-statements. An intriguing possibility is that self-enhancing types of self-deceptive coping may be associated adaptive outcomes, whereas energy directed toward the *unrealistic denial* of all negative and critical evaluations of the self may be tied to maladaptive outcomes.

Returning to the research on self-deception that has been conducted, we detect an interesting and perhaps critical link between the situation of self-deceivers facing unambiguous failure and the suicidal individual confronting a devastating personal setback. In particular, we contend that the process that leads up to the mental state preceding completed suicide (if there is one such state) may be qualitatively very similar to the mental state that arises in individuals whose self-deceptive illusions are shattered by an unavoidable encounter with a threatening self-awareness. In both cases it seems the individual encounters a setback to self-esteem or self-understanding that cannot be gainsaid. In the absence of more palatable ways of construing the situation, the individual is faced with a difficult choice: to accept the self-damaging facts of the matter or to somehow shut them out. It is suggested that when the damage to be sustained would be too great and the capacity to deny the negative reality is too limited, individuals employing self-deceptive coping strategies may consider suicide as an acceptable solution.

THE SELF-PROTECTIVE FUNCTION OF SUICIDE

Self-deception and suicide both appear to be profoundly paradoxical acts—paradoxical because both self-deception and suicide are reflexive activities in which the self seems to commit a destructive act against itself. The enigmatic question, assuming for the moment that individuals seek pleasure and avoid pain, remains: Why do some people aim to "destroy themselves"? Freud (1925) referred to this enigma as "the riddle of the tendency to suicide," in that "we cannot conceive how the ego can consent to its own destruction" (p. 252). He suggested that a splitting of the ego allows a person to kill oneself; not in a complete sense of self, but just the part that is identified with a lost (now "bad") loved one. This riddle endures as suicidology's great paradox. We suggest that a variation to the solution of this riddle is that, psychologically, people do not destroy themselves. Suicide has commonly been viewed as the ultimate act of self-destruction. However, from the perspective presented here, this may not always or even usually be the case. In the context of the stylistic motivation to avoid or escape negative, highly salient, publicly/ privately evaluative, and now unambiguous and unavoidable self-awareness, it may be more accurate to view suicide as the ultimate act of *self-protection*. Shneidman (1985) has noted that people tend to die as they have lived, and suicide is no exception. Similarly, Nuland (1993) has recently observed that "the uniqueness of each of us extends even to the way we die" (p. 3). Egression and consistency are among suicide's commonalities. Like self-deception and perhaps largely through it, the idea of suicide becomes congruent with one's usual defenses. It is another way of protecting the self from aversive insight.

Self-deception appears to succeed as a coping strategy when events threatening to one's positive self-image are embedded in ambiguous contexts. An important implication of this finding is that those who rely on self-deception may be more likely to display extreme outcomes in their adaptations to stressful life events. If the events occur in a sufficiently ambiguous context, self-deception is likely to provide a more than adequate coping response. Conversely, when a threatening event occurs in a stark and unambiguous fashion, individuals who typically rely on self-deceptive coping may find themselves both unable to employ this usual style and without ready or accessible alternative strategies. In short, self-deceivers are effectively adopting a strategy that allows them to succeed in most instances, but that leaves them unprepared for others and faced with cognitive disruption in the face of such adversity. This may be the precise scenario in the suicidal mind.

The notion of suicide as self-protection is consistent with Baumeister's view of suicide as escape from self, in that the "self" one flees from is highly negative and contemptible if brought into conscious awareness. Yet it is an unknown self. It is the familiar self that is further protected through suicide by the now absolute avoidance of facing unbearable self-awareness. This perspective stands against the view of suicide as masochistic acting out, where one supposedly wishes to suffer physical harm in the way we might experience unwanted pain. Indeed, Freud wrote in 1932 that "masochism quite especially [presents] a truly puzzling problem to the libido theory," and as a result ended up placing suicide within his death instinct theory (cited in Litman 1970, p. 572). Consider in this regard the fact that many who commit acts of self-harm may not actually be seeking pain and suffering per se. Physical damage incurred during periods of emotional intensity is often not experienced as painful at the time, such as by the soldier who sustains cutaneous or other injury during battle or the athlete during sport, or the borderline person who slashes yet reports not only an absence of physical pain but the experience of "feeling better" emotionally. It is well known that tears can soothe the hurt. It is as though physical pain and emotional pain serve to partially cancel each other out. In the case of the borderline person, voluntary self-injury not only serves a communicative function but is also a method of emotional pain management; it is not just to "make the pain worse all around because I want to feel hurt." Suicide in escape theory is thus more closely related to the avoidance of pain, as in the extreme intolerance of criticism vividly portrayed by Hendin (1994) in his intriguing case of one business executive's suicide. However drastic, suicide is, in the end, both face-saving and effective pain management.

Although the majority of people with clinical depression will never kill themselves, depression (viz. extremely low self-esteem) has been found to be the most common affective syndrome preceding suicide (Klerman 1987, Shafii et al. 1985). Clinically depressed individuals with the self-deceptive/ repressive coping style, for whom this form of self-protection has been present in the absence of depression, may be particularly vulnerable to incorporating the escape idea of suicide into their otherwise low range of options during threats to one's integrity. Given that most suicidal people are also likely depressed, it seems reasonable to inquire about self-schemas during depression and the likelihood that the idea or action-schema of suicide might correspond with these. In a review of the relevant literature, Segal and Muran (1993) reported that the depressed person's accessible self-schemas are predictably highly negative and self-disparaging. They found that research evidence supports the relationship between mood and the accessibility of corresponding self-schemas from memory, and noted that since "depressed individuals are in a chronic state of negative mood activation, negative self-constructs will come to mind more easily than will positive or neutral alternatives. It is also likely that the activation of one negative element will increase the chances of similar elements coming to mind" (pp. 139–140). Accessibility of these self-constructs may increase vulnerability to depression (Segal and Ingram 1994).

There is also some evidence that a primary goal in depressive self-presentation is self-protection from perceived negative evaluation by others (Hill et al. 1986, Weary 1988). It may be that the searing, negative self-awareness, highly salient and threatened with unambiguous exposure, is so painful and unbearable that the familiar route of escape, together with agitating cognitive disruption, serves to make suicide a logically compatible option. One aspect of this state is a sense of unbearable shame, one of the complex emotions that by its very nature *requires* self-reflection and exposure to oneself (Lewis 1992, 1995, Lynd 1958). Perturbation is heightened in light of the mismatch between an uncovered self and the familiar and public self. One's usual resilience is now compromised, given the finding that a strong component of adaptive coping is the congruence of contextual, public meanings, including others' opinions of us, with our own sense of self (see Rutter 1985, Swann et al. 1992).

CONCLUSION

The convergence of the theoretical and empirical work presented here suggests that there may be a psychology of suicide worthy of investigation in the concept of self-deception. There may be a type of person whose defensive style makes suicide a compelling choice when the usual becomes impossible. Unambiguous confrontation with failure together with potential "public" exposure will be deeply cutting for those with low self-esteem (e.g., during depression) whose typical style is to avoid and escape such self-awareness. The autonomic rush and negative self-awareness they now experience are unfamiliar, frightening, overwhelming, perhaps even panic-inducing, and seen as ultimately inescapable within one's usual escape repertoire. And the deep, now felt experience of the suicidal person's aloneness (Buie and Maltsberger 1989) only reinforces the belief that reaching out to someone is quite pointless. In a depressed state, the idea of suicide may thus appear as a subjectively logical choice. Suicide becomes the ultimate act of self-protection.

Much has already been written on the thought processes of suicidal individuals. Shneidman (1985) has indicated that, because thinking during a suicidal crisis is rather shaky, one should never kill oneself when suicidal. "It takes a mind capable of scanning a range of options greater than two to make a decision as important as taking one's life" (p. 139). The now deconstructed/ disrupted cognitive state described by Baumeister (1990) contributes to the perception of no other choice and increases the motivation to act. Further work is needed in the area of self-deception and suicide to explore and understand this potentially deadly link in the apparent similarity of thinking and defensive strategy. Indeed, discussion of interventions directed at this self-deceptive style with suicidal individuals has already begun (e.g., Zinberg 1989).

The controversy regarding the adaptive versus maladaptive aspects of various forms of self-deception, as in the role of overly positive illusions about the self, continues. These two sides of self-deception, adaptive and maladaptive (e.g., Colvin and Block 1994, Taylor and Brown 1994) now need to be explored particularly in the area of suicide. Are some people who employ a particular form of self-deception at higher risk for suicide when confronted with certain kinds of stress? Suicidologists are noting that certain self-discrepancies are strong candidates for membership among the core commonalities in suicide, particularly discrepancies between public and private selves (e.g., Shneidman's cognitions regarding self; see Leenaars 1987) and between bodily and psychic selves (Maltsberger 1993). Studies of self-representation in lethal people, within the broader framework of a cognitive unconscious, should shed more light on the psychology of completed suicide.

ACKNOWLEDGMENTS

Most of Michael Kral's contribution was written during a summer leave at the Center for Advanced Study in Theoretical Psychology, University of Alberta; thanks are extended to its director, Leendert Mos, for making this experience both possible and highly enjoyable. Edward Johnson would like to express thanks to his co-author for inviting him to work on what has been a truly collaborative "meeting of minds." Johnson's initial writing on the chapter was carried out during his tenure as a postdoctoral fellow at the Centre for Applied Cognitive Science at the Ontario Institute for Studies in Education, University of Toronto. Thanks are extended to the centre and to David Olson for their support. Thanks also to Erik Woody for his helpful suggestions at various stages of this work, and to Antoon Leenaars, David Lester, Robert James, and M. David Wallace for comments on earlier drafts.

REFERENCES

Ader, R., Weiner, H., and Baum, A., eds. (1988). *Experimental Foundations of Behavioral Medicine: Conditioning Approaches.* Hillsdale, NJ: Lawrence Erlbaum.

American Psychiatric Association. (1980). *Diagnostic and Statistical Manual of Mental Disorders*, 3rd ed. Washington, DC.: American Psychiatric Association.

Asendorpf, J. B., and Scherer, K. R. (1983). The discrepant repressor: differentiation between low anxiety, high anxiety, and repression of anxiety by autonomic-facial-verbal patterns of behavior. *Journal of Personality and Social Psychology* 45:1334–1346.

Avrill, J. R. (1986). The acquisition of emotions during adulthood. In *The Social Construction of Emotions*, ed. R. Harre, pp. 98–118. New York: Basil Blackwell.

Baars, B. (1983). Conscious contents provide the nervous system with coherent, global information. In *Consciousness and Self-Regulation: Advances in Research and Theory*, vol. 3, ed. R. J. Davidson, G. E. Schwartz, and D. Shapiro, pp. 41–79. New York: Plenum.

Baechler, J. (1975). *Suicides*, trans. B. Cooper. New York: Basic Books, 1979.

Baumeister, R. F. (1990). Suicide as escape from self. *Psychological Review* 97:90–113.

Baumeister, R. F., and Cairns, K. J. (1992). Repression and self-presentation: when audiences interfere with self-deceptive strategies. *Journal of Personality and Social Psychology* 62:851–862.

Baumeister, R. F., and Scher, S. J. (1988). Self-defeating behavior patterns among normal individuals: review and analysis of common self-destructive tendencies. *Psychological Bulletin* 104:3–22.

Beck, A. T., and Steer, R. A. (1989). Clinical predictors of eventual suicide: a 5- to 10-year prospective study of suicide attempters. *Journal of Affective Disorders* 17:203–209.

Berger, E. M. (1953). Relationships among expressed acceptance of self, expressed acceptance of others, and the MMPI. *American Psychologist* 8:320–321.

——— (1955). Relationships among acceptance of self, acceptance of others, and MMPI scores. *Journal of Counseling Psychology* 2:279–283.

Bonnano, G. A., and Singer, J. L. (1990). Repressive personality style: theoretical and methodological implications for health and pathology. In *Repression and Dissociation: Implications for Personality Theory, Psychopathology, and Health*, ed. J. L. Singer, pp. 435–470. Chicago: University of Chicago Press.

Bowers, K. S., and Meichenbaum, D., eds. (1984). *The Unconscious Reconsidered*. New York: Wiley.

Buie, D. H., and Maltsberger, J. T. (1989). The psychological vulnerability to suicide. In *Suicide: Understanding and Responding*, ed. D. Jacobs, and H. N. Brown, pp. 59–71. Madison, CT: International Universities Press.

Clark, D. C., and Horton-Deutsch, S. L. (1992). Assessment in absentia: the value of the psychological autopsy method for studying antecedents of suicide and predicting future suicides. In *Assessment and Prediction of Suicide*, ed. R. W. Maris, A. L. Berman, J. T. Maltsberger, and R. I. Yufit, pp. 144–182. New York: Guilford.

Colvin, C. R., and Block, J. (1994). Do positive illusions foster mental health? An examination of the Taylor and Brown formulation. *Psychological Bulletin* 116:3–20.

D'Andrade, R. G. (1992). Schemas and motivation. In *Human Motives and Cultural Models*, ed. R. G. D'Andrade, and C. Strauss. New York: Cambridge University Press.

Davies, M., and Humphreys, G. W., eds. (1993). *Consciousness: Psychological and Philosophical Essays*. Oxford, UK: Blackwell.

Davis, M. H., and Franzoi, S. L. (1987). Private self-consciousness and self-disclosure. In *Self-Disclosure: Theory, Research, and Therapy*, ed. V. J. Derlega, and J. H. Berg. New York: Plenum.

Demos, R. (1960). Lying to oneself. *Journal of Philosophy* 57:588–595.

Dingman, C. W., and McGlashan, T. H. (1988). Characteristics of patients with serious suicidal intentions who ultimately commit suicide. *Hospital and Community Psychiatry* 39:295–299.

Ellenberger, H. F. (1970). *The Discovery of the Unconscious: The History and Evolution of Dynamic Psychiatry*. New York: Basic Books.

Epstein, S. (1994). Integration of the cognitive and psychodynamic unconscious. *American Psychologist* 49:709–724.

Erdelyi, M. N. (1990). Repression, reconstruction, and defense: history and integration of the psychoanalytic and experimental frameworks. In *Repression and Dissociation: Implications for Personality Theory, Psychopathology, and Health*, ed. J. L. Singer, pp. 1–31. Chicago: University of Chicago Press.

Eysenck, H. J. (1994). Neuroticism and the illusion of mental health. *American Psychologist* 49:971–972.

Fingarette, H. (1969). *Self-Deception*. London: Routledge & Kegan Paul.

Fiske, D. W. (1957). The constraints on intra-individual variability in test responses. *Educational and Psychological Measurement* 17:317–337.

Franzoi, S. L., and Brewer, L. C. (1984). The experience of self-awareness and its relation to level of self-consciousness: an experiential sampling study. *Journal of Research in Personality* 18:522–540.

Franzoi, S. L., Davis, M. N., and Markwiese, B. (1990). A motivational explanation for the existence of private self-consciousness differences. *Journal of Personality* 58:641–659.

Fremouw, W. J., de Perzel, M., and Ellis, T. E. (1990). *Suicide Risk: Assessment and Response Guidelines*. New York: Pergamon.

Freud, S. (1917). Mourning and melancholia. *Standard Edition* 14:237–258.

Frijda, N. H. (1986). *The Emotions*. New York: Cambridge University Press.

Glassock, E. M. (1955). An investigation of the value of the Minnesota Multiphasic Personality Inventory as a prognostic instrument (Doctoral dissertation, Washington University, 1954). *Dissertation Abstracts* 15:874–875.

Greene, R. L. (1991). *The MMPI-2/MMPI: An Interpretive Manual*. Boston: Allyn & Bacon.

Greenwald, A. G. (1988). Self-knowledge and self-deception. In *Self-Deception: An Adaptive Mechanism?*, ed. J. S. Lockard, and D. L. Paulhus, pp. 113–131. Englewood Cliffs, NJ: Prentice-Hall.

Gur, M. D., and Sackheim, H. A. (1979). Self-deception: a concept in search of a phenomenon. *Journal of Personality and Social Psychology* 37:147–169.

Gynther, M. D., and Brilliant, P. J. (1968). The MMPI K+ profile: a re-examination. *Journal of Consulting and Clinical Psychology* 32:616–617.

Hacking, I. (1986). The invention of split personalities. In *Human Nature and Natural Knowledge*, ed. A. Donagan, A. N. Perovich, and M. V. Wedin, pp. 63–85. New York: D. Reidel.

———— (1992). Multiple personality and its hosts. *History of the Human Sciences* 5:3–31.

Harre, R., ed. (1986). *The Social Construction of Emotions*. Oxford: Basil Blackwell.

Heilbrun, A. B. (1961). The psychological significance of the MMPI K scale in a normal population. *Journal of Consulting Psychology* 25:486–491.

Hendin, H. (1994). Fall from power: suicide of an executive. *Suicide and Life-Threatening Behavior* 24:293–301.

Higgins, E. T. (1987). Self-discrepancy: a theory relating self and affect. *Psychological Review* 94:319–340.

Hill, M. G., Weary, G., and Williams, J. (1986). Depression: a self-presentation formulation. In *Public Self and Private Self*, ed. R. F. Baumeister, pp. 213–239. New York: Springer-Verlag.

Jahoda, M. (1958). *Current Concepts of Positive Mental Health*. New York: Basic.

Janoff-Bulman, R. (1992). *Shattered Assumptions: Toward a New Psychology of Trauma*. New York: Free Press.

Johnson, E. A. (1994). *Self-deception or self-esteem? An investigation of the sources of adaptive coping*. Paper presented at the annual conference of the Canadian Psychological Association, Penticton, BC, June.

———— (in press). Self-deceptive responses to threat: adaptive only in ambiguous contexts. *Journal of Personality*.

Johnson-Laird, P. N. (1983). *Mental Models*. Cambridge, MA: Harvard University Press.

Jones, R. B. (1969). Suicidal out-patients: the MMPI and case file data (Doctoral dissertation, University of Oregon, 1968). *Dissertation Abstracts* 29:2635-B.

Jorgensen, R. S., Filipowski, D. M., Gelling, P. D., and Langer, A. W. (1991). Defensiveness and low levels of disclosed type A behavior and anger: repressive coping and the discrepancy between cardiovascular and affective responsivity. *Psychophysiology* 28:8.

Jorgensen, R. S., Schere, G. E., Baskin, L., and Kolodzeij, M. (1992). Denial and discrepancy between heart rate and reported negative affect: a study of convergent and discriminant validity. *Psychotherapy and Psychosomatics* 58:202-207.

Jourard, S. M., and Landsman, T. (1980). *Healthy Personality: An Approach from the Viewpoint of Humanistic Psychology*, 4th ed. New York: Macmillan.

Kahneman, D., Slovic, P., and Tversky A., eds. (1982). *Judgment under Uncertainty: Heuristics and Biases*. Cambridge: Cambridge University Press.

Kihlstrom, J. F. (1990). The psychological unconscious. In *Handbook of Personality: Theory and Research*, ed. L. A. Pervin, pp. 445-464. New York: Guilford.

Klerman, G. L. (1987). Clinical epidemiology of suicide. *Journal of Clinical Psychiatry* 48:33-38.

Kral, M. J. (1992). *Using the MMPI mindfully*. Paper presented at the annual conference of the Canadian Psychological Association, Quebec, QC, June.

–––––– (1994). Suicide as social logic. *Suicide and Life-Threatening Behavior* 24:245-255.

Kral, M. J., and Dyck, R. J. (in press). Public option, private choice: impact of culture on suicide. In *The Impact of Suicide: A Comprehensive Handbook*, ed. B. F. Mishara. New York: Springer.

Kuhn, D. (1989). Children and adults as intuitive scientists. *Psychological Review* 96:674-689.

Lazarus, R. S. (1983). The costs and benefits of denial. In *Denial of Stress*, ed. S. Breznitz, pp. 1-30. New York: International Universities Press.

Leenaars, A. A. (1987). An empirical investigation of Shneidman's formulations regarding suicide: age and sex. *Suicide and Life-Threatening Behavior* 17:233-250.

Levenson, R. W., Ekman, P., Heider, K., and Freisen, W. V. (1992). Emotion and autonomic nervous system activity in the Minangkabau of West Sumatra. *Journal of Personality and Social Psychology* 62:972-988.

Lewis, M. (1992). *Shame: The Exposed Self*. New York: Free Press.

–––––– (1995). Self-conscious emotions. *American Scientist* 83:68-78.

Lewis, M., and Haviland, J. M., eds. (1993). *Handbook of Emotions*. New York: Guilford.

Litman, R. E. (1970). Sigmund Freud on suicide. In *The Psychology of Suicide*, ed. E. S. Shneidman, N. L. Farberow, and R. E. Litman, pp. 565-586. New York: Science House.

Lutz, C., and White, G. M. (1986). The anthropology of emotions. *Annual Review of Anthropology* 15:405-436.

Lynd, H. M. (1958). *On Shame and the Search for Identity*. New York: Science Editions.

Maltsberger, J. T. (1993). Confusions of the body, the self, and others in suicidal states. In *Suicidology: Essays in Honor of Edwin Shneidman*, ed. A. A. Leenaars, pp. 148-171. Northvale, NJ: Jason Aronson.

Mandler, G. (1983). Emotion and stress: a view from cognitive psychology. In *Emotions in Health and Illness: Theoretical and Research Foundations*, ed. L. Temoshok, C. Van Dyck, and L. S. Zegans, pp. 195-205. New York: Grune & Stratton.

Mandler, G., Mandler, J. M., Kremen, I., and Sholiton, R. D. (1961). The response to threat: relation among verbal and physiological indices. *Psychological Monographs: General and Applied* 75(513).

Maris, R. W. (1981). *Pathways to Suicide: A Survey of Self-Destructive Behaviors*. Baltimore, MD: Johns Hopkins University Press.

–––––– (1992). How are suicides different? In *Assessment and Prediction of Suicide*, ed. R. W. Maris, A. L. Berman, J. T. Maltsberger, and R. I. Yufit, pp. 65-87. New York: Guilford.

Markus, H. R., and Kitayama, S. (1991). Culture and the self: implications for cognition, emotion, and motivation. *Psychological Review* 98:224-253.

Meehl, P. E., and Hathaway, S. R. (1946). The K factor as a suppressor variable in the MMPI. *Journal of Applied Psychology* 30:525-564.

Mele, A. R. (1983). Self-deception. *Philosophical Quarterly* 33:365–377.

Melnechuk, T. (1988). Emotions, brain, immunity, and health: a review. In *Emotions and Psychopathology*, ed. M. Clynes and J. Panksepp, pp. 181–247. New York: Plenum.

Menninger, K. (1938). *Man Against Himself.* New York: Harcourt Brace.

Monts, J. K., Zurcher, A., and Nydegger, R. V. (1977). Interpersonal self-deception and personality correlates. *Journal of Social Psychology* 103:91–99.

Morgan, H. G., and Priest, P. (1984). Assessment of suicide risk in psychiatric inpatients. *British Journal of Psychiatry* 145:467–469.

Niaura, R., Herbert, P. N., McMahon, N., and Sommerville, L. (1992). Repressive coping and blood lipids in men and women. *Psychosomatic Medicine* 54:698–706.

Nisbett, R. E., and Ross, L. (1980). *Human Inference: Strategies and Shortcomings of Social Judgement.* Englewood Cliffs, NJ: Prentice-Hall.

Nuland, S. B. (1993). *How We Die: Reflections on Life's Final Chapter.* New York: Knopf.

Paulhus, D. L. (1986). Self-deception and impression management in test responses. In *Personality Assessment via Questionnaires: Current Issues in Theory and Measurement*, ed. A. Angleitner, and J. S. Wiggins, pp. 143–165. New York: Springer Verlag.

Paulhus, D. L., and Reid, D. B. (1991). Enhancement and denial in socially desirable responding. *Journal of Personality and Social Psychology* 60:307–317.

Pennebaker, J. W. (1989). Stream of consciousness and stress: levels of thinking. In *Unintended Thought*, ed. J. S. Uleman, and J. A. Bargh, pp. 327–350. New York: Guilford.

Piattelli-Palmarini, M. (1994). *Inevitable Illusions: How Mistakes of Reason Rule our Minds.* New York: Wiley.

Reis, H. A. (1966). The MMPI K scale as a predictor of prognosis. *Journal of Clinical Psychology* 22:212–213.

Rogers, A. H., and Walsh, T. M. (1959). Defensiveness and unwitting self-evaluation. *Journal of Clinical Psychology* 15:302–304.

Roth, D. L., and Ingram, R. E. (1985). Factors in the self-deception questionnaire: associations with depression. *Journal of Personality and Social Psychology* 32:680–691.

Rutter, M. (1985). Resilience in the face of adversity: protective factors and resistance to psychiatric disorder. *British Journal of Psychiatry* 147:598–611.

Sackheim, H. A. (1983). Self-deception, self-esteem, and depression: the adaptive value of lying to oneself. In *Empirical Studies of Psychoanalytical Theories*, ed. J. Masling, pp. 101–157. Hillsdale, NJ: Analytic Press.

Sackheim, H. A., and Gur, R. C. (1978). Self-deception, self-confrontation, and consciousness. In *Consciousness and Self-Regulation: Advances in Research*, vol. 2, ed. G. E. Schwartz, and D. Shapiro, pp. 139–197. New York: Plenum.

——— (1979). Self-deception, other-deception, and self-reported psychopathology. *Journal of Consulting and Clinical Psychology* 47:213–215.

Sartre, J.-P. (1943). *Being and Nothingness*, trans. H. Barnes. London: Methuen, 1958.

Schafer, R. (1992). *Retelling a Life: Narration and Dialogue in Psychoanalysis.* New York: Basic Books.

Schwartz, G. E. (1986). Emotion and psychophysiological organization: a systems approach. In *Psychophysiology: Systems, Processes, and Applications*, ed. M. G. H. Coles, E. Donchin, and S. W. Porges, pp. 354–377. New York: Guilford.

——— (1990). Psychobiology of repression and health: a systems approach. In *Repression and Dissociation: Implications for Personality Theory, Psychopathology, and Health*, ed. J. L. Singer, pp. 405–434. Chicago: University of Chicago Press.

Schwartz, T., White, M., and Lutz, C. A., eds. (1992). *New Directions in Psychological Anthropology.* New York: Cambridge University Press.

Searle, J. R. (1992). *The Rediscovery of the Mind.* Cambridge, MA: MIT Press.

Segal, Z. V., and Ingram, R. E. (1994). Mood priming and construct activation in tests of cognitive vulnerability to unipolar depression. *Clinical Psychology Review* 14:663–695.

Segal, Z. V., and Muran, J. C. (1993). A cognitive perspective on self-presentation in depression. In *The Self in Emotional Distress: Cognitive and Psychodynamic Perspectives*, ed. Z. V. Segal, and S. J. Blatt, pp. 131–163. New York: Guilford.

Shafii, M., Carrigan, S., Whittinghill, J. R., and Derrick, A. M. (1985). Psychological autopsy of completed suicide in children and adolescents. *American Journal of Psychiatry* 142:1061–1064.

Shevrin, H., and Bond, J. A. (1993). Repression and the unconscious. In *Psychodynamic Treatment Research: A Handbook for Clinical Practice*, ed. N. E. Miller, L. Luborsky, J. P. Barber, and J. P. Docherty, pp. 308–325. New York: Basic Books.

Shneidman, E. S. (1969). Prologue: Fifty-eight years. In *On the Nature of Suicide*, pp. 1–30. San Francisco: Jossey-Bass.

––––––– (1985). *Definition of Suicide*. New York: Wiley.

Shneidman, E. S., and Farberow, N. L. (1961). Statistical comparisons between attempted and committed suicides. In *The Cry for Help*, pp. 19–47. New York: McGraw-Hill.

Singer, J. L. (1990). A fresh look at repression, dissociation, and defenses as mechanisms as personality styles. In *Repression and Dissociation: Implications for Personality Theory, Psychopathology, and Health*, ed. J. L. Singer, pp. xi–xxi. Chicago: University of Chicago Press.

Spanos, N. P. (1994). Multiple identity enactments and multiple personality disorder: a sociocognitive perspective. *Psychological Bulletin* 116:143–165.

Stengel, E. (1964). *Suicide and Attempted Suicide*. Baltimore, MD: Penguin.

Swann, W. B., Stein-Seroussi, A., and Giesler, R. B. (1992). Why people self-verify. *Journal of Personality and Social Psychology* 62:392–401.

Sweetland, A., and Quay, H. (1953). A note on the K scale of the MMPI. *Journal of Consulting Psychology* 17:314–316.

Taylor, S. E. (1989). *Positive Illusions: Creative Self-Deception and the Healthy Mind*. New York: Basic Books.

Taylor, S. E., and Brown, J. D. (1988). Illusion and well-being: a social psychological perspective on mental health. *Psychological Bulletin* 103:193–210.

––––––– (1994). Positive illusions and well-being revisited: separating fact from fiction. *Psychological Bulletin* 116:21–27.

Tolstoy, L. (1886). The death of Ivan Illich. In *The Death of Ivan Illich and Other Stories*, trans. A. Maude, pp. 95–156. New York: New American Library, 1960.

Tov-Ruach, L. (1988). Freud on unconscious affects, mourning, and the erotic mind. In *Perspectives in Self-Deception*, ed. B. P. McLaughlin, and A. O. Rorty, pp. 246–263. Berkeley: University of California Press.

Turner, R. G. (1978). Self-consciousness and speed of processing self-relevant information. *Personality and Social Psychology Bulletin* 4:456–460.

Uleman, J. S., and Bargh, J. A., eds. (1989). *Unintended Thought*. New York: Guilford.

Weary, G. (1988). Depression and self-presentation. In *Self-Representation*, ed. S. L. Zelin, pp. 31–51. New York: Springer Verlag.

Weinberger, D. G. (1990). The construct validity of the repressive coping style. In *Repression and Dissociation: Implications for Personality Theory, Psychopathology, and Health*, ed. J. L. Singer, pp. 337–386. Chicago: University of Chicago Press.

Weinberger, D. G., Schwartz, G., and Davidson, R. (1979). Low-anxious, high-anxious, and repressive coping styles: psychometric patterns and behavioral and physiological responses to stress. *Journal of Abnormal Psychology* 88:369–380.

Weiner, D. N. (1951). A control factor in social adjustment. *Journal of Abnormal and Social Psychology* 46:3–8.

Zinberg, N. E. (1989). The threat of suicide in psychotherapy. In *Suicide: Understanding and Responding*, ed. D. Jacobs, and H. N. Brown, pp. 295–327. Madison, CT: International Universities Press.

Part III
STUDIES OF THE UNCONSCIOUS
AND SUICIDE

There is a wealth of research about suicide, but it has failed to provide us with an adequate understanding of the suicidal mind. Simple explanations are insufficient, and the study of broader perspectives that include the unconscious is only beginning. The examination of the unconscious, however, is appropriate and can be done in many ways. Part III consists of three chapters: an examination of how literature can illuminate the role of the unconscious in suicide, a study of psychological testing that taps the unconscious, and a nomothetic study of unconscious content in suicide notes.

6: THE UNCONSCIOUS AND SUICIDE
IN LITERATURE

David Lester

There is a long history of using literature to illustrate and sometimes test psychological theories. For example, theories of suicide have been tested using the content of suicide notes (Leenaars 1988). Occasionally, suicides (for example, Sylvia Plath) leave a book or poem describing their behavior, and this kind of material may be of use in exploring the unconscious psychodynamics of the suicidal act. In other fields of psychology, folk tales of primitive societies have been studied, for example, for evidence of the societal need for achievement or power (McClelland et al. 1966).

Before focusing on the use of literature in the study of suicide, let us explore a few of these general areas of interaction between psychology and literature in a little more detail.

PSYCHOLOGY AND LITERATURE

Understanding Human Behavior in Historical Times

The psychological study of history has created a new discipline, called psychohistory. Psychohistory seeks to enlarge our understanding of historical events and persons by applying psychological theory and knowledge (Hoffer 1979). Crosby (1979) defined the field as "the form of history which makes explicit use of the concepts, principles, and theories of psychology in order to enhance our understanding of particular people and events in the past" (p. 6).

This joining of psychology and history had long been advocated (Barnes 1925, Smith 1913) but developed in depth only in the 1970s. The major psychological theory applied to history has been psychoanalysis (for example, Erikson's [1962] study of Martin Luther), but other theories, such as cognitive theory and trait theory, have been utilized. Although psychohistorians can use a variety of materials to make inferences about the psychological state of historical individuals and cultures, occasionally literature has been used.

For example, Hoffer (1974) analyzed school textbooks from the first half of the nineteenth century to show how threats to national unity appeared to influence textbook writers to minimize divisive and unruly episodes in earlier American history, a decision consistent with Festinger's (1957) theory of cognitive dissonance.

McClelland (1958) illustrated the possibility of incorporating quantitative methods into psychohistory. For example, McClelland scored a variety of Greek writings for the need to achieve and found that this need declined steadily in Greece from 700 B.C. to 250 B.C., which fits with the historical events of that period. Hull and colleagues (1978) used the manuscripts left by loyalists and revolutionaries in the Revolutionary era in New York to identify differences in a variety of traits, including need for order, submissiveness, and conformity, and they related these to the writers' political affiliation.

History and psychology can also interact through literature in attempts to categorize historical events and epochs in psychological rather than in political or economic terms. For example, Manuel (1967) took utopian novels from the last five hundred years and argued that they fall into three clear psychological periods: the utopias of calm felicity (pre–nineteenth century), the open-ended utopias of the nineteenth century, and the contemporary utopias based either on the hypothesis of a growing spiritualization of man (the humanistic psychology influence) or on a fantasy of greater sensate gratification (the psychoanalytic influence).

Psychological Analyses of Literature

Psychoanalytic theory (and other psychodynamic theories) have been applied in order to understand better the unconscious motivations of the fictional characters. For example, Antigone's motives in Sophocles's play of the same name have been analyzed by Faber (1970).

Oedipus accidentally murdered his biological father and married his biological mother, without any conscious awareness of what he was doing. He had four children by his mother/wife, Jocasta: Eteocles, Polynices, Ismene, and Antigone. When he found out what he had done, his mother/wife hanged herself, and Oedipus took the brooches from her dress and blinded himself with them. Oedipus then went into exile.

Antigone was with Oedipus in his exile, helping to take care of him. After his death, his two sons fought against each other for the control of Thebes, killing each other in the process, leaving Oedipus's uncle, Creon, as King. Creon ordered that Eteocles should be buried with honor, but that

Polynices, the rebel, should be left to rot without burial. He ordered that anybody who tried to bury Polynices would be executed.

In Sophocles's play, Antigone decides to bury Polynices, her brother. At first she tries to enlist the help of her sister Ismene, but Ismene refuses to go against the law. So Antigone decides to bury Polynices herself, knowing that the penalty is death. She says she will be happy to die if she is caught.

She buries him, covering him with a layer of dirt, and the fact of his token burial is reported to Creon. After Polynices's body is cleaned off, Antigone tries to bury him again, this time screaming as she does it, with the result that the sentries discover her in the act.

When Creon questions Antigone, she admits the act. There is the feeling that Creon would pardon her, but Antigone provokes his anger against her, so that he sentences her to be walled up in a cave to be left to die, even though she is engaged to his son, Haemon. Ismene tries to join Antigone in being blamed for the act, but Antigone refuses to let Ismene accept any responsibility. She wants to be punished alone.

As Antigone talks to the chorus of her impending death, she compares herself to Niobe, the daughter of Tantalus, but the chorus reminds Antigone that Tantalus's daughter was a goddess whereas Antigone is a mortal. As she talks of her death, she refers to it as her bridal bower. She looks forward to seeing her father, mother, and brothers again.

Creon orders her to be removed to a cave and sealed in it. Later he has a change of heart and rushes to the cave with his son to save her. They find that she has already hanged herself. Haemon tries to slay his father but, missing, turns his sword onto himself, killing himself in front of his father.

Antigone's death can be seen as a case of *victim-precipitated homicide*, a term coined by Wolfgang (1958). Antigone, perhaps unconsciously, commits suicide by getting Creon to execute her. The penalty for burying Polynices is death, yet Antigone's screaming draws the attention of the sentries. When Creon looks as if he might pardon her, she seems to goad him into ordering her execution. It is by no means clear that these psychodynamic processes are conscious to Antigone, however.

Once Antigone is imprisoned in the cave, she hangs herself rather than die slowly of starvation. Interestingly, she chooses the same method of suicide employed by her mother. (The men in Sophocles's plays use swords or other piercing instruments for their self-destructive acts.) The suicides of young people often show an imitation effect, much more so than the suicides of older people.

At the time of her death, Antigone has had a succession of losses. All of her family is now dead. The stain on the family name, beginning with the actions of Oedipus and ending with the civil war of her brothers, has grown enormously. Her family has lost its honor, and Antigone to a large extent does restore some honor to the family by her actions and death. She is primarily concerned with her status after death, which makes sense given her psychological pain (shame, grief, and humiliation) on earth. Her death will restore her nobility. Interestingly, the chorus tries to restrain her fantasies.

Although her death satisfies her general reunion fantasies, her reunion with Polynices seems to be the central goal. She refers to her deathbed as her bridal bower. She says she can easily find a husband, but where could she find another brother like him? She does not mention Eteocles. Incestuous desires between brother and sister are not uncommon, especially when the two are separated during their childhood and adolescence (Lester 1972a).

A frequent task in the psychological study of literature has been the tracing of a significance of a symbol or an idea through its many manifestations in literature, perhaps identifying in the process a Jungian archetype. For example, McClelland (1963) started with the idea that not all people fear death. Indeed, some people, often women, actually seem to look forward to death, with a sense of excitement as well as fear, as if death could be an unconscious equivalent for the final sexual union with the ideal mate (Bromberg and Schilder 1933, 1936). McClelland's student, Greenberger (1965), found that dying women were more likely to gives stories involving illicit sexuality to cards from the Thematic Apperception Test than women who were not dying. Women students in his classes rated "a gay seducer" as more appropriate as a description of death than did the men.[1] Stimulated by these findings, McClelland traced the development of the Harlequin theme in literature. In the typical Harlequin story, Harlequin pursues Columbine, his love, despite obstacles placed in his way by her father, Pantaloon. In the dark scenes, Harlequin is definitely connected to underworld figures, and often Columbine dies at the end of the story.

The Harlequin figure seems to derive from an old French character called Herlequin, who is the devil (Driesen 1904). In an eleventh-century manuscript by Ordericus Vitalis, there is a Herlequin family in the underworld, which sometimes appears on earth. In a play written in 1262 by Adan de le Hale, Herlequin is a single character and, in time, variants of the Harlequin story were acted in pantomime and danced in ballet, from the Arlecchino tradition in Italy to the bullfight tradition in Spain, all the way to modern equivalents, such as Agatha Christie's stories of love and death in *The Mysterious Mr. Quin* (Christie 1930) and the 1961 Hollywood film *The Last Sunset*.[2]

---

[1]Subsequent research has not always confirmed these empirical findings (Lester 1966, Lester and Schumacher 1969).

[2]Other manifestations of the Harlequin complex can be found in older times, as in the story of Hades coming up from hell to take Persephone off to the underworld and the fear of witches both in Europe and North America, and in modern times, as in the stories about the hypnotist Svengali, the mystique of the foreign psychoanalyst who allies himself with the dark side of the

Literary styles have also been studied. For example, Skinner (1941) attempted to estimate whether the amount of alliteration in Shakespeare's sonnets exceeded chance expectations, and Rokeach and colleagues (1970) analyzed *The Federalist Papers* to ascertain the authorship of the disputed papers.

Psychological Studies of the Author and the Reader

Psychoanalysis (and other psychodynamic theories) have often been applied to fictional works in order to better understand the author. The first example of the use of psychoanalysis to this end was by Freud (Niederland 1960), who applied his theory to the novel *Die Richterin* by the Swiss writer Conrad Ferdinand Meyer (1825–1898). Freud sent an essay to his friend, Wilhelm Fliess, on June 20, 1898, in which he suggested that the novel was an unconscious defense against the writer's memory of an affair with his sister (Freud 1954). In the novel, a mother murders her husband and rules in his place until her stepson returns and unmasks his stepmother as the murderer. The stepmother thereupon commits suicide, but, in the course of the novel, the avenging stepson has an affair with his half-sister. Niederland notes that Meyer's father died when Meyer was 15. His early efforts to write were thwarted by his mother but encouraged by his sister. After his mother's suicide, Meyer lived with his sister in a close and personal relationship until he married in his late forties. She acted as his housekeeper, companion, secretary, and advisor.

There have been many studies of the psychological state of individual authors. Bellak (1963), for example, treated the short stories of Somerset Maugham as if they were stories written to stimuli such as those in the Thematic Apperception Test, scoring the stories to measure the psychological needs of Maugham. For example, the *descriptive theme* in "Footprints in the Jungle" is that Bronson brings Cartwright home because he is temporarily in hard circumstances. Bronson's wife has an affair with Cartwright and persuades Cartwright to murder her husband. Although the police discover the crime, they do not have enough evidence to try the couple, who then live happily ever after. Bellak saw the *interpretive theme* as that women can come between men and cause trouble and that sexual passion can motivate murder even in decent people, who may not even suffer remorse. At the *diagnostic level*, Bellak suggested that Somerset Maugham perceived, perhaps unconsciously, women as sources of trouble for men, separating them and destroying them. There is also an oedipal theme here in which a man has to kill another man

---

unconscious (Bakan 1958), and most recently, Dr. Jack Kevorkian, the "Doctor of Death," who initially helped mostly women commit suicide.

in order to obtain a mate, and, finally, passion can overpower the superego, leading to lack of control over aggression.

In general, after an analysis of ten of Maugham's ninety-one short stories, Bellak suggested that Maugham had a continual struggle with his sexual and aggressive impulses. To control them, Maugham tried for emotional isolation and detachment, playing the role of an onlooker toward others. His resulting self-image is that of a mild, ineffective person pushed around by external forces. Maugham saw women as domineering and demanding, leading men to feel inadequate, a view that is perhaps a projection of his own strong unconscious aggressive drives. Maugham suffered from a conflict between activity and passivity, conformity and nonconformity, and male and female identification, leading to embarrassment and shame, a feeling of inadequacy and a fear of failure. Bellak noted that his conclusions from his thematic analysis of Maugham's short stories was consistent with biographies of Maugham's life, although Bellak's knowledge of Maugham's life may have affected the conclusions he drew from his thematic analysis of Maugham's short stories!

Research on the impact of literature on the reader is illustrated by the studies stimulated by the Commission on Obscenity and Pornography (Anon. 1970), which produced a number of studies of the effects of pornography on people.

Other Points of Contact

Goodman (1963) has noted two other areas in which psychology and literature relate. First, psychologizing can be seen itself as a literary genre. A psychoanalytic case history is, for Goodman, a real novel or adventure story. A second relationship that Goodman saw between psychology and literature is in the way writers have been affected by psychological thought. Goodman noted, for example, how contemporary writing takes into account such psychodynamic ideas as the continuity of dream life, daydreams, waking life, slips, fantasy, and wishful thinking.

A Dissenting Voice

Not everyone approves of this interaction between psychology and literature. For example, Jaffe (1967) has argued that a work of literature is contrived, serving only the writer's intent. The literary structure of a play forces the character into particular acts and mannerisms. Thus we cannot learn about real people from a study of literary characters. We can learn only about unreal people. For example, "responses in literature are not only responses *per se*, they are responses to stimuli which have been inserted, so to speak, *in order to* elicit them. It is precisely this which is not true of life" (p. 7). Jaffe pointed out that the situation that causes neurosis in a client was not designed to produce the neurosis.

In Franz Kafka's *The Trial*, K refuses to kill himself. This, noted Jaffe, is not a sign of strength or of weakness. K cannot kill himself for reasons that have nothing to do with some person "K" who does not exist. K cannot kill himself because of the nature of suicide and the way it functions in the text. In *The Trial*, suicide by an individual implies that the person has chosen to kill himself after considering, and rejecting, the alternative of continuing to live and because his experience in the course of the text indicates to him that death is the preferred alternative. The act of suicide is a symbol of redemption, postulates values to be redeemed, and requires an agent who can assimilate experience and understand these values. K cannot assimilate experience because, in the text, he is the experience itself. He cannot be an agent because of his function in the novel. If K committed suicide, it would falsify the novel. The novel would be a different novel, and *The Trial* would not exist. Suicide is not a choice that is open to K or even to Kafka, the novelist. Thus, we cannot learn about the reasons people may have for not committing suicide from *The Trial*.

Furthermore, we must beware of rediscovering "facts" from a study of literary works that incorporated those facts. For example, we would be fools indeed to use Huxley's novels to provide support for Sheldon's theory of the relationship of physique to temperament, since Huxley was well aware of Sheldon's theory and depicted his characters so as to be consistent with the theory.

However, perhaps we can demonstrate in this chapter that, with care and forewarning, the psychologist can find a rich source of materials for the study of suicide in the realm of literature.

STUDYING SUICIDE (AND THE UNCONSCIOUS) THROUGH LITERATURE

Understanding Suicide

Faber (1970) has provided several examples of how an examination of suicide in literary characters can throw light on our understanding of suicide. In doing this, Faber views literary suicides as case studies (although he places the words in quotes) that may serve as archetypes of suicidal behavior and may provide insights into suicidal behavior. He states that he is not interested in how the suicides further the literary aims or "esthetic contraptions" of the authors, their esthetic implications, or how they might throw light on the attitudes toward suicide of the society in which the novel or play was written.

In Faber's analyses of the suicide of Haemon in Sophocles's *Antigone* and the self-blinding of Oedipus in his *Oedipus the King*, Faber provides good insights into the unconscious motivation for suicide. (Sophocles appears to have anticipated Freud's insights by some two thousand years.) However,

Freud's theory could just as easily have been illustrated with modern cases. On the other hand, many of the suicides in the plays of Euripides are altruistic suicides, which are rare in modern times. Few case studies appear in print, and many suicidologists have suggested removing altruistic and fatalistic suicide from Durkheim's (1897) theory since these types of suicide are so rare in modern society (Johnson 1965).

The suicide of Alcestis, Queen of Thessaly, illustrates some of the possible unconscious psychodynamics of voluntary altruistic suicide. Apollo learns that Alcestis's husband, Admetus, is to die prematurely and makes a deal with the Fates to spare his life. The Fates demand another death in Admetus's place, and only his wife, Alcestis, volunteers to die for him.

The central theme in the play appears not to be that Alcestis has offered to die in place of her husband, but that her husband has accepted her offer! After Alcestis realizes that Admetus is going to accept it, she is filled with resentment toward him. She acts so as to induce guilt in him to punish him for accepting her offer. However, her aggression is expressed in part consciously and in part unconsciously.

On the day of her death, Alcestis does not emphasize the voluntary nature of her death. She speaks of herself as one who is about to be destroyed, implying that Admetus should have protected her from this destruction. She hints of betrayal and abandonment, focusing for example on her soon-to-be-motherless children. She expresses the hope that her daughter will marry a noble husband, implying that her own husband is not so noble.

In Admetus's presence, Alcestis breaks down and weeps, whereas with others she is more controlled. As soon as Admetus begins to experience the guilt and to suffer, Alcestis recovers her composure rapidly. She then extracts a promise from Admetus that he will not remarry, so that he will be less likely to forget Alcestis and her sacrifice.

Faber notes that Admetus is very dependent upon his wife, and it is this dependence that leads him in part to ask for and accept her sacrifice. However, his dependence on Alcestis makes her loss unbearable. He ends up begging her not to abandon him. We have, therefore, a relationship between a dependent person with few inner resources and a self-sacrificing person who resents being involved with a man who needs her in an infantile way as an object. Admetus uses Alcestis's sacrifice to stop living rather than anticipating the construction of a new life without her.

So, a clinical hypothesis generated by Faber's analysis is that voluntary altruistic suicides stress that they are victims; in contrast, obligatory altruistic suicides tend to protect their egos by transforming the will of others into their own will, that is, they see themselves as martyrs. I doubt that this hypothesis could have been formulated using cases of suicidal behavior found among the clinical material in the files of psychiatric hospitals or psychotherapists' offices.

Understanding a Culture

Suicides in literature have also been used to study a culture. Lester (1972b) examined the suicides that occur in the plays of Ibsen to see if they conform to the patterns described by Hendin (1964) for suicides in Norway, Sweden, or Denmark. Hendin used his clinical judgment to argue that suicide in Sweden was usually the result of failure to achieve a high level of performance, suicide in Denmark was the result of the loss of significant others, and suicide in Norway was the result either of loss of a significant other upon whom the suicide was dependent or of guilt over transgressions.

Apart from a brief mention in *Cataline* of the suicide of a woman after rape, there are seven suicidal deaths in Ibsen's plays—five victim-precipitated homicides and two equivocal deaths. In general, Lester found that the suicides had suffered from dependency loss, whereas the victim-precipitated murders were experiencing guilt over transgressions. The suicides also appeared to be motivated by the desire to preserve or restore an ideal self-image.

For example, in *The Wild Duck*, Hedvig is very attached to her parents, especially her father. Because of her poor eyesight, she does not go to school and has no friends her own age. Hedvig's suicide occurs after her father realizes that she is not his daughter, considers leaving home, and verbally rejects her. Hedvig shoots herself shortly after her father tells her to go away and not to come near him. Her suicide is clearly provoked by the rejection from her father. It would seem to be a dependency-loss suicide, which fits Hendin's description of Norwegian suicides.[3]

Understanding a Suicidal Writer

There are several suicidal writers whose fiction appears to be somewhat autobiographical and, therefore, provides us with some insights into their unconscious psychodynamics, which increases our understanding of them; examples are Ernest Hemingway and Cesare Pavese. However, Sylvia Plath wrote a poem, "Daddy" (in Plath 1981) in the months prior to her suicide that provides a startling insight into the unconscious psychodynamics of her suicide. Plath casts herself as a Jew in a concentration camp versus her father as a Panzer man and as a devil who bit her heart in two. She says that she has always been scared of him, and she calls him a bastard. Yet she says that her suicide attempt at age 20 was an attempt to be reunited with him. She then made a model of her father and married him, but she calls this person a vampire who drank her blood for seven years. Indeed, her marriage to the British poet, Ted Hughes, lasted about seven years. At the end of her poem,

---

[3]Interestingly, Ibsen considered moving to Denmark, but never did so. Furthermore, according to Meyer (1971), Ibsen did contemplate suicide during one stressful period in his life.

she tells her father that he can lie back now, perhaps because, as she says a few lines earlier, she is finally through.

The oedipal theme in the poem is clear. The motivation for her first suicide attempt was to be reunited with the father who died when she was 8 (the poem says 10). And, in case he is jealous of her marriage to Ted Hughes (why else is Daddy sitting up in his grave?), she is now finally through and, presumably, going to be reunited with Daddy for sure this time (and so he can lie back down to await her).

However, there are other elements in the poem. The ambivalence toward her father is evident throughout, but most exquisitely expressed in the final line, where she uses the words, "Daddy" and "bastard," a juxtaposition of affection (Daddy) and anger (bastard). Plath also says that she has killed two men. Who are these two? Daddy and her husband? Plath's father died of natural causes when she was 8, but perhaps Sylvia had wished his death when she was angry at him and believes, magically, that her death wish for him contributed to his death, a common belief in children. Or perhaps she feels guilty over other of her actions toward her father before he died? But then, how did she kill her husband? Perhaps psychologically as her stature as a poet grew to equal, and perhaps surpass, his?

There is an interesting feature to this poem in that Plath uses the word *black* six times, a frequency much higher than in her first book of poems (Lester 1989). According to Piotrowski's (1974) method for interpreting the Rorschach ink-blot test, the use of dark shading predicts a tendency to act out, rather than quieten down, when anxious or under stress. Lester (1991) noted a similar tendency in the poems of Anne Sexton, who also committed suicide.

DOES CREATIVE WRITING HARM SUICIDAL PEOPLE?

Is writing therapeutic for creative writers or it is a stressor that contributes to their psychological disturbance? Silverman and Will (1986) analyzed the life and suicide of Sylvia Plath and concluded that, although she tried to control her suicidal impulses by means of her poetry, she failed in this endeavor. Silverman and Will argued that poetry is successful when it bridges the inner worlds of the creative person and the audience. (Presumably they mean critically successful, for even poor poetry can serve a useful psychological function for the writer, even if it is merely cathartic.) To be successful, poetry must first achieve a balance between the writer's use of the audience to serve his or her own narcissistic needs (a type of exhibitionism) and the desire to give others a way of structuring the terrors and anxieties that afflict us all (a homonymous desire on the part of the writer to use a term coined by Andras Angyal [1965]).

The writer must also achieve a balance between the potentially destructive conscious and unconscious forces motivating the writing and the constructive desires to harness these forces for the purpose of writing creatively. Related to this, the writer must balance primary and secondary process mechanisms. The writer must also compromise between the fantasy permissible in writing and the acceptance of reality necessary for successful living.

When they apply their ideas to Sylvia Plath, Silverman and Will assert that the successful creative process is successful only when the unconscious forces in the writer operate silently and remain hidden from view. This assertion represents a rather traditional view of creative writing. It would seem to express a preference on the part of Silverman and Will for a particular type of literature rather than expressing a universal truth. For example, the unconscious forces motivating Ernest Hemingway may be under control in his writing, but they are certainly not hidden. More pertinently, the confessional style of poetry developed by W. D. Snodgrass and Robert Lowell and pursued by Anne Sexton is in direct opposition to Silverman and Will's view.

Silverman and Will see the transitional period in Plath's poetry as being her final years in the United States. Plath may have had her confidence undermined by the frequent rejections that writers must endure so that she changed her style. In her new style, she revealed her deepest feelings in her poems, using her experiences to create the poem rather than to simply transform it. Silverman and Will note that she described her early poems as "proper in shape and number and every part" but not alive. Her poems moved from being a reordering and reshaping of experience with a poetic purpose toward becoming expressions of herself. She identified with her poems, which made their rejection even more painful, and Silverman and Will label this change as a "narcissistic regression."

The causal sequence that Silverman and Will propose for Plath has no evidence for or against it. It is simply one reading of Plath's life. Other, equally plausible, alternative paths can be proposed. For example, it is quite likely that Plath's participation (along with Anne Sexton with whom she became very close) in a poetry workshop run by Robert Lowell, had a major impact on her writing style. Several members of his workshop adopted a more self-revealing content for their poems, and two received Pulitzer prizes for their work (Lowell and Sexton).

Furthermore, Plath, as she herself clearly recognized, was prone to recurring depressions. In all probability, Plath had an affective disorder, possibly bipolar, and her depressions were likely to recur periodically. It is evident from the severity of her depression in 1953, which led to a very serious suicide attempt, that she would likely become suicidal again with each new depression (much as Virginia Woolf had).

What is interesting is that, whereas in the early 1950s, her writing may not have helped her cope with the stressors, external and intrapsychic, with which she was confronted, in the later 1950s her switch to a more revealing and personalized style of writing may have helped her survive. Silverman and Will claimed that her writing failed to prevent her suicide. Perhaps it may have postponed her suicide?

In the months prior to her suicide, Plath wrote feverishly, sometimes producing several poems in one day. (This feverish activity in the months prior to a suicide was apparent also in Anne Sexton's life.) What would Silverman and Will suggest as a more appropriate strategy for a person confronting intrapsychic turmoil who is not under professional care? It is very likely that the writing helped Plath control her inner turmoil, and some commentators think that the poems she produced were among her finest.

In seeking to formulate a general hypothesis about the role of writing for the depressed and distressed person, it is obviously important to discuss more than one case. In the present context, the life and suicide of the poet Anne Sexton is relevant.

Lester and Terry (1992) argued that writing poetry can be useful with suicidal clients. Writing poems *per se* may not be helpful to the client, but the revision of the initial drafts of poems may be therapeutically useful. Revising poems may serve a similar function for clients as the journal assignments devised by cognitive therapists by giving the clients intellectual control over their emotions and distance from the traumatic memories.

Sexton revised her poems extensively and, in the process of revision, had to concentrate on form rather than content. This allows for both the action that therapists deem to be therapeutic and the distancing of the self from one's problems. Because Sexton ultimately chose the moment of her death, one should not discount the therapeutic help her writing afforded her.

Anne Sexton illustrates the dialectic in poetry as therapy, between expression and catharsis on the one hand and cognitive control on the other. Sexton, as long as she was able to stay psychiatrically stable, was able to apply the craft of poetry to her creative productions. Both Sexton and Martin Orne, her first therapist, believed that her poetry had helped her recover. Only toward the end of her life, as her ability to craft her poems declined, did her mental stability dissipate.

Interestingly, both Plath and Sexton showed manic trends prior to their suicides, writing poems furiously, poems with more emotional expression and less poetic crafting. Rather than arguing that writing poetry contributed in part to their suicides, it makes much more sense to say that, in their final breakdowns, poetry was no longer able to help them deal with the intrapsychic forces driving them as it had in the past. As their inner turmoil increased, both wrote feverishly, almost like a safety valve letting out the steam under pressure in a boiler, but to no avail since the pressure was building up faster than they could release it.

But this final failure of the craft of poetry to keep Sylvia Plath and Anne

Sexton alive does not, as Silverman and Will argue, signify total failure. Both were outstanding poets and functioned quite well given their probable affective disorders. I would argue that the craft of poetry kept both poets alive for many years after their self-destructive impulses first manifested themselves, and so signifies success.[4]

REFERENCES

Andreasen, N. C. (1987). Creativity and mental illness. *American Journal of Psychiatry* 144:1288–1292.

Angyal, A. (1965). *Neurosis and Treatment*. New York: Wiley.

Anon. (1970). *Report on the Commission on Obscenity and Pornography*. New York: Bantam.

Bakan, D. (1958). *Sigmund Freud and the Jewish Mystical Tradition*. Princeton, NJ: Van Nostrand.

Barnes, H. E. (1925). *Psychology and History*. New York: Century.

Bellak, L. (1963). Somerset Maugham. In *The Study of Lives*, ed. R. W. White, pp. 142–159. New York: Atherton.

Bromberg, W., and Schilder, P. (1933). Death and dying. *Psychoanalytic Review* 20:133–185.

———— (1936). The attitudes of psychoneurotics towards death. *Psychoanalytic Review* 33:1–128.

Christie, A. (1930). *The Mysterious Mr. Quin*. New York: Dodd Mead.

Crosby, F. (1979). Evaluating psychohistorical explanations. *Psychohistory Review* 7(3):6–16.

Driesen, O. (1904). *Der Ursprung des Harlekin*. Berlin: Alexander Duncker.

Durkheim, E. (1897). *Le suicide*. Paris: Felix Alcan.

Erikson, E. (1962). *Young Man Luther*. New York: Norton.

Faber, M. (1970). *Suicide and Greek Tragedy*. New York: Sphinx Press.

Festinger, L. (1957). *The Theory of Cognitive Dissonance*. Palo Alto, CA: Stanford University Press.

Freud, S. (1954). *The Origins of Psychoanalysis: Letters to Wilhelm Fliess, Drafts and Notes, 1887–1902*, ed. M. Bonaparte, A. Freud, and E. Kris. New York: Basic Books.

Goodman, P. (1963). The psychological revolution and the writer's life view. *Psychoanalytic Review* 50(3):17–24.

Goodwin, D. W. (1988). *Alcohol and the Writer*. Kansas City, MO: Andrews & McMeel.

Greenberger, E. (1965). Fantasies of women confronting death. *Journal of Consulting Psychology* 29:252–260.

Hendin, H. (1964). *Suicide in Scandinavia*. New York: Grune & Stratton.

Hoffer, P. C. (1974). *A case study of the reduction of cognitive dissonance*. Paper read at the Ohio Academy of History, April.

———— (1979). Is psychohistory really history? *Psychohistory Review* 7(3):6–12.

Holden, C. (1987). Creativity and the troubled mind. *Psychology Today* 21(4):9–10.

Hull, N. E. H., Allen, S. L., and Hoffer, P. C. (1978). Choosing sides: a quantitative study of the psychological determinants of political affiliation in Revolutionary New York. *Journal of American History* 65:344–366.

Jaffe, A. (1967). *The Process of Kafka's Trial*. East Lansing, MI: Michigan State University Press.

Johnson, B. D. (1965). Durkheim's one cause of suicide. *American Sociological Review* 30:875–886.

Kammann, R. (1966). Verbal complexity and preferences in poetry. *Journal of Verbal Learning and Verbal Behavior* 5:536–540.

Leenaars, A. A. (1988). *Suicide Notes*. New York: Human Sciences.

---

[4]It should be noted in passing that creative writing has been found to be strongly associated with both affective disorder (Andreasen 1987, Holden 1987) and with alcohol abuse (Goodwin 1988), and these disorders may adversely affect the psychological health of writers.

Lester, D. (1966). Checking on the Harlequin. *Psychological Reports* 19:984.

_____ (1972a). Incest. *Journal of Sex Research* 8:268–285.

_____ (1972b). Suicide in Ibsen's plays. *Life-Threatening Behavior* 2:35–41.

_____ (1987). Psychology and literature. *Psychology* 24(1/2):25–27.

_____ (1989). Application of Piotrowski's dark shading hypothesis to Sylvia Plath's poems written before her suicide. *Perceptual and Motor Skills* 68:122.

_____ (1991). Dark-shading in the poems of Anne Sexton. *Perceptual and Motor Skills* 73:366.

Lester, D., and Schumacher, J. (1969). Schizophrenia and death concern. *Journal of Projective Techniques and Personality Assessment* 33:403–405.

Lester, D., and Terry, R. (1992). The use of poetry therapy. *Arts in Psychotherapy* 19:47–52.

Manuel, F. E. (1967). Toward a psychological history of utopias. In *Utopias and Utopian Thought*, pp. 69–98. Boston: Beacon.

McClelland, D. (1958). The use of measures of human motivation in the study of society. In *Motives in Fantasy, Action, and Society*, ed. J. W. Atkinson, pp. 518–552. Princeton: Princeton University.

_____ (1963). The Harlequin complex. In *The Study of Lives*, ed. J. W. White, pp. 94–119. New York: Atherton.

McClelland, D., Davis, W., Wanner, E., and Kalin, R. (1966). A cross-cultural study of folk tale content and drinking. *Sociometry* 29:309–337.

Meyer, M. (1971). *Ibsen*. New York: Doubleday.

Niederland, W. G. (1960). The first application of psychoanalysis to a literary work. *Psychoanalytic Quarterly* 29:228–235.

Piotrowski, Z. A. (1974). *Perceptanalysis*. Philadelphia: privately published.

Plath, S. (1981). *The Collected Poems*. New York: Harper & Row.

Rokeach, M., Homant, R., and Penner, L. (1970). A value analysis of the disputed Federalist Papers. *Journal of Personality and Social Psychology* 18:245–250.

Silverman, M. A., and Will, N. P. (1986). Sylvia Plath and the failure of emotional self-repair through poetry. *Psychoanalytic Quarterly* 55:99–129.

Skinner, B. F. (1941). A quantitative estimate of certain types of sound-patterning in poetry. *American Journal of Psychology* 54:64–79.

Smith, P. (1913). Luther's early development in the light of psychoanalysis. *American Journal of Psychology* 24:360–377.

Wolfgang, M. (1958). *Patterns in Criminal Homicide*. Philadelphia: University of Pennsylvania.

7: ASSESSING THE ROLE OF THE UNCONSCIOUS IN SUICIDAL PSYCHIATRIC PATIENTS

Charles N. Lewis

This chapter examines the unconscious in a particularly tragic type of person through the use of the Rorschach test, a psychological assessment technique. If we compare our means of assessment to a lens, we might say that here the lens is both dimmed and sharpened by such a person's psychological condition, which complicates observation of the unconscious. Since we are looking at psychiatric patients, the likelihood of a thought disorder might mean that unconscious processes are more florid and psychological defenses are weaker, thus opening up the possibility of perceiving unconscious material. At the same time, since the "suicidal" state often involves depression, unconscious expression might be limited by a lack of energy and/or by the dominating presence of obsessive, pessimistic, conscious thoughts.

Most of the discussion focuses on the Rorschach test as the most direct means of uncovering access to the unconscious through fantasy. The Rorschach is a projective test, which often draws upon a subject's internal images, free fantasy, and associations, thereby helping to organize the test's otherwise ambiguous inkblot stimuli. Theoretically, the response to the inkblot plates reflects the subject's reactions to reality by sampling the psychological resources that the person brings to organize an awareness and understanding of other unfamiliar life situations including those that bring unconscious fantasies and motivations to expression.

The unconscious is always an elusive object. One currently popular technique of Rorschach analysis has developed a scale to predict suicidal behaviors while elsewhere minimizing the importance of specific response contents, questioning the validity of the projective hypothesis, and ignoring the importance of looking directly for unconscious motivations behind

Rorschach imagery (Exner 1978, 1989). This will not be the strategy used here. Rather, an attempt is made to show how we may detect unconscious psychological meanings, which are expressed symbolically through Rorschach response contents, so as to understand the role of the unconscious in the psychodynamics of suicidal behaviors.

Both the interpretation of Rorschach symbolism and the nature of the unconscious itself are influenced by the theoretical framework used to understand personality. In the personality theories described here, the unconscious may be seen in one case as expressing either disturbing or pathological material disowned by consciousness, or in the other as a potentially creative or destructive force, revealed in imagery, that may be opposite in nature to a one-sided or skewed conscious awareness. To understand the symbolism associated with Rorschach contents, I use both a psychoanalytic theory of the unconscious and another, based on Jungian ideas, that offers an understanding of how Rorschach perception may be influenced by unconscious archetypical sources in the psyche.

PSYCHOANALYTIC PERSPECTIVE

According to psychoanalysis, the unconscious contains primarily repressed contents, governed by primary process (drive dominated, autistic, unrealistic) functioning, whose force of energy seeks to reenter consciousness. The unconscious can achieve expression only after having undergone distortion of especially disturbing material in order to bypass a psychic censor.

Although the Rorschach test did not arise from psychoanalytic theory, its unstructured quality may favor a disguised expression of the unconscious, which can then be analyzed with Freudian personality theory. It is important to remember that the evocative stimulus characteristics of each of the ten Rorschach plates have been established through normative data (what is statistically expected). Thus, the examiner has a set of expectations about what constitutes consciously determined reality-oriented responses that are close fits to blot areas, and those that are more unusual or bizarre and more likely reflective of unconscious inner stimuli, less related to actual blot contours.

Rorschach response contents have been evaluated in terms of levels of psychological functioning, from a primitive level of unconscious expression to that of familiar reality-oriented ego adaptation (Schafer 1954). These levels are said to correspond to a particular relationship of id, ego, and superego forces. It has been suggested that the human movement response (M) can reflect the amount and personal quality of deeply embedded, inner fantasy (Piotrowski 1957). Following such reasoning, we would look for unconscious sources in unusual response contents especially those involving movement (Lerner 1991, Schafer 1954) that can be grouped together to express a common theme, or where there are a high number of sexual or aggressive responses that reflect unneutralized drive energy (Holt 1977). The particular symbolic meaning expressed outside the subject's conscious awareness can then be integrated into other clinical data through a formal analysis, as opposed to a content analysis, of the Rorschach record, as well as through what is revealed in psychotherapy and in case history material. This enables us to begin to define the dynamics behind a person's suicidal behavior, and perhaps to help alter its potentially severe progression.

It should be noted that the response qualities arising from the unconscious that we have called bizarre or unusual may first be noted in quite subtle shifts from normative verbalizations or usual response expectancies. We must attempt to link the implications of such a response to possible symbolically similar responses in the record so as to form a common pattern that can then be interpreted.

A 41-year-old depressed man saw "a bird or winged creature flying" seen in an uncommon inkblot location on card IX that was described as having a "tailbone." Statistically this is an unusual characteristics to mention ("tailbone" refers to the coccyx possessed by humans and certain tailless primates). Both a bird flying and the word *tailbone* may have sexual connotations. Using references to antiquity, folk beliefs, and linguistic expression, Freud (1910) discussed how dreams of flying symbolized a disguised wish for sexual potency, and how the words *tail* and *bird* are familiar substitutes for the penis in a variety of languages. Since Freud and most Rorschach theorists have cautioned against analysis through universal symbols, we must look for additional associations. Elsewhere in the Rorschach record a futuristic airplane is seen with "motors in the tail section," and there is a manta ray with a single tail that is changed to a moth with a dual tail section. A commonly seen animal skin on card IV has "what's left of front feet." This pattern of responses may, in a male subject, be suggestive of concerns over sexual potency and possibly of castration fantasies according to Freud's theory.

Since such unconscious fantasies are disguised from conscious awareness, they may use displacement whereby one detail stands for the conflict as a whole through a chain of associations. Thus a concern about the integrity of the phallus may be displaced to Rorschach responses involving characteristics of "tails" or other body appendages—their bony structure or missing elements.

However, such a statement is still a generalization that can be descriptive of many adult males. We can take a further step in discovering unconscious meaning by noting the words a person uses to embellish his description of these Rorschach responses. Elaborating on the futuristic airplane with its energized tail section, our subject said "I was surprised by what they used in the Gulf War." This uncommon remark may also involve associations to his own sexuality. One could speculate on the question of what else happened in this person's life in early 1991 (when he was diagnosed as having a genetic abnormality and began taking sexual hormones) that may have "surprised" him. We should also look at the intrinsic qualities natural to types of responses given (how does a moth differ from a manta ray?), and at indications of the person's conscious ego functioning elsewhere in the Rorschach record.

In some cases, we may be able to determine how unconscious expressions, which arise from highly individualized sources, may reflect a psychological reaction to past experiences, which contributes to a current psychological crisis with symptomatic suicidal behaviors. Sometimes a Rorschach response may arise from an unacknowledged source of anger or unresolved sexual needs and present as a disguised image that also reflects a chronic sense of guilt through a process of superego censorship.

> For example, a man secretly hated his stepmother who was a nurse and, reading about a nurse's murder when he was 25 years old, began to believe that he was a suspect and felt compelled to confess to the crime. He developed depressive symptoms, suffered a nervous breakdown, and became uncommunicative for fear that, if he told authorities that he was the murderer, they would believe him. Years later he took an overdose of pills after his stepmother died, and later overdosed on medication again when a female nurse refused to give him a barium enema to treat chronic constipation. In psychotherapy he talked about how his stepmother had been obsessed with giving the children enemas for fear that they would die from fecal impaction. When given the Rorschach test he was 58 years old and had recurrent self-destructive thoughts without any accompanying affective response. Here are his responses to cards I to III:

I. 3 seconds

1. Two dogs' heads on the side. Q. (Examiner asks for elaboration.) Dog or wolf, mouth with teeth.
2. Middle looks like a Jack-O-Lantern . . . Halloween. Q. Halloween face, two eyes, mouth on both sides.
3. Some kind of animal's mouth and two little claws. Q. Mouth here and claws.
4. Thing looks like a shaving brush. Q. Shaving brush . . . handle of the brush . . . soap on it.

II. 3 seconds

1. Two elephants with trunks together. Q. Trunks together.
2. Center looks like a hanging lamp . . . red parts don't look like anything to me. Q. Hanging lamp . . . light and that shape. Pendant at the bottom and thing it hangs by.

III. 5 seconds

1. Looks like two human figures. Q. Human figures, legs, arms, head, feet.
2. Red thing looks like a bow tie. Q. Bow tie, the shape.
3. Bottom looks like a face with eyes covered by mittens or boxing gloves. Q. Face with two hands over eyes . . . the head, mouth.

His Rorschach record showed him to be emotionally inhibited with obsessive-compulsive character traits, and to be chronically depressed, which contributed to a low ideational productivity for a man of high intelligence. His Rorschach movement responses were passive (on card IV he saw a gorilla "bending forward away from you") in an unusual way, perhaps oriented to contain his own unconscious aggression through reaction formation (replacement of a repressed wish by a defensive character trait that stands in opposition to the original impulse). Several times he saw a whole response of an animal with an intrinsic aggressive quality, which was followed by a small detail located off to one side (considered a diversionary looking away from a source of anxiety) as in his last response to card I. He saw on card III (turned upside down) the unusual response, "The bottom looks like a face with eyes covered by mittens or boxing gloves."

In psychotherapy we concentrated on this stance conveyed in his Rorschach image of "not seeing" certain emotionally sensitive issues, and how he had learned to control anger by suppressing it, often with its opposite (inoffensive humor), but not without a sense of foreboding anxiety. We reviewed childhood incidents (he had destroyed a pet kitten and had been severely punished), and the antics of cartoon characters (one developed into a monster) that he had drawn as an adult that seemed to touch on his defenses against suppressed rage. After several months he recalled for the first time incidents where his stepmother had masturbated him and his older brother, while both were infants, in order, he believed, to calm them and keep them from crying.

It was not possible to substantiate these reported memories of sexual abuse, but interestingly he has shown a lifelong intellectual interest in creating childhood toys, and has shown an awareness of child abuse but always displaced from himself.

As an adult he has constructed tops that turn over when they are spun, and obtained a patent for a toy in human shape that wobbled down an inclined board through shifting balance, powered only by gravity. He also maintained for sixty years a fascination with the Loeb-Leopold murder and the Lindbergh kidnapping, which involved crimes against boys committed before the patient had reached adolescence. These behaviors could suggest a form of unconscious identification with the victim, and a continued attempt to deal intellectually with the emotional issues of a child's helplessness to manipulation by outside forces through the means available to a child.

One might say from his Rorschach response to card III that guilt ("I always hated my stepmother but now I feel guilty") had caused him to develop an unconscious attitude of finding ways of hiding his anger through a prohibition involving "not seeing" his potential for violence and turning instruments of aggression back against the self (using boxing gloves as a blindfold). Sensitization was blocked (mittens on the hands) to an unconscious hatred toward his stepmother (the perpetrator who he reports had "used her hands" on him sexually). Such displacement of anger served to diminish guilt, which had inhibited aggressive action. In the past this permitted suicidal angry actions to focus on the self (the self-described victim who perhaps had enjoyed an imposed illicit pleasure).

These first two cases illustrate how a specific Rorschach content can provide a symbolic clue that then can be interpreted through psychoanalytic theory. However, there is the danger with isolated contents of engaging in "wild analysis," of seeing something that is not there, perhaps by projecting one's own unconscious and preconscious preoccupations (Schafer 1954). For this reason, the Rorschach contents that form the basis of speculation about the unconscious should be firmly embedded in case history data, including other psychological behaviors that can have projective meaning (artworks, remembered dreams, actions that by repetition point toward an emotionally significant event), and, if possible, with data communicated in psychotherapy—all of which join together so that similar implications point toward the same conclusion.

A further example of this multifaceted understanding of personality is Lewis and Arsenian's (1982) study of a suicidal paranoid schizophrenic inpatient who was seen in psychotherapy in order to cope with unexpressed feelings about his murder of his wife ten years previously. The man, who was a trained artist, was given a Rorschach test prior to psychotherapy and after one year of therapeutic work. He had killed his wife as she slept, using a baseball bat and a wood carving knife; he was under the delusion that she had been sleeping with hippies. Psychotherapy brought out his memories of the murder, and in this way encouraged a "reliving" of the event and an expression of unconscious feelings and associations.

Here are his responses on his first Rorschach test to cards I to III:

I. 5 seconds

1. I don't know, a bat. Q. Spread out—the wings, but doesn't look like it anymore. Not a good inkblot. I like the pretty ones.

2. Don't know what else, don't know . . . way in the middle looks something like a woman. Woman's body, hips, breast, no head, no feet, or no shoes — just legs coming down, no shoes. Q. Woman in the middle with hip, no head or feet. Two legs without feet, breasts here and no head.

II. 15 seconds

1. Don't know, I see a butterfly. Butterfly, I see a red, looks like a butterfly. Q. Butterfly, looks like a butterfly in there, red and sort of darkish at top.
2. Looks like a couple of elephants with trunks together . . . or dogs. Head, no body, just the neck. Q. Two elephants or looks more like dogs rubbing noses. Like two dog's heads without body, profile of dogs.
3. Looks like red ice, red icicles. Q. Part here in a cave, stalagmites. Don't know how they are formed. Didn't study that, saw in a book once. Wouldn't be red in a cave but white, stone-like. Drips down from moisture in the ground.

III. 5 seconds

1. Looks like two men, both the same because it's an inkblot. Looks like doing some kind of dance. Two figures, don't know if they are male or female, looks like men I guess. Q. Two men dancing, middle looks like a fire pot or cushion chair.
2. Looks like a butterfly in the middle, a red butterfly. Don't know, nothing else. Q. In the middle . . . symmetrical, both sides are parallel. An abstract, not real idea of wingspread.

Following a year of psychotherapy, his second Rorschach was less constricted, with a greater number of good form responses including those with human movement (suggesting more access to inner fantasy), and an expanded productivity to color cards (suggesting a greater freedom to express feelings). A comparison of the Rorschach responses before and after psychotherapy showed an increase in the number of pointed objects ("icicles," "wood chisel," "bird with a beak," "pointed shoes with high heels"), and a decrease in disowning statements ("don't know how they are formed, didn't study that") used to describe these responses. Since he had stabbed his wife to death, this is consistent with an unconscious repetition of the event through intrusive fantasy that parallels the conscious repetition through memories. On the second Rorschach, on card I, he saw the unusual response of two men seducing and copulating with the same woman, followed by the statement "I remember it from long ago." That he killed his wife in a state of paranoid jealousy offers additional evidence that psychotherapy has had an "uncovering effect."

In addition, themes in his artworks during this period paralleled his attempts in psychotherapy to grasp the variable emotions engendered by remembering the murder. These themes included a man being punished by women (talion anxiety), the drawing of apotropaic faces to frighten away evil persons (an attempt to project bad feelings outward), and drawings interpreted as a wish fulfillment to see himself as the victim. Choice of subject matter for artworks seemed to assist in developing unconscious mental associations to the murder into themes communicated in psychotherapy that attempted to express or in some way alleviate his guilt.

Art therapy and psychotherapy probably lessened the force of self-punishing and often potentially suicidal behaviors that also threatened to express themselves. This repetition compulsion of symbolic behaviors that "repeat the crime" continued until he both expressed his sense of inner evil and achieved an integration of good and bad self-images into a more stable ego identity, enabling him to spend time painting and living outside the hospital.

In examining unconscious motivations with the Rorschach, we have emphasized that the implications of several separate responses should point toward the same conclusion. This requires a somewhat elaborate record with certain unusual contents that use determinants (color, movement, shading) rather than a simple attention to readily seen inkblot forms. Often, however, a depressed suicidal psychiatric patient produces a much sparser record, with a below-average number of responses. These consist of unelaborated simple forms. Although such responses may show injured or dead contents (that seem pertinent to the question of suicide), these reflect obsessive pessimistic ego attitudes that are obvious even in a casual interview, and probably do not disclose specific unconscious motivations. The Rorschach provides little information about the unconscious in these instances. A procedure called "testing the limits" can sometimes "flesh out" a record for interpretation by asking questions that help elicit further responses (whether popular, or human contents can be seen), or by asking for free associations to responses already given.

A psychoanalytic interpretation of the Rorschach may better disclose unconscious motivations in certain types of suicidal cases than in others. Freud (1917) discusses how, rather than mourning a loved one who is lost, in melancholia there is an unconscious representation of the lost object that becomes introjected into the self so that rage at being abandoned is directed inward against the patient's own ego. According to psychoanalytic theory, suicidal behaviors could be a potential outcome from depression that originated in ambivalent or hostile feelings toward a lost love object that the person turned back on himself. It is my impression in dealing with psychiatric patients who share these psychodynamics of loss, depression, and poor self-object differentiation that in these cases the Rorschach is often flat and meager, producing little information about the unconscious. A patient's expressed fear of death (Maltsberger 1986) might be the only indication of a reaction to an unconscious wish to die in response to unbearable self-condemnation. In such cases there is often a projection of this self-contempt to a delusional outside source of persecution. Here symptoms frequently take on the form of a psychotic depression.

In the two case history examples presented earlier, there was a struggle that accompanied suicidal behaviors, over a "return of the repressed" in response to an earlier traumatic experience. Unconscious expression was at first repressed and then disguised as the ego struggled toward a restitution of psychological functioning. Such unconscious influences that push toward reentry into consciousness would theoretically be much more likely to be reflected in a projective test such as the Rorschach.

Psychoanalytic understanding of unconscious psychological processes initially grew out of case studies of neurotic patients and was subsequently extended to paranoid behavior (Freud 1911) and psychosis. A psychoanalytic interpretation of the unconscious (employing the Rorschach test) may be more limited where the psychological state of mind did not result from neurotic conflict, but where neurotic mechanisms are used in an attempt at psychological restitution (Holzman 1975). Schizophrenia, where there is a profound deficiency in psychological functioning, may represent one such limiting condition. The unconscious interference by mental traces of archetypal experiences from the evolution of human consciousness, as presented in the next section, may be another such condition.

ARCHETYPALLY INFLUENCED PERCEPTION

We now look at the unconscious from a dramatically different perspective. Following Jungian ideas, McCully (1971, 1987) has proposed that the unconscious, in addition to containing individual psychodynamics, is a repository of collective common human experiences grouped together into discrete archetypes that can express themselves in Rorschach imagery. According to McCully, the Rorschach has the power to activate archetypal energy in the psyche and, when this occurs, the perception of images is influenced by that energy. These archetypal experiences represent repeated essential features in human psychosocial evolution and include, for example, birth, mothering, male, female, death, love, good, evil, and other shared collective human activities repeated over time. Once stimulated, these archetypes have the potential to influence perception and reveal themselves to consciousness through symbolism in certain Rorschach responses.

Before hesitating to attach such significance to Rorschach imagery, one should consider that various cross-cultural images, themselves the product of innumerable acts of human fantasy, may be carriers of such archetypal meaning. For example, the image of the moon is expressive in many cultures of intrinsic but varied female qualities (McCully 1977). We often project female qualities onto the moon based on observations of their essential qualities repeated over generations (their common monthly period of cyclical changes involved in "giving birth" to the child or full moon). A man's or woman's unconscious may project female qualities onto the moon despite the fact that these behaviors are closed to males as actual experiences.

In the imagination, the moon that brings refreshing dew and the woman's breast may become representative of immortal life fluid. At the same time, the link in folklore of the witch (the destructive side of the female) to the black night (negative energy) and the crescent moon (a harbinger of growth) point toward representations in various cultures of the terrible mother (Neumann 1972) who carries within her negative form the truth that nature is not all beneficent but maintains life through a process of both creation and destruction.

Hypothetically, these archetypes can be traced back to prehistorical time, when consciousness was beginning to emerge and when symbolic effects (activating psychic behaviors much as instincts guided physical behavior patterns) could be more easily glimpsed.

Similar symbolic or metaphorical imagery in mythology often reflects archetypal sources (Jung 1969). Schizophrenic delusions can be seen as resulting from the conscious ego's passive relationship to a flooding from these unconscious sources. However, here the unconscious can be seen as both a potentially creative and destructive force. Primary process functioning and the unconscious in general are no longer linked primarily to psychological symptoms of pathology. Elements of the collective unconscious, unlike those of the personal unconscious, never undergo repression by an individual's ego, and there is no hypothetical psychic censor to demand a disguised expression of unconscious motivation.

The ego's relationship to these collective unconscious sources usually determines whether they will exert a destructive or beneficial influence. For example, the power of the sexual opposite within, or anima (Jung 1973), may overwhelm a man having a strict narrow definition about what constitutes masculinity, whereas in other cases it may become a source of creative power.

Suicidal behavior results from the ego's inability to deal with a strongly negative effect from the power of a particular archetype.

The Rorschach encourages a free association of visual images and it allows consciousness to be temporarily bypassed, enabling archetypal energy to influence resulting perception. When this happens, these images carry a symbolic imprint of their unconscious sources. We will look for archetypal sources in particular in original Rorschach responses or where common images are viewed in an idiosyncratic way. This requires a grasp of symbolic language. With archetypal imagery the patient's free associations are usually not helpful in finding meaning, since they did not originate from either the personal unconscious or conscious sources.

As presented in a recent paper (Lewis and McCully 1994) there are several Rorschach characteristics that, when taken together, suggest there is an archetypal unconscious meaning being communicated, common to the scope of human experience, rather than a personal unconscious meaning:

1. The Rorschach response content should show a combination figure (one with an intermixture of human, animal, or mythological elements) engaged in some type of movement. Animal movement (scored FM) when present should show activity inappropriate to the species of animal at hand. Piotrowski and Abrahamsen (1952) first noticed that particular psychological traits within a subject appear to be expressed when animal content is seen on the Rorschach with a quality and type of movement that is incongruous with the natural behavior of the animal. This relationship was explored further in a lucid and detailed analysis of Adolf Eichmann's Rorschach (McCully 1980).

When human movement responses (scored M) in such a combination figure are described with rich and unusual qualities, one must be alert to the effects of archetypal energy impinging on the nature of perception. For example, the response on card I of "two witches flying away with carrion, or the remains of a female body" raises the question about the patient's relationship to matriarchal power, and how the negative side of that power effects interpersonal adaptation.

2. The Rorschach response may show content with unusual features that result once consciousness is bypassed, permitting archetypal energies to influence perception. The unconscious can express itself in visual images that are blended together to form a symbolic meaning. Similarly, two or more Rorschach perceptions, arising from unconscious sources, may be brought together into a single response whose unusual relationship challenges our means of interpretation. The literal meaning of such response content often does not conform to everyday reality. This Rorschach content may feature animals behaving unnaturally, mythological imagery, or humans showing highly unusual qualities. The interpretation of meaning in such Rorschach imagery requires a feeling for symbolic language such as Zimmer (1948) employed in an "imaginative understanding" of myth and folklore.

3. Such unusual archetypally influenced Rorschach responses are typically described without customary conscious judgments. Instead fantasy, sometimes pleasant and sometimes gruesome in quality, is allowed to unravel from a naive uncritical viewpoint without evaluations (no words such as *evil* or *ugly* that pronounce a judgment), or conscious reactions (no adjectives such as

menacing or *disturbing*). The special language of the unconscious features an indifference to reality, doubt, certainty, and the fine discriminations of intellectual reasoning for which consciousness takes responsibility.

4. Rorschach content with suspected unconscious sources (for instance, "a woman with a dragon's head running . . .") may be related to similar but consciously determined imagery (for instance, "a female spider running . . .") elsewhere in the record. The words used to describe such related Rorschach contents (which are referred to as "paired responses") may reflect the effect on consciousness of unconscious symbolic meaning and influence. Rorschach imagery reflecting unconscious sources may show humans or animals engaging in unrealistic or fanciful actions, sometimes with mythological characteristics. In contrast, more consciously determined imagery is often less unusual, may or may not show movement, and may be related to unconsciously influenced contents as a paired response based on a similar pattern (things fighting, or ascending, or surrounding an object), or by the mention of a common gender (male or female), or by some other shared but distinctive feature. The occurrence of such a paired response allows us to compare related images, and thereby attempt to sample the contributions of unconscious and conscious psychic sources.

In a previous publication (Lewis 1990) the Rorschach record of a 58-year-old psychiatric patient with a chronic suicidal history was examined to detect signs of archetypally influenced symbolism (McCully 1971, 1987). As a young man he had worked as a medical corpsman aboard ship, and had taken on the persona of a doctor, often describing to strangers his fictitious position as a physician. When he failed at a school to provide certification as an independent medical corpsman, he returned to his deceased mother's apartment and attempted suicide by ingesting her leftover medications mixed together in a large bowl. Since then he had attempted suicide on several other occasions, and has in various ways punished himself "for letting my lying ego lead me into disaster."

Recently he had returned in winter to his boyhood home with the resolution to die outside from exposure. Crippled by arthritis he crawled into the woods but his nerve failed and he admitted himself to a hospital. When he began psychotherapy and received psychological testing he was depressed, feeling he had failed in life, and that he had little hope for the future.

Here are his responses to Rorschach cards I, V, and VII:

I. 4 seconds

1. Two witches, middle part looks like a scarab . . . tearing it apart, or a beetle. Q. Whole thing. Both sides, cap and cloak . . . holding unto a beetle . . . torso, buttocks, and feet.

2. Silhouette of a female torso from the shoulders down. Big word floating in my mind "Valkyries," the witches. Q. Within the scarab is a silhouette of a woman's torso, curvaceous but no head.

V. 5 seconds

1. Looks like a rabbit being attacked by two beasts laterally. Could be warthogs. Q. Ears, splayed legs, running for its life. Two devils have got him in the carotid area I would say.

VII. 11 seconds

1. Two Scottie dogs. Tail, feet, square type faces. Whatever this is, it's nibbling on it. Q. Scotty, tail, ears and legs. Keenly interested in this, sniffing or devouring it.

Card VII shows a conscious paired response as described in criterion 4. This can be compared to Rorschach imagery on cards I and V that is more violent, and more likely to be symbolic of unconscious turmoil (as described by criteria 1, 2, and 3). The response on card I of two witches tearing apart a scarab, which contains the image of a woman's headless torso, suggests a chronic psychological struggle between a weaker male principle and dominant negative forces associated with more powerful matriarchal energies within his unconscious. It also suggests his choice of the impostor role as a compensatory fantasy of masculine power. The patient is familiar with world history and mythology. The scarab in Egyptian mythology has the meaning of spontaneous creation, as it was believed that all scarab beetles were males and that they reproduced by themselves. This further suggests conflict with the primal role of the power of the destructive side of the Great Mother.

When he began psychotherapy he was completing a long epic poem entitled "An Atlas or Anatomy of the Psyche," describing the evolution of consciousness in primitive human beings. In this poem there were many phrases that reflected the failure of an ego-inflated persona once primitive man was no longer guided by his instincts. It paid homage to the earth as the source of life, and denigrated civilization and consciousness, which made a slave of the individual to group fashion and the dictates of leaders:

By wiles and by threat these leaders did thrive
Utilizing all forms of submission
While the rest chose to plod semi-alive
In the raw, ego killing conditions.

We speculate that his poem is a conscious creation, that touches on his own life trauma, and is fueled by unconscious sources.

There are various indications that his ego has a negative relationship to archetypal energies associated with the maternal and feminine within his unconscious. His passive longings for nurturance are spoiled by the inner-directed violence of the destructive side of matriarchal power. We can see these forces in his choice of means of suicide—drinking his dead mother's medications from a bowl (a shape symbolic of the maternal essence), and lying down on the earth to die. His response to card V shows a graphic picture of the violence done to his passive longings for nurturance. Here the attacking outer figures that surround a victim have become warthogs attacking a rabbit—an unnatural behavior for such animals. We would speculate that such an illogical combination results from the fusion of two separate images whose joining together has an unconscious symbolic significance. These images of warthogs have symbolic meaning probably connected with the witches seen on card I. Thus warthogs are pigs—usually symbolic of fertility where an archetypal female is often involved in sacrificial life renewal. Pigs also root out corpses, thus resembling the Valkyries (also seen on card I) who retrieve slain warriors. The tusk of the pig, shaped like a crescent, links it to the witch, a mythological female creature of black magic (negative mother) connected with symbols of night (negative) and the crescent moon (positive).

On card VII, this arrangement of two outer figures surrounding a smaller center detail is repeated again. Much as in his poem, the behavior of the dogs emphasizes a reliance on primitive instinct and senses—taste and smell. This time the image (commonly seen and of good form) seems consciously determined, yet eager for what appears to be an intense need for nurture or satisfaction of appetite. The violence and illogical imagery seen in cards I and V are relatively reduced in scale, yet egocentric affective hunger, not relatedness, still predominates psychically. Rorschach imagery whose source in the unconscious is the destructive side of matriarchal power may be perceived by consciousness as just such an empty unfulfilled hunger.

In many cases a Rorschach record contains rich imagery that Freud's libido theory fails to decipher, so that one suspects that Rorschach perception has a source wider than personality dynamics alone. As shown here, archetypal sources in the unconscious may produce symbolism in Rorschach imagery and other forms of self-expression that likewise are more than merely a disguised expression of personality conflict. Additionally, these symbolic expressions arising from the templates of human psychosocial evolution may alert us to conditions that affect a person's suicide potential. An exclusive reliance on psychoanalysis to understand unconscious influences on Rorschach perception would blind us to these implications.

FINAL NOTE

This assessment of unconscious expression in suicidal psychiatric patients explores an important relationship within a much larger field. We should mention the obvious fact that not all persons with suicidal behaviors are psychiatric patients, and not all motivations to self-harm arise from unconscious sources. We should also acknowledge the difficulties that encompass an exploration of the unconscious through Rorschach imagery. Since we need a self-expressive Rorschach record to assess unconscious meanings, a banal record gives us little clue to the underlying unconscious. It is also possible that certain aspects of the unconscious, coming from deeper, more archaic areas of the psyche, have no means of expression in either self-revealing "accidents" of behavior, symbolic imagery, or through a person's inexplicable portent of unease. There is nothing to be interpreted or measured, only what may be noticed as startling in retrospect.

A 43-year-old depressed man attempted to kill himself by setting fire to the furnace in his house after making sure that his family would be gone for the day. He was saved when the water pipes burst, putting out the fire. The physician who treated him said that he had never before seen a person survive such a serious case of smoke inhalation. This suggests a tremendous unconscious will to live underlying, in this case, a psychological struggle over whether to live or die. A Rorschach record obtained one month after the incident gave nothing unusual or revealing in either content or formal response characteristics. "The will to live" as well as Freud's hypothetical death instinct may represent unconscious, conflicting, opposite components of life that remain hidden and inexpressible on the Rorschach test.

A source of both hidden expression and permanent mystery as vast and oceanic as the unconscious, revealed to consciousness through symbolic imagery and associative fantasy, needs an assessment technique that gives unlimited play to these means of communication. The Rorschach test can provide this open arena, but only if our means of Rorschach analysis is also open to unconscious meanings and goes beyond a presentation of what is statistically apparent. Two theories have been presented to help understand such symbolic imagery. These theories do not exhaust the reservoir of unconscious meaning; but, in my opinion, they are the best available, and each may have superior merit in a particular case.

Because of the complexity of motivations (unconscious and otherwise) that may underlie suicidal thoughts and actions, no specific Rorschach indicator (neither a specific content or determinant) is likely to emerge as a universal single sign to predict suicide (Eyman and Eyman 1992). Using the Rorschach, as we have done, to examine the unconscious in suicidal psychiatric patients may uncover how intrapsychic conflicts can overwhelm a vulnerable ego. This may give us discriminative power in treating suicide. On the other hand, looking directly for some unconscious sign of suicide may be simplistic and fails to focus on understanding such behaviors. Instead we must actively explore the role of the unconscious through varied means of Rorschach interpretation, in corroboration with other clinical data, to help understand how the psychodynamics of the individual person may be formed or bypassed, leading in some instances to suicidal inclinations and actions.

REFERENCES

Exner, J. E. (1978). *The Rorschach: A Comprehensive System*. New York: Wiley.

———— (1989). Searching for projection in the Rorschach. *Journal of Personality Assessment* 53:520-536.

Eyman, J. R., and Eyman, S. K. (1992). Personality assessment in suicide prediction. In *Assessment and Prediction of Suicide*, ed. R. W. Maris, A. L. Berman, J. T. Maltsberger, and R. I. Yufit, pp. 183-201. New York: Guilford.

Freud, S. (1910). Leonardo da Vinci and a memory of his childhood. *Standard Edition* 11:57-137.

———— (1911). Psychoanalytic notes on an autobiographical account of a case of paranoia (dementia paranoides). *Standard Edition* 12:9-82.

———— (1917). Mourning and melancholia. *Standard Edition* 14:237-258.

Holt, R. R. (1977). A method for assessing primary process manifestations and their control in Rorschach responses. In *Rorschach Psychology*, ed. M. Rickers-Ovsiankina, 2nd ed., pp. 375-420. New York: Krieger.

Holzman, P. S. (1975). Problems of psychoanalytic theories. In *Psychotherapy of Schizophrenia*, ed. J. G. Gunderson, and L. R. Mosher, pp. 209-221. New York: Jason Aronson.

Jung, C. G. (1969). The structure of the psyche. In *Collected Works*, ed. B. H. Read, M. Fordam, and G. Adler. 8:139-158. London: Routledge and Kegan Paul.

———— (1973). The syzygy: anima and animus. In *Collected Works*, ed. B. H. Read, M. Fordam, and G. Adler. 9:11-22. London: Routledge and Kegan Paul.

Lerner, P. M. (1991). *Psychoanalytic Theory and the Rorschach*. Hillside, NJ: Analytic Press.

Lewis, C. N. (1990). Psychological assessment of an artist and impostor. *Journal of Personality Assessment* 54:656-670.

Lewis, C. N., and Arsenian, J. (1982). Psychological resolution of homicide after 10 years. *Journal of Personality Assessment* 46:647-657.

Lewis, C. N., and McCully, R. S. (1994). Archetypally influenced perception and Rorschach symbolism. *British Journal of Projective Psychology* 39(1):1-9.

Maltsberger, J. T. (1986). *Suicide Risk*. New York: New York University Press.

McCully, R. S. (1971). *Rorschach Theory and Symbolism*. Baltimore: Williams & Wilkins.

———— (1977). Jung's depth psychology and Rorschach patterning. In *Rorschach Psychology*, ed. M. Rickers-Ovsiankina, 2nd ed., pp. 513-534. New York: Krieger.

———— (1980). A commentary on Adolf Eichmann's Rorschach. *Journal of Personality Assessment* 44:311-318.

———— (1987). *Jung and Rorschach: A Study in the Archetype of Perception*, 2nd English ed. Dallas: Spring.

Neumann, E. (1972). *The Great Mother*. Princeton, NJ: Princeton University Press.

Piotrowski, Z. (1957). *Perceptanalysis*. New York: Macmillan.

Piotrowski, Z., and Abrahamsen, D. (1952). Sexual crime, alcohol, and the Rorschach test. *Psychiatric Quarterly Supplement* 26:248-260.

Schafer, R. (1954). *Psychoanalytic Interpretation in Rorschach Testing*. New York: Grune & Stratton.

Zimmer, H. (1948). *The King and the Corpse*. Princeton, NJ: Princeton University Press.

8: AN EMPIRICAL INVESTIGATION OF THE UNCONSCIOUS PROCESSES IN SUICIDE NOTES

Antoon A. Leenaars, Brenda McLister, and Susanne Wenckstern

At the threshold of any attempt to evaluate the doctrines of psychoanalysis is a curious and significant difficulty. If the theory be true, the prosaic business of considering pros and cons may itself be an expression of unconscious motives, and any objections that rise to a critic's attention may be unconscious defenses against unwelcome revelations.

From the standpoint of science, the question of evidence constitutes the most serious obstacle in the way of judging the theory. Attempts have been made, to be sure, in some cases by psychoanalysts but for the most part by academic psychologists, to submit some of the concepts of the system to the experimental and statistical procedures of science (Heidbreder 1933).

Freud (1915) Shneidman (1981, 1985), Leenaars (1992) and others have indicated that important unconscious psychodynamic forces are present in the motivation of people committing suicide although some theorists (e.g., Skinner 1964) would argue *a priori* that such concepts are mere explanatory fiction. A series of studies investigating the manifest content of suicide notes (Leenaars 1987, 1988, Leenaars et al. 1985) or utilizing a logical empirical (protocol sentence) approach (Carnap 1931, Leenaars and Balance 1984a) indicated that important unconscious psychodynamic forces were judged to be present not only in most suicide notes (i.e., at least half of the time) across various samples but also were observed significantly more frequently in genuine suicide notes than control data (i.e., simulated suicide notes). Leenaars (1986) further demonstrated not only interjudge reliability among clinical judges but also score-rescore agreement for such content in suicide notes.

These preliminary findings strongly suggested the need to develop procedures for identifying such latent concepts, by providing structured classifications or operational definitions about the nature of the latent content and decision rules or guidelines for assigning a vote to the classifications. This chapter provides *operational definitions* of unconscious forces, whereas previous observations were based on clinical judgments. It would be anticipated that considerable training and practice sessions between raters would be needed to establish adequate reliability in such procedures.

Dreams have often been subjected to latent analysis, and since both dreams and suicide notes can be seen as a response, as it were, to the blank card of the Thematic Apperception Test, both are amenable to the rules of thematic interpretation in general. The primary difficulty in conducting research on latent concepts is that observation and interpretation tend to be subjective (Kerlinger 1964); unconscious dynamics cannot be assessed directly (Freud 1915) but only analyzed from the distorted manifest content. Freud (1901, 1917) proposed that wishes, needs, and motivation that are related to psychological conflict are frequently repressed into the unconscious and, subsequently, expressed in dreams and, although the mental processes are different in some ways, everyday life (e.g., verbal expressions, writings). These expressions are, however, distorted and thus the unconscious forces (latent content) cannot be assessed directly (Freud 1915). However, they can be assessed indirectly from the distortions in the verbalizations, associations, and so on (Freud 1916).

Based on this perspective, Foulkes (1978) attempted to develop *objective* general principles to describe the types of distortions that commonly occur in the manifest content of dreams, and these principles can be equally applied to suicide notes and other thematic material. Foulkes's scoring system for latent structure is objective and explicit. He proposed that unconscious forces are presented in linguistic form in psychologically meaningful units, namely subject-verb-object relationships. Table 8–1 presents a summary of Foulkes's scoring classifications that focus primarily on interpersonal factors. As an analysis technique, Foulkes's scoring system is unique and innovative because it attempts to establish a reasonable and orderly set of rules for the analysis of latent content.

This chapter examines genuine suicide notes and simulated suicide notes (as control data), utilizing Foulkes's scoring system for the interpretation of the latent content in these personal documents. Based on previous research (Leenaars 1986, 1987, 1988), it is predicted that unconscious forces would be present in the statements of the genuine suicide notes more frequently than in the simulated notes, that is, more distortions would be identified in genuine notes according to established operational definitions. Two types of distortions are evident in Foulkes's system, either when associative statements result in transformations of interactive statements or when interactive statements

TABLE 8–1

FOULKES'S SCORING CLASSIFICATIONS

Classifications	Examples
Interactive Verbs:	
Moving Toward	Loving, wanting, needing, accepting, liking, helping
Moving From	Withdrawing, disconnecting, disenfranchising, detaching from
Moving Against	Being aggressive toward, rejecting, dominating, controlling, exploiting
Creating	Discovering, nurturing, inventing
Associative Verbs:	
With	Associated with
Equivalence	Being identical to
Means	Acting as the means/medium
Nouns:	
Father	Father, older man, grandfather, males in positions of authority
Mother	Mother, older woman, grandmother, nurturing females
Parent	Scored when sex of parent is unknown
Sibling	Siblings
Spouse	Spouse, peer of opposite sex in long-term relationship
Peer Male	Males of approximately same age
Peer Female	Females of approximately same age
Children	Males/females of younger age
Ego	Self
Symbolic	Animals, material objects, thoughts, ideas

Author's note: This table is based on material from the work of David Foulkes and is used here with Dr. Foulkes's permission.

cannot be scored directly from the text and decision rules must be applied (such as whether ego is subject or object or when an authority figure is scored as Father). It is hypothesized that both types of distortions will occur more frequently in genuine suicide notes than simulated suicide notes.

METHOD

Judges

Two independent individuals, who have had graduate training in psychology, served as the judges. The judges were blind to the purpose of the study. As suggested by Leenaars (1986) and recommended by Foulkes (1978), these individuals received considerable instructions in the scoring system and were trained on a sample of 63 suicide notes. The judges' scoring agreement reached at least 90 percent on all classifications before initiating the current study.

The judges were then asked to score Shneidman and Farberow's (1957) thirty-three genuine suicide notes, which they had randomly obtained (with the cooperation of the Los Angeles County's coroner's office) from a sample of 721 suicide notes, and thirty-three simulated notes, which they had subsequently obtained from independent, nonsuicidal individuals who were matched by sex, age, and occupation. The judges were unaware of the use of simulated notes as control data.

As recommended by Foulkes (1978), the judges scored the suicide notes independently, and subsequently met to reconcile their scoring to minimize deviation from the scoring rules. The reconciled scores were employed in the data analysis.

Instructions

The judges read Foulkes's (1978) description of the rules for the scoring system for latent structure. Every sentence in a note is not free to be scored based on intuition or theoretical tenets; rather it is scored based on rules with relationships as the conceptual unit of analysis. Every sentence is scored for subject (noun), verb, and object (noun), as follows:

Verbs are scored either Interactive or Associative (see Table 8-1). Interactive statements are scored for subject-verb-object relationships with the verb categories of Moving Toward, Moving From, Moving Against, and Creating. Associative statements are scored when nouns are linked by relationships defined as With, Equivalence, and Means. Interactive verbs can be modified. Modifications that enhance the intensity of the relationship are scored + and those that diminish the intensity of the relationships are scored − .

Foulkes lists the various noun categories (see Table 8-1). Self is scored as Ego. Persons older than Ego, and persons who are described as authority figures or nurturant figures are scored as Father or Mother, or Parent if sex is not specified. Persons of the same generation as the Ego are scored as Sibling, Spouse, Peer Male, or Peer Female depending on their sex and relationship to Ego. Persons younger than Ego are scored as Child. A symbolic noun category is included for animals and inanimate objects. Nouns can be modified. Nouns described in terms that are positive or enhance their adequacy are scored + , and nouns described in terms that are negative or diminish their adequacy are scored − .

The decision rules for scoring Ego are described by Foulkes (1978). Every interactive statement is considered to be a self-statement, so either the subject or the object must be scored as Ego. Every interactive statement is considered to describe an interpersonal relationship, so Ego may be the subject or the object, but may not be both. Thus, the scoring system requires that the writer of the note "is located in, at least, one pole of every scored interactive relationship" (Foulkes 1978, p. 208). This assumption is based on Freud's statement that "dreams are completely egoistical."

A similar assumption has been made about other expressions of a person (Freud 1916) and can be readily applied to suicide notes. Ego is either stated directly in a note or can be inserted into the context by being represented in a note in several ways and/or times through identification with extraneous persons (and/or other objects). Other things being equal, since the suicidal person is the author of the note, he/she is the subject of each sentence. The principle is called active voice; that is, the subject is Ego, although this can be "modified by 'identification' rules which align Ego with persons of like age and sex" (Foulkes 1978, p. 210). If the object of the sentence is clearly the writer, the object is scored as Ego. Ego can be scored only once in each sentence, even in sentences like "I hate myself." The later reflexive type sentences are scored as modifying Ego (as in our case, Negative or –) but do not constitute interactive statements.

When neither the subject nor the object is explicitly described as Ego in a note, the following decision rules are applied to infer Ego: If the subject and the object are of the same generation and are both the same sex, the active voice is assumed, and the subject is scored as Ego. If the subject and object are opposite sexes, sex role identification is assumed, and Ego is scored in the position of the character if the same sex as Ego. If the subject and object are of the same sex but different generations, age role identification is assumed, and Ego is scored in the position of the character of the same generation as Ego. Thus, the primary identifications are by active voice, by sex, and by age. Other changes can occur, such as authority figures scored as Father (see Table 8-1). More complex rules are also provided when statements describe interactions between third persons and symbolic nouns. All interactive statements that cannot be scored directly from the text and for which decision rules must be applied constitute one type of distortion.

Foulkes also explains that, under certain circumstances, associative statements lead to a transformation of interactive statements, following Freud's dictum that associations or contextual data are given a priority if available. Nouns in interactive statements can be replaced (transformed) with nouns that have been linked to them only with associative statements. For example, if in a note the person writes "I hate x" and "x goes with spouse," then one can conclude "I hate spouse." Associative sentences are exempt from the rule that Ego must be scored in each sentence; that is, third-person sentences can occur, following Freud's resolution that associations are not always ego-cathected (nor significant). The example above illustrates the exemption.

When associative statements result in transformations of interactive statements, this implies that a distortion has occurred (although different from distortions related solely to interactive statements). Thus, there are two types of distortions scored in the system — one related to associative transformations and the other referring to cases in which interactive statements cannot be scored directly from the text.

The scoring rules are complex and are described in detail by Foulkes (1978).

RESULTS

The judges' scoring was in agreement for 85.4 percent of the content of the thirty-three matched genuine and simulated notes — 86.13 percent for the genuine notes and 84.06 percent for the simulated notes. Following Foulkes's (1978) results, this level of agreement is seen as reflecting adequate reliability.

The results of a Wilcoxon rank sum test indicated that the genuine suicide notes contained more interactive statements than the simulated notes ($z = 2.46$, $p < .05$), suggesting the need to control for this variable (i.e., by covariance) in subsequent, appropriate statistics. The mean number of interactive statements per note was 11.55 for the genuine notes and 6.15 for the simulated ones.

The results of a chi-square test for independent groups using the Yates correction for continuity (Ferguson 1976) indicated that genuine and simulated suicide notes did not differ in distortions related to associative transformations ($\chi_1^2 = 0.12$, n.s.). With regard to the interactive statements only 7.87 percent of the genuine notes and 5.42 percent of the simulated notes contained such transformations. Subsequent references to distortions refer to cases in which interactive statements could not be scored directly from the text.

The results of a chi-square test for independent groups using the Yates correction for continuity indicated that genuine suicide contained significantly more distortions than the simulated notes ($\chi_1^2 = 3.88$, $p < .05$, $C = 0.24$). An analysis of covariance to control for the effect of the greater number of interactive statements in genuine notes in this and subsequent analysis (S.A.S. Institute 1985) indicated that genuine suicide notes contained significantly more distortions than the simulated notes ($t_{63} = 1.93$, one-tailed $p < .05$). The covariant (i.e., number of interactive statements) in this analysis and every instance in this study was significant at the .05 level. The adjusted mean number of distortions per note was 2.20 for the genuine notes and 1.32 for the simulated suicide notes. The slopes of the regressions were tested and in no case in this study were they different, suggesting that there were no relationships between the covariant and variables tested.

Of the genuine suicide notes, twenty-one contained distortions — almost two-thirds of the notes — and distortions were associated with 25.2 percent of the interactive statements. Of the simulated suicide notes, twelve contained distortions — about one-third of the notes — and distortions were associated with 11.82 percent of the interactive statements. A large proportion of the distortions in both the genuine (86.40 percent) and simulated (80.77 percent) notes involved the employment of the decision rules to determine whether the Ego should be scored in the position of subject or object of an interactive relationship between two third persons or between a third person and an object.

No differences were found in the frequency with which each interactive verb (Moving Toward, Moving From, and Moving Against) was noted in genuine and simulated notes. Moving Toward was scored most frequently; Moving Toward accounted for 67.45 percent of the interactive statements in the genuine notes. Table 8-2 presents the frequencies of interactive verbs in genuine and simulated suicide notes.

Creating relationships accounted for fewer than 1 percent of the statements. Ambivalent assertions (both Moving Toward and Moving From or Moving Against relationships) did not differ in the genuine and simulated notes. An analysis of covariance indicated that genuine and simulated notes did not differ significantly in the frequency of each relationship.

The number of times each noun category was employed in the interactive statements of each note is presented in Table 8-3.

As specified in the scoring rules, Ego was scored as the subject or object in 100 percent of the interactive statements. As Table 8-3 indicates, Spouse was the next most frequently employed noun; relationship between Ego and Spouse accounted for 57.22 percent of the interactive statements in the genuine notes. Chi-square analysis for independent groups using the Yates correction for continuity indicated that only Father ($\chi^2_1 = 5.07$, $p < .05$, $C = 0.27$) and Spouse ($\chi^2_1 = 5.78$, $p < .05$, $C = 0.28$) were significantly more often scored in genuine notes. Spouse was employed in thirty-two genuine notes (although this, in part, is likely reflective of the fact that Shneidman and Farberow's notes were written only by married individuals). Mother, Sibling,

TABLE 8-2

FREQUENCY OF INTERACTIVE VERBS IN GENUINE AND SIMULATED SUICIDE NOTES

Verbs	Genuine		Simulated	
	No. of Notes	Statements (%)	No. of Notes	Statements (%)
Moving Toward	32	67.45	30	59.11
Moving From	19	11.81	22	19.70
Moving Against	24	20.21	18	20.69

TABLE 8-3

FREQUENCY OF NOUNS IN INTERACTIVE STATEMENTS OF GENUINE AND SIMULATED
SUICIDE NOTES

Nouns	No. of Notes	Statements (%)	No. of Notes	Statements (%)
Father	13	5.77	4	2.46
Mother	7	4.20	2	1.97
Sibling	3	1.57	0	0
Spouse	32	57.22	24	51.72
Peer Male	12	6.30	5	2.46
Peer Female	4	2.36	0	0
Child	10	9.71	11	9.85
Symbolic	22	12.86	29	31.53

Peer Male, Peer Female, Child, and Symbolic noun categories did not differ. An analysis of covariance indicated that genuine and simulated notes did not differ significantly in frequency of Mother, Sibling, Spouse, Peer Female, and Child. Genuine notes contained more references to Father ($F_{1,63}$ = 4.48, p < .05) and references to Peer Male ($F_{1,63}$ = 4.24, p < .05), whereas simulated notes contained more references to symbolic nouns ($F_{1,63}$ = 8.39, p < .01).

A chi-square test for independent groups using the Yates correction for continuity indicated that genuine and simulated notes did not differ significantly in use of positive (χ^2_1 = 0.90, n.s.) or negative (χ^2_1 = 0.18, n.s.) modification of interactive verbs. An analysis of covariance indicated that genuine and simulated notes did not differ significantly in frequency of positive and negative modification of interactive verbs, although it was significant at a borderline level in frequency of negative modification ($F_{1,63}$ = 3.20, p < .07) such that negative modifiers occurred more in simulated suicide notes.

A chi-square test for independent groups using the Yates correction for continuity indicated that genuine and simulated suicide notes did not differ significantly in use of positive modification of Ego, negative modification of Ego, positive modification of nouns other than Ego, negative modification of nouns other than Ego, or ambivalent modifications of nouns. The results of the analysis of covariance were not significant — only negative modification of Ego reached borderline significance ($F_{1,63}$ = 3.49, p < .06) in the direction of the simulated suicide notes containing more.

Finally, the total number of positively and negatively modified terms in the interactive statements of each note was computed. A chi-square test for independent groups using the Yates correction for continuity indicated that the genuine and simulated notes did not differ significantly in use of positive or negative modifiers. An analysis of covariance indicated that genuine and simulated notes did not differ significantly in frequency of positive modification of terms, but simulated notes contained significantly more negatively modified terms ($F_{1,63} = 4.49$, $p < .05$). The adjusted mean frequency of negatively modified terms per note was 4.73 for the genuine notes, and 6.09 for the simulated notes.

Table 8-4 presents a summary of all significant findings in the various analyses of covariance. The table contains (1) frequency of nouns in interactive statements, and (2) frequency of positive or negative modifiers in interactive statements adjusted for number of interactive statements. (No differences were found in frequency of interactive verbs.) The number of tests performed raises a problem, and the likelihood of a type I error may well be higher than .05.

Table 8-5 presents a suicide note scored by Foulkes's system as an illustration.

TABLE 8-4

SUMMARY OF SIGNIFICANT FINDINGS IN VARIOUS ANALYSES OF COVARIANCE
OF FREQUENCY OF NOUNS IN INTERACTIVE STATEMENTS AND OF
FREQUENCY OF POSITIVE OR NEGATIVE MODIFIERS IN INTERACTIVE STATEMENTS
OF GENUINE VERSUS SIMULATED SUICIDE NOTES ADJUSTED FOR NUMBER OF
INTERACTIVE STATEMENTS

I. Frequency of Nouns in Interactive Statements

Noun	Source	SS	d.f.	MS	F	P	Note
Father	Type of Note	2.83	1	2.83	4.48	.05	Genuine
	Error	39.84	63	0.63			
Peer Male	Type of Note	3.11	1	3.11	4.24	.05	Genuine
	Error	46.15	63	0.73			
Symbolic	Type of Note	15.95	1	15.95	8.39	.01	Genuine
	Error	119.75	63	1.90			

II. Frequency of Positive or Negative Modifiers in Interactive Statements

Modified Term	Source	SS	d.f.	MS	F	P	Note
Verb/Negative	Type of Note	9.13	1	9.13	3.20	.07	Simulated
	Error	179.66	63	2.85			
Ego/Negative	Type of Note	2.91	1	2.91	3.49	.06	Simulated
	Error	52.50	63	.83			
Total Negative	Type of Note	27.35	1	27.35	4.49	.05	Simulated
	Error	383.95	63	6.09			

Note: No differences were found in analysis of covariance of frequency of interactive verbs.

TABLE 8-5

AN ILLUSTRATION OF A SUICIDE NOTE SCORED BY FOULKES'S SYSTEM

Text	Scoring	Distortions
Dear Mary,		
I am writing to you	Ego, Moving Towards, Spouse	
as our divorce		
is not final,		
and will not be		
till next month,	Negative/Moving From, Ego, Spouse	
so the way things	Negative/Moving From, Spouse, Ego	
stand now		
you are still my wife,	[Ego, Positive/With, Spouse]	
which makes you		
entitled		
to the things		
that belong to me,	[Ego, With, Positive/possession]	
and I want you		
to have them.	[Positive/Spouse, Negative/With]	
Don't let anyone	Positive/possessions	
take them from you	Ego, Negative/Moving Against,	Anyone
	Spouse	to Ego
	[Positive/possession, Negative/	
	Equivalence, Ego (Peer Male),	
	Moving Against, Spouse]	
as they are yours.	[Spouse, With, Positive/possession]	
Please see a lawyer	Spouse, Moving Toward, Ego	Lawyer
and get them		to Ego
as soon as you can.	Spouse, Positive/Moving Toward,	
	Positive-Negative/Ego	
I am listing		
some of the things,		
they are:		
a blue davenport	[Ego, With, Positive/davenport]	
and chair,	[Ego, With, Positive/chair]	
	[Positive davenport, With Positive/chair]	
a Magic Chef stove,	[Ego, With, Positive/stove]	
a large mattress,	[Ego, With, Positive/mattress]	
an Electrolux cleaner,	[Ego, With, Positive/Vacuum cleaner]	
a 9 × 12 rug,	[Ego, With, Positive/rug]	
reddish flower design,		
and pad.	[Ego, With, Positive/pad]	
	[Positive/rug, With, Positive/pad]	
All of the things		
listed above		
are almost new.		

(continued)

TABLE 8-5 (*continued*)

Text	Scoring	Distortions
Then there is		
my 30-30 rifle,	[Ego, With, rifle]	
books,	[Ego, With, Positive/book]	
typewriter,	[Ego, With, Positive/typewriter]	
tools,	[Ego, With, Positive/tool]	
and a hand contract	[Ego, With, contract]	
for a house	[Contract, With, house]	
in Chicago,	[House, With, Chicago]	
a savings account	[Ego, With, account]	
in Boston, Mass.	[Account, With, Boston]	
William H. Smith		

Associative statements are demarked in the scoring by being placed within brackets.

DISCUSSION

The procedures outlined appear to have been useful in investigating the unconscious processes in suicide notes and would very likely be so with other clinical material that is thematic in nature. Even if one does not accept the psychoanalytic assumptions in this chapter, one is still confronted with the fact that blind judges scored latent content (i.e., distortions) more frequently in genuine notes than simulated ones. The procedures in this study subjected the investigation of unconscious psychodynamic forces in suicide notes to the first reported structured, objective analysis in the literature, although further validity studies are warranted with the system. Because the current study and a previous one (Leenaars 1986) with clinical judgments report similar findings, and because Foulkes's system can be applied to dream reports, suicide notes, and likely other thematic material, the idea that the distortions as operationally defined may well measure what they report to measure is supported.

But are we indeed, measuring what we are reporting to be measuring? Interjudge agreement addresses only (one aspect of) reliability, and maybe the measures are not valid. It may well be, as some would argue, that we are simply measuring the confusion associated with the mental state that precedes suicide. The suicidal person may simply be unaware (unconscious) of aspects of his/her information processing. However, such a perspective is in contrast to Freud's (1916) when he suggested that distortions (as well as displacements, bizarreness, etc.) measure the *dynamic unconscious*. The focus in this view — implied in Foulkes's system — is on repressed unconscious contents (e.g., wishes, needs). As Eagle (1987) has noted, this is an issue of markedly different theoretical tenets, that is, different conceptions of the unconscious.

The ideas in this chapter are largely based on a number of tenets of psychoanalytic psychology. They accept the distinction between manifest and latent. They accept that latent implications are important in understanding a suicidal person. They accept that there are procedures to infer the latent implications from the manifest content in suicide notes. For example, it is implied that distortions are symptomatic of unconscious forces.

In contrast, the more cognitive-behavioral view would be one that accepts that the person is *only* unaware (unconscious) of processes that influence behavior, such as what would occur when the suicidal person decides to end his/her life due to mental constriction, unbearable pain, or hopelessness-helplessness. We do not mean to suggest that such processes espoused by the cognitive view do not occur; rather, we believe that both these processes and others (e.g., biological, sociocultural, philosophical) occur in an individual who defines an issue for which suicide is perceived as the best solution.

It is possible to structure suicide notes and, by implication, suicide from a psychoanalytic perspective of unconscious forces as, we believe, our results objectively show. Indeed, we believe that the driving forces behind an individual's suicide are largely the *dynamic unconscious* ones, although there is almost continuous interaction with these forces and other variables that may be related to the suicide (Leenaars 1988, 1992). Further analysis with thoughts and observations of various diverse theorists on latent content is needed, although a critical shortcoming of such investigations, as in all studies of completed suicide, is the availability of adequate data (e.g., associations) (Maris 1981). Simply stated, if we could put the suicide notes in the context of the authors' lives, we could make greater use of associations to understand the event.

Our results support the observation of Leenaars (1986, 1987, 1988) that genuine suicide notes contain more unconscious psychodynamic implications than simulated notes. The current results substantiate the finding of Leenaars by utilizing an objective scoring system. We found significantly more distortions in the interactive statements of individuals who wrote genuine suicide notes than matched individuals who wrote simulated suicide notes. Distortions are reflections of latent content (Foulkes 1978, Freud 1916). No support was found for one type of distortion, namely when associative statements result in transformations of interactive statements. This finding is likely related to the fact that free associations cannot be obtained for suicide notes as they can be for dreams and that this type of distortion is generally dependent on associations.

Significant support was found for the other critical types of distortion. Genuine suicide notes more often called for decision rules to be applied about the latent meaning in the interactive statements. A large proportion (86.4 percent) of the distortions involved deciding whether the Ego should be scored in the position of object or subject of an interactive relationship between two third persons or between a third person and an object. One possible interpretation of these findings is that the manifest content of a suicide note may not be identical with all of the writer's wishes and needs. By analyzing the latent content, we may be able to uncover some of these underlying forces. For example, it may be assumed that identifications, as noted elsewhere (Leenaars and Balance 1984b), are important in suicide.

Suicide is often interpersonal in nature (Freud 1921, Leenaars 1987, 1988, Leenaars et al. 1985, Shneidman 1985). Leenaars (1986, 1992) has suggested that dynamic unconscious processes are related to this interpersonal aspect of suicide. The current results clearly suggest that the dynamics are related to a key significant other and other people (e.g., father), often more than two people. Further, the wish in these relations is often one of moving toward (attention, approval, gratitude, affection, love, sex, etc.) rather than moving against or moving away. According to Horney (1950), from whom Foulkes developed his schema for interactive verbs, such a person evaluates his/her life according to how much he/she is liked, needed, wanted, or accepted. This type of person is self-effacing and has a continual wish (or need) for attachment—attention, approval, gratitude, affection, love, sex. To be loved is to be safe. This type of person will sacrifice all to be loved.

> While curtailed in any pursuit on his own behalf, he is not only free to do things for others but, according to his inner dictates, should be the ultimate in helpfulness, generosity, considerateness, understanding, sympathy, love, and sacrifice. In fact, love and sacrifice in his mind are closely intertwined: he should sacrifice everything for love—love is sacrifice. [Horney 1950, p. 220]

Other theorists have cited other factors. Freud, for example, would cite intense identification with a lost or rejecting object (e.g., person) and aggression turned inward. Shneidman, for another example, would cite intense unbearable psychological pain, with accompanying constriction, hopelessness, push for egression, and so on, sparked underneath by dramatically frustrated needs.

Our own tentative position (Leenaars 1986, 1988, 1989, 1992) is that the unconscious dynamics in suicide are most related to intense (identification) attachment wishes and needs in a relation (e.g., person, freedom, employment, good health) and, despite ambivalence, a deep loss/rejection, with accompanying unbearable pain, of the *moving toward* in this same relation. A history—or as Maris (1981) stated a "suicidal career"—is implied in these processes.

To conclude, unconscious psychodynamic implications are often present in the act of killing oneself, and as Heidbreder (1933) suggested, the experimental and statistical procedures of science can be used to evaluate this concept of the psychoanalytic system.

REFERENCES

Carnap, P. (1931). Psychology in physical language. In *Logical Positivism*, ed. A. Ayer, trans. G. Shick, pp. 165-198. New York: Free Press, 1959.

Eagle, M. (1987). Revisioning the unconscious. *Canadian Psychology* 28:113–116.

Ferguson, G. A. (1976). *Statistical Analysis in Psychology and Education*, 4th. ed. New York: McGraw-Hill.

Foulkes, D. (1978). *A Grammar of Dreams*. New York: Basic Books.

Freud, S. (1901). The psychopathology of everyday life. *Standard Edition* 6:1–310.

––––––– (1915). The unconscious. *Standard Edition* 14:159–215.

––––––– (1916). Dreams. *Standard Edition* 15:83–228.

––––––– (1917). General theory of neurosis. *Standard Edition* 16:243–483.

––––––– (1921). Group psychology and the analysis of the ego. *Standard Edition* 18:67–146.

Heidbreder, E. (1933). *Seven Psychologies*. New York: Appleton-Century-Crofts.

Horney, K. (1950). *Neurosis and Human Growth*. New York: Norton.

Kerlinger, F. N. (1964). *Foundations of Behavioral Research*. New York: Holt, Rinehart, & Winston.

Leenaars, A. A. (1986). A brief note on the latent content in suicide notes. *Psychological Reports* 59:640–642.

––––––– (1987). An empirical investigation of Shneidman's formulations regarding suicide: age and sex. *Suicide and Life-Threatening Behavior* 17:233–250.

––––––– (1988). *Suicide Notes*. New York: Human Sciences Press.

––––––– (1989). Suicide across the adult life span: an archival study. *Crisis* 10:132–151.

––––––– (1992). Unconscious processes. In *Suicidology: Essays in Honor of Edwin Shneidman*, ed. A. Leenaars, pp. 125–147. Northvale, NJ: Jason Aronson.

Leenaars, A. A., and Balance, W. D. G. (1984a). A logical, empirical approach to the study of suicide notes. *Canadian Journal of Behavioural Science* 16:249–256.

––––––– (1984b). A predictive approach to Freud's formulations regarding suicide. *Suicide and Life-Threatening Behavior* 14:275–283.

Leenaars, A. A., Balance, W. D. G., Wenckstern, S., and Rudzinski, D. (1985). An empirical investigation of Shneidman's formulation regarding suicide. *Suicide and Life-Threatening Behavior* 15:184–195.

Maris, R. (1981). *Pathways to Suicide*. Baltimore, MD: Johns Hopkins University Press.

S.A.S. Institute. (1985). *S.A.S. User's Guide: Statistics*, 5th ed. Cary, NC: S.A.S. Institute.

Shneidman, E. S. (1981). *Suicide Thoughts and Reflections: 1960–1980*. New York: Human Sciences Press.

––––––– (1985). *Definition of Suicide*. New York: Wiley.

Shneidman, E. S., and Farberow, N. L., eds. (1957). *Clues to Suicide*. New York: McGraw-Hill.

Skinner, B. F. (1964). Behaviorism at fifty. In *Behaviorism and Phenomenology: Contrasting Basis of Modern Psychology*, ed. W. Wann. Chicago: University of Chicago Press.

Part IV
CASE CONSULTATIONS

The intense personal study of suicidal lives has been supported by Gordon Allport, Henry Murray, and Edwin Shneidman, and the case study has a significant place in suicidological understanding. There is much one can glean from the idiographic approach, both to refine clinical theory and to suggest practical strategies for prevention, as one is not limited by statistics, psychological autopsies, third-party interviews, or other indirect methods of study. One listens to the suicidal person him/herself. Part IV consists of four chapters: a study of a suicide attempt in a child, a case consultation with a suicidal adolescent, an illustration of suicide in adulthood, and an intensive study of suicide in an older adult.

9: JUSTIN: A SUICIDE ATTEMPT IN A 4-YEAR-OLD BOY

Antoon A. Leenaars

Hello. Dr. Leenaars . . . This is Dr. Smith in Windsor. I'm calling to see if you would accept a referral from our hospital. We have a patient who attempted to kill himself by hanging. He needs to be seen as soon as possible. . . . He is a 4-year-old boy, the son of Dr. Susanne Jones, one of our psychologists.

That was my first contact with a most extraordinary boy, Justin, who was in deep pain. Indeed, the pain had become so unbearable for him that he wanted to "go away." The case is perplexing and bewildering. Why would Justin, a bright and energetic 4-year-old boy, want to hang himself?

Many people do not believe that a 4-year-old — or even an 8- or 10-year-old — could kill himself. They simply deny the event; they would say, "Justin did not make a suicide attempt. It was an accident or suicide-like behavior." Yet, children do commit suicide. Although suicide is rare in children younger than 12, it occurs with greater frequency than most people imagine. Unlike the relatively low number of children who commit suicide, there is a much higher percentage of children who attempt suicide and an even greater number who think about suicide. Pfeffer (1986) reported in a study of elementary school children that 11.9 percent of the children had thought about suicide. To my knowledge, there are no figures for completions and attempts.

How do we understand suicide in children? Defining suicide is a complex endeavor, even in adults. Shneidman (1985) has provided the following definition: "Currently in the Western world, suicide is a conscious act of self-induced annihilation, best understood as a multidimensional malaise in a needful individual who defines an issue for which suicide is perceived as the best solution" (p. 203).

Pfeffer (1986) has suggested that the definition of suicide needs to be clarified somewhat for youth, providing the following comment: "It is not necessary for a child to have an understanding of the finality of death but it is necessary to have a concept of death, regardless of how idiosyncratic it may be" (p. 14).

To understand Justin's behavior, one should keep Shneidman's definition in the foreground, but also keep in mind Pfeffer's clarification about death. Much has to do with children's understanding of death. Although nobody (unconsciously) understands death, people's view of it shifts across the life span and children have their own perspectives. Research (Nagy 1948, Pfeffer 1986) suggests that children's views differ depending on their age. Young children (up to age 7) see death as temporary. Children around 10 years of age see death as personified and temporary; an outside agent causes death. By the time a child is 12 years old — a young adolescent — he/she sees death as final; internal biological processes cause death. Yet, even older adolescents may misunderstand the finality of death.

To begin to understand suicide in children, I will outline the case of Justin as an idiographic study. Next, I will attempt to show how the concept of the unconscious is necessary to understand both Justin's suicide attempt and suicide in children in general. It is necessary because the child's conscious mind has a large number of lacunae. The consciousness of the child cannot explain his/her suicide as completely as in the adult.

Consciousness, as already shown in this volume, affords an insufficient explanation of behaviors. Only by presupposing other processes can one understand suicide. For a person of any age, consciousness is only a small part of the mind. From a developmental perspective, this is especially true in children. The assumption of the unconscious, in fact, is necessary to understand suicide in children. It allows one to better comprehend the enormous complexity of suicide in youth.

THE CASE: AN EXAMINATION

Justin is a 4-year-old boy, attending a preschool setting. The chief reason for referral was the suicide attempt. Justin had attempted to hang himself, still showing the rope marks upon intake. That attempt, however, was his mother's reason for referral, not Justin's. When asked, Justin was unsure initially why he was seeing a therapist (i.e., "a doctor").

Based upon his mother's report, Justin appeared to have been experiencing distress for two years. His behavior began to be regressive at times. Changes were noted in level of play, sleep patterns, level of activity, and anxiety. The identified stress was marital discord. She reported that Justin's father, Michael Jones, had been abusive, both emotionally and physically, toward Justin and herself. She described these incidents as severe, escalating in the last two months. Yet, the precipitating event was a quite chaotic fight between them four weeks ago. At that time, a chair was broken and furniture was thrown, after which Mr. Jones left the house and has not returned since. Through telephone calls, Dr. Susanne Jones had learned that her husband had decided to separate and to leave the house. Subsequently, Justin's behavior deteriorated, becoming quite depressed. The suicide attempt occurred about four weeks later.

Justin had no previous mental health history. Dr. Jones denied any disturbance or treatment. However, she reported that she now believes Mr. Jones was psychiatrically disturbed, likely having a narcissistic personality disorder.

Justin's medical history was unremarkable; he had the usual childhood illnesses. Only the reaction to the abusive father was identified as problematic. Dr. Jones reported that Justin was probably depressed. She knew of no psychiatric illness in her or her husband's family.

Mr. and Dr. Jones met at university about two years before they married. Dr. Jones described the relation as positive, "not like with other men." They were both Catholic and socially established. When married, they were financially supported by Mr. Jones's family. She reported that there were no problems until she decided to get pregnant. Mr. Jones had wished to delay a family; nevertheless, Justin was conceived. She reported that after his birth, things changed, with her having less time for Mr. Jones. She needed to be with Justin. By the time Justin was 2, the marriage was "dysfunctional."

Dr. Jones is a psychologist, practicing at a hospital. At the hospital, she has a position of responsibility in an adult inpatient unit. She reports no problems at work.

Mr. Jones was not seen at intake because, according to Dr. Jones, he was not interested in Justin. Dr. Jones reported that her husband owned a clothing store. The business did well, with the support and involvement of Mr. Jones's father.

Justin was the only child in the marriage. Dr. Jones reported that she was isolated from her family of origin, with little involvement with them at this time. She did, however, report that Mr. Jones's parents were involved in her family, often too much.

Dr. Jones's reaction to the attempt was one of distress, and she reported that she was overwhelmed. She did not believe that children could make suicide attempts, finding the event highly perturbing. She reported that she was unsure of Mr. Jones's reaction, suggesting that he probably did not care.

Justin's personal history was generally unremarkable until the age of 2 when the conflicts in the home arose. Pregnancy and birth were normal, although Dr. Jones reported that her husband did not want the pregnancy. Early motor and speech development were normal. Dr. Jones suggested that Justin began to speak at an early age. Justin began to read by the age of 3. She reported that there were problems at school, namely relating to other children, not following directions, and being overactive. She reported that Justin had no problems at nursery school earlier. In the last year, Dr. Jones reported that Justin was more clingy to her when she brought Justin to the school, and Justin had been even more so during the last four weeks. Aside from the abuse and rejection from Mr. Jones, Dr. Jones saw no other problems with Justin.

The Process

Utilizing a time sequence format, I will outline the complexity of the case as it arose in treatment.

Dr. Jones, visibly agitated, brought in her son. The rope marks were evident upon his neck. While Justin played in the playroom, she described the incident, telling me that she and her husband had been separated for four weeks, following a severe conflict in the home. She said that Justin was unhappy about the separation, especially since his father had not seen him during the four weeks. Justin was described as agitated and overactive. He frequently experienced "anxiety attacks," looking numb. "He often doesn't focus for minutes, as if he is out of touch with reality," she said. She described frequent crying spells at home and at nursery school. Sleep disturbances occurred, requiring her frequently having to sleep with Justin. He had been experiencing school problems lately, often not following directions and just "asking for me." Her diagnosis was a childhood depression as a result of her husband's neglect and abuse. I agreed with the diagnosis, not necessarily the reason.

When I saw Justin alone, he was cooperative; he enjoyed the playroom. However, he was unfocused, going from one toy to another. When I asked how he was feeling he said, "I don't know." When I asked if he was happy, he said "no." Upon enquiry, he said he wanted to see his father. I asked if he sees his father. He said, "I don't know." But he then revealed that he saw his father "last Sunday."

When I asked about the rope marks, he said "I don't know." Since I primarily wanted to build an attachment, I allowed him to keep this inhibiting approach for now. We merely turned to drawing. Figures 9–1 to 9–3 are some of Justin's first pictures in treatment.

Although I will not address assessment in this chapter, a few observations about Justin's drawings may be helpful. The contrast between Justin's picture of himself being happy (e.g., sun) and the picture of his mother's being depressed (e.g., rain) is critical. It reflected, largely unconsciously, Justin's perception of who was depressed. One can

FIGURE 9-1.   Justin's picture of himself.

even note the greater slashes on Dr. Jones's neck, something Richman (1986) has associated with suicidal behavior. Figure 9-3 of the house is not that unusual for a child of Justin's age (although it was more primitive than his ability with words). The house might be remarkable because of the lack of smoke, which, like the inaccessible door, raises question about what was occurring in the house.

Justin was obviously perturbed, but how lethal was his act? Understandably, there are no observations or tests that will allow us to know how suicidal Justin was (Maris et al. 1992). Suicide is too complex, and

FIGURE 9-2. Justin's depressed mother.

even more complex in very young children. One needs to use one's clinical skill to evaluate the risk. Many questions arose: What was so traumatic for Justin? What were the dynamics in the family? What were the unconscious processes that caused such a young boy to attempt to hang himself?

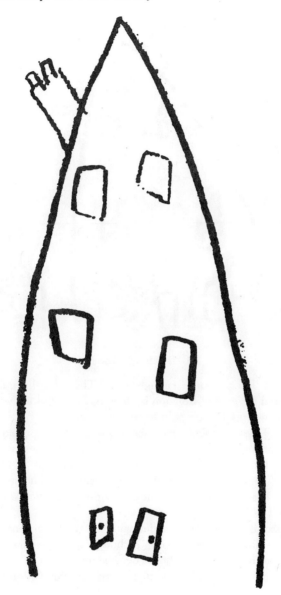

FIGURE 9–3. A house.

Justin returned the next day. He brought me a picture (Figure 9–4) that, like the ones he had drawn for me the previous day, was quite revealing. It was a picture of "a house on fire" that he had drawn at school. The teacher had written Justin's story for me: "There is a fire. It was on Dandurand, in Windsor. The people died. But except the

FIGURE 9-4.   The fire.

8-year-old. He got out in enough time." The symbolism about his own family and his pain of isolation is obvious. Drawings are windows to the mind. How was Justin's pain to be addressed?

Dr. Jones revealed more about Justin. She reported that he had said, "I am going to see God," before the attempt. These words had been repeated for weeks. Perseveration was a hallmark of Justin's mind. He would often repeat acts and words in treatment. The statement about God had been occurring since the day of the separation, which Dr. Jones described as "very violent."

Justin became more familiar with the playroom, and, as he would do every day, he read books. Although he occasionally drew other pictures at my request, the books became our vehicle of communication. Treating children is often just that — a relationship within the context of play.

A few days later, I saw Justin and his mother. The mother started to talk about her depression, describing her feelings as reactions to her husband's "abuse." My own impression, however, was that the depression was more endogenous. Justin himself was more perturbed; again, he had not seen his father.

At a next visit, Dr. Jones was seen by herself, allowing me to discover more. She appeared to be a very dependent person, who struggled with that need. She described years of abuse by her husband, suggesting that the conflict began upon Justin's birth. When queried what she thought the reason might be for the conflict at that time, she said, "Justin needed me." Justin had often experienced verbal and physical conflicts in his family since the day of his birth.

She revealed in response to seeing Justin's picture (Figure 9-2) that she had realized that she was depressed. She said that she had been crying for months, suffering from severe sleep disturbance. She reported increasing isolation, with Justin as her only companion.

The next few weeks, the following events occurred:

1. Justin arrived for therapy with a fire truck that he had received from his father. He was most eager to show me the toy, whereas his mother was "having a hard time."
2. Justin read books. Only after I asked about his father did he show his agitation. Dr. Jones again revealed that his father had not seen Justin.
3. Dr. Jones came in, very frustrated. She expressed extreme anger at her husband. At the same time, she reported that Justin had been acting out at school; for example, he was biting some other children.
4. Justin arrived happier again, reporting that he saw his father. He talked about people being "mean." However, he was very vague about *who* was mean.

Toward the end of three months in treatment, Justin arrived with some drawings for me (Figure 9-5), which I believe was an expression of the increasing closeness in the therapeutic relationship.

For the first time, he spoke about his parents' fighting, stating, "I hate his [father's] butt." Upon saying this, he became more withdrawn, almost frightened. Justin was unable to come in for his next session, owing to his mother's illness, so he and I spoke on the telephone. It is sometimes critical to maintain ongoing contact with young children in treatment. The next session Justin said, "I hate it," the "it" being his parents' fighting. He now began to verbalize more and revealed that he was feeling "sad." Justin began to trust me enough to talk about his feelings.

The next five sessions were much the same. Justin began to talk about "divorce," asking, "Who will I live with?" and "What if dad gets remarried?" Justin also spoke about visits with his father that were more frequent now.

At about four and a half months into treatment, Dr. Jones arrived alone, visibly agitated. She reported, "I want to let Michael [her husband] have custody." She wanted to get out of the situation, stating that "everything was too much." She was more willing to talk. She requested to see me individually, an idea that is not that unusual in my practice. Often seeing the parent speeds the child's healing.

FIGURE 9-5.   Justin's hero "Ninja Turtle."

The next session Justin decided to read Dr. Seuss's *Horton Hears a Who*. His favorite line was "a person is a person no matter how small." Justin's self-esteem needed a lot of reinforcement.

The following sessions were unremarkable. However, at the end of five months, Justin informed me that Barika, the class hamster, died. He said, "I felt sad," which led to talk about death. Justin's idea of death was much like that of younger children. He saw death as temporary; he understandably did not grasp its adult meaning. Throughout his treatment, death was a recurrent theme, something Pfeffer (1986) has also observed in suicidal children.

At about six months into treatment, Dr. Jones began to reveal more about herself. She reported a very conflictual relationship with her mother. She recalled her mother saying, "You'll never amount to anything." Her parents were divorced. These issues and others as well as her own extreme inner anger became the focus of our therapeutic work, which seemed to result in a noticeable difference in Justin. The more Dr. Jones attempted to work through her own pain, the less Justin's pain became.

One other important shift occurred with Dr. Jones's increasing participation in treatment—Mr. Jones became more involved with Justin. Justin, in fact, had his first overnight visit with his father, which he enjoyed, although he was "lonely" for his mother.

Regrettably, however, these advances were short-lived. Appointments were soon canceled by Dr. Jones. When she finally arrived, she revealed that her husband had a new girlfriend, stating that it was "not moral." Her ups and downs were cyclical.

At about seven months into treatment, Justin's work centered on the announcement of a divorce. He talked, for example, about a classmate whose parents were divorced. At school, Justin began to act out more. For example, he urinated on another boy in the washroom. His mother's work in treatment became less productive. Her anger intensified and began to be expressed toward many people. However, she was most angry at Mr. Jones, stating that she was often upset at home. She attempted to increase her mental separation from Mr. Jones, stating, "I've outgrown him," despite her increasing anxiety and insecurity.

Within days Justin's problems at school increased. He described the teachers as "not fair." He stated that he was being punished (with time-outs) "even when I'm good." His agitation increased.

Despite Dr. Jones's agitation, she was responsive to the school's and my concerns about Justin's behavior. She reprocessed the suicide attempt, stating, "I don't want him to die." Yet, she said, "There is nothing we can do."

Dr. Jones was, in fact, mentally constricted. There was a narrowing of the range of perceptions or opinions or options that occurred to her conscious mind. She used words like *only, always, never,* and *forever.* One had to attempt continually to widen her view. She was generally unconscious of Justin's and her own psychodynamics.

Upon Dr. Jones's request, at about eight months into treatment, Mr. Jones was seen for his first visit. I had previously requested that Mr. Jones be involved in Justin's treatment, but Dr. Jones had either refused or indicated that her husband did not want to be involved. When I saw him, he was solely focused on Justin, asking for help. He wanted to know what he could do, suggesting that he wanted to be involved with Justin. Mr. Jones was an anxious individual. He often let things get to him and was passive and dependent. His father, despite retirement, often ran the business, similar to what he described as his parents' overinvolvement in Justin's life. The separation had been very difficult for Mr. Jones. A half year after the separation, he had finally began to socialize and date again.

He genuinely loved Justin, although, both when married and after the separation, he was in conflict with Dr. Jones over child-rearing practices. The slightest event resulted in conflict — swimming classes, birthday parties, anything. Mr. Jones described Dr. Jones as "going on and on" in such situations, demanding her way. Although earlier agreeing to her wishes, in the last few years of the marriage he began to express his disagreements with her. At such times, he would "lose it," and yell repeatedly. On a few occasions, he reported that he broke objects, including a rocking chair on the day that he left. However, he denied any physical violence toward Dr. Jones or Justin.

Mr. Jones disagreed with Dr. Jones about issues of access to Justin (i.e., visitation rights). He reported that he had been refused access. He suggested that he was aware that Justin was upset about the separation and not seeing him on a regular basis. Yet, he said, "I didn't know what to do. She wouldn't let me see him."

After that visit, Justin and I spoke about his father's visit here. However, he would quickly switch topics, wanting only to play. Talking about his father was anxiety-producing.

Next week, Mr. Jones and Justin were seen together. That visit was productive for them, but Dr. Jones, at her next visit, was agitated. We discussed her needs. A colleague had suggested that she was in need of an antidepressant. This suggestion was immediately rejected: "I have no problems."

Over the next months, Justin and his mother were seen together or individually. Dr. Jones was often upset, talking about "the game" Mr. Jones was playing. Attempts at providing support were increasingly rejected. Her defensiveness increased and so did Justin's acting out both at home and at school. On one such visit Justin arrived upset; he said that his father "broke a promise." He said, "He doesn't keep promises," stating that his father had not called him. He said, "I'm angry at him."

On one of Dr. Jones's visits, when she was more introspective than usual, she tearfully revealed some memories of her childhood. She described her mother as neglectful, recalling how she got no birthday cake on her seventh birthday. She revealed now that her mother was "a manic-depressive," despite having denied any family history of mental illness at intake. This was to be her last discussion about her mother, and thereafter she focused only on her husband and his emotional abuse.

Shortly after, Justin revealed that his father had come to the house and moved "his stuff" out. Justin was visibly agitated. For the first time, in fact, he became angry at me. We were reading a book, and he suddenly grabbed the book and slammed it down. "You did that wrong," he said. His next visit continued to be centered on my reading the book wrong. When I asked if he was angry at someone, he said "Yes." He said, "My father is a thief." He suggested that his father stole his mother's money, adding, "You talk to him for 6 hours. I hate him."

Dr. Jones, in her own meetings, expressed similar anger, suggesting that I might speak to Mr. Jones. When I saw him, his story was quite different. He was perplexed about the problem, suggesting that the real issue was an attempt at financial settlement in the divorce proceedings. Our focus with Mr. Jones became one of how to solve current problems and how to have Justin return for visits.

Next meeting, Dr. Jones informed me that Justin had said, "I want to kill Dad." Indeed, a visit to his father had been conflictual, "as I predicted," she said. Justin had refused to listen to his father, being very demanding. This resulted in Mr. Jones yelling at Justin. Justin, of course, had problems handling his feelings, as did Dr. Jones. Dr. Jones offered a memory of a girl in grade 4 who had abused her. This experience had been overwhelming, and she stated that her expressions toward the other girl was like Justin's today. Even today, she harbored homicidal wishes toward the girl.

The next week, Justin and his father were seen. Justin stated, "I don't want to see my father any more." He was quite angry and refused to talk. Later that same day, Dr. Jones called, stating that a custody dispute had been started in court.

In our next visit, Dr. Jones became focused on the issue of custody, stating that Mr. Jones had filed for custody of Justin. However, Mr. Jones on a later occasion announced that he was not seeking custody. He suggested that his wife was overreacting, and that he was only asking for reasonable access to Justin. However, Dr. Jones maintained her anger. She stated, "I wish I could kill him."

Despite that focus, for a few weeks during this time, she became more relaxed and focused on herself. She described herself as "an insecure, crying little girl." During such periods, Justin was more at ease and visited his father. However, it was a labile situation. Often, the focus was only on her husband's abuse.

During these weeks, Justin's problems at school mirrored the home situation. Questions arose whether he had an attention deficit disorder, a diagnosis that was not accurate.

Justin's behavior in my office equally mirrored that at home. On one such occasion, he talked about "the fight" that had occurred four weeks before the attempt. He said that his parents were fighting that day. They were pushing each other. "My father grabs a rocking chair," he said. "He breaks it and says 'Eat this.'" This story, after its first telling, became repetitive. It was quite meaningful to Justin and was symbolic of his broken family. Figure 9-6 shows a picture of Justin in his home. The inner turmoil is expressed by the heavy lines (or chaos) inside his body. Equally the "Eat this" was reflective of the unresolvable problem—a

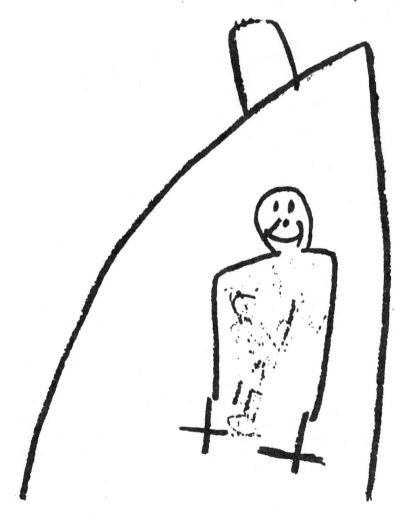

FIGURE 9-6.   A house with Justin boxed in.

situation that is beyond a child's ability to solve, something that Orbach (1988) has isolated as a repetitive theme in many suicidal children. Destructive events are a necessary prerequisite to a suicidal solution in a child.

Both parents recalled the event for me in treatment, although quite differently. Neither recalled the statement about the chair, although a chair had been broken by Mr. Jones. It was the day that he left. During one of Mr. Jones's visits, I confronted him about the event. He agreed that Justin witnessed a lot of "yelling," although he described both his wife and himself as participating in the turmoil that day. He left that day because he felt that the conflicts were destructive for Justin.

Justin announced, "I'm angry," talking about the fights between his parents. He vacillated between anger toward his father versus anger toward both parents. It was the first expression of anger, albeit ambivalently, toward his mother. Figure 9-7 shows a picture of Justin's mother. From my view, the picture shows anger. The mother's face with the plentiful teeth and the wide open engulfing mouth suggests being incorporated (chewed up).

Ten months into treatment, in response to Justin's problems at school (e.g., questions about his diagnosis, etc.), a school meeting was planned. Dr. Jones and Mr. Jones were at that meeting, the only time

FIGURE 9-7. Justin's "Angry" mother.

that I ever saw them together. Indeed when Justin saw them, he showed his biggest smile.

Justin was described as very bright; he was estimated to be "gifted." Yet, he was seen as inattentive and unable to concentrate. He was described as "hyper," being aggressive and acting out frequently, especially toward a female teacher.

His diagnosis was explored. The teachers suggested that Justin had an attention deficit disorder (ADD). Reviewing criteria, an alternative was proposed, a posttraumatic reaction within the context of a childhood depression. I discussed the events leading to the separation, the family's conflicts, the evening of the broken chair, and Justin's inability to cope, leading to a childhood depression. Although nosological classifications with children is problematic, they can be useful as a metaphorical communication. The school seemed to accept the posttraumatic label and the ideas about depression.

During the school interview Dr. Jones became irate several times, yelling and screaming at Mr. Jones. She focused on his lack of support for Justin's swimming classes, a repetitive theme over the last few months. Mr. Jones, despite his frustration, remained appropriate. The meeting ended with satisfaction for the school, but not for Dr. Jones. It was agreed by all that everyone had to work together.

The next appointment for Dr. Jones and Justin at my office was not kept. Dr. Jones arrived for the following appointment alone, although such visits became rare. She was solely focused on the fact that Mr. Jones had abused her, refusing to discuss the school meeting. Subsequent visits alone or with Justin were characterized by the repetitive ups and downs.

Mr. Jones, on the other hand, started attending meetings more frequently and asked for a referral for treatment. He suggested that his father was not loving, adding, "I don't want to be like him." Mr. Jones said that he wanted to work on his relationship with Justin. However, he was at times deflective, avoiding questions about the family's past experiences.

During one of Justin's visits, after his pet bird had died, he asked what would happen if he fell out of the window of my eighth floor office. He said, "My brain would fall out and you (I) would see this." Death became a preoccupation for Justin. After one visit to his father, Justin's mother was not home to receive him. Justin stated "Mom is dead." On another occasion he stated to his father, "You hate me. You want me dead." He also asked me on occasion if I would die. Figure 9–8 shows an expression of Justin's wish to be away. He wanted to be on a spaceship to "go away."

At about one year into treatment, Justin's preoccupation with death

FIGURE 9-8.   An expression of Justin's wish to "go away."

resulted in Dr. Jones's returning to see me alone; she had taken a lengthy hiatus from therapy after the visit at school. She was very worried about Justin. She reported that Justin had asked if the rope burns were still on his neck. However, her concern was short-lived.

Dr. Jones also announced that she had been dating Dr. Clark, a psychiatrist at her hospital who was being supportive of her. She said that he discouraged her attending sessions with me. "The problem," she said, "is Mr. Jones." Dr. Clark had confirmed her belief that she had no problems. When asked about Justin's reaction to Dr. Clark, she said, "It's not upsetting." Subsequent meetings were generally canceled, although Justin continued individually.

At the next session, Justin introduced the topic of Dr. Clark to me, suggesting a vague, nonrevealing reaction to him. Justin revealed that he had been told not to mention Dr. Clark to me. Dr. Jones's lack of participation was increasingly having an impact on treatment. Justin became less active. Mr. Jones, on the other hand, became more concerned, focusing on how he could best handle situations.

Dr. Jones arrived to see me, announcing that she felt better and had no need for help, except for Justin. On one occasion, Justin said to his mother, "I'm angry at you. You don't let me . . ." That proved to be very problematic. Dr. Jones became quite upset at Justin. She said, "You don't hate me! You hate your dad."

On a later visit, she stated, "I don't want to be here. I can solve all my problems." However, five days later, she called about an incident

with Mr. Jones. They again were arguing over Justin. Justin was to go
to a birthday party during a visit with Mr. Jones. Dr. Jones had not told
Mr. Jones and that resulted in Justin being quite upset. Dr. Jones
claimed Mr. Jones was being abusive.

A new issue arose about school. Dr. Jones wanted Justin to go to a
private school, but Mr. Jones suggested the public system. This became
a very conflictual issue. As in the past, Justin was caught in the middle,
as symbolized by the broken chair. He felt upset. It is likely that without
support, his thoughts would have escalated again toward death.

On one of Mr. Jones's visits, I confronted him about physical abuse.
Despite his defensiveness, he revealed a different story. "She was
abusive," he said. He admitted to being verbally abusive but again
denied any physical abuse. He said that he was often cornered, feeling
helpless. He said, "There was no way out." He said that he felt
"castrated," feeling the "push, push" from his wife as unbearable.

Mr. Jones also revealed now that Dr. Jones had often been suicidal.
He stated that she would talk in front of Justin about killing herself. She
would say, "I'll hang myself." At other times, she would say, "I'll kill
myself." In fact, he described his wife as very depressed at times and
aggressive at other times. "She swings up and down," he said.

At about 14 months into treatment, Justin and Dr. Jones arrived
together; it had just been Justin's sixth birthday. We spoke and read his
favorite book, *Horton Hears a Who*. He said, "I feel better."

That was the last meeting with Justin. Dr. Jones had come to
announce that she was moving back to London, Ontario, with her
mother. Her relationship with Dr. Clark had failed, and she felt that she
needed change. "That will solve the problem," she said. She suggested
that her family would be supportive, hoping finally to be away from Mr.
Jones.

Mr. Jones continued his contact. He and Dr. Jones divorced; he
remarried. He continued to see Justin, with access being spelled out in
the divorce agreement. These visits were often positive, he suggested.

Six months after Justin's abrupt termination, I was contacted by Dr.
Berger, a therapist in London. Dr. Jones had followed my recommendation for continued treatment for Justin.

Three years after my contact, Mr. Jones called. He reported that
Justin was doing well, continuing to see his therapist. Dr. Jones,
however, he reported, had been hospitalized, following a period of highly
lethal thoughts of suicide by hanging. The hospitalization resulted in
greater intervention. Dr. Jones was prescribed lithium and is still being
seen for psychotherapy. Mr. Jones also carried a message from Justin:
"Hello."

CASE DISCUSSION

Preliminary Considerations

We should not view suicide from a single perspective. Suicide, regardless of the patient's age, is a multidimensional malaise. It is a complex event. I will outline a few comments about Justin's developmental age, present a few notes about lethality and perturbation, provide a general frame to understand suicide, discuss how the unconscious is a necessary concept to explain suicide in children, highlighting attachment, and make a few points about treatment.

A Developmental Perspective

People are developing beings. Erikson's (1963, 1968) outline of human development is the best known developmental perspective although alternative models have been presented (e.g., Freud, Jung, Charlotte Buhler). Erikson's model "provides one view of the 'river of life' and its major turning points and forks, so that we might have a sense of what the crucial challenges are for the individual at various points along the stream" (Kimmel 1974, p. 23). To frame Justin's points on the life span, a brief outline of Erikson's view will be presented with approximate chronological ages noted, although no development age can be rigidly defined. Some people mature earlier, some later, depending on the ego's structures (as related to familial function, brain damage, etc.).

From approximately birth to the age of 2, one develops a sense of the world. The world is related to the primary caregiver, the mother in American culture. The experience with the parents is crucial; the child develops either trust or mistrust. It is an early stage of individuation, the early beginnings of an identity. It is also the beginning of a child's experience of pain. The capacity to adjust begins almost immediately and, out of that, one's ego, the part of the mind that reacts to reality and has a sense of individuality, begins to form as does one's earliest structures for attachments. Strength is primarily derived from the ego strength of the parents. With trauma, a growing inability to cope may occur, and one may learn a basic mistrust.

From the ages of 2 to 4, the child matures, exerting greater control over self and the outside world (Frager and Fadiman 1984). The child develops a sense of autonomy. The child begins to test his/her trust or mistrust. Some children become overly rigid or controlled by developing a demanding conscience with the earliest signs of self-punishment in a few. Rather than adjust, they develop a strong sense of shame or self-doubt. The child feels deficient, having a lack of esteem with weaknesses being constantly exposed. On the other hand, with a supportive environment, even during trauma, other children develop autonomy. The child develops a sound and healthy will. In Justin's case, there is no question about the lack of autonomy. Indeed, one even wonders about the earlier stage; how did Dr. Jones and/or Mr. Jones address Justin's earliest needs? Justin probably experienced early traumatic events, and his needs were frustrated. After all, Dr. Jones was focused on her own depression. A climate of detachment must have prevailed.

After Erikson's second stage (i.e., autonomy vs. shame and doubt), the child develops initiative or guilt. The child experiences greater conscious mobility. One's ability to adjust expands. One develops mastery and responsibility. Language is a prime example. Equally, the child learns to plan ahead, to have purpose (Ginsberg and Opper 1969, Piaget 1968, Piaget and Inhelder 1969). However, a child's ability to cope can be hampered. The child must do more, and his/her learning can be hindered by the parents (for example, as would be experienced in the home of an alcoholic parent). With weakened mobility and inquisitiveness, the child develops anxiety, a deep sense of pain. The parents, for example, may support self-guidance and/or self-punishment. If a parent is highly suicidal, the child may equally introject that destructiveness. In some, the anxiety and guilt are too much to withstand, and the pain becomes unbearable. Justin obviously showed such early signs, especially at age 5. For example, he often had people respond to him as if he were "bad." At the earliest meeting, Justin was self-critical. He knew no direction. Everything had collapsed, symbolized by the "broken chair."

It is important to remember that development does not stop here. Development is continuous, not discontinuous. Development occurs across the life span (Erikson 1963, 1968, Piaget, 1968). Development is dynamic, ongoing, and serial. The suicidal person, even at Justin's age, does not respond anew to each crisis in life, but his/her reactions are highly consistent. There is an *elliptical* nature to one's development (Shneidman 1985).

Preliminary Concepts

There is no *one* definitive behavior in children — or people of any age — that is predictive of suicide. Suicide is a multidimensional event across the life span. Two concepts that are very useful and helpful to understand suicide are *lethality* and *perturbation* (Shneidman 1985). Lethality, a psychological state of mind, refers to the probability of a person killing him/herself and on a quantitative scale ranges from low to moderate to high. Perturbation refers to subjective distress (irritated, disturbed, agitated, "boxed in") and can also be rated from low to moderate to high. Both concepts are needed in order to understand the depth of pain — or psychopathology — of suicidal children. Lethality kills, not perturbation. All sorts of children are highly perturbed but not suicidal. Perturbation is often relatively easy to observe, even in children. Lethality is not. This is especially true in children, in part, because of their developmental stage. Tests for risk assessment in children have been shown to be of little use to assess lethality (Leenaars and Wenckstern 1994, Lewinsohn et al. 1989, Maris et al. 1992). In the case of Justin, his perturbation on quantifiable scales would be high. His lethality, based on clinical judgment, would be moderate on a few occasions and not high. Overall, his lethality on a day-to-day basis was low.

A Psychological Theory of Suicide

To understand suicide, like any behavior, one must go beyond general development and even psychopathology in children (Achenbach 1974, Bemporad 1980, Cameron 1963, Eissler et al. 1977, A. Freud 1965, Horney 1950). A psychology of suicide is needed (Leenaars 1988). Shneidman (1985) suggests that to develop such a model—a psychological theory regarding suicide—one must begin with the question, What are the interesting common psychological dimensions of suicide?—rather than, What kind of people, even as a child, commit suicide? This question, according to Shneidman, is critical; for these common dimensions are what suicide is. Not necessarily the universal, but certainly the most frequent or common characteristics provide us with a meaningful conceptualization of suicide. This question, he says, is as true for children as for adolescents and the elderly (Shneidman 1991):

> Of course, blacks, females, unemployed, AIDS patients—and, apropos the human life course—children, youth, adults and oldsters commit suicide, and it is often useful to group suicides under such rubrics. But it is meaningful only if one goes further and looks at underlying patterns. In my analysis of suicide, there are no separate youth suicides, adult suicides, gerontological suicides; there is only human suicide and all of it is to be understood in terms of the same principle. [p. 40]

Most frequently, nonprofessionals identify external causes as the reason for a child's suicide (e.g., ill health, being abandoned by a parent, divorce) as what is common in suicide. A recent downhill course (e.g., divorce, death of a parent, a suicide) can, indeed, be identified in suicide. However, although there are always situational aspects in every suicidal act, these are only the precipitating events. Suicide is more complex, even in children. Suicide is a multidetermined event. How can we understand these psychological complexities?

To begin to answer this question, I agree with Shneidman (1985) that the psychological dimensions of suicide are the "trunk" of suicide. "The psychological component, the problem-solving choice—the best solution for the perceived problem—is the main "trunk" of suicide" (Shneidman 1985, p. 203).

As for all people, suicide for children is an intrapsychic drama on an interpersonal stage. From this psychological view, I believe that suicide in children relates to the following components (Leenaars 1988, 1996):

Intrapsychic

Unbearable Psychological Pain.   The common stimulus in suicide is unendurable psychological pain (Shneidman 1985). The enemy of life is pain. The suicidal child is in a heightened state of perturbation. Although, as Menninger (1938) noted, other motives (elements, wishes) are evident, the child primarily wants to flee from pain—a trauma, a catastrophe. The fear is that the trauma, the crisis, is bottomless—an eternal suffering. The child feels boxed in, rejected, deprived, forlorn, distressed, and especially hopeless and helpless. It is the emotion of impotence, the feeling of hopelessness-helplessness, that is so painful for many suicidal children. The situation is unbearable and the child desperately wants a way out of it (even if the child's concept of death is not fully developed). The suicide, as Murray (1967) noted, is functional because it abolishes painful tension for the individual. It provides relief from intolerable suffering expressed, for example, as "I can go to sleep" or "I can go see God."

How is it possible for a 4-year-old child to be in so much pain? Was Justin's pain unbearable? These are difficult questions. Yet, my own opinion and others (Orbach 1988, Pfeffer 1986) is that children, indeed, can experience unbearable pain. At even younger ages, children experience pain, as, for example, in the case of failure-to-thrive infants (Fraiberg 1980). At as young as 8 months, individual differences can be objectively noted in children's behavior in play (Wenckstern et al. 1984). There are various reasons for such differences including trauma (Fraiberg 1980), consistent with theory (e.g., Erikson 1963, 1968). Justin was perturbed, agitated, and troubled. He felt boxed in. Everything was broken. He, as well as his mother, wanted it to go away.

Cognitive Constriction.   The common cognitive state in suicide is constriction (Shneidman 1985). Constriction—rigidity in thinking, narrowing of focus, tunnel vision, concreteness—is the major component of the cognitive state in suicide. This is heightened in children because of the level of cognitive development (Piaget 1968). The child is figuratively intoxicated or drugged by the constriction, resulting in dysfunction in emotions, language, perception, and even bodily functions. Significant regression(s) may occur. The suicidal child exhibits at the suicidal moment only permutations and combinations of a trauma (e.g., poor health, rejection by a parent) (Sullivan 1962, 1964). The suicidal mind is, thus, in a special state of relatively fixed purpose and of relative constriction. In the face of the trauma—pain—a possible solution becomes the solution. This constriction in children is one of the most dangerous aspects of the suicidal state of mind.

Justin was mentally constricted. The constriction was probably associated with his inability to assimilate all of the trauma—the abuse, the abandonment by father, the depression of the mother. Justin was often singly preoccupied with one event, such as the fact that I read something wrong. Of more concern was his preoccupation with death. His emotions, perceptions, and language reflected this state of mind. One often witnessed regression, mainly as a reaction to the state of mind of his mother. Dr. Jones was equally constricted: The problem was Mr. Jones. Her only solution was to punish her husband, which Justin expressed, for example, in my need to speak to his father for six hours.

Indirect Expressions. Complications, ambivalence, redirected aggression, unconscious implications, and related indirect expressions (or phenomena) are often evident in suicide. The phenomena are oblique. The suicidal person is ambivalent (Shneidman 1985). There are complications, concomitant contradictory feelings, attitudes, and/or thrusts, often toward a person and even life (Shneidman 1985). Love and hate clash. Yet there is much more. What the child is consciously aware of is only a fragment of the suicidal state of mind. There are more reasons to the act than the suicidal person is consciously aware of when making the decision. Suicide is complex, more complicated than the child's conscious mind can been aware of (Leenaars 1993). The driving force, as I will discuss below, may well be unconscious processes.

Justin was ambivalent; he often expressed contradictory feelings and attitudes toward his father. Sometimes he was happy, whereas other times he was not happy. His love and hate clashed, which, I believe, was equally true with respect to his mother. He expressed his anger toward her on a few occasions. However, Justin was punished for this, and Dr. Jones prohibited such expressions, although she did not succeed in banishing these feelings in Justin. He needed to repress these emotions, for only love toward her was allowed. Dr. Jones was equally ambivalent, even toward Justin. She expressed, for a period of time, the wish to abandon Justin, a fact that Justin knew. More frequently, if Justin did not meet her expectations, he was rejected. Her aggression was redirected toward Justin and, obviously, at Mr. Jones. However, her deep anger toward her own mother (and an obviously absent father) was buried. The family's dynamics were primarily indirect and, as I will discuss in detail, unconscious.

Inability to Adjust. People with all types of problems (pain, losses, etc.) are at risk for suicide. Although a large percentage of suicidal children exhibit depressive disorders, other syndromes (conduct or behavioral problems, childhood schizophrenia, panic disorders, attention deficit disorders, learning disabilities, to name a few possibilities) have been also related to suicide in children (Leenaars 1988, Sullivan 1962, 1964). Most importantly, in fact, suicidal people of all ages see themselves as unable to adjust (Adler 1910). His/her state of mind is incompatible with a discerning recitation of what is going on. These children reject everything except escape—they do not survive life's difficulties. Children, given their developmental age, are often insufficiently developed to cope with the pain.

First and foremost, as a relevant aside, it should be understood that not all suicidal children are depressed and that not all depressed children are suicidal. Depression and suicide are *not* equivalent. Yet, Orbach (1988) and Pfeffer (1986, 1993) have noted that depressive disorders distinguish many suicidal children from nonsuicidal groups. Depression can be noted in mood and behavior (ranging from feeling dejected and some hesitancy in social contacts, to difficulty in contacting, isolation, serious disturbance of appetite and sleep), verbal expression (ranging from talk about being disappointed, excluded, blamed, etc., to talk of suicide, being killed, abandoned, helpless), and fantasy (ranging from being disappointed, excluded, mistreated, etc., to suicide, mutilation, loss of a significant person). Behaviors such as excessive aggressiveness, change in school performance, decreased socialization, somatic complaints, loss of energy and regressive change in behavior (e.g., toilet habits, talk) have all been associated with depression (Pfeffer 1986), although the mode of expression will depend upon the child's developmental age (Leenaars 1991b, Pfeffer 1993). However, not all depression is overt. Children can exhibit "masked depression" (Leenaars and Wenckstern 1991). This was certainly the case with Justin, as in his acting out at school. He was depressed. Data suggested that this had been true for several years, exacerbated by his parents' separation.

Justin was unable to cope, and the breakup of his family was too much to bear. He was, in part because of his age, unable to discern accurately what was going on. Justin was depressed. He had been weakened by a steady toll of trauma. Dr. Jones was even more weakened.

If one wishes to use a nosological classification, Justin exhibited a childhood depression (American Psychiatric Association 1987). Posttraumatic symptoms were evident, a fact that I have observed in most suicidal children. Justin had experienced an unusual event for him, namely the breakup of the family. However, this event was a culmination of ongoing abuse. He persistently experienced intrusive recollections of the broken-chair incident. To give another example, in the case of one 6-year-old, the recurrent event was an abandonment by the father (Berman et al. 1991). Justin reexperienced his trauma in his play. There was the ever-present fear of losing his mother as had occurred on the evening that his father returned Justin from a visit and Justin's mother was not at home. Mr. Jones took Justin back to his home. His mother finally called Mr. Jones two hours later. During those two hours, Justin perseverated over his mother's death (which she herself often expressed in the talk of suicide). Justin avoided talking about his pain, often being numb. He had difficulty sleeping, was irritable, and had difficulty concentrating. He often exhibited dissociative behaviors. Needless to say, Justin was traumatized by the age of 4, and his depression was deep. However, Dr. Jones's depression (a major affective disorder) was even deeper.

Ego.   The suicidal child's ego is a critical aspect in the suicidal act. Ego strength is a protective factor against suicide. In children, the ego is often not sufficiently developed. Suicidal people frequently exhibit a relative weakness in the capacity to develop constructive tendencies and to overcome their personal difficulties (Menninger 1938). These children have been emotionally deprived of mature growth. Their egos have probably been weakened by a steady toll of traumatic events (e.g., loss, rejection, abuse). This implies that a history of traumatic disruptions, even for a young child, places the person at risk for suicide. It disrupts the child's ability to develop mechanisms (or ego functions) to cope. A weakened ego correlates positively with suicide risk (Jung 1921). The child's ego is, thus, a critical factor in the suicidal scenario.

A child's earliest relationships are critical for the development of an ego (Mahler 1968). Justin's ego was inadequately developed—it offered little strength to cope with events. Even his earliest time lines were hampered; his mother's own ego strength was lacking. If one examines Justin from Erikson's (1963, 1969) model of development the deficits are obvious. Justin learned mistrust. He lacked autonomy (as did Dr. Jones). These earliest years placed Justin at risk; he had not developed the necessary function to adjust. Mr. Jones, although more adequately developed, had clear lacunae in his ego, being susceptible to regression during periods of conflict. He would be verbally aggressive at such times. Dr. Jones was even more hampered in her development and, I suspect from a generational perspective, that her mother was also troubled.

Interpersonal

Interpersonal Relations.   The suicidal child has problems in establishing or maintaining relationships. There is a disturbed, unbearable familial situation (Sullivan 1962, 1964, Zilboorg 1936, 1937). A calamitous relation in the family has prevailed. A positive development in those same disturbed relations is held as the only possible way to reduce the pain, but such development is seen as not forthcoming (Sullivan 1962, 1964). Suicide appears to be often related to unsatisfied or frustrated attachment (affiliation) needs, although other needs may also be evident, such as achievement, autonomy, and dominance. The child wants, for example, only that the family be together. The person's psychological needs are frustrated, exemplified in the often dysfunctional family. Suicide is committed because of the thwarted or unfulfilled needs (such as attachment, nurturance, and safety in this case), needs that often become frustrated in the family (Murray 1938, 1967). Almost always, if not always, the relationships of the parents themselves are disturbed, and the children express that dysfunction.

Thus, as supported by ample studies (e.g., Corder and Haizlip 1984, Corder et al. 1974, Leenaars 1988, Leenaars and Wenckstern 1991, Orbach 1988, Pfeffer 1981a,b, 1986, 1993, Toolan 1981), the family system is a central factor associated with suicide and suicidal behavior in children, although by no means do all families of suicidal children display all characteristic patterns of dysfunction. I will outline these dysfunctions in more detail here because of their central role in childhood suicide. Based on a review of the above-cited references, here are a few common observations regarding suicidal children and their families (although the list should not be construed as exhaustive):

1. There is, at times, a lack of generational boundaries in suicidal families. There is an insufficient separation of the parent from his or her family of origin. For example, grandparents take over the parenting role.

2. The family system is often inflexible. Any change is seen as a threat to the survival of the family. Denial, secretiveness, and especially a lack of communication is seen in the family. Additionally, such families have strict discipline patterns and limit-setting, which restrict the individual in early development. In some cases, even basic behaviors such as eating, toilet use, and playing are excessively controlled.

3. At times, there is a symbiotic parent–child relationship. A parent is too attached to the child. Not only is such a relation disturbing, but furthermore the parent does not provide the emotional protection and support that a parent usually provides intuitively to a child as he or she grows. Sometimes the parent treats the youth as an "adult." One can see such problems especially at ages 4 to 5 when the child needs to separate from the parents. Additionally, it has been noted over and over that, if a symbiotically enmeshed parent exhibits an emotional dysfunction, such as suicidal behavior, the child may exhibit similar behavior, such as a wish to be magically united with that parent if the parent dies. Indeed, the child may act out the pathology of the parent(s).

4. Long-term disorganization (malfunctioning), such as maternal or paternal absence, divorce, alcoholism, and mental illness, has been noted in families of suicidal children. Sexual abuse is more prevalent than in the general population. Often these problems are generational.

Justin's family was dysfunctional. People in Justin's family had problems in establishing and maintaining relationships. This was true for Dr. Jones and Mr. Jones. There was an unbearable, disturbed, familial situation. All was calamitous. There was a lack of individuation in both parents, more so in Dr. Jones. The family was inflexible—everything had to be the way Dr. Jones wanted. Justin's parents lacked communication. Justin's behavior was extremely controlled. Only certain aspects of his abilities were promoted, for example, his verbal skills. There was an overly symbiotic relationship between

Justin and his mother (which I will discuss in detail below). The Jones family had a history of malfunctioning, for example, abuse and mental illness. In the familial context, Justin's needs were not met, and, I suspect, neither were Dr. Jones's or Mr. Jones's needs. Justin's pain was an expression of the family dysfunction.

Rejection-Aggression. The rejection-aggression hypothesis was documented by Stekel in a famous 1910 meeting of the Psychoanalytic Society in Freud's home in Vienna (Friedman 1910). Adler, Jung, Freud, Sullivan, and Zilboorg have all expounded variations of this hypothesis. Loss is central to suicide. It is often a rejection that is experienced as an abandonment. It is an unbearable narcissistic injury (Zilboorg 1936). It is a traumatic event that leads to self-directed aggression. The child is deeply ambivalent. In addition to being ambivalent, a characteristic in some suicides is the turning back upon oneself of murderous impulses (wishes, needs) that had previously been directed against a traumatic event, most frequently someone who had rejected him or her (Freud 1917). However, in such families the child must deny such feelings. Anger is often unacceptable for the child, whether toward a person or in general. Suicide may be veiled aggression — it may be murder in the 180th degree.

Loss was central in Justin and not only loss of his father. I believe that Justin experienced an ongoing abandonment in his home. He was often narcissistically injured by his parents (especially Dr. Jones) who themselves were narcissistically deprived (Miller 1981, 1986). There were deep ambivalences. Aggression was often expressed outwardly, especially toward Mr. Jones. Dr. Jones had murderous impulses toward her husband (and her mother). However, equally, the aggression was turned inward. Her suicidal behavior was likely veiled aggression, and Justin's own act, as I will show, was intertwined with her anger.

Identification-Egression. Freud (1917, 1920) hypothesized that intense identification with a lost or rejecting person is crucial in understanding the suicidal person. Here, identification is defined as an attachment (bond), based upon an important emotional tie with another person (Freud 1921) or any ideal, often toward a parent. This is especially true if that parent is suicidal — or had died, killed herself/himself, or abandoned the family. If this emotional need is not met, the suicidal child experiences a deep discomfort (pain) and wants to egress, that is, to leave, to be gone, to be elsewhere (Murray 1967). The suicidal child wants to leave, to exit, to get out, to get away, to be gone, to be elsewhere, not to be, to be dead, within the context of the child's idiosyncratic concept of death. Suicide becomes the only egression or solution, and the person plunges into the abyss.

Justin was deeply attached to his mother, and so was she to him. There was an intense identification (bond). However, this emotional need was doomed since Dr. Jones herself was not able to form a healthy relationship. It is likely that Justin had only partly differentiated himself from his mother so that he was his mother and she was him to a great degree. Mr. Jones, on the other hand, was hindered in developing a close relationship to his wife because of Dr. Jones's pathology (as well as the family dynamics generally and his own ego weaknesses). Mr. Jones was constantly pushed away as the bad parent (or person), which Anna Freud (1966) has called a splitting of the parents. One parent is bad, whereas the other is good in such families. In such an atmosphere, it would be impossible for Justin to have his emotional needs met. His attachments were deeply troubled and he wanted to go away. Even more so, Dr. Jones wanted to egress, to be gone. The suicide attempt of Justin was an expression of both of their wishes.

But suicide in children is more than these common elements. Suicide is not simple; it is not due only to external stress. The suicide has a history. The common thread in suicide is the child's development of adjustment patterns (Leenaars 1991b, Shneidman 1985). It is not only coping with unbearable pain. It is coping with a history of that pain, consciously and unconsciously, often generational.

With the commonalities of suicide in mind, it is possible to structure suicidal phenomena from a developmental point of view. Although suicide is in many ways the same across the life span, as Shneidman (1991) argued, it is productive to view Justin's behavior equally from a developmental view. Simply put, I believe that it is useful to frame a suicidal child's characteristics within a developmental perspective. Yet, the differences that we observe across the life span may not be the presence or absence of a characteristic, but the mode of expression of that characteristic. The suicide of children is both different and *the same* from older people.

UNCONSCIOUS PROCESSES

The concept of the unconscious is, I believe, necessary to understand Justin's suicide attempt. It is necessary because the conscious has a large number of gaps. The manifest content of the act cannot explain his suicide attempt. It provides an insufficient explanation of Justin's behavior. Only by including additional factors can one understand Justin. The assumption of the unconscious is, in fact, necessary. It allows us to understand the enormous complexity of Justin's and his family's behaviors. It allows us to dig into the deeper aspects of the "trunk."

My perspective here is largely based on a number of tenets of dynamic psychology. It accepts the distinction between conscious and unconscious. It accepts the distinction between manifest and latent and that there are therapeutic techniques for inferring the latent implications from the manifest content. For example, it implies that Justin's representation of the broken chair is an expression of the unconscious. The broken chair has an obvious latent meaning: the broken family. I do not mean to suggest that the unconscious singly explains suicide (or any behavior) of a child. My point is that it is possible to understand Justin's suicide attempt from a perspective that includes the unconscious. One needs to go beyond the manifest level, such as his mother's explanation of Mr. Jones's abuse. We must put Justin's suicide attempt within the context of his and his family's latent lives.

Research (Chapter 8 of this volume; Leenaars 1986, 1993, McLister and Leenaars 1988) supports this view. This research showed that there are significant unconscious implications in suicide. Specifically, it showed that clinicians judged genuine suicide notes to be more frequently reflections of unconscious meaning than control data (i.e., simulated notes). It also showed that latent content (Foulkes 1978, Freud 1916) could be objectively scored more frequently in genuine notes than simulated ones. Although further research is needed, this research established that one can use the concept of unconscious to understand suicide.

Suicide is an interpersonal event. I recently suggested that significant unconscious processes are related to the interpersonal aspects (Leenaars 1986). Indeed, the most significant unconscious processes may well be interpersonal (Leenaars 1993, Maltsberger 1986). Freud (1920) had already speculated on the latent interpretation that leads someone to kill him/herself: "Probably no one finds the mental energy required to kill himself unless, in the first place, in doing so he is at the same time killing an object with whom he had identified himself and, in the second place, is turning against himself a death wish which had been directed against someone else" (p. 162).

The suicidal person, even the child, has had to develop a strong identification with other people. Attachment, based upon an important emotional tie with another person, was Freud's (1921) early meaning for the term of identification. The person (or other ideal) does not merely exist outside; rather, he/she becomes introjected into one's own personality. Although the word *identification* has different meanings in the literature (see Hartmann 1939, Meissner 1981), I have here retained Freud's early use of the term. Freud (1921) speculated:

> Identification is known to psychoanalysis as the earliest expression of an emotional tie with another person. . . . There are three sources of identification. First, identification is the original form of emotional ties with an object. Secondly, in a regressive way it becomes a substitute for a libidinal object tie, as it were by means of introjection of the object into the ego, and thirdly, it may arise with any new perception of a common quality shared with some other person who is not an object of the sexual instinct. [p. 105]

Freud's (1940) own use of the concept changed. In his later writings, he reserved the concept of identification as a mechanism of structuralization, namely the superego. Although I am not suggesting that these views are not relevant, I wish to preserve identification to mean a deep primary attachment to significant people (e.g., parents) or some other ideal. Identification is a means of identifying with an object consciously and/or unconsciously, making it part of one's own internal world. It has a psychic existence.

Identification becomes a hallmark of one's early development. The attachment is deep within one's mind. Regrettably, the attachment is often symbiotic. As Litman (1967) noted, our "ego is made up in large part of identification" (p. 333). These identifications in children are associated primarily with one's parents, especially the primary caregiver. With loss, abandonment, excessive dependency, and other traumatic experiences in the relationships, the attachment becomes dysfunctional. The development is hampered; the child may develop mistrust, shame and doubt, and guilt. He/she experiences pain and may become hopeless and helpless (Fenichel 1954). The child, for example, may express the pain as being "boxed in" (Orbach 1988).

The importance of attachment in Justin is obvious. It was his relationship to his mother, Dr. Jones, that was especially painful. This relationship was critical in hampering Justin's development, and then the loss-abandonment by his father was too much for his fragile ego to bear. Attachment is, I believe, the basic process in suicide in children, although not the only one. A death wish may occur, but it is less primary. Although aggressive wishes, directed both inward and outward, occurred in Justin, it is primarily identification (i.e., attachment) that is a key to understanding his behavior. The suicide attempt for Justin was more an outcome of frustrated attachment needs (wishes) than of aggressive ones. The earliest attachments were dysfunctional; the relation to the mother was deeply problematic. Indeed, Justin's family showed many of the familial dynamics that have been related to suicide (e.g., Orbach 1988, Pfeffer 1986, Trad 1990). Then, the loss of his family, experienced as abandonment, at both the broken rocking chair level and the deeper latent level, fueled both his pain and his mother's pain. His mother could not cope: no family, no life.

Indeed, it was Justin's mother who was especially hopeless and helpless. Her attachments were fragile, obviously related to her earliest relationships. For example, the experience with the cake on her seventh birthday was even now unbearable for her. She continued to exhibit overly painful attachments. She needed the regressive relationship between her and Justin. Justin's and his mother's dynamics were intermeshed. She had been suicidal for years. It is likely that Justin's attempt was more an expression of her death wish than his own. Justin acted out the nature of the relationship.

The dynamics in Justin's suicide attempt, I believe, are thus related to key significant others (i.e., his mother and his father). The need in his relationships was one of attention, approval, validation, affection, and love.

That was equally true for his mother. According to Horney (1950) such a person evaluates his/her life according to how much he/she is liked, needed, wanted, or accepted. This type of person is often self-punishing, even by the age of 4. One's development is hampered. There is a continued need for attachment. In Justin's mind, as in most children of his age, love and family are closely intertwined. His family was everything. Dr. Jones equally exhibited such a need. She would sacrifice everything—even her son. Although other needs may be present, it is the need for attachment, within both of their developmental contexts, that was critical in the suicidal behavior.

It is likely that as a group, suicidal children are, in fact, quite pathological in their love and that is equally true of their caregivers. In his analysis of Freud's speculations on suicide, Litman (1967) writes: "Freud often referred to certain dangerous ways of loving in which the 'ego is overwhelmed' by the object. Typically, the psychic representation of the self and others are fused and the other is experienced as essential to survival" (p. 340). Dr. Jones's love of Justin was dangerous. Justin even introjected her suicidal wishes. She was overwhelmed, as the case presentation outlined. Her obvious affective disorder was catastrophic in the family. Dr. Jones was often intoxicated by her emotions and thoughts. She had problems developing constructive, loving attachments. She needed Justin's existence. She was overly narcissistic, being unable to provide for the development of a sound sense of self or identity for Justin (Miller 1981). A mental breakdown was an ever-present reality, despite her denial. For her, the problem was often only Mr. Jones. She was so constricted. Even more regrettably for Justin, Dr. Jones and Justin were emotionally fused. The fusion was, as is so common, fragile. The broken chair—and Justin's association "Eat this"—was experienced, for example, as an end to their survival. Dr. Jones's problems, such as with Justin's expression of anger to her in treatment, only added to the pain. Dr. Jones and Justin simply could not cope—they could not eat the chair.

We term such attachments *symbiotic* (Mahler 1968) and it is likely that symbiotic love is a potential precursor of suicide (Litman 1967). Justin's family exhibited unhealthy love. For them, love was a trauma, the separation, that Dr. Jones and, by identification, Justin could not bear. Dr. Jones's pain was probably related to her mother, who sounded equally disturbed. The trauma in the Jones family was so complete that there was little hope. There was an overwhelming level of perturbation. The pain in the family was unbearable.

Suicide occurs in needful children. It occurs in children whose development has been shackled.

> It is difficult to conceptualize an individual committing suicide apart from the individual seeking to satisfy inner felt needs; . . . there can never be a needless suicide; . . . it focally involves an attempt to fulfill some urgently felt psycho-

logical needs. Operationally, these heightened unmet needs make up, in large part, what the suicidal person feels (and reports). [Shneidman 1985, pp. 208–209]

This is equally true of suicidal children (Trad 1990). If we use the perspective of the unconscious, we learn that Justin's suicide attempt is largely related to loving, needing, wanting, liking, and accepting. In the suicidal child, love is the driving force. Justin needed love.

TREATMENT: A FEW OBSERVATIONS

Intervention with children depends on the developmental age of the specific child. Each child has his/her own unique pain, attachments, needs, and relationships. Specific interventions are based not only on the child but also on the family. Although I utilize play activities (e.g., Axline 1947, Caplan and Caplan 1974) with children in therapy (Reisman 1973), I almost never see only the child. As the case of Justin shows, even greater complexity is added. One must consider the parents' (and even siblings') pain and needs, which can be complicated by a host of factors such as divorce in Justin's case (or in paternal abandonment in a case that I discussed elsewhere under the name of David [Berman et al. 1991]). Factors such as long-term instability, alcoholism, and imprisonment are just a few other examples of events that can be traumatic and affect a child's pain and development in general.

Often I see the child and parent(s) separately. Often the parent needs to discuss the child, and the therapist serves as an auxiliary ego. Even more so, the parents' own pathology, as with Dr. Jones, makes such treatment necessary (Leenaars 1991a, 1995, Leenaars et al. 1994). Although joint sessions with the parents are desirable for some issues, often that may be complicated, as in the separation — experienced as "hate" — in Justin's family (Haley 1971).

Freud (1909) was the first to show the utility of seeing parent(s) individually in the case of Hans, a 5-year-old boy. Little Hans's problem was not unlike Justin's. Hans's trauma dated back to the age of 2. Hans developed a deep attachment to his mother early on. At 3½ two traumatic events occurred for Hans: his mother threatened to castrate him, and his sister was born. At age 5, Hans woke up one morning in tears. He had dreamt that his mother had abandoned him. The more problematic the relationship(s) became to his mother and others in the family, the more the attachment became symbiotic at an unconscious level for even the mother. Hans became erratic and very perturbed. The family was dysfunctional, although much less, I believe, than Justin's. Indeed, Hans never exhibited suicidal behavior; instead, his pain was expressed in a phobia.

In Freud's case and my case, the parents needed assistance. In Justin's case the assistance went beyond parenting skills. Dr. Jones exhibited a significant affective disorder in her life. Indeed, in the case of Justin, I foresaw little gain for Justin without treatment for Dr. Jones. One needed to reduce Dr. Jones's pain in order to reduce Justin's.

Often extensive family treatment with suicidal families is needed (Richman 1986). Addressing the family's dysfunctions, as outlined earlier, is necessary. However, despite my attempts, this was difficult with Justin's family; the family had separated.

Equally, one may need to address system issues, beyond the family, especially within the school (Leenaars and Wenckstern 1990). In Justin's case, this became increasingly necessary and the joint meeting at his school was most useful. It allowed the teacher to reframe Justin's problem and introduce better remediation. After all, one uses different techniques with attention deficit disorders than with deep pain. In other cases, such as David's (Berman et al. 1991), a social welfare agency and treatment center were needed. I strongly believe, in fact, that one should use the help of all associated people — medical doctors, siblings, the elders, ministers, teachers — in the treatment of suicidal children and, indeed, people in general (Leenaars 1994). Consultation with a peer is often useful especially when treating suicidal children. One may discuss one's treatment, the family's dysfunction, one's countertransference, the patient's need for medication and hospitalization, and so on (Shneidman 1981).

On the issue of medication and/or hospitalization, each case needs to be evaluated individually. Especially if there are medical/physical complications, medication may be necessary. Hospitalization should be used only in the very highly lethal cases of the child and/or parent. Hospitalization is always a complicated event in the treatment of suicidal children and the quality of care from doctors, nurses, and others is crucial (Shneidman 1981).

CONCLUSION

Miller (1981) reports the following account of a patient about her pain as a child in a dysfunctional family:

> "I lived in the glass house into which my mother could look at any time. In a glass house, however, you cannot conceal anything without giving yourself away, except by hiding it under the ground. And then you cannot see it yourself either." [p. 21]

Even at the age of 4, Justin had buried much. Yet, with the broken chair, he could no longer bear the pain. His attachments were disrupted. He was boxed in and needed to get out. His mother's own suicidal wish was acted out by Justin. Unconscious processes, within the context of unbearable pain, cognitive constriction, and egression, were a driving force in Justin's and his mother's suicidal behavior. Justin and his mother had hid so much from themselves.

To conclude, if one attempts to explain suicide in children at a manifest level, one will understand little; one would accept, for example, Dr. Jones's hypothesis of Mr. Jones's abuse, a belief that was, in fact, more fantasy than reality. Regrettably a current popular formulation regarding suicide in children is that it is simply due to an external event or stress such as a divorce or abuse. Although these events do occur in the lives of suicidal children, there is much more than the manifest level. Suicide is complex and, to understand such complexity, the concept of the unconscious is necessary. Without the unconscious, developmental suicidology will be overly barren.

REFERENCES

Achenbach, T. (1974). *Developmental Psychopathology*. New York: Ronald.

Adler, A. (1910). Contributions to discussion of Vienna Psychoanalytic Society—1910. In *On Suicide*, ed. P. Friedman, pp. 109–121. New York: International Universities Press, 1967.

American Psychiatric Association (1987). *Diagnostic and Statistical Manual of Mental Disorders*, 3rd ed., rev. Washington, DC: American Psychiatric Association.

Axline, V. (1947). *Play Therapy*. New York: Random House.

Bemporad, J., ed. (1980). *Child Development in Normality and Psychopathology*. New York: Brunner/Mazel.

Berman, A., Leenaars, A., and Schutz, B. (1991). David: a case consultation. *Suicide and Life-Threatening Behavior* 21:299–306.

Cameron, N. (1963). *Personality Development and Psychopathology: A Dynamic Approach*. Boston: Houghton Mifflin.

Caplan, F., and Caplan, T. (1974). *The Power of Play*. Garden City, NY: Anchor.

Corder, B., and Haizlip, T. (1984). Environmental and personality similarities in case histories of suicide and self-poisoning in children under ten. *Suicide and Life-Threatening Behavior* 14:59–66.

Corder, B., Parker, P., and Corder, R. (1974). Parental history, family communication and interaction patterns in adolescent suicide. *Family Therapy* 3:185–190.

Eissler, R., Freud, A., Kris, M., and Solnit, A. (1977). *Psychoanalytic Assessment: The Diagnostic Profile*. London: Yale University Press.

Erikson, E. (1963). *Childhood and Society*, 2nd ed. New York: Norton.

———— (1968). *Identity: Youth and Crisis*. New York: Norton.

Fenichel, O. (1954). *The Psychoanalytic Theory of Neurosis*. New York: Norton.

Foulkes, D. (1978). *The Grammar of Dreams*. New York: Basic Books.

Frager, R., and Fadiman, J. (1984). *Personality and Personal Growth*, 2nd ed. New York: Harper & Row.

Fraiberg, S., ed. (1980). *Clinical Studies in Infant Mental Health*. New York: Basic Books.

Friedman, P., ed. (1910). *On Suicide*. New York: International Universities Press, 1967.

Freud, A. (1965). *Normality and Pathology in Childhood: Assessments of Development*. New York: International Universities Press.

———— (1966). *The Ego and the Mechanisms of Defense*. New York: International Universities Press.

Freud, S. (1909). The case of little Hans. *Standard Edition* 9:101–147.

———— (1916). Dreams. *Standard Edition* 15:83–220.

———— (1917). Mourning and melancholia. *Standard Edition* 14:239–260.

———— (1920). A case of homosexuality in a woman. *Standard Edition* 13:147–172.

———— (1921). Group psychology and the analysis of the ego. *Standard Edition* 18:64–147.

———— (1940). An outline of psycho-analysis. *Standard Edition* 23:137–207.

Ginsberg, H., and Opper, S. (1969). *Piaget's Theory of Intellectual Development*. Englewood Cliffs, NJ: Prentice-Hall.

Haley, J., ed. (1971). *Changing Families*. New York: Grune & Stratton.

Hartmann, H. (1939). *Ego Psychology and the Problem of Adaptation*. New York: International Universities Press.

Horney, K. (1950). *Neurosis and Human Growth*. New York: Norton.

Jung, C. G. (1921). Psychological types. In *The Collected Works of C. G. Jung*, vol. 6, ed. H. Read, M. Fordan, and G. Adler, pp. 1–617. London: Routledge & Kegan Paul, 1974.

Kimmel, D. (1974). *Adulthood and Aging*. New York: Wiley.

Leenaars, A. (1986). A brief note on the latent content in suicide notes. *Psychological Reports* 57:640–642.

_____ (1988). *Suicide Notes*. New York: Human Sciences.

_____ (1991a). Suicide notes and their implications for intervention. *Crisis* 12:1–20.

_____ , ed. (1991b). *Life-Span Perspectives of Suicide*. New York: Plenum.

_____ (1993). Unconscious processes. In *Suicidology: Essays in Honor of Edwin Shneidman*, ed. A. Leenaars, pp. 125–147. Northvale, NJ: Jason Aronson.

_____ (1994). Crisis intervention with highly lethal suicidal people. In *Treatment for Suicidal People*, ed. A. Leenaars, J. Maltsberger, and R. Neimeyer, pp. 45–59. Washington, DC: Taylor & Francis.

_____ (1996). Suicide: A multidimensional malaise. Presidential address presented at the Conference of the American Association of Suicidology, St. Louis, Missouri, April.

Leenaars, A., Maltsberger, J., and Neimeyer, R., eds. (1994). *Treatment of Suicidal People*. Washington, DC: Taylor & Francis.

Leenaars, A., and Wenckstern, S., eds. (1990). *Suicide Prevention in Schools*. Washington, DC: Hemisphere.

_____ (1991). Suicide in the school-age child and adolescent. In *Life-Span Perspectives of Suicide*, ed. A. Leenaars, pp. 95–107. New York: Plenum.

_____ (1995). Helping lethal suicidal adolescents. In *Threat to Life, Dying, Death and Bereavement: The Child's Perspective*, ed. D. Adams and E. Deveau. Amityville, NY: Baywood.

Lewinsohn, P., Garrison, C., Langhinrichsen, J. and Marsteller, F. (1989). *The Assessment of Suicidal Behavior in Adolescents: A Review of Scales Suitable for Epidemiological Clinical Research*. Rockwell, MD: National Institute of Mental Health.

Litman, R. (1967). Sigmund Freud on suicide. In *Essays in Self-Destruction*, ed. E. Shneidman, pp. 324–344. New York: Jason Aronson.

Mahler, M. (1968). *On Human Symbiosis and the Vicissitudes of Individuation*. New York: International Universities Press.

Maltsberger, J. (1986). *Suicide Risk: The Formulation of Clinical Judgment*. New York: New York University Press.

Maris, R., Berman, A., Maltsberger, J., and Yufit, R. (1992). *Assessment and Prediction of Suicide*. New York: Guilford.

McLister, B., and Leenaars, A. (1988). An empirical investigation of the latent content of suicide notes. *Psychological Reports* 63:238.

Meissner, W. (1981). *Internalization in Psychoanalysis*. New York: International Universities Press.

Menninger, K. (1938). *Man Against Himself*. New York: Harcourt, Brace.

Miller, A. (1981). *Das Drama des Begabten Kindes*. (*The Drama of the Gifted Child*, trans. R. Ward). New York: Basic Books.

_____ (1986). *Thou Shalt Not Be Aware*. New York: Meridian.

Murray, H. (1938). *Explorations in Personality*. New York: Oxford University Press.

_____ (1967). Death to the world: The passions of Herman Melville. In *Essays in Self-Destruction*, ed. E. Shneidman, pp. 7–29. New York: Science House.

Nagy, M. (1948). The child's view of death. *Journal of Genetic Psychology* 73:3–27.

Orbach, I. (1988). *Children Who Don't Want to Live*. San Francisco: Jossey-Bass.

Pfeffer, C. (1981a). Suicidal behavior in children: a review with implication for research and practice. *American Journal of Psychiatry* 138:154–160.

———— (1981b). The family system of suicidal children. *American Journal of Psychotherapy* 35:330–341.

———— (1986). *The Suicidal Child*. New York: Guilford.

———— (1993). Suicidal children. In *Suicidology: Essays in Honor of Edwin Shneidman*, ed. A. Leenaars, pp. 175–185. New York: Jason Aronson.

Piaget, J. (1968). *Structuralism*. New York: Harper Torchbooks.

Piaget, J., and Inhelder, B. (1969). *The Psychology of the Child*. New York: Harper Torchbooks.

Reisman, J. (1973). *Principles of Psychotherapy with Children*. New York: Wiley.

Richman, J. (1986). *Family Therapy for Suicidal People*. New York: Springer.

Seuss, Dr. (1954). *Horton Hears a Who!* New York: Random House.

Shneidman, E. (1981). Psychotherapy with suicidal patients. *Suicide and Life-Threatening Behavior* 11:341–348.

———— (1985). *Definition of Suicide*. New York: Wiley.

———— (1991). The commonalities of suicide across the life span. In *Life-Span Perspectives of Suicide*, ed. A. Leenaars, pp. 39–52. New York: Plenum.

Sullivan, H. S. (1962). Schizophrenia as a human process. In *The Collected Works of Harry Stack Sullivan* vol. 2, ed. H. Perry, N. Gawel, and M. Gibbon, pp. 1–363. New York: Norton.

———— (1964). The fusion of psychiatry and social science. In *The Collected Works of Harry Stack Sullivan*, vol. 2, eds. H. Perry, N. Gawel, and M. Gibbon, pp. 1–346. New York: Norton.

Toolan, J. (1981). Depression and suicide in children: an overview. *American Journal of Psychotherapy* 35:311–322.

Trad, P. (1990). *Treating Suicide-like Behavior in a Preschooler*. Madison, CT: International Universities Press.

Wenckstern, S., Weizman, F., and Leenaars, A. (1984). Temperament and tempo of play in eight-month-old infants. *Child Development* 55:1195–1199.

Zilboorg, G. (1936). Suicide among civilized and primitive races. *American Journal of Psychiatry* 92:1347–1369.

———— (1937). Consideration on suicide, with particular reference to that of the young. *American Journal of Orthopsychiatry* 7:15–31.

10: CASE CONSULTATION WITH A SUICIDAL ADOLESCENT

David A. Jobes and Mary Pat Karmel

Since the late 1970s, when adolescent suicide rates reached their historic peaks, there has been a steadily growing public and professional awareness about issues related to adolescent suicide. The attention of public and mental health professionals during these years has centered on some of the startling epidemiological data as well as the ground-breaking empirical results of various psychological autopsy studies. From the epidemiological research perspective, we know that youth suicide rates have tripled since the 1950s and that there are approximately 5,000 completed youth suicides each year in the United States and probably hundreds of thousands of suicide attempts. Alternatively, from the psychological autopsy research perspective, we have learned that the typical adolescent suicide completer is a male who uses a gun, has a diagnosable mental disorder, may well abuse substances, and often shares his suicidal intent with others (Brent et al. 1988). While our increasing knowledge in these areas has been invaluable, clinicians must nevertheless find ways to integrate these nomothetic data with the idiographic data of an individual patient — a living suicidal young person who is not yet a statistic and who may or may not look "typical" according to the empirical research literature (Berman and Jobes 1991).

Shneidman (1993) has argued that a thorough clinical assessment of any suicidal person requires a comprehensive understanding of the idiosyncratic nature of each suicidal individual's struggle with unbearable psychic pain, emotional "perturbation," and experiences of various "presses." To further understand the suicidal adolescent patient, the clinician must also conduct a thorough functional analysis of the young patient's suicidality in an effort to ascertain the psychological *meaning* of suicide, at a particular point in time, for a person who is living through the critical developmental period of adolescence. Furthermore, this functional analysis must consider both the patient's conscious suicidal experience as well as important unconscious forces that may underlie the patient's suicidality. To this end, we will endeavor throughout the following case consultation to analyze, understand, and ultimately bring clinical meaning to one suicidal young person's life-and-death struggle, particularly as it pertains to suicide and the unconscious.

THE CASE OF SARAH

Sarah is a 15-year-old white girl who was admitted to an inpatient psychiatric unit of a suburban hospital in upstate New York. She was admitted by her outpatient therapist for evaluation and treatment of severe drug and alcohol abuse, depression, chronic suicidal ideation, and self-injurious behavior. Her chemical dependency reportedly began in the fifth grade and has never been formally treated. There is some evidence of a posttraumatic stress disorder related to recurrent and intrusive recollections of severe past sexual traumas and abuse. Sarah's efforts to avoid and/or deny her traumatic thinking and fearful feelings have proven to be unsuccessful, resulting in general feelings of detachment, estrangement, and diminished interests in pleasurable activities. Further diagnostic work to rule out a possible dissociative disorder as well as personality disorders is indicated.

Sarah, a physically attractive girl, appears older than her stated age of 15. Upon admission Sarah was dressed in 1960s-style clothing with a tie-dyed T-shirt, a long, flowing skirt, an ankle bracelet of silver bells, and a tattoo of teddy bears encircling her other ankle. She considers herself a "Dead-Head" — a follower of the Grateful Dead rock band. Prior to admission, Sarah had been living with her mother, had contact with her stepfather, and only rarely saw her biological father. In her initial interview, Sarah presents as a likable and friendly girl who enjoys creative and artistic activities that enable her to express her "inner self." Alternatively, there is evidence during the interview that Sarah can become emotionally labile, hostile, and quite sullen. Sarah's grades in school have been typically good, particularly in math. She describes herself as athletic and reports that she once won a junior downhill skiing medal. Sarah states that she is popular among her peers and has numerous girlfriends and various boys who are romantically interested in her.

General Family History

Sarah is the eldest of four children. Her parents were separated when she was 8 years old, shortly after the birth of her youngest brother. Her alcoholic father was also addicted to cocaine and reportedly had a number of extramarital affairs during his marriage to her mother. Sarah reported that her father called her his "Little Princess" and treated her with special attention. Sarah states that she was a "good little girl" who always tried to be "perfect" for her parents. Sarah's father had an extensive history of violence and had been repeatedly accused of beating his ex-wife and current wife. She describes her mother as inattentive and self-centered, stating, "She never gave me anything . . . no time, no attention, no love . . . nothing."

Sarah's mother worked as a waitress after separating from Sarah's father and intermittently received welfare until she met her second husband, whom she married when Sarah was 10 years old. The family's financial status changed significantly at this time since Sarah's new stepfather was quite wealthy. Sarah's mother reportedly left her second husband three years into the marriage, but has since pursued marital therapy in an effort to salvage the marriage.

Chemical dependency has been a prominent feature in Sarah's family history. Her father was a polysubstance abuser, and several of her mother's siblings have histories of alcohol and drug abuse. Sarah's maternal grandmother and grandfather were both chronic alcoholics. Suffering through years of depression and multiple treatment failures, Sarah's grandfather had evidently hanged himself following a drinking binge on his eightieth birthday.

Major Presenting Symptoms

Sarah's presenting symptoms at the time of her admission were depressed affect, sleep disturbance, feelings of hopelessness, and flashbacks of previous sexual traumas. She has an extensive history of engaging in a range of dysfunctional behaviors such as drug and alcohol abuse, sexual acting-out, and various self-destructive behaviors. Sarah reported that she had intense urges to use drugs throughout a previous two-month psychiatric hospitalization and further noted that she had recurrent dreams about using marijuana, LSD, cocaine, mushrooms, and alcohol during this hospitalization. At one point during this inpatient treatment, Sarah snorted the contents of a pixie stick because "it reminded me of cocaine."

History of Sexual Abuse

After her initial adjustment to the inpatient unit, Sarah began to discuss her extensive history of sexual promiscuity and described several rapes that she had experienced while using drugs. These previous sexual activities and assaults were both difficult to recount and painful for her to describe. Sarah stated that there were many times in which she felt like a "sexual predator" who hunted, dominated, and abused her sexual partners by "forcing" them to have sex with her. Alternatively, however, Sarah also reported that her repeated experiences of sexual abuse and exploitation sometimes made her feel like "sexual prey"—helplessly "consumed" by men who left her feeling dirty and degraded.

About two weeks into her hospitalization, Sarah began to describe memories of "sex games" with her father (which had sometimes included his friends). These games were conducted late at night when her father (typically drunk and/or high on drugs) would force her to select a "toy" (e.g., a vibrator, dildo, handcuffs) that they would "play" with that night. Any reluctance on Sarah's part to participate in "games" (which usually involved oral sex, vaginal intercourse, and sometimes anal intercourse) would result in severe physical punishment. As an alternative form of punishment, Sarah's father would use the "silent treatment," acting as if Sarah had died and making statements such as, "I'm so lonely now that my Little Princess is dead." Sarah reported that her mother was always asleep when the abuse occurred and that she had no idea about the father's abuse of Sarah. The father's ritualized sexual abuse, in combination with her mother's systematic negligence, plainly injured Sarah deeply, leaving behind an unusually traumatic legacy.

Psychological Testing

Psychological testing indicated that Sarah had a Full-Scale IQ of 120 (in the superior range of intelligence). She appeared to have good academic potential and was insightful and verbally articulate. There was no evidence of any neuropsychological deficits. Projective testing provided some striking results. From a purely content-oriented standpoint, her Rorschach and Thematic Apperception Test (TAT) responses were filled with sexual, destructive, and morbid images. For example, Rorschach responses such as "HIV-infected sea horses being hung" (card III) and "a vagina after a shot-gun blast" (card VI) may provide some insight into her primitive unconscious world. Themes of interpersonal betrayal, abuse, explosive rage, and murder were evident throughout her TAT responses. For example, card XV elicited a story about "an evil psycho-man, the devil's son on earth . . . who goes around to graves . . . raises the dead . . . rapes them and kills them all over again." While it is apparent that Sarah has some excellent cognitive resources and an ability to be interpersonally engaging and appropriate, her projective testing results suggest a haunting unconscious internal world filled with primitive images, chaos, and terror.

Self-Destruction and Suicide

Sarah, from the onset of puberty, had routinely engaged in frequent self-injurious behaviors such as scratching and biting her biceps and wrists, and banging her hands and head. She had made multiple suicide attempts (e.g., various overdoses, an attempt to hang herself with her bra, and an attempt to cut her wrists with a kitchen knife). She had more recently became fixated on obtaining a gun to kill herself because she knew "it would get the job done once and for all." Sarah reported that she had regressed in her previous hospitalization to a point where she needed help getting up in the morning and had difficulty maintaining proper hygiene. During this period she obsessed about suicide and was placed on a suicide watch. Referring to this experience, Sarah recalled that she simply wanted to give up, wishing for death so that she would no longer have to endure her internal suffering. Over the past three years, Sarah had numerous experiences of intense self-destructive impulses that she described as "coming out of nowhere." However, Sarah did acknowledge that these episodes of intense suicidality seemed to be related to her recent psychotherapy work that was increasingly focused on her history of sexual abuse.

Case Summary

Sarah, a severely disturbed young woman, had limited psychological resources to contain, manage, and understand her profoundly chaotic and traumatic past. Her main difficulties seemed to increasingly center on her inability to manage her overwhelming thoughts and feelings related to her past abuse. These thoughts and feelings typically triggered paralyzing fear, anger, and sometimes profound feelings of depression. Sarah was also having increasingly frequent dissociative episodes and intrusive thoughts about past traumas. Sarah appears to be vulnerable to severe regression and suicidality when she actively explored her traumatic history in psychotherapy.

HISTORICAL TRAUMA AND THE UNCONSCIOUS

For many years psychoanalytically oriented theorists have asserted that historical trauma effects the individual at the unconscious level, fundamentally influencing subsequent psychological and emotional adjustment in later life. As discussed by Blum (1987), traumatic experiences often create "a state in which the ego is so overwhelmed that it cannot cope, is reduced to archaic modes of defense, and is forced into regression" (p. 610). Needless to say, children are especially vulnerable to trauma since their limited ego development does not provide the coping mechanisms that are necessary to combat affronts of this kind to the psyche.

Among the range of traumata encountered by the relatively defenseless child, incestuous sexual abuse is perhaps the most devastating. From a developmental perspective, incestual sexual abuse undermines (and sometimes even destroys) the child's entire sense of psychological well-being. As discussed by theorists including Bowlby (1979), Kohut (1977), and Guntrip (1971), the child's essential development of self, or ego, relies on the appropriateness, constancy, and nurturance of one's "primary object relations" (i.e., the infant's mother, father, or primary caregiver). Early attachments are thought to be central to the organization of a child's internal and external world. Under normal circumstances, a child who enjoys good and consistent nurturing from his or her caregivers may well come to view others and the world as open, responsive, reliable, and just.

However, as seen in a case like Sarah's, poor parenting that involves active abuse and passive neglect may contribute to the development of a very different view of others and the world. For Sarah, and others like her, the trauma of incest is often a twofold phenomenon in that there is both the incestuous act by a trusted parental object and the failure of another trusted parental object to protect the innocent child from physical and emotional harm. Certainly, in Sarah, we see this dual violation of a father who engaged in inappropriate and exploitive sexual acts while a mother failed to protect and intervene in the systematic sexual abuse of her vulnerable child. In these situations, the helpless child must invariably find ways to psychologically survive this form of abject abuse and neglect. To this end, psychoanalytically oriented theorists assert that various unconscious defense mechanisms and intrapsychic processes evolve to minimize the impact of the trauma and provide some measure of subjective control.

INTRAPSYCHIC SURVIVAL

The unconscious defenses and intrapsychic processes that help a child survive severe trauma are often quite complex. For example, in the case of Sarah, we see a range of apparently inconsistent behaviors. At times she acts out toward her environment and significant others in her life; at other times her anger and frustration is directed at herself. Given the trauma incurred in her childhood, one may wonder why Sarah seems to be drawn as a young adult to place herself in abusive, or potentially abusive, situations. While such behavior may seem counterintuitive, Sarah's risk-taking, self-abusiveness, and suicidal behaviors are not uncommon among some severely abused adolescents and adults.

To gain a deeper understanding of these complex behaviors we must consider how the unconscious attempts to maintain intrapsychic survival. In

Sarah's case it is important to grasp the unconscious processes of introjection, ego splitting, and identification as they relate to the apparently contradictory nature of her self-descriptions of being a "sexual predator" and being "sexual prey." In these seemingly conflicting self-perceptions we see the essence of an unconscious conflict that ultimately is at the heart of Sarah's intrapsychic survival and, alternatively, her life-and-death suicidal struggle.

Introjection and Ego Splitting

From the perspective of object relations theory, Sarah's response to her abuse may be seen as a process of introjection and splitting of the ego. Within the tradition of the British school of object relations theory, there are various conceptual notions about healthy and maladaptive development that are important for us to briefly review.

In a significant departure from traditional psychoanalytic drive theory and ego psychology, Fairbairn (1954) argued that infants are object seeking from the start of life. The ego is thought to develop through introjections (an internal absorption) of various facets of the primary love object (typically, the mother). Through the child's experience of relating, and being in relationship to this "primary object," the ego evolves and develops.

Fairbairn reasoned that appropriate nurturance of the infant, who is naturally whole, leads to good object experiences that results in healthy ego development. Such children become secure in the belief that their primary caregiver will provide sustenance, love, warmth, and a stable environment.

Yet, in abusive situations where the primary object relations are consistently hurtful, neglectful, and painful, the child must deal with overwhelming feelings of fear and rage in such a manner that continued positive attachments to the abusive primary object are still possible. Within the language of object relations theory this is unconsciously achieved by introjecting the perceived "badness" of the primary object into the structure of the ego, resulting in a perception (conscious and/or unconscious) that the parental object is good and the self is bad. Ideally, the child divides his or her experience into good and bad feelings within his or her inner world by introjecting the good and projecting the bad. When the infant experiences an unsatisfying parental episode, it may well internalize the "bad mother" resulting in a good and bad split within the ego. The negative aspects of the experience are absorbed intrapsychically while the idealized internal object (the mother) is used to fend off a sense of hopelessness, emptiness, and futility. For a child whose caregiver is inconsistent, neglectful, and/or abusive this process is difficult to achieve, because the abused child (unlike an abused spouse) has limited resources and no viable options for leaving the relationship. Being wholly dependent on the abusive caregiver, the child must do everything possible to sustain the attachment, despite its detrimental effects.

The result is that the good aspects of the caregiver are projected onto the parent and the bad aspects are introjected into the ego of the child, resulting in a child who feels that he or she is bad while the parent remains good.

How then do these notions relate to Sarah? Over years of abuse, Sarah came to learn painful lessons about what it is like to be a victim. Survival instincts of young children inherently compel them to seek and do whatever is necessary to maintain attachments to their primary caregivers. Central to this notion of intrapsychic survival is the idea that it is better to have a bad object than to have no objects at all (Guntrip 1968). From this perspective, it is understandable that Sarah would resist viewing her father as purely bad because, despite his abusive behavior, the alternative of being vulnerable and alone is more frightening. Sarah was thus forced to figure out a way to understand this attachment, which she both desired and feared.

One early unconscious psychological maneuver Sarah's psyche undertook was to construe her father's abuse as a result of her own bad behavior, not his. In this manner she could claim his badness and make it her own, thereby maintaining a perception that he was good and therein provide herself some sense of control over her abject victimization. In her mind, if she could only clean her room better, help out more, or play nicely with her siblings, then she could avoid the abusive and neglectful "punishment" inflicted upon her by her parents. The continuous evidence that she could not control her abusers through her "perfect" behaviors led to intense feelings of frustration, anger, and lowered self-esteem. As a young child, Sarah was baffled as to why, despite her many attempts to be good and please her abusers, she was continually violated and neglected. As Sarah reached puberty, she was compelled to find others ways of surviving intrapsychically.

Identification with the Aggressor

As discussed by Anna Freud (1936), there is a range of unconscious defenses that enable hapless victims to psychologically survive traumatic experiences. "Identification with the aggressor" represents a defensive maneuver that separates the self and object by projecting one's aggressive drives onto external objects as well as the self (Orgel 1974). Anna Freud emphasized that a certain level of identification is part of normal superego development. However, profound psychological and/or physical abuse in childhood may lead to an automatic process of unconscious identification with one's aggressor to a much greater degree, resulting in a hyper-punitive superego. To master the stress and shock of a severe emotional or physical trauma, the ego attempts to become active where it was formerly (and forcibly) passive. As discussed by Blum (1987), the victim unconsciously identifies with the aggressor in order to gain control over an abusive situation, to overcome feelings of fear and helplessness, and to obtain aggressive (libidinal) satisfaction. The victim's aggressive fantasies help compensate the ego through a role reversal in which the victim becomes the perpetrator with the power to assert his or her will over another victim. This phenomenon has been well documented among victims of the Holocaust (Kestenberg 1992) and has also been commonly seen in abused children (Daldin 1988).

Sarah's description of herself as a "sexual predator" is therefore a classic example of identification with the aggressor. Anna Freud (1936) states, "Here, the mechanism of identification or introjection is combined with a second important mechanism. By impersonating the aggressor, assuming his attributes or imitating his aggression, the child transforms himself from the person threatened into the person who makes the threat" (p. 113). This unconscious process may well be seen as understandable and an adaptive response to an experience of abuse, but ultimately, this method of coping can lead to destructive behaviors.

Childhood sexual abuse invariably leaves the child with an enormous sense of betrayal, not only by his or her abuser but also by the world at large. This experience may lead to a form of identification with the aggressor that is referred to as a "sadomasochistic compromise formation" (Larson 1993).

There are various elements that contribute to this complex form of identification. First, the child is full of rage in that he or she has been betrayed and deprived of much needed love, nurturance, and autonomy. Yet, the violent and intrusive nature of sexual abuse provides a hyperarousal of aggression in the victims. Faced with overwhelming "sexual and aggressive stimulation, the child is compelled to identify with the aggressor not simply to discharge massive physical tension but in order to relieve intolerable rage, regain psychic equilibrium, and restore a tolerable self-image" (Larson 1993, p. 139). It is not unusual for such children to have discipline problems in school, poor impulse control, violent tempers, and to display excessively violent behavior. Through this form of identification with the aggressor, the child can experience the power of being a frightful person, which affords the child the opportunity to experience control and a sense of self-protection. Daldin (1988) reports a case of a boy who was severely physically abused by his father, and sexually abused by trusted others. In the second year of therapy the boy stated that he became aware of how he identified with father, because the father was so powerful and frightening, and that by becoming "like him" he would be able to protect himself as well as his mother and sister.

THE SELF AS VICTIM AND ABUSER

It is clear that a childhood of victimization may well lead to similar experiences in adolescence. It is not uncommon for survivors of child abuse to become both victims and abusers as adolescents and adults. When a child is abused, particularly in the case of sexual abuse, one result is an extreme rage on the part of the child in response to the adult's betrayal of the child's trust and physical and psychological integrity. The child learns that relationships are based on power, dominance, and humiliation. As the child grows, he or she may learn that the way "to seek and find pleasure and self-validation [is] within personal exploitation, whether manifested sexually or not" (Larson 1993, p. 138).

Self as Victim

Incest survivors often become unconsciously and deeply identified with the experience of being a victim. In Sarah's case, growing up in an abusive and neglectful family taught her a great deal about life as a victim. Tragically, while victimization is painful and humiliating, systematic abuse (especially when it occurs over time) can become familiar, almost comforting, in its predictability. Certain expectations are established and the child knows what to expect and is guaranteed attention (albeit negative). Moreover, it is not uncommon for victims to have the perception that they are special in the eyes of their abusers — they may come to feel needed and important to their abuser (e.g., Sarah's recollection of being Daddy's "Little Princess"). If, as a child, the victim experience and sense of specialness becomes deeply ingrained and unconsciously familiar, then the compulsion to replicate and/or control the experience as an adult may become quite compelling. For Sarah, acting out sexually as a young adult provided some sense of the control and power that was denied her as a child-victim of sexual abuse, yet ironically this behavior also perpetuates her victimization.

Self as Abuser

As we have discussed, it seems that Sarah fends off anxiety and her pervasive sense of helplessness by unconsciously identifying with her aggressor. When she functions as the perpetrator of abuse, she finally experiences power over others. Tragically, however, her identity as "the predator" invariably leads to perpetrating crimes against herself. Thus, she becomes both victim and perpetrator of abuse; this satiates her aggressive libidinal impulses and simultaneously placates her superego, which predominantly functions to denigrate her. Certain passive and active manifestations emerge from this interactive dynamic of self-abuse and victimization.

Passive Manifestations

Passive manifestations of Sarah's abuse are those psychiatric symptoms, conditions, and disorders that are basically rooted in the unconscious experience of being a victim. These include poor self-esteem, depression, dissociation, and delayed-stress (posttraumatic) symptomology. Each of these

manifestations reveal the injured, beaten, traumatized, version of Sarah—
that part of her that yearns for death, to be put out of her own internal
misery. Sarah loathes this "pathetic" part of her self and, perhaps not
surprisingly, deeper exploration of this victim-self in psychotherapy has led to
increased suicidal preoccupations. Yet, paradoxically, her passive victimized-
self has not been able to take the active step of ending her life. Victimization
and suffering has become all too familiar, expected, and understood as a way
to be oriented to life itself.

Active Manifestations

Far more destructive to Sarah's general health and life are the active
manifestations of her abuse history. With reference to our earlier discussions
of identification and introjection, these active responses were largely developed within the unconscious to provide a sense of control, mastery, and even
dominance over herself and others. These active manifestations are therefore
associated with Sarah's abuser-self and implicated in all of her overt
risk-taking behaviors such as her sexual acting out, substance abuse, physically self-damaging acts, and suicidality. As will be discussed further on,
suicide thus becomes a "siren song" (cf. Clark and Fawcett 1992) to Sarah the
abuser, representing the ultimate way of seizing control and mastery over the
helpless despair of the pathetic victim within.

SUICIDE AND SELF-DESTRUCTION

Before we discuss more specifically the unconscious nature of Sarah's
suicidality, it is important to place Sarah within a larger context of what we
know about adolescent suicide. Over the past two decades there has been an
extensive proliferation of articles and books about adolescent suicide within
the general literature. As discussed by Berman and Jobes (1991), this
literature covers a broad range of topic domains but can be essentially divided
into five main areas of concern—adolescent suicide epidemiology, theory,
empirical research, assessment and treatment, and prevention/postvention. A
brief review of these topic domains is important to provide both context and
a larger understanding about the topic so that we may more fully understand
young people like Sarah.

Epidemiology

Epidemiological research in adolescent suicide has been responsible for
alerting practitioners to the problem of adolescent suicide. Generally speaking, epidemiologists endeavor to study the incidence of suicide completions
and attempts (Centers for Disease Control 1986, 1991), examine historical

trends in suicidal behaviors (Rosenberg et al. 1987), and provide important demographic information about these behaviors (Berman and Jobes 1991).

Theory

Perhaps not surprisingly, there is no unified theory of adolescent suicide. However, the theories that do exist tend to fall into three major traditions. The first tradition is the classical sociological approach, first advanced by Durkheim (1897), which posits that suicides result from society's strength or weakness of control over the individual. A second major theoretical tradition is the psychological approach, which largely evolved out of psychoanalytic theorizing and early studies of suicide notes and psychological autopsies (Leenaars 1988, Litman et al. 1963, Menninger 1938, Shneidman 1993, Shneidman and Farberow 1961). Theories within this tradition are not limited to dynamically oriented constructs; subsequent theories within this tradition have included behavioral (Ferster 1973), cognitive (Beck et al. 1989), and integrated cognitive-behavioral approaches as well (Linehan et al. 1991). A final contemporary theoretical approach is biological, and primarily focuses on serotonin and the role that this key neurotransmitter plays in depressive disorders and suicidal behaviors (Asberg 1990).

Various authors (Hendin 1987, Lester 1988, Mack 1986) have proposed different integrative theoretical models with varying degrees of utility. Finally, some integrative approaches also examine some of the above constructs in relation to the unique features of adolescent development (cf. Berman and Jobes 1991, Leenaars and Wenckstern 1991).

Empirical Research

The majority of empirical studies conducted in the area of adolescent suicide tend to focus on psychosocial risk factors for inpatient and outpatient samples of suicide ideators and attempters; see Berman and Jobes (1991) for a review of some of these studies. Critically, since the 1970s the psychological autopsy technique has been increasingly employed as a valuable tool to better understand adolescent suicide *completers*. With a number of funded psychological autopsy studies currently under way, the seminal work of Brent and colleagues (1988), Shaffer (1974), and Shaffi and colleagues (1985) has provided some of our best data about adolescent suicide, data that are relevant to both practicing clinicians and prevention-oriented health professionals. As summarized by Berman and Jobes (1991), the totality of the empirically based risk-factor research in adolescent suicide can be thematically grouped into one of the following seven research areas: (1) negative personal history; (2) psychopathology and significant negative personality attributes; (3) stress; (4) breakdown of defenses and affect/behavioral dysregulation; (5) social and interpersonal isolation and alienation; (6) self-deprecatory ideation, dysphoria, and hopelessness; and (7) method availability, accessibility, and knowledgeability.

Assessment and Treatment

A great deal has been written on the assessment and treatment of the suicidal adolescent. Perhaps even the majority of the published literature on adolescent suicide centers on various assessment, treatment, and management techniques with this population. As it is beyond the scope of this chapter to fully review this extensive literature, the reader is advised to consider any of a number of references related to the topic of youth suicide (e.g., Alcohol, Drug Abuse, and Mental Health Administration 1989, Berman and Jobes 1991).

Prevention/Postvention

A final area within the general adolescent suicide literature is prevention and postvention. With regard to prevention, much has been written about federal and public health initiatives (CDC 1986, 1988, 1992), community approaches (Berman 1990, Cantor 1989, Clarke and Lester 1987), crisis intervention and hotline services (Franklin et al. 1989), and school-based prevention programs (Leenaars and Wenckstern 1990). A great deal has also been written about suicide "postvention"—those interventions made after a suicide to facilitate appropriate grieving and prevent further "copycat" suicidal behaviors. In this area, various authors from the Centers for Disease Control and Prevention have made valuable contributions to the literature that provide practical recommendations and guidance if a suicide should occur within a specific interpersonal or larger community system (CDC 1988, 1992).

SUICIDE, SELF-DESTRUCTION, AND THE UNCONSCIOUS

In Sarah we see a troubled adolescent engaged in an intrapsychic life-and-death battle that is primarily waged at the unconscious level. The heart of Sarah's suicidal struggle centers around two different, yet related, experiences of the self—as victim and as abuser. Before more fully exploring this notion, with implications for clinical work, it is important to consider four additional conceptualizations of suicide and the unconscious that are germane to Sarah's experience.

Melanie Klein's (1935, 1940) notions about suicide are highly pertinent to Sarah. Within the object relations tradition, she argued that early parenting experiences are fundamentally important in that good or positive primary-object internalizations are necessary to help counter subsequent losses and injuries to the ego. According to Klein (1935), in cases where there are impoverished parental object internalizations and representations, the death instinct can be turned on the self. Therefore, suicide can be seen as a desperate act, aimed at protecting internalized "good" objects from the death instinct and the destructive effects of one's internalized badness. It follows that when there are few good objects internalized into the self, the person may become extremely vulnerable to hating the bad self (and associated objects), such that the death instinct attempts to murder these bad introjects to protect good object representations (and the associated good self).

In an extreme case like Sarah's, limited positive parental internalizations throughout her childhood left her with ego resources that are inadequate to deal with her many painful experiences and internalizations. Thus, her attachments to her abusive father and neglectful mother may have led to the development of splits within the ego. Within object relations theory it is thought that painful internalizations may be split off into an "antilibidinal" ego that internally reproduces the hostility of punishing and rejecting objects, fundamentally thwarting libidinal gratification. The libidinal ego is therefore hated and persecuted by the antilibidinal ego, in effect dividing the ego against itself (Fairbairn 1954, Guntrip 1968). Sarah's various self-punishing behaviors and her compulsions to place herself consistently in abusive and punishing situations may be seen as manifestations of the split-off antilibidinal ego.

From a somewhat different perspective, Maltsberger (1986) has argued that understanding suicide vulnerability requires an appreciation of the two core components of the psychology of despair. First, suicidal people experience absolutely intolerable affective states so painful that they cannot be endured. Second, suicidal people recognize their condition and give up, abandoning the self as hopeless and unworthy of further concern. According to Maltsberger, many suicidal people have not developed their internal resources to self-soothe, and must therefore rely solely on external resources for comfort. In cases where external resources are absent, there can be a profound sense of aloneness, which puts ongoing survival in danger. Sarah seems to embrace both psychological components of despair; she experiences an unendurable affective state of pain and she has given up on herself, seeing herself as a hopeless case. Throughout her history it is clear that she has never had the opportunity to learn about self-soothing. Her abusive and neglectful early object relations compelled her to seek comfort in unreliable external resources that ultimately fail her (e.g., sexual relationships and substance abuse).

From yet another perspective, Smith's (1985) "ego vulnerability" approach to suicide seems especially relevant to Sarah. This approach emphasizes intrapsychic mechanisms within a context of a particular pattern of ego organization. Central to this approach is the assumption that a matrix of unconscious dynamics and ego organization make an individual vulnerable to suicidal crises. Thus, for a suicide to occur there must be a special loss of an unconscious life-guiding abstraction (one's "life fantasy" of internalized views of self and others) and a rigid, inflexible, vulnerable ego that chooses the denial of death as means of gaining intrapsychic control.

When we ask the critical assessment question of "Why now?" regarding Sarah's increasing suicidality, the answer may lie in her evolving conscious awareness of her abuse history in the absence of internal coping resources. Using Smith's (1985) language, it seems that Sarah has survived her painful history by developing a life fantasy, a fiction, that she was powerful and in control; as a sexual predator, she "forced" others to have sex with her. Similarly, as a chronic substance abuser, she has been able to manipulate and control her phenomenological conscious experience. Ultimately, as an actively self-destructive and suicidal young woman, she has controlled her own physical abuse and her fate in life. As mentioned, recent psychotherapy for Sarah had become intensely painful, perhaps because the exploration of her abuse and victimization challenged her fiction of being in control as the abusing perpetrator of others and herself. With her guiding life fantasy shattered, she was increasingly forced to deal with her history of being a terrorized victim at the hands of those she desperately sought to trust and protect her from harm. In these situations, it can become simply too painful to give up one's life fantasy/fiction, and suicide may then be used as a defense. As discussed by Smith (1990), suicidal people may feel compelled to maintain their preferred (and familiar) view of themselves and others with various defense processes. From this perspective, suicide may not reflect a patient's giving up as much as a refusal to give up preferred views of self and others; suicide therefore functions as a defense against change.

Finally, Hendin's (1991) psychodynamic examination of youthful suicides emphasizes the importance of affective and cognitive meanings that are embedded in suicidal behaviors. In terms of affect, Sarah clearly exhibits intense feelings of rage, hopelessness, despair, and guilt. For her, suicide has great meaning as it represents an escape from the rage connected with her abuse and those who betrayed her, the guilt for having "caused" it, and the hopeless despair that her feelings will never change. On both conscious and unconscious levels, suicide also represents a means for Sarah to seek revenge against her father, retaliatory abandonment against her mother, and punishment of herself. In the single act of self-destruction, revenge and atonement are magically and simultaneously achieved.

SUMMARY AND RECOMMENDATIONS

The case of Sarah dramatically portrays various unconscious components of one young person's suicidal struggle. Sarah's story is both tragic and clinically complex. Diagnostically, Sarah meets criteria for a number of *DSM-IV* axis I disorders—mood and polysubstance-related disorders are primary, and posttraumatic stress and dissociative disorders are also evident. While Sarah may not fully meet criteria for any one specific axis II personality disorder, a number of cluster B personality features are nevertheless present. Antisocial, borderline, histrionic, and narcissistic traits are evident throughout her dramatic, emotional, and erratic lifestyle and character structure.

As discussed throughout this case consultation, Sarah is yet another tragic example of the hazardous effects of poor parenting that was both actively abusive and passively neglectful. In such cases, early emotional injuries may be largely managed at the level of the unconscious through various defense mechanisms and unconscious maneuvers. Throughout this chapter we have attempted to understand and bring meaning to Sarah's unconsciously driven self-destructive behaviors and overt suicidal impulses. In our view, Sarah's suicidality is connected to an unconscious intrapsychic struggle to psychologically survive her profound abuse and neglect. Fundamental for Sarah are unconscious defensive processes that include introjection, ego splitting, and identification. Critically, out of Sarah's unconscious, emerge two distinctly different and interactive selves—the victim-self and abuser-self. In Sarah's experience of being prey and predator we see both the passive-submissive and the active-aggressive aspects of self that ultimately compel her to engage in a range of self-destructive behaviors. Over time, and through treatment, Sarah's efforts to cling to her self-as-predator identity has rapidly slipped away; her increasing awareness of her victim-self and associated feelings of rage, shame, guilt, and self-loathing have made life increasingly unbearable. Thus, the ultimate act of suicide for Sarah becomes loaded with multidimensional meaning; it represent a way to simultaneously kill off the bad self, reap revenge, punish herself, give up, find atonement, and maintain some final semblance of power and control over her own life.

From the interventionist's perspective Sarah's case is indeed daunting. Treatment will continue to be painful as Sarah will need to further confront her history of trauma and betrayal. Nevertheless, with a thoughtful and well-integrated program of treatment, even profoundly wounded adolescents like Sarah can survive their history and find relative mental health over time. To achieve this worthy goal for Sarah, a well-coordinated treatment program that emphasizes structured living, psychotherapy, group support, and pharmacotherapy is indicated.

Sarah clearly needs more structure in her life to keep her behaviorally safe and emotionally supported while she continues to engage in treatment. Ideally, this would occur in an inpatient or residential treatment setting, perhaps a structured group-home treatment facility where behaviors can be monitored and support is available around the clock. While structure is critical, appropriate psychotherapy is the central component of her integrated treatment program. In our view, this psychotherapy should be both cognitive-behavioral and psychodynamic in nature. As described by Linehan and colleagues (1991), cognitive-behavioral treatments that emphasize the development of skill-based coping strategies can help increase behavioral safety by providing concrete tools to better cope with life stressors. As described elsewhere (Jobes 1995, Smith 1991), psychodynamically oriented psychotherapy holds the promise of treating and healing the underlying causes of suicidality. By providing the patient with the potentially novel experience of being in an appropriate, supportive, consistent therapeutic relationship, the patient has the opportunity to grow through the transference relationship, as well as the real relationship, with the therapist.

For any individual psychotherapy effort to be successful, however, a solid program of substance-abuse sobriety must be firmly established. Therefore, specific substance abuse treatment and twelve-step program involvement are essential to Sarah's overall recovery. Typically, substance abuse treatment involves various forms of group work, which Sarah plainly needs to develop a different sense of self and self-in-relation-to-others. In addition, the support provided in a group context by peers can be an invaluable adjunct to the work of individual psychotherapy. Finally, the appropriate and judicious use of pharmacotherapies is indicated to help manage some of Sarah's more acute psychiatric symptomology (especially with regard to her symptoms of depression).

In reality, the recommended multidimensional treatment program broadly discussed above would be difficult to implement effectively. It represents a challenging (and potentially expensive) undertaking that requires a great deal of patient commitment and clinician dedication to succeed over time. Yet, with hard work (and a bit of luck) a gradual therapeutic momentum can be built over time that might enable Sarah to experience a slow emotional growth process that could ultimately liberate her from the unconscious demons that were born in the wake of her traumatic childhood. Even for cases as challenging as Sarah's, there are healers who have developed the necessary will, capacity, and empathic fortitude, to help such patients recover from deep historic unconscious wounds inflicted by trusted others (Jobes and Maltsberger 1995). When these patients are fortunate enough to find these healers, the patient's unconsciously driven suicidal impulses may give way to a hard-earned conscious desire to both live and realize a healthy and positive sense of self, others, and the world.

REFERENCES

Alcohol, Drug Abuse, and Mental Health Administration. (1989). *Report of the Secretary's Task Force on Youth Suicide*. DHHS Pub. No. (ADM) 89-1622. Washington, DC: U.S. Government Printing Office.

Asberg, M. (1990). *The biology of suicide*. Paper presented at 23rd annual conference of the American Association of Suicidology, New Orleans, LA, April.

Beck, A. T., Brown, G., and Steer, R. A. (1989). Prediction of eventual suicide in psychiatric inpatients by clinical ratings of hopelessness. *Journal of Consulting and Clinical Psychology* 57:309–310.

Berman, A. L., ed. (1990). *Suicide Prevention: Case Consultations*. New York: Springer.

Berman, A. L., and Jobes, D. A. (1991). *Adolescent Suicide: Assessment and Intervention*. Washington, DC: American Psychological Association.

Blum, H. P. (1987). The role of identification in the resolution of trauma: the Anna Freud Memorial Lecture. *Psychiatric Quarterly* 61:609–627.

Bowlby, J. (1979). *The Making and Breaking of Affectional Bonds*. London: Tavistock.

Brent, D. A., Perper, J. A., Goldstein, C. E., et al. (1988). Risk factors for adolescent suicide. *Archives of General Psychiatry* 45:581–588.

Cantor, P. C. (1989). Interventions strategies: environmental risk reduction for youth suicide. In *Report of the Secretary's Task Force on Youth Suicide: Volume 3. Prevention and Interventions in Youth Suicide*, ed. Alcohol, Drug Abuse, and Mental Health Administration, pp. 285–293. (DHHS Publication No. ADM 89-1623.) Washington, DC: U.S. Government Printing Office.

Centers for Disease Control. (1986). *Youth Suicide in the United States, 1970–1980*. Atlanta, GA: CDC.

———— (1988, August 19). CDC recommendations for a plan for the prevention and containment of community clusters. *Monthly Morbidity and Mortality Weekly Report: Supplement* 37 (suppl S-6):1–12.

———— (1991). Attempted suicide among high school students—United States, 1990. *Mortality and Morbidity Weekly Report* 40:633–635.

———— (1992). *Youth Suicide Prevention Programs: A Resource Guide*. Atlanta: CDC.

Clark, D. C., and Fawcett, J. (1992). Review of empirical risk factors for evaluation of the suicidal patient. In *Suicide: Guidelines for Assessment, Management, and Treatment*, ed. B. Bongar, pp. 16–48. New York: Oxford University Press.

Clarke, R. V., and Lester, D. (1987). Toxicity of car exhausts and opportunity for suicide. *Journal of Epidemiology and Community Health* 41:114–120.

Daldin, H. (1988). The fate of the sexually abused child. *Clinical Social Work Journal* 16:22–32.

Durkheim, E. (1897). *Suicide: A Study in Sociology*. New York: Free Press, 1951.

Fairbairn, W. R. D. (1954). *An Objects Relations Theory of the Personality*. New York: Basic Books.

Ferster, C. B. (1973). A functional analysis of depression. *American Psychologist* 28:857–870.

Franklin, J. L., Comstock, B. S., Simmons, J. T., and Mason, M. (1989). Characteristics of suicide prevention/intervention programs: analysis of a survey. In *Report of the Secretary's Task Force on Youth Suicide: Volume 3. Prevention and Interventions in Youth Suicide*, ed. Alcohol, Drug Abuse, and Mental Health Administration, pp. 93–102. (DHHS Publication No. ADM 89-1623.) Washington, DC: U.S. Government Printing Office.

Freud, A. (1936). *The Ego and the Mechanisms of Defence*. New York: International Universities Press.

Guntrip, H. (1968). *Schizoid Phenomena, Object Relations, and the Self*. New York: International Universities Press.

———— (1971). *Psychoanalytic Theory, Therapy, and the Self*. New York: Basic Books.

Hendin, H. (1987). Youth suicide: a psychosocial perspective. *Suicide and Life-Threatening Behavior* 17:151–165.

———— (1991). Psychodynamics of suicide, with particular reference to the young. *American Journal of Psychiatry* 148:1150–1158.

Jobes, D. A. (1995). Psychodynamic treatment of adolescent suicide attempters. In *Treatment Approaches with Suicidal Adolescents*. ed. J. Zimmerman and G. M. Asnis, pp. 137–154. New York: Wiley.

Jobes, D. A., and Maltsberger, J. T. (1995). The hazards of treating suicidal patients. In *A*

Perilous Calling: The Hazards of Psychotherapy Practice, ed. M. Sussman, pp. 200–214. New York: Wiley.

Kestenberg, J. (1992). Children under the Nazi yoke. *British Journal of Psychotherapy* 8:374–390.

Klein, M. (1935). A contribution to the psychogenesis of manic-depressive states. *International Journal of Psycho-Analysis* 16:145–174.

_____ (1940). Mourning and its relation to manic-depressive states. *International Journal of Psycho-Analysis* 21:125–153.

Kohut, H. (1977). *The Restoration of the Self*. New York: International Universities Press.

Larson, L. R. (1993). Betrayal and repetition: understanding aggression in sexually abused girls. *Clinical Social Work Journal* 21:137–150.

Leenaars, A. (1988). *Suicide Notes*. New York: Human Science Press.

Leenaars, A., and Wenckstern, S., eds. (1990). *Suicide Prevention in Schools*. Washington, DC: Hemisphere.

_____ (1991). Suicide in the school-age child and adolescent. In *Life-Span Perspectives of Suicide*, ed. A. Leenaars. New York: Plenum.

Lester, D. (1988). One theory of teen-age suicide. *Journal of School Health* 58:193–194.

Linehan, M., Armstrong, H., Suarez, A., et al. (1991). Cognitive-behavioral treatment of chronically parasuicidal borderline patients. *Archives of General Psychiatry* 48:1060–1064.

Litman, R. E., Curphey, T., Shneidman, E. S., et al. (1963). Investigations of equivocal suicides. *Journal of the American Medical Association* 184:924–929.

Mack, J. E. (1986). Adolescent suicide: an architectural model. In *Suicide and Depression Among Adolescents and Young Adults*, ed. G. L. Klerman, pp. 55–76. Washington, DC: American Psychiatric Association.

Maltsberger, J. T. (1986). *Suicide Risk: The Formulation of Clinical Judgment*. New York: New York University Press.

Menninger, K. (1938). *Man Against Himself*. New York: Harcourt Brace.

Orgel, S. (1974). Fusion with the victim and suicide. *International Journal of Psycho-Analysis* 55:531–538.

Rosenberg, M. L., Smith, J. C., Davidson, L. E., and Conn, J. M. (1987). The emergence of youth suicide: an epidemiologic analysis and public health perspective. *Annual Review of Public Health* 8:417–440.

Shaffer, D. (1974). Suicide in children and early adolescence. *Journal of Child Psychology and Psychiatry* 15:275–291.

Shafii, M., Carrigan, S., Whittinghill, J. R., and Derrick, A. (1985). Psychological autopsy of completed suicide in children and adolescents. *American Journal of Psychiatry* 142:1061–1064.

Shneidman, E. S. (1993). *Suicide as Psychache*. Northvale, NJ: Jason Aronson.

Shneidman, E. S., and Farberow, N. L. (1961). Some comparisons between genuine and simulated suicide notes in terms of Mowrer's concepts of discomfort and relief. *Journal of General Psychology* 56:251–256.

Smith, K. (1985). Suicide assessment: an ego vulnerabilities approach. *Bulletin of the Menninger Clinic* 49:489–499.

_____ (1990). *Treating suicidal impulses within psychotherapy*. Paper presented at the Suicide Advanced Seminar at the University of Calgary, Alberta, Canada, February.

_____ (1991). Therapeutic care of the suicidal student. In *Suicide Prevention in Schools*, ed. A. Leenaars and S. Wenckstern, pp. 135–146. New York: Hemisphere.

11: A CASE OF SUICIDE IN ADULTHOOD

Gernot Sonneck and Elmar Etzersdorfer

The following case history of suicide is a very long disease history of a man who was treated by one of the authors (G.S.) at the Crisis Intervention Center in Vienna, primarily in a social therapeutic setting and to a lesser extent in psychotherapy. It never involved classic psychotherapy or psychoanalysis, as this was not possible owing to the circumstances, the client's personality structure, the difficulties of the patient (alcohol abuse and frequent depressive phases with numerous hospital stays), and transference and countertransference problems that were not adequately dealt with by the therapist. This is the history of a difficult patient.

CASE HISTORY

In 1973, W., a corpulent, charming, and friendly single man who worked as a locksmith came to the outpatient department of the psychiatric department of the University of Vienna after several inpatient psychiatric stays in different hospitals because of serious alcohol problems and falls resulting from his intoxication. After several serious relapses and further inpatient stays, the patient's brother, himself a doctor, contacted the first author, the head of the Crisis Intervention Center, and requested that he take over the care of the patient.

W., the elder of two brothers, grew up in the Tyrol, a western Alpine region of Austria. No particular psychological peculiarities are known from his childhood, which occurred in the difficult time of the Second World War. His mother was a housewife and his father a craftsman. The father had alcohol problems all his life, and he disappeared after the war and perished. The Second World War had already started when W. started school. The father joined the armed forces, and the mother tried as well as she could to survive with the two boys. After the end of the war, W. was 11 years old and very emaciated and sick. He went to Switzerland for recuperation, where he received sufficient food. But he had to work very hard. He received no help for his anxieties or problems, as food and work assumed primary importance. There was no formal education available, and only when he returned to the Tyrol could he complete his education and his apprenticeship as a locksmith. The younger brother was allowed to study, and he became a teacher and later a doctor.

During his apprenticeship W. experienced periods of anxiety and a peculiar feeling of being lost, which caused him much anguish. At such times, since he could not work nor talk with others, he withdrew to a small hut high in the mountains, hid there, hardly daring to go out, and ate little. These states would pass after a few days, and he would return to his family in the valley where the incident was not mentioned at all. At this time he discovered the relieving effects of alcohol, and the first excessive use of alcohol occurred. There were problems at work, which led to reproaches about this at home and finally to his dismissal. His mother reproached him, time and again, for being like his father. He left home in an attempt to escape from this closeness to his mother and moved to the capital, where his brother was studying. He lived in a small apartment, and his plans to move to a larger one were thwarted by his instability. More than once he lost his job, although he always found a new job soon.

When he came for treatment to the psychiatric outpatient department, he had lost his apartment. In Vienna, his excessive use of alcohol led to inpatient stays in the casualty department and in the psychiatric hospital as a result of severe intoxication or falls and injuries. These episodes were followed by days of severe restlessness and anxiety. At the psychiatric department he was diagnosed with manic-depressive disorder and chronic alcoholism and treated with lithium and neuroleptics, which brought about some stability and which W. experienced as helpful. He also attended group therapy at the Crisis Intervention Center with the aim of raising his self-esteem.

Regularly, at times of severe intoxication, suicidal thoughts arose that, until his death, never led to suicidal behavior. After such episodes, he was generally completely sober, sometimes for several weeks, and contrite and full of good intentions.

As a result of his Tyrolean dialect, W. was well received in Vienna. He could show his winning side, but only as long as he felt well. He withdrew at the slightest mood swing, no longer kept appointments, and disappeared for days at a time. It became apparent that he was no longer in a position to handle money, for he spent it either on drink or prostitutes. Because of this, an agreement was reached whereby his money was administered at the Crisis Intervention Center and was paid to him three times a week. This agreement proved helpful, for, with support, W. finally found an apartment and kept it in good condition. His feelings of responsibility were supported by his borrowing books from the Crisis Intervention Center that he returned regularly. He gradually began to manage his own money once again, was completely dry for months, became acquainted with a woman, and looked after an old, seriously ill bedridden man who lived in the same house.

During this 10-to-15 year period in Vienna W. came to his therapist two to three times a week for 30-minute therapy sessions. These sessions mainly dealt with the daily problems of living and provided support in an atmosphere of mildly positive transference, which, in itself, was not the focus of the therapy. Imperceptibly to the therapist, the sessions became more political in content, with W. criticizing various politicians who appeared to be too pragmatic and to be without character. These discussions intensified when Kurt Waldheim's candidacy for the state presidency came under fire in the 1980s in Austria as a result of his Nazi associations during World War II and the subsequent international criticism of him. Within Austria, the discussion led to severe polarization and brought up the question of Austria's role in the war. The arguments finally reached a climax when the candidate received the majority of the votes in the election. Both the therapist and the patient were morally outraged. The sessions had, by now, moved away from psychotherapy in the strictest sense of the word.

During this time the patient moved in with his girlfriend, who had a son. He looked after the boy and took his paternal duties seriously. He was also, once again, a guest at his brother's house where he was popular as the friendly uncle. The brother, a doctor, had earlier become involved in health politics and, since the 1970s he had, with the help of the media, highlighted numerous abuses in medicine, influenced important reforms, and, as a result, achieved a certain reputation.

At this time W. lived on a little social security that did not cover his basic living expenses. Because of this he repeatedly received allowances from the Crisis Intervention Center's resources, which had to be carefully allocated since they were limited.

In a session in November 1989, after almost 17 years of continual and very close care, a drastic complication arose. W. had already sat down when the therapist had to leave the room briefly before beginning the session. This offered W. the opportunity to steal the wallet from the therapist's jacket. W. spent all the money and cashed three checks. Early the next day he tried to cash another check. However, the account had been closed as soon as the loss had been discovered, and so W. was detained by the bank employee. The bank employee consulted the account holder by telephone and, when W. noticed this, he demanded to speak to "the Doc" since he knew him. On the phone they agreed, at the suggestion of the therapist, that W. would come that day to the Crisis Intervention Center in order to discuss the matter. The therapist assured him that the matter would be settled between them, but that the bank would certainly file a report.

W., as agreed, arrived and could not explain why he had taken the wallet. He had seen it in the inner pocket, and he said he only wanted to see what was inside. He could not say why he took it. He was conscious of his guilt, and the two finally agreed that W. would compensate the therapist for the loss. They discussed how this would be done given the chronically strained financial position of the patient. It was decided that the financial support of the Crisis Intervention Center until the end of the year would be divided, and that W. could make up at least part of the sum. The therapist had the impression that the incident concerned rivalry with the brother, which had been transferred to the relationship with the therapist. These issues were not completely dealt with. Three weeks after the incident, just before Christmas, W. surprisingly failed to appear, something that had not occurred in recent years. A few hours later it was discovered that he had fatally poisoned himself with the exhaust fumes of his girlfriend's car the previous night. It was subsequently learned that, for a long time, he had also stolen money from both his girlfriend's son and the old man he had cared for.

DISCUSSION

The unconscious is the central tenet of psychoanalysis. "If Freud's discovery had to be summed up in a single word, that word would without doubt have to be 'unconscious.'" (Laplanche and Pontalis 1973, p. 474). The concept had been used before, and nowadays is sometimes used in very different ways, but only Freud constructed a system around it, without which our understanding of the psychological processes would remain rudimentary.

> The division of the psychical into what is conscious and what is unconscious is the fundamental premise of psycho-analysis; and it alone makes it possible for psycho-analysis to understand the pathological processes in mental life, which are as common as they are important, and to find a place for them in the framework of science. To put it once more, in a different way: psychoanalysis cannot situate the essence of the psychical in consciousness, but is obliged to regard consciousness as a quality of the psychical, which may be present in addition to other qualities or may be absent. [Freud 1923, p. 13]

Psychoanalytic theory differentiated three ways of using the adjective *unconscious*. In the topical model, Freud contrasted the unconscious as a system with the conscious and the preconscious. Quite early, he differentiated *unconscious* from *subconscious*, a term that was used by Janet and other authors. In his nineteenth introductory lecture on psychoanalysis, he wrote, "And I should like to hear you admit that our terms, 'unconscious,' 'preconscious,' and 'conscious' prejudge things far less and are far easier to justify than others which have been proposed or are in use, such as 'subconscious,' 'paraconscious,' 'intraconscious,' and the like" (Freud 1917b, p. 296).

While the unconscious is seen as its own system in the topical concept, in the dynamic sense it is used to describe subject matter that is not capable of becoming conscious at a given point of time, despite great mental effort. With the introduction of the structural theory (Freud 1923) and the differentiation of the ego, id, and superego, it became necessary to state that parts of the ego and the superego are also unconscious. "We perceive that we have no right to name the mental region that is foreign to the ego 'the system Ucs.,' since the characteristic of being unconscious is not restricted to it" (Freud 1933, p. 72). What had been called the "system unconscious" corresponds to the id, the representation of drives, in the structural theory (Freud 1923).

In the third mode of use, the descriptive sense that is predominant in Freud's writing and represents the most frequent mode of use today, subject matter that is not at present contained in the conscious is described as unconscious. "The oldest and best meaning of the word 'unconscious' is the descriptive one" (Freud 1933, p. 70). The preconscious is, therefore, unconscious when viewed descriptively but not when viewed dynamically. Each of these modes of use of the word unconscious cannot, in any case, be isolated from other psychoanalytic concepts, especially those of transference, countertransference, defense mechanisms, and resistance, which are inconceivable without the unconscious.

In discussing the above case history, the unconscious will be spoken about primarily in the descriptive sense. The reader will notice, first of all, that the details of the life history and the therapeutic relationship remain fragmentary. This is remarkable since the therapist can look back on more than 1,000 contacts with W. It is not so much a matter of the inherent restrictions of every case history; rather, many details of the patient's life remained hazy and unclear to the therapist during those years of contact. Much never became clear, and many areas, for example, sexuality, could never be discussed despite many attempts and offers from the therapist to talk about them. Childhood and adolescence were barely considered. It was obviously an unspoken condition of the therapeutic relationship with W. that much material that could have made his personality, his life, and his relationships easier to understand was not addressed. Even if the therapist was aware of this, it was certainly unconscious for W. in the descriptive sense, for these issues were never spoken about and this state of affairs did not change over the years. At the same time these omissions seemed to be a precondition for the continuation of the therapeutic relationship between the therapist and W. It was unconscious for W. also in the dynamic sense and topical sense. There were repressed instinctual wishes in W. whose access to consciousness was barred. Expressed in the more recent psychoanalytic view of psychological conflict, there was an interplay between instinctual demands, defense mechanisms, demands of the superego, and negative emotions (in the form of anxiety and/or depressive affect), which finally led to compromise formations (Brenner 1982). W.'s concrete unconscious demands, wishes, and fantasies can only be hypothesized as the therapeutic setting did not allow the therapist to detect them empirically.

Even though the implied (unconscious) precondition for W.'s continuing therapy impeded our understanding of his unconscious and its significance for his suicide, it is impossible to understand the ultimate confusion of the therapeutic relationship without using the theory of the unconscious, even if some suggestions have to remain speculative.

According to the psychotherapeutic orientation of the authors, Adlerian (individual psychology) and psychoanalytic aspects of the unconscious are relevant for understanding suicidal behavior. An individual psychology view states that deeply rooted feelings of inferiority, unsuccessful compensation, antithetical schemata of apperception (Ansbacher and Ansbacher 1956), dichotomizing judgments, all-or-nothing thinking, a lack of social interest, and considerable activity stand at the center of suicidal behavior. W. clearly had an especially strong feeling of inferiority (Adler 1907)—he was a poor Tyrolean who had to live in Switzerland, a poor craftsman who achieved nothing, and a recipient of social security. In an attempt to compensate, he tried to realize his fictional life goal, which was, unconsciously, to be good, noble, and morally blameless. However, he did not succeed in maintaining or realizing this goal—alcohol excess, difficulties in relationships, and minor swindles stood in the way. In therapy, he falsely led the therapist toward his fictional life goal through his good behavior, then unconsciously destroyed it (by the theft of the wallet), and was no longer able to live in this "disgraced" state. The therapist stood by him for a long time, helped him, made no reproaches, and tolerated almost everything. The therapist became, therefore, someone toward whom some degree of trust slowly arose, as contrasted with W.'s earlier brief therapeutic relationships.

This newly begun relationship, however, did not help him to build on the trust further and to develop it. He had to test it (through alcohol abuse and loss of both work and his apartment). Rigid dichotomous thinking (very good versus very bad) and a restricted behavior repertoire are indications of patterns of apperception that are counterbalanced unstably, which brought him again and again to the same situations. However, the therapist tolerated everything, with the result that the feelings of inferiority increased further as the therapist became even "greater." The last test seemed to be, How will he react if I take his money? The reaction was still relatively positive, but the distance between W. and his therapist became too great, and suicide was inevitable. W. felt hostile toward the people by whom he felt threatened, abandoned, and scorned, but he never acted aggressively, something that his physical size and weight would facilitate. Ultimately he did not trust the therapist—he could not confide in him without fearing that he would be completely exposed, which for him would probably be incompatible with living. Consequently, if it is not possible to gain access to this "inner insecurity," the hope that the "outer development" would bring improvements is bound to be dashed. The increased activity that repeatedly occurred, leading to severe states of unrest, did not, however, help W. to develop a sense of social interest, but rather led to further defeats.

What can psychoanalysis contribute to our understanding of W.? In Freud's extensive work there is, with the exception of the introduction and conclusion to the suicide discussion (Freud 1910), which took place at the Viennese Psychoanalytic Society in 1910 and appeared as a pamphlet in the same year (Wiener Psychoanalytischer Verein 1910), no known work that explicitly deals with suicide. Freud's main contribution to the question of suicide can be found in *Mourning and Melancholia* (1917a). Freud deduced that the attacks on the person that can ultimately lead to suicide correspond to hate tendencies that were originally directed toward an object but were subsequently drawn back to the ego.

> The analysis of melancholia now shows that the ego can kill itself only if, owing to the return of the object-cathexis, it can treat itself as an object—if it is able to direct against itself the hostility which relates to an object and which represents the ego's original reaction to objects in the external world. [p. 252]

Freud described two opposed situations when the ego is engulfed by the object: when intensely in love and in suicide. To differentiate between the normal reaction of mourning and that of depression, Freud described a particular object relation for the latter, which he called "object-choice of the narcissistic type." Freud described this more fully in his earlier work *On Narcissism* (Freud 1914) as a relation where one unconsciously seeks in the other person (the object) what oneself is, would like to be, or was. A person with a predominance of this kind of relation obviously looks for a replica of himself or herself as a love object. This relationship is, however, easy to damage since the object remains idealized (the person has to perceive the similarities between himself/herself and the love object at least in fantasy), and the feeling of self-esteem is regulated through the supply of this idealized object. The other type of object relation is characterized by the unconscious search for similarities with the first caring person, usually the mother, and has been called a "type of anaclisis" (Freud 1914).

In the course of time this theory has become common knowledge in the area of suicide — in this context Litman spoke of it as a cliché produced by continual repetition. "Freud is quoted as support of a relative overemphasis on aggression and guilt as components of suicide, with underemphasis of the helplessness, dependency, and erotic elements" (Litman 1970, p. 340). In contrast to Litman, we do not view this position as intermediate between instinct theory and the death instinct concept; rather, it is firmly rooted in his instinct theory. Later, Freud did not explicitly formulate or revise his view, neither when he developed the death instinct hypothesis nor in his structural theory. The death instinct theory especially, which is not accepted by all psychoanalysts, had little influence on psychoanalytic theories of suicide, with the exception of Menninger (1938), perhaps because it is not very helpful clinically.

The theory of the "turning of aggression," as it is widely known, is helpful in understanding W. Through his relationship to the therapist, we know that his kind of object relationship was a slightly idealizing one and was in a state of constant positive transference, whereby some of the characteristics of the brother, which he wished for himself, were mirrored in the therapist (both doctors, both successful), while W. himself, as his mother rightly reproached him, compared himself to the unsteady father who was an alcoholic and simply disappeared.

In the beginning the patient also frequently "disappeared" from therapy as he did not keep appointments and relapsed so that a classical psychotherapeutic setting was not tenable. The therapeutic relationship was still unstable, even after many years, and was in danger of breaking up. Important aspects of his experience had to remain outside the therapeutic situation because he feared being disappointed with the therapist's response or because he was not able to confide in him. On the other hand, the therapist also feared endangering the continuity of the relationship by using conflict-oriented techniques. His countertransference led the therapist to confine himself to being helpful and to overcoming current conflicts and, in this way, unconsciously colluded with the patient, whereby both put the unconscious conflicts to one side.

The relationship was clearly like the one that Freud (1914) described for the object choice of the narcissistic type and the above-mentioned condition for the development of depression (Freud 1917a). W. looked for someone who understood and accepted him, whatever he was doing. This seemed to be an idealized self-representation (an ideal he demanded from himself) and thus different from his own actual behavior. W.'s other relationships were similar, as evidenced by the countless breakups of relationships in the face of minor disappointments, partly rationalized through alcohol. He had a very unstable narcissistic equilibrium that was constantly in danger of collapsing. The structure of his personality would have fit the diagnosis of a borderline personality disorder (complicated by an affective disorder).

W.'s self-destructive way of living revealed itself in his lifelong history of excessive abuse of alcohol. Since his youth, W. suffered from depressive episodes, during which he would withdraw and later resort to alcohol. Although his self-destructiveness had never led to open suicidal behavior before, he tried, through alcohol, to escape from depression and inflicted upon himself various psychological stressors (reproaches of the mother, relationship problems), social stressors (dismissals, apartment evictions), and physical disadvantages (illnesses accompanying alcohol abuse). Menninger (1938) viewed alcohol abuse as a form of "chronic suicide," an expression that has become common in suicide theory. W.'s suicide was preceded by covert aggressive acts—he stole the wallet from the therapist and he embezzled money from people who had trusted him (from the old man whom he had looked after and from the adolescent son of his girlfriend). The suicide itself expressed aggression toward the girlfriend whose car exhaust he used for suicide. Seen from an individual psychological viewpoint, here could lie an unconscious purpose of the suicidal act. Of course, the conscious purpose lies in avoiding, through one's own death, the experience of the ultimate social defeat.

The psychoanalytic concept of ambivalence with depressed patients, as aptly described by Fenichel (1945), can also contribute to an understanding of W.

> The depressed patient is ambivalent toward himself as he is toward objects. But the two components of the ambivalence are stratified differently. In relation to the object, the love impulses (or at least the impulses toward being loved) are more manifest, while the hate is hidden. In relation to his own ego, it is the hate that becomes vociferous, while the primary narcissistic overestimation of the ego remains concealed. [p. 392]

After some chaotic years, which were characterized by excessive alcohol abuse and repeated depressive episodes, W. was able to maintain a long, outwardly stable, therapeutic relationship. Dynamically, it followed the above-described concurrence of, on the one hand, strong dependence on the object (therapist) and, on the other hand, strong hostile feelings toward the same object. The dependence and the wish to be loved were clear and distinct—they were expressed in an atmosphere of a slight positive transference by W., who always respectfully called his therapist "Doc." The aggressive side was somewhat hidden. For a long time the relationship revolved around unconscious issues—How much responsibility can I assume for myself and how much should or must the others do for me? (Can I manage money myself? Can I maintain an apartment? Can I receive financial allowances? etc.) On the one hand, W. demanded much—in terms of time (two to three contacts per week) and intensity (relapses, very difficult social relationships). He was not a patient who strengthened the therapeutic self-esteem of the therapist—he was much more like an infant who demands without giving anything and leaves the mother exhausted. Like many mothers, the therapist protected himself from this exhaustion by the misleading narcissistic gratification of viewing himself as successful where many other colleagues had not succeeded. In addition to these conditions, which are very difficult to fulfill, he required the support of an appropriate institution. The milieu of a crisis intervention center (working on psychosocial crises through appropriate intervention so that a better level of psychological and social functioning is reached), can seduce one into being content with these short-term, achievable therapeutic goals. This raises the important question of therapeutic goals, especially with acute and chronic self-destructive behavior.

Fenichel also writes about the narcissistic overestimation of the ego in depressed patients. If their needs are not immediately satisfied, their self-esteem is reduced to a dangerous level. In spite of their ambivalent feelings, depressed patients are forced to secure attention for themselves through servility and adaptation. They crave love. Although they themselves are unable to actively love, they have a strong need to be passively loved. They tend toward dependence on others. They look for all-powerful objects with whom they can identify, but they continually choose new people, because no object can give them the necessary gratification.

More recent psychoanalytic theories of suicide deal more directly with narcissism and narcissistic crises (Henseler 1974). In addition to the many other meanings of narcissism, which have led to criticism of the concept as a whole (Pulver 1970), the identification of narcissism with self-esteem is stressed. It is not within the scope of this chapter to discuss whether this would create a new theory or whether Freud's concepts, in which narcissism is also used in the sense of self-esteem but discussed with somewhat different terminology, have been simply translated into a different language.

W.'s feeling of self-esteem had always been very unstable—light blows had always led to renewed, excessive consumption of alcohol and relationship breakups (including the therapeutic relationships). As Fenichel (1945) described, not only is the dependence of the self-esteem on others characteristic of these patients, but so is their vital need, their huge hunger, for narcissistic gratification. The depressed individual moves through the world with a continual craving for gratification of this need, which can never be satisfied. The alcohol abuse can be understood as an attempt to achieve this gratification through external means. The "oralness" of alcoholics and depressed patients can be understood in W. as an attempt to achieve a little more independence from the object. Perhaps it is no coincidence that the method of suicide consisted of incorporating something orally—deadly fumes. The suicide proceeded in a manner that was "lifestyle typical." The life-threatening danger of emptiness, if the external supply is denied, found itself once again in the early phases of self-withdrawal, as in the Alpine hut that became a place of retreat.

A similar withdrawal (but internal instead of external) later took place in therapy, where W.'s avoidance of getting into contact might fit the description of a "psychic retreat" as given by Steiner (1993). It reflects the activity of pathological organizations of the personality with the unconscious aim of creating a state of mind that provides protection from anxieties and pain, which otherwise would be experienced.

Likewise the theft of the wallet seems to express both unconscious tendencies—on the one hand, the longing to fuse (to live from the same money) or at least to experience forgiveness, and on the other hand, hate, envy, and the wish to take something away from the other (which he himself did not have). Melanie Klein (1957), unlike other analysts, saw a connection between envy and the earliest external manifestations of the death instinct. It seems noteworthy that W. himself could not clearly say why he had actually taken the wallet and that he repeated through this embezzlement an act that, as it only became known afterward, he had for a time done to others who were also important to him. Can this be explained by the fact that the aggressive instincts finally gained the upper hand and that he ultimately did his utmost to destroy all important relationships? (His final aggressive act toward his girlfriend has already been mentioned.) Was it a last desperate act of communication with the idealized therapist, so that the therapist would find him out and help him out of the other financial difficulties? Or was it the unconscious wish to destroy the last intact relationship so as to enable him to commit suicide? W.'s behavior at the bank mirrors an unconscious wish to be caught and also an unconscious need to be punished, as if he wanted to say, "Please, love me. But you cannot love me. You must hate me for what I have done, and I will give myself the punishment I deserve."

This case history not only underlines that the unconscious is essential to an understanding of suicide, but it also shows clearly that unconscious motives express themselves in the therapeutic relationship in transference and countertransference, and, therefore, influence the therapeutic process in a significant way. The condition for W.'s therapeutic relationship was the avoidance of a therapeutic relationship that would have focused more on understanding the patient more fully. The sociotherapy engaged in could have significantly improved the external conditions for W.'s survival, but it failed to change his personality structure, solve unconscious conflicts, or alter his lifestyle so that the destructive tendencies would no longer play a role. To achieve this, another therapeutic setting was needed, but this was not seriously considered. The need for an alternative therapeutic strategy drifted more and more away from the therapist's attention during the course of therapy. Therefore, the sociotherapy and the therapist's offer of an amicably permissible and distanced relationship could only delay, but not prevent, W.'s suicidal development.

ACKNOWLEDGEMENT

The authors want to thank Monika Korber, who translated this chapter and gave us several helpful comments and suggestions.

REFERENCES

Adler, A. (1907). *Studie über die Minderwertigkeit von Organen.* Frankfurt a. Main: Fischer.

_____ (1937). Selbstmord. *Internationale Zeitschrift für Individualpsychologie* 12:1–5. [Translated as Adler, A. (1958). Suicide. *Journal of Individual Psychology* 14:57–61.]

Ansbacher, H. L., and Ansbacher, R. R., eds. (1956). *The Individual Psychology of Alfred Adler.* New York: Basic Books.

Brenner, C. (1982). *The Mind in Conflict.* New York: International Universities Press.

Fenichel, O. (1945). *Psychoanalytic Theory of Neurosis.* New York: Norton.

Freud, S. (1910). Contributions to a discussion on suicide. *Standard Edition* 11:231–232.

_____ (1914). On narcissism: an introduction. *Standard Edition* 14:67–102.

_____ (1917a). Mourning and melancholia. *Standard Edition* 14:237–258.

_____ (1917b). Introductory lectures on psycho-analysis. *Standard Edition* 15:1–239, 16:241–463.

_____ (1920). Beyond the pleasure principle. *Standard Edition* 18:1–64.

_____ (1923). The ego and the id. *Standard Edition* 19:1–66.

_____ (1933). New introductory lectures on psychoanalysis. *Standard Edition* 22:1–182.

Henseler, H. (1974). *Narzisstische Krisen: Zur Psychodynamik des Selbstmordes.* Opladen: Westdeutscher Verlag.

Klein, M. (1957). Neid und Dankbarkeit. In *Das Seelenleben des Kleinkindes.* Stuttgart: Klett Cotta, 1983.

Laplanche, J., and Pontalis, J. B. (1973). *The Language of Psychoanalysis.* New York: Norton.

Litman, R. E. (1970). Sigmund Freud on suicide. In *The Psychology of Suicide,* ed. E. S. Shneidman, N. L. Farberow, and R. E. Litman, pp. 324–344. New York: Science Books.

Menninger, K. A. (1938). *Man Against Himself.* New York: Harcourt, Brace, & World.

Pulver, S. (1970). Narcissism: the term and the concept. *Journal of the American Psychoanalytic Association* 18:319–341.

Steiner, J. (1993). *Psychic Retreats.* London: Routledge.

Wiener Psychoanalytischer Verein (Hg.). (1910). *Über den Selbstmord insbesondere über den Schüler-Selbstmord.* Amsterdam: E. J. Bonset, 1965.

12: THE FAMILY AND UNCONSCIOUS DETERMINANTS OF SUICIDE IN THE ELDERLY

Joseph Richman

Dreams were once seen as the royal road to the unconscious (Freud 1900–1901). Now, the unconscious is seen as the royal road to healing (e.g., Erickson 1983). In this chapter, I offer a view of the unconscious that is applicable to the family and other social groups for both healing and understanding.

This concept of the unconscious as an interaction between the family and the suicidal individual is indebted to two main sources. One is the writings of psychoanalysts, such as Freud and Klein, and other investigators. The other is my experiences for the past thirty years in conducting family therapy with hundreds of suicidal people, including the old. I shall review some of the salient literature, present case histories of seriously suicidal elderly patients who were seen in psychotherapy, and discuss the theoretical and practical implications. I have selected examples of elderly patients because the dynamic and unconscious determinants for suicide in the aged have been inexcusably neglected. Parts of the case histories have been presented elsewhere (Richman 1993, 1994), but without a central focus upon the unconscious.

The unconscious has been broadly defined as psychological events that are out of awareness; but that comprises the great majority of all that we know and do (Whyte 1960). These experiences are hypothesized as occurring within an individual, and validly so. In psychoanalytic theory, unconscious events are seen as dynamically determined and based upon psychic mechanisms such as repression, denial, and dissociation.

Melanie Klein (1975a,b) discussed the development of the individual in terms of such mechanisms as introjection, projection, and projective identification. These are universal processes that occur so early that they precede consciousness. One inevitable result of early human development is the splitting of people into good and bad figures. Klein emphasized the interpersonal, object relations nature of these processes, even though they occur shortly after birth.

Klein and her followers, especially those who have been trained in family therapy, have made contributions that are central to the concept of a family unconscious. Scharff (1992), for example, observed that "shared unconscious assumptions about family life eventually lead to the identification of parts of family experience inside individual personalities" (pp. 37–38). Scharff added that, as part of the same process, individual aspects are projected onto the intrafamily group unconscious. These Kleinian concepts help us understand the unconscious basis of family conflicts, not only in the first year of life, but throughout the entire life span.

Freud (1921) recognized the presence of an unconscious that operates in social or group relationships. He also suggested that there are dreams "from above" that are not derived primarily from the individual's unconscious, as Whyte (1960) has discussed. The concept of unconscious ideas that are derived from a source other than the individual might also be applicable to the family and its influence.

THE CONCEPT OF A FAMILY UNCONSCIOUS

I hypothesize the presence of a family-based unconscious consisting of automatic and out-of-awareness beliefs and principles of the family system. This family unconscious guides the values and behavior patterns of its members through the unconscious of the individuals. The unconscious is a systems phenomenon, and the individual unconscious cannot be fully understood outside of the systems context.

The content of the family unconscious includes the fantasies, beliefs, myths, and stories that are shared by family members. The existence of these ideas and their origins may be unconscious. The reconstruction of unconscious elements in the family is inferred from the relationship between family interactions and their past history. Family members are aware of conflict and dissension, but not of their unconscious family origins. Nevertheless, they appear to react in accordance with the following nine characteristics, which have been observed most frequently in family interviews with suicidal patients.

1. The fear of separation, which can best be understood in the light of a long family history of losses and separations.
2. The loss of family continuity, with a resulting threat of dissolution of the family structure, which further feeds the separation anxiety.

3. The symbiotic nature of the family attachments, where individual identities become merged. Separation then arouses an almost literal feeling of losing the self as well as the family.

4. An inability to grieve appropriately, leading to the pervasiveness of unresolved mourning.

5. A fear of change, with maladaptive efforts to preserve the status quo.

6. Disturbances in roles, relationships, communication, and the expression of emotions, in order to maintain an untenable family homeostasis. These include the myth of exclusiveness and high expressed emotion, discussed below.

7. A breakdown in the family homeostasis, often with a heartless exploitation of family members and others, concomitant with the breakdown of family traditions and social values.

8. A loving and protective aspect, especially the need to save a fragile family member.

9. A developmental lag in the spouses, in which the husband and wife maintain their primary attachments instead of making the commitment to a new marriage and family.

In summary, the themes of early separation and loss, the failure to grieve for these losses, the resulting loss of continuity, the arousal of early unresolved parent–child conflicts, and the craving for love, which is countered by a fear of abandonment with rage ready to explode, are based upon unconscious family dynamics. The loss of continuity includes the family relationships, traditions, and values. Not only the suicidal individual is affected, but the entire family. Family members have all been traumatized, which is why maladaptive roles and relationships develop outside the family. One such unexamined belief is the *myth of exclusiveness* — the idea that there can be only one intimate attachment, which is destroyed when another intimate relationship develops. Therefore, if a family member forms a close attachment to someone outside the family, it means the total destruction of an intimate relationship inside the family. Such beliefs illustrate how fragile and insecure the family organization is, and how easily it is threatened by outside forces, even positive ones. The unconscious beliefs lead to a closed system, where the family tries to shut itself off from the larger society.

Another example of disturbed roles and relationships is found in the concept of expressed emotion (Leff and Vaughn 1985), where the family members are critical, hostile, and overinvolved with the patient. The participants are not aware that they are being critical, hostile, or overinvolved. They react with surprise and denial should someone describe their behavior in such terms. The usual response is, "I am only pointing out the truth." The participants are still less aware of the unconscious function of high expressed emotion, which is to maintain the prevailing family pattern. While the suicidal state is active, high expressed emotion is needed to deal with the stress, which is based upon separation problems in the family. With the reduction of separation anxiety during therapy, high expressed emotion is also reduced.

A comparison of the family determinants with other risk factors at the time of a suicidal state (Richman 1986, 1993) presents a thought-provoking picture. The risk factors for individual suicidal potential are more overt and in conscious awareness, while the risk factors in the family are more covert and out of awareness. The less-conscious family dynamics are the primary source of the vast tension and anxiety behind the suicidal state. These anxieties, in turn, can be traced to the effects of early experiences, including the experiences of previous generations, which are repeated and handed down from one generation to the next. The therapeutic applications of these concepts are illustrated in the following examples of elderly suicidal individuals. Contact with the unconscious determinants is made through recognizing and empathizing with the conscious fears and feelings.

UNCONSCIOUS DETERMINANTS IN A HOLOCAUST SURVIVOR

My most vivid memory of Peter V. was his insistence in group therapy that he would jump out of the window of his apartment on the seventeenth floor, and his adept refusal of all suggestions by other group members to consider alternatives. I arranged to see him alone the next day, when he continued to voice suicidal and deeply despairing statements. He then recalled how he was drafted into the Russian Army during World War II and returned home to his shtetl in Poland when the war was over. The visit confirmed what he already been told, that his entire family—mother, father, brother, and sister—had been killed by the Nazis. After reliving that terrible visit, he burst into tremendous uncontrolled sobs and expressed regrets that he was the one that survived. It should have been his brother, who was an educated man and a professional, while Peter had left school and home at age 16 and wandered around the country, working at odd jobs.

That session marked the turning point in his therapy. I had been seeing him in individual and group psychotherapy (combined with medication) for about six months prior to the above sessions. He had come to my attention after he told a social worker at the hospital where his wife was dying that he intended to commit suicide. He was walking around with a suicide note. The social worker requested that I call Mr. V., which I did. He welcomed my contact and made an appointment to see me. Unknown to both of us, his wife was expiring at the time of our talk. After the mourning period, he kept his appointment and became my patient.

Mr. V. was 78 years old but had never resolved the conflicted symbiotic relationship with his mother. He reacted to the terminal illness and death of his wife with a revival of his survivor guilt. His suicidal reaction served as a form of atonement. Nevertheless his ambivalence toward his wife was prominent. It was a repetition of the unresolved symbiosis, which was combined with a forbidden resentment he felt toward his idealized mother.

For example, when he was 10 years old he returned home from school and prepared to go out to play soccer. However, his mother told him that a poor man whose shoes were torn and filled with holes came to the door, and she gave the man her son's soccer shoes. He told this story to illustrate how saintly was his mother.

It was not only the unconscious survivor guilt, but the repetitive experiences of loss, leading to rage at being abandoned, that were behind his suicidal state. He dealt with anger by almost automatically turning it against himself. He did so again when I retired and had to leave as the leader of the therapy group. His first response was, "I'm going to kill myself!" Fortunately, we had planned a gradual transition to a new group therapist. His reaction was met with understanding, and an encouragement to remain in treatment. The group continued with a new therapist, and Mr. V. continued to do well. He left a year later to live in an adult home.

A SUICIDAL REACTION TO LOSS AND FAMILY EFFORTS AT PROTECTION

Mrs. Rose A. was an 80-year-old woman with a complex life history, who took a lethal drug overdose and barely survived. I received a phone call one evening from her daughter-in-law, who stated that her mother-in-law had just been hospitalized. Mrs. A.'s 50-year-old daughter had died six months ago, and Mrs. A. was told she had died suddenly from a blood clot.

Mrs. A. entered into individual and family therapy, which included her son, daughter-in-law, and grandchildren, and, in one session, the husband of her deceased daughter. The family sessions disclosed that, unknown to Mrs. A., her daughter had become an alcoholic and, in reality, had died from a fall down the cellar steps of her home while drunk. The family had rallied to "protect" the patient from this information, and made up the story of the blood clot.

However, it was an enormous strain for the family to maintain this lie. That was especially true of her grandchildren, the daughters of the deceased daughter. Therefore, they reacted to every effort by Mrs. A. to talk about her beloved daughter by becoming extremely distressed. Mrs.

A. blamed herself for their unhappy state and felt that her existence was harmful. The conviction that she was a great burden, combined with the blocking of the grief process and her escalating depression led to the decision to kill herself.

In therapy her son, and especially his wife, who was a vital therapeutic resource, insisted upon telling Mrs. A. the truth about her daughter's alcoholism and other disturbed behaviors, in seemingly brutal detail. In fact, it was not brutal but loving. I asked Mrs. A. if she would rather not hear these unpleasant details. She declared that she wanted to hear them; she wanted to know the truth.

Mrs. A. said that she had felt suicidal when her husband died fifteen years ago. She also reported many distressing early family situations. She was raised by an alcoholic father and an overburdened mother. Her mother had told Mrs. A. that she had considered aborting her because she did not want another child while her husband was an alcoholic. When Mrs. A. married in her early twenties, her father was not allowed to attend her wedding for fear that he would shame them.

Nevertheless, her relationship with father was very loving. She was the only family member who felt sympathetic and understanding of his condition. He, in turn, became intensely attached to her. In several individual therapy sessions she returned to memories of his telling her that if she rejected him he would commit suicide.

Her family saw close relationships as dangerous and to be avoided. That was an unconscious theme based upon destructive family triangles. Her son, Kevin, reported a typical outcome of the myth of exclusiveness. He had to leave home as a teenager because his father seemed to become upset and threatened by the sheer existence of his son. As Kevin expressed it, "I had to leave or else one of us would have died."

The grandchildren told some relevant family history during the family sessions. Mrs. A.'s mother came from a very large family. One of her mother's sisters married a man who subsequently became involved in a fiery love affair with another sister. This husband was preparing to divorce his wife to marry her sister, but this sister changed her mind. The husband murdered her and then killed himself. Mrs. A. never mentioned that event, and evidently had dissociated the memory of the session where it was told. When I asked about that family tragedy during an individual session, she became extremely upset and asked how I knew this family secret.

Meanwhile, Mrs. A. improved symptomatically, was not clinically depressed, and resumed her social activities. However, she was very fearful of becoming feeble and dependent upon others. She began to ruminate about her wish that I as her therapist, "pull the plug if I should ever become sick and helpless." She did not want to become a burden and did not want to rely upon others. There was a third, and less conscious reason, as illustrated in the following incident.

During one of the family sessions with Kevin, she expressed her fears of becoming ill and disabled, repeating "I would rather be dead." I asked Kevin how he would feel about taking care of an aged and helpless mother. He said that he, too, would rather she were dead, and Mrs. A. nodded her head in agreement. I accepted their views and the session continued. Toward the end of the hour I commented to Kevin that he was still relatively young and inexperienced; once he is older and knows more about life he might feel differently. Kevin heartily agreed, adding that he had been asked about a situation that he knew nothing about. When they left, Mrs. A. lagged behind and said to me, "I have such a feeling of well-being."

Mrs. A's conscious awareness that she wanted to die and be the recipient of assisted suicide covered up an unconscious theme that ran through her life, as well as the life of her mother, her alcoholic father, her son, and her numerous relatives: to be loved and accepted without reservations. The love was experienced during therapy, through the acceptance by her son with whom there had been over thirty years of alienation and misunderstanding. The hope aroused in therapy that her son would always be there for her provided a direct reassurance that caring relationships could continue to the very end. Such intervention is less possible when the family is not seen directly. It is likely that similar unexamined dynamics are behind many actual cases of euthanasia and assisted suicide.

Effective treatment that touched upon unconscious family dynamics was conducted with both Mr. V. and Mrs. A. during individual sessions. It is evident that the therapist can contact the family unconscious in individual therapy, with the patient serving as a conduit between the therapist and the family system.

The positive and protective aspects that are prominent in suicidal patients was illustrated by both Mr. V. and Mrs. A. Behind their problems concerning rejection and abandonment on the one hand and of being a burden on the other, was the wish to shield family members from pain. That emerged most clearly with Mrs. A., in her testing of whether her son wanted her to be dead should she become dependent upon him. I have seen over and over again that the wish of the suicidal person to be loved and cared for is dominant in the entire family unit.

The therapist cannot satisfy these wishes. However, the therapist can facilitate the healing process and be a catalyst for the emergence of the forces of love and caring. In a study of veterans who attempted or committed suicide, Valente (1994) noted that the affective state of some suicidal individuals included positive emotions such as love. In my experience, these positive emotions are present in the majority of suicidal patients and their families. However, the positive feelings of the family are often covered over by negative emotions that feed the turmoil that frequently erupts in the early family sessions.

Anger, rage, and despair combine with scapegoating, double binding, blaming, accusations, and the expression of death wishes. These extreme reactions are often a necessary prelude to healing. At some level, the family members are aware that they are dealing with their inability to cope with separation and loss, but they are less aware of the degree to which the normal tasks of the family members that inevitably require change represent a threat that increases the separation anxiety to unmanageable proportions. That is why the message that they do not have to separate until ready is so therapeutic.

The proper therapeutic intervention, conducted with positive regard, good humor, and a sense of timing, reduces the tension. My positive emphasis includes an initial approval of the expression of the negative emotions, because they must be expressed, followed by relabeling, monitoring, and other procedures. Then, the positive and caring forces of the family can emerge. I deal only with the conscious derivatives of the unconscious and make no effort to interpret the unconscious determinants. The emphasis, instead, is on the here and now, with the goals of stress reduction, alleviation of symptoms, and an increase in social cohesion (see Richman [1986, 1993] for a more detailed account).

Unconscious family determinants are also seen in many disruptive crises other than suicide. I found dramatic examples in cases of marital conflict in response to a terminal illness (Richman 1981). The illness of one spouse was reacted to with an escalation of conflict and anger between both spouses. Both participants used anger and conflict to deny their awareness of the true situation. The unconscious dynamic features were very similar to those seen in suicidal situations. With the terminally ill, however, the fears of separation and loss and the imminence of an irreparable loss are all too real. In psychotherapy, with the reduction of tension and fear, and an opportunity to face the true situation, the families were helped toward a positive and loving end.

These experiences, too, are related to the question of assisted suicide. A failure to recognize the unconscious determinants is sometimes prominent in the medical professions, with reactions that may be similar to that of relatives.

A 55-year-old woman was hospitalized with amyotrophic lateral sclerosis. A team of doctors, social workers, and lawyers was working to legally remove her life supports, at her request. I suggested a family session before this final solution. The doctor replied, "Her family has no interest in this patient, and she has no contact with them." He added, somewhat inconsistently, that she chose to die because she felt she was a burden. The fact was that the family—and the doctors—could not deal with the illness and approaching death. This case was consistent with the clinical experience that severely suicidal patients feel that they are a burden to their families *and* to their doctors.

A conscious altruistic wish to support a patient's wish to die may be based upon a lack of knowledge of how to treat such situations, combined with more unconscious motives. The unconscious desire to be rid of such a patient is known as countertransference.

UNCONSCIOUS FAMILY DETERMINANTS OF COUNTERTRANSFERENCE

In psychotherapy, the role of unconscious processes and communications has received increasing attention. Freud and other therapists became gradually aware that the most influential relationships in treatment occur below the level of consciousness (see, e.g., Epstein and Feiner 1979). To a large extent, transference and countertransference reactions are based upon the unconscious of the patient interacting with the unconscious of the therapist. Effective psychotherapy begins when the therapist can confront his or her countertransference reactions. These reactions determine how the therapist deals with the family and social determinants of the suicidal state. Therefore, the broader social context, including their unconscious determinants, cannot be disregarded. The perceptive therapist can contact the family unconscious, even in individual therapy.

An awareness of the family unconscious may be particularly valuable because a countertransference that the therapist does not recognize is one of the most frequent problems in therapy. One example is the accurate perception by the therapist that the family interaction is destructive and contributes to a suicidal state. The outcome may be an attitude of condemnation followed by a recommendation that the suicidal person be removed from the family. That is often based upon a countertransferential interference with the realization that the disturbed family relationship may be treatable, and that the family can then exert a far-reaching positive and suicide preventing influence.

Group therapy with homogeneous groups of severely depressed and suicidal elderly patients has been particularly effective in my experience (Richman 1993). Because of the responsiveness of the suicidal elderly to the process and their need for social stimulation and a sense of belonging, it is surprising that such therapy is not more prevalent.

Reiss (1968) noted that when two suicidal people get together, they encourage each other to commit suicide. However, when three or more suicidal people gather together in a therapy group, they help each other to live. The group unconscious is healing and life oriented, while suicidal persons as individuals or in dyads are destructive and death oriented. Mr. V. kept insisting he was suicidal and wanted to die. In the group, however, he put his energies and considerable skill into helping others who were suicidal to accept life.

I know of no reports of terminally ill patients in group psychotherapy who opted for assisted suicide. Many assisted-suicide patients might have decided differently had they been placed in a homogeneous therapy group consisting of more than two people. In one-to-one therapy, in contrast, there may be no one to challenge a therapist's unexamined countertransference.

DISCUSSION

The description of the conscious as awareness and the unconscious as out of awareness implies a polarity that is misleading. There is an awareness in dreams, poetry, and other manifestations of the primary process, which is different from the awareness of conscious waking thought rather than an absence of awareness. The interaction of family members when they are emotionally engaged with each other is closer to that primary process awareness. Similar thoughts apply to the therapist, who must confront his or her countertransference reactions. To confront does not mean that everything in the unconscious must or should become conscious. It does mean a therapeutic contact with the kind of self-awareness that depends upon a *different* kind of consciousness. All effective self-awareness is built upon this covert foundation.

The basic components of the suicidal situation outlined earlier are all based upon the covert family dynamics, which I defined as the family unconscious. It became evident in family sessions that avoidance and denial are family system defenses, not just individual ones. The reasons for suicide that are given are more often conscious efforts to explain what is unknown because the primary determinants are part of a shared family unconscious. That is why family interviews offer the best opportunity to understand and deal effectively with the basic origins of the suicidal state.

The concept presented here is unrelated to the Jungian theory of an inborn collective unconscious (Jung 1959). Rather, the family unconscious emerges out of lived experiences that are learned and handed down from one generation to the next.

An understanding of unconscious determinants, especially of the family-based unconscious, throws into question the belief that is fostered by the media, that pain or any one motive is the sufficient reason for suicide. The big problem for the supporters of such views arises when the life of the suicidal person is examined, including the one who is terminally ill or severely disabled. The view of suicide as solely an individual right, and that the social and family determinants can be disregarded, then becomes untenable.

The problem for society is compounded by the failure of television and the press to present this reality. The one-sided defense of assisted suicide by the media raises questions about the existence of a societal unconscious whose reach is immeasurably greater than that of any individual, family, or other subgroup unconscious. We are obligated to contact the unconscious at all levels, from the individual to the social. The task of therapists and all of us who strive for a better world is to tap the life-affirming forces of individuals, families, and the larger society in the service of all people at all ages.

REFERENCES

Epstein, L., and Feiner A., eds. (1979). *Countertransference: The Therapist's Contribution to the Therapeutic Situation.* New York: Jason Aronson.

Erickson, M. H. (1983). *Healing in Hypnosis,* ed. E. L. Rossi, M. O. Ryan, and F. A. Sharp. New York: Irvington.

Freud, S. (1900-1901). The interpretation of dreams. *Standard Edition* 5:339-751.

_____ (1921). Group psychology and the analysis of the ego. *Standard Edition* 18:67-143.

Jung, C. G. (1959). *The Archetypes and the Collective Unconscious.* New York: Pantheon.

Klein, M. (1975a). *Love, Guilt, and Reparation, and Other Works.* New York: Delacorte.

_____ (1975b). *Envy and Gratitude and Other Works.* New York: Delacorte.

Leff, J., and Vaughn, C. (1985). *Expressed Emotion in Families.* New York: Guilford.

Reiss, D. (1968). The suicide six: observations on suicidal behavior and group function. *International Journal of Social Psychiatry* 14:201-212.

Richman, J. (1981). Marital psychotherapy and terminal illness. In *Questions and Answers in the Practice of Family Therapy,* ed. A. S. Gurman, pp. 445-449. New York: Brunner/Mazel.

_____ (1986). *Family Therapy with Suicidal Persons.* New York: Springer.

_____ (1993). *Preventing Elderly Suicide: Overcoming Personal Despair, Professional Neglect, and Social Bias.* New York: Springer.

_____ (1994). Family therapy for the suicidal elderly. In *Now I Lay Me Down. Suicide in the Elderly,* ed. D. Lester, and M. Tallmer, pp. 73-87. Philadelphia: Charles Press.

Scharff, J. S. (1992). *Projective and Introjective Identification and the Use of the Therapist's Self.* Northvale, NJ: Jason Aronson.

Valente, S. M. (1994). Messages of psychiatric patients who attempted or committed suicide. *Clinical Nursing Research* 3(4):316-333.

Whyte, L. L. (1960). *The Unconscious Before Freud.* New York: Basic Books.

Part V
GENDER AND CULTURAL CONSIDERATIONS

To understand suicide, the suicidologist must give special consideration to an array of factors, especially gender and culture. Among the efforts to develop explanatory patterns of suicidality, it is noticeable that female suicidal behavior, including unconscious aspects, has received little attention. Research into culture has also been neglected. Although there are probably different unconscious dynamics involved in suicide in people from different cultures, mainstream Western psychology continues to ignore the cultural matrix as well as gender. This part presents three chapters: a comprehensive analysis of gender, suicide, and the unconscious; a discussion of the cultural dynamics of suicide in Japan; and a presentation of suicide and self-destructive behavior in traditional native societies in America.

13: THE UNCONSCIOUS MOTIVATION OF SUICIDALITY AMONG WOMEN

Benigna Gerisch

In his repression theory developed from his studies of hysteria, Freud (1896, 1920) asserted that an existing cause was only traumatic if it actualized repressed conflict matter (cf. Gerisch and Köhler 1993). As early as 1905 Gaupp also doubted whether a simple causality pattern of suicidality was conclusively able to define the motive and real cause. He emphasized that "traumatic situations trigger the action but can never cause them" (p. 18; cf. Linden 1969). Henseler and Reimer (1981) examined this assumption in depth and asserted that a fundamental discrepancy existed between the consciously communicated motive and the generally unconscious motive.

Suicidologists of differing schools of thought agree at least on one point: for suicidal acts to take place, extremely varying factors and unconscious conflicts can be involved. This central question of what the motives were was one of the primary reasons why the phenomenon of suicidality became an interdisciplinary object of research for philosophers, physicians, psychologists, psychoanalysts, sociologists, and social scientists, all of whom were attempting to develop explanatory patterns of suicidality. Suicidologists are largely in agreement that it is extremely problematic to formulate a general definition of suicide. It can, in fact, only deal with "the dynamic references of occurrences leading to death," which can actually only give an "analysis of the individual case" (Krebs 1982, p. 10).

The complexities of individual cases, however, also generate new interpretation difficulties and, repeatedly, undefined aspects and combinations. As we know, Freud (1900), saw dreams as the "royal way" to discovering the unconscious. In the same way as in the unconscious, the contents of a dream are distorted by specific mechanisms such as condensation and displacement and are always, therefore, determined or overdetermined by many levels. For this reason, Freud (1900) concluded that one could never be certain "to have totally interpreted a dream, even if the solution appears satisfying, [for] it is still possible that another sense can appear from the same dream" (p. 285).

Among all of these efforts to develop explanatory patterns of suicidality, it is noticeable that the phenomenon of female suicidality, including the unconscious motivation in medical-psychiatric as well as in psychodynamic concepts, has received little attention. Research into female suicidality is analogous with the long — and still existent — tradition of patriarchal history of culture and science in which women have always been defined by men, with no trace of women's own subjectivity, that is, women's self-reflecting, acting being (cf. Gerisch 1994). Even though Schwarz stated in 1946 that the involvement of both genders was perhaps the most interesting aspect of suicide, it is remarkable that the high rate of attempted suicides by women — twice as many as by men — is hardly dealt with as a subject in itself, despite the enormous numbers of papers on suicide (cf. Lester 1979). It is hardly necessary to mention that the few publications dealing with female suicidality in Germany are by women — for instance, the psychodynamically oriented study of suicidal problems of young girls by Dührssen (1967) and the sociological studies by Kneissl (1984, 1985) and Lindner-Braun (1990).

Descriptions of female suicidal behavior are generally presented by male authors whose studies not only contain implied constructions of their own regarding the differences between the genders, but also attempt to place female suicidal behavior at the perimeter of male suicidal behavior, whereby women are defined by, and dependent on, the male. Moreover, on reviewing epidemiological and medical psychiatric suicide literature, it becomes evident that, without exception, biologically oriented hypotheses have been formed to explain the suicidal behavior of women but not that of men (cf. Durkheim 1987, Kneissl 1984, Schmidke 1988). Accordingly, women are primarily governed by the influences of menstruation, pregnancy, and menopause, but hardly by social-cultural processes that are also of intrapsychic significance. Interestingly, social-cultural aspects were only then considered significant if they presented the prospect of a partial liberation of women. Therefore, emancipation, secularization, and gainful employment are still maintained to be the cause of the increased rate of female suicides and also for the rise in violent acts by women (cf. Wiese 1993).

In her recent critical survey of Anglo-American scientific studies of gender-specified suicidal behavior, Canetto (1992) presented the provocative claim that the supposed objective facts of suicidal behavior need only be interpreted as a reproduction of stereotyped gender roles. The scientific vicious circle lies in the fact that the scientific viewpoint, and its resulting traditional suicide theories, are greatly influenced by male and female gender stereotypes that, in turn, evoke norm-conforming male or female suicidal behavior and, vice versa, form suicidologists' preconceptions (cf. Gerisch and Köhler 1993, Kuhn 1962).

The traditional explanatory patterns often give the impression that the causes of suicide, whether supportive or repressive, should be solely sought in the so-called biological nature of women. This deeply rooted identification of women with the traditional division or dichotomy of "women and nature" on the one hand, and "men and culture" on the other (cf. Laqueur 1990) was responsible for the fact that women have always misused their bodies, even to the state of self-annihilation, in rebelling against this stipulation process. Pious female anorexia nervosa sufferers, hysterical women, female eating disorders, and female suicide victims provide the historical proof (cf. Braun 1985, 1989, 1992).

PERSONAL THEORIES ON THE UNCONSCIOUS MOTIVATION AND PSYCHODYNAMIC UNDERSTANDING OF SUICIDALITY AMONG WOMEN

I believe that a differentiated understanding of suicidality will only be possible if the traditional explanations are rigorously questioned, and if an adequate differentiation is made between men and women concerning the conditions causing suicidality (cf. Gerisch 1993a).

My deliberations stem partly from the traditional male myths concerning gender and femininity, which have also been the object of critical examination by neighboring social sciences (Adorno and Horkheimer 1947, Bovenschen 1979, von Braun 1985, 1989, 1992, Foucault 1976, Hardach-Pinke 1982, Hausen and Nowotny 1986, Laqueur 1990, Rohde-Dachser 1991, Schuller 1990, Weigel 1989, Weigel and Stephan 1983). I make the same assumptions as these authors, namely that differences in gender cannot be legitimized by invoking nature; masculinity and femininity will be interpreted as dialectically created social categories. The reconstruction process of traditional gender differentiation illustrated that women were always defined as what the man is not, or in the sense of Beauvoir (1951) as "The Second Sex," and that their allocated identities were always derived from men.

Continuation of this scientific discussion in recent decades produced new concepts and theories concerning gender differentiation and female development, predominantly by female psychoanalysts, that can be reasonably applied to the subject of female suicidality (Benjamin 1986, 1988, 1993, Chasseguet-Smirgel 1964, 1986, Chodorow 1978, Fast 1984, Gilligan 1982, Kestenberg 1988, Mitscherlich 1985, Mitscherlich-Nielsen 1978, Olivier 1980, Rohde-Dachser 1989a,b, 1990, 1991).

Although their theoretical argumentation differs greatly, the female authors attempt to present alternate or complementary female gender identity models by critical reflection on existing concepts. In summary — and almost unanimously — their basic criticism is directed at the classical psychoanalytical femininity theory still represented within mainstream psychoanalysis, in which women are thought to be inferior in terms of the concepts of phallic monism and penis envy, and dependent on men for their psychosexual identity. Freud's theory of female development (e.g., 1905) is also called the theory of phallic monism because it is based on the assumption that, until girls and boys discover the gender differences, they all presume that there is only one genital type, namely that of the male. In addition, some of the female authors (e.g., Rohde-Dachser 1989b) reject the "bad" mother overestimation or hypertrophy whose power during the early childhood development period is not only overemphasized, but is also always connected with an implicit placing of blame (cf. Konnertz 1987) for the faults in the child's development. The analogy of power and the mother's/woman's blame that legitimizes her degradation anew results, among other things, from the constant confusion between the real mother and the internal psychic image created in the child, the mother-imago.

Kneissl (1985) came to the conclusion that social interpretation of the individual act is not only permissible but also essential if dealing with the recognition of social subjectivity. Women have been characterized as a social group especially discriminated against. "It would, therefore, be nonsensical, because of their socially acquired behavior repertoire, to accuse them of individual failure in private conflicts by certifying them with inferior psychic strength [that is, psychologically able only to stand a limited amount of stress] without providing further details" (p. 287). An interpretation of suicide acts, and also other psychic and psycho-vegetative disturbances in women, can only take place under special consideration of the overburdened and conflicting conditions under which they live. Attempted suicide as a specifically female conflict-solving strategy does not, therefore, document an individual fate but the "reaction to specific interdependent life conditions to which women are exposed to a greater degree than men" (p. 288).

When I deal with the unconscious motivation of female suicidality in the following pages, it is always with consideration of the traditional gender arrangements on the one hand, and the intrapsychic working-out of social-cultural and interactional processes, in the sense of psychic reality, on the other. The difficulty with which one is repeatedly faced in such an attempt, is the question of "how social reality interaction reaches the depths of the unconscious with its imaginary scenarios and phantasms" (Konnertz 1987, p. 9). For this reason alone, I lay no claim to totality and am fully aware of the hypothetical character of my deliberations.

Suicidality as an Expression of the Desire for a Change in an Object Relationship

As Canetto (1992) succinctly commented, "she died for love and he for glory" is an almost unanimous premise; that is, the motivation for women to attempt suicide lies in their partnership problems, whereas for men it is serious problems in their working life. The dependency on, and the breakdown of romantic relationships are not attributed to their possible dysfunctional structure but to assumed natural female personality traits, such as weakness and dependency, whereby the perception of women as pathological beings on the one hand, and the perpetuation of the weak female stereotype on the other, is sustained.

Taking traditional gender arrangements into consideration, as well as the conclusions of more recent feminity theories (Chodorow 1978, Fast 1984, Gilligan 1982, Rohde-Dachser 1991) the female relationship pattern — "she died for love" — could be decoded in such a way that, because of the mother and daughter's shared gender, the process of formation of a girl's identity can best be defined through attachment, "self-in-relation" (Jordan and Surrey 1986), which encourages the development of particular abilities, such as relationship orientation and empathy. As opposed to masculine morals, Gilligan (1982) assumes the existence of specifically female morals whose ethical principles derive from the care of, and relationship for, others. The formation of the male identity, on the other hand, is, from the very beginning, based on the central experience that he differs from his mother because of his gender, and is characterized by separation (cf. Gerisch 1993b). A high level of social and communicative competence is an initial characteristic of women and they generally pursue a different autonomy ideal from men, one that is based not on independence from others but on reciprocal appreciation, in the sense of "referred individuation" (Stierlin 1978) and autonomy (cf. Benjamin 1993, Braun 1992). Women are, therefore, more likely to have difficulties with their separation and individuation, and men more probably with proximity and intimacy.

Rudolf and Stratmann (1989) as well as Grande and colleagues (1992) reached similar conclusions in their studies of male and female patients with psychogenetic and psychosomatic disturbances. While women suffered more often because of difficult relationships from which they were not able to release themselves internally, and to which they attributed disappointment and grievance even after a real separation, male patients more often demonstrated difficulties in restricting their autonomy and in forming emotional attachments and social relationships.

As a result of my own experience with suicidal patients, I now wish to combine this viewpoint with Kind's (1992) theory on suicidality including his extremely important addition to the term *appeal function*, in the sense of securing the object and changing the object relationship.

My theoretical deliberations include those female patients who, either as a result of a separation or highly conflictive relationships, have attempted suicide or experienced suicidal thoughts and feelings and who, during the initial contact, expressed the conviction of not being able to continue living without the respective man. A dual subject presence with a relatively unconnected parallel existence was remarkable in these female patients — on the one hand, self-loss due to the problems of separation, and, on the other, a relatively good social and occupational integration.

From a theoretical object relations theory perspective, Kind (1992) holds the view that every suicidal act — including the accomplished suicide — represents an actualization of pathological object experiences in early childhood, and is motivated by conflict dissension with inner and outer objects. Object relations theory deals primarily with the internalization of innerpsychic representations of a child's relationship experiences with the parents.

Each suicidal act is, therefore, an immanent interactional function that is applied as a last resort if intrapsychic or interpersonal crises do not seem able to be solved in any other way. In contrast to Freud's suicide theory — which according to him was basically an object relations theory of suicidality — Kind (1992) assumes that the suicidal act is not only an attempt to kill an introjected object but also an attempt to secure and change it. Object securing defines the suicidal person who, with his weakened sense of self-worth, is dependent on the real presence of another person; object changing describes how an uncaring and rejecting person becomes caring and attentive. These wishes and needs can be directed toward real reference persons, as well as toward therapy.

The female autonomy ideal in reverse appears to find one form of expression in women feeling bound by a deeply seated imperative to create and maintain relationships, even in contradiction to their own needs (cf. Goldner 1992). Thus, women lapse into many more interpersonally caused crises than men, which cannot be dealt with by any other means than a suicide attempt. Women appear to have a tendency to remain object directed also in hopeless and unbearable situations, in the hope that by risking their lives they will be able to force the other to reconciliation and change.

In addition, women are often under the identity-forming illusion that only the man as father, brother, partner, and son is entitled to justify female existence, as Rousseau-Dujardin (1987) stated in her short essay "Outside Herself." In her practice she also observes how women "step outside themselves" and decompensate with suicidality as a result of separation and loss, while men's initial defense reaction to loss of a possession is anger and revenge. She admits that men experience extreme suffering in unhappy love affairs. However, in contrast to women, a threat to their identity is not of primary importance but rather an attack of their "phallic right," that is, the male concept of the woman as man's rightful possession. Rousseau-Dujardin concludes: "But perhaps they were not as threatened as these women were, whose place in life was characterized by functioning in a position determined by a man, their man, which, when it was questioned, led them to experience an acute identity crisis" (p. 60).

The author describes how the fixation of the mother on the father already creates a normative reality for a daughter, in which the man is always at the center of importance and desire. The mother's inner and outer direction toward the father prevents the daughter from feeling sure of the mother's attention and from being able to experience a certain period with the mother exclusively. The hope, therefore, of an exclusive intimacy with the mother is always destroyed by the real or indirect presence of a third person. The intrapsychic working out of this rejection causes the daughter to experience herself as unsatisfactory or bad, and the conviction is sustained that she herself does not satisfy the mother but that only the man and father can do so.

A patient described, for example, how she, after having listened to her mother intensively, always registered the mother's abrupt disregard as her own failure. These situations were particularly painful because the mother complained to her exclusively about the insults and disappointments she had suffered from her husband and son, only then, visibly relieved, to return her attention to the alleged malefactors — those very people (husband, son) whom she had accused of being the cause of her pain.

In summary, Rousseau-Dujardin (1987) holds the view that women's agonizing doubts concerning their self-value after a separation, including the feeling of emptiness, should not be interpreted as an expression of penis envy. The mother is, in fact, identified with the impression that only the man is entitled to justify female identity. She transfers this identity-forming wish by delegation to the father onto the daughter. Should then male confirmation be refused or, because of separation, withdrawn, an existential threat of self-loss would occur so that suicide would appear to be the only solution.

Suicidality as an Expression of the Desire to be Present in Another Person

In my psychotherapeutic work with suicidal patients I have often heard grievances from female patients who feel that "the way I am," that is, their narcissistic need, is not seen,[1] a grievance expressing the existential "desire for recognition" (Balint 1968). What these patients seemed to be lacking was the

---

[1] In consideration of the specifically female problems, this aspect proves to be doubly determined. In this context the individual fate is locked into social reality, where the woman's place is hardly visible or, only by making a great effort to adapt to the needs of others, is a place conceded to her.

basic feeling of being permitted to be in the world at all; in this sense they had no "self-representative of justifiable existence" (Kind 1992, p. 95), which results from the inability to establish an internal empathetic object as a psychic structure (cf. Rohde-Dachser 1986).

In her essay "Struggle Towards Empathy" Rohde-Dachser (1986) interpreted the sadomasochistic fantasy productions — in the sense of coping — to be the result of an inadequate empathy mirroring in early childhood. These patients could evidently only then feel alive if their fantasy included causing themselves or others physical pain. I will take that point up here and put forward the thesis that the functionalization of the body as an object, and an anal-narcissistic defense — in the sense of achievement-oriented — could illustrate a similar attempt to compensate for this structural deficit. When it was no longer possible to maintain the usual coping pattern, the above patients reacted with suicidal decompensation. My patients and those described by Rohde-Dachser, therefore, differed from each other not in the narcissistic trauma they experienced but in the mechanism to cope with this deficit. The motivation in both groups of patients was to trigger a reaction and not to be ignored (Stolorow 1975).

The biographical anamnesis showed that these female patients were traumatized very early. Due to these traumatic situations, the patients' suicidality can also be interpreted as an expression of a latent early death wish directed against themselves (Federn 1929, Klemann 1983). One patient, for instance, was placed with foster parents at birth, and the foster mother died shortly afterward. Another patient was left alone at home by her mother without sufficient care. In three other patients there was an identification with a "dead mother" as Green (1993) named this complex, that is, the identification with an externally present but, due to depression, internally absent mother. In all these cases the father was either not physically present or was not emotionally available for the child, so that the narcissistic trauma could not be compensated by a third object.

Not only satisfying a child's basic instinct needs is relevant (Eagle 1984) for its development, but also experiencing an unqualified resonance to the totality of its person (cf. McDougall 1978, Spitz 1963).

> To be able to develop a reliable, coherent image of itself and, the closely connected feeling of personal identity, a child, practically from birth on, needs to experience an adequate empathetic response to its presence and 'the way it is' from its mother in a continuous, mutually satisfying dialogue . . . , whereby visual contact between mother and child plays a special role, particularly in the first few years. [Rohde-Dachser 1986, p. 45]

Before an infant is in the position to have an image of itself, it must experience that another person has an image of it. In this sense the "object constancy begins in another person" (Kind 1992, p. 78). This experience is a necessary requirement for establishing a coherent and integrated self-representative. In addition, this existential basis helps the child in later years to master real separation from, in most cases, the mother object and to feel itself existent beyond time and place. If the often quoted "glow in the mother's eye" (Kohut 1967) is missing, and if these early development steps are traumatically disturbed or prevented, only an inadequate self and object constancy develops, as well as a permanent dependency on a real external object. In this context, Benedetti (1983) speaks of a dumb area in the psyche that as "death holes" erode the individual's feeling of identity. Habermas (1971) interprets these psychic gaps as a lack of integration of pre-speech paleo- or protosymbols into the regulated system of language associations. If this transition is not achieved the paleosymbols encapsulate themselves within the psychic structure, becoming "internal foreign parts" (Freud 1933b, p. 62), no longer accessible to the subject.

According to Rohde-Dachser (1986) the continuous search for an "empathetic object" results from the early childhood traumatic experience of never having been sought and found by an "almighty" or "adequate object confirming that is how I am," thereby giving the child a "feeling of justified existence" essential for the development of its identity (p. 46).

One patient described it in the following words: "Sometimes I want to hide myself so that my parents look for me and find me."

Another patient: "An enormous loneliness spreads through me, like a desert increasingly destroying good land. I am in the middle, and nobody can reach me. No one is able to find the way to me, there are no signs. Nobody is close enough to me to reach me. I have the feeling that the void is consuming me."

> In one patient, due to the unavailability of a real object, the "own body as an object" (Hirsch 1989) is functionalized and given quasi-existence-securing attributes. The patient believed herself to be incapable of going outside and mixing with people unless she was wearing very conspicuous sunglasses and exposing her tattoos, as she feared she would otherwise not be seen. After the fifty-fifth therapy session, this patient dreamt that her sunglasses had melted in a fire and could no longer be used. To her astonishment she realized in her dream that she was in a crowded street and no longer felt panic about disappearing into the mass.

One can assume that the first buds of a secured self and object representatives had sprouted, enabling the patient to feel her own self and existence among others without the exterior attributes.

Kind (1992) summarizes this aspect as follows:

> Disappearing in the crowd is not only the fear of being mediocre, it is not only a narcissistic insult, it is also an anxiety not to exist that is directed against the self. To be unique should not be understood here as a fantasy of grandeur, but as an essential experience for any person striving for individuation, and it is

vital for the development of a core identity. The "I am different to others" expression is a basic feeling necessary for individuation. To be able to be found, recognized, and located . . . articulate[s] this basic need. [p. 82]

The case of the following patient will demonstrate why aggression can, and may, only be directed against oneself and not against others: On the one hand, the presence of a real object is experienced as essential and, on the other, the patient identifies herself with her rejection by others because of her massive self-degradation. The object loss is, therefore, experienced as a result of her own inferiority. "When nobody reacts to me any more, even if I rave and scream, when I have the feeling that the other person has lost all interest in me, I feel destructive and killed. I could ram a knife into his or her flesh, but at the same time I feel that the other person is right, I am nothing. Then I prefer to kill myself. My suicide is the logical reaction to the feeling that I have already been destroyed."

In another group of patients the feeling of not being perceived and cathected as "the way I am" was dominant, independent of beauty or achievement. "If you are not as she wants you to be, she does not see you and you are not in the world" (Hammer 1978, p. 35) seemed to be the existential anxiety common to all of the patients. In contrast to the previously mentioned patients, these women had experienced being seen, at least partially and selectively, although only under the condition of specific achievements.

A 39-year-old patient wrote the following to her mother who had given her to foster parents shortly after her birth: "What do you imagine becomes of a person who is only marginally liked when she has fulfilled certain demands and expectations, and never simply because someone is glad that she exists?" Due to the early traumatization and emotional deprivation this patient was convinced that she had to repeatedly justify her existence, for example, by adapting or achieving.

In another patient who expressed something similar, the maternal wish for achievement and beauty was delegated to a predominant position: "I probably did not receive something important in my childhood, the feeling of really being in the world, to have a place in life and simply feel comfortable in my existence. I learned that I always had to do something in order to be happy or right in the world. That is it. I have the feeling that I cannot simply 'be.'"

In her daughter role this patient felt functionalized by her mother as a narcissistic self and identification object. Narcissistic identification describes an identification process in which the functions that a child can have for its mother vary. It can be seen as what the mother herself is, what she was, or what she would like to be or not like to be, for example, "bad or malicious." The mother of this patient, who was also unhappy with her life and marriage, appears to have delegated all of her unlived desires and hopes, in the sense of an extension of her own self. Various authors (e.g., Balint 1963, Chodorow

1978, Fliess 1961) have pointed out that this form of narcissistic identification is particularly encouraged in mother–daughter relationships because of the shared gender. However, I feel that, not the narcissistic identification itself, but the included message of implied rejection of the daughter, namely "do not be like me, become someone else," in the sense of preventing "identification love" (Benjamin 1993), can have traumatic effects and encourage the development of a foreign or "false self." According to Winnicott (1990a), the false self is created by the fact that it is not the mother who has a sympathetic understanding for the child's world, but instead that the child adapts to the mother's real or fantasized reactions, needs, or desires.

The conviction not to have been seen contrasts singularly when patients are conspicuously attractive. I had the impression that the exaggerated adoption of current fashions and beauty ideals, or the wearing of extremely odd clothing, was not to be understood as an expression of the typical female vanity attributed to women, but that it was an existential desire to be seen by others, and to be identifiable as an unique individual. In this case it appears as if women who, unlike men, are obliged to have aesthetic bodies, utilize them for an existential function. In other words, the "beautiful body" is linked with interactional and intentional meaning and secures, at least temporarily, the existential feeling of "being in the world."

One patient said, "Every mirror is mine, not to check on how I look, but whether I am still here!"

I therefore doubt that women's choice of less-disfiguring suicide methods means that, even beyond death, women are vainer and, for that reason, avoid behavior that would damage their bodies (Diggory and Rothman 1961). Certainly female aestheticism of the body cannot be claimed as unevidenced fact without considering that the female body is, on the one hand, obliged to be aesthetic, and, on the other, is proclaimed to be especially susceptible to mishap due to its specifically female functions. According to Freud (1933a) "the woman's narcissistic vanity" should be seen as a compensatory reaction to her inferior anatomy. Furthermore, women rarely look at themselves in the mirror to admire themselves, but more likely to inspect themselves self-critically in search of their failings, in which the anticipated male glance is already present (Akashe-Böhme 1992).

When I listened to female patient's fantasies about "the beautiful corpse" (Bronfen 1994), I gained the impression that it was a narcissistic restoration attempt that was connected, on the one hand, with the notion of not being capable of anything but wanting to die beautifully, and, on the other hand, with the hope to reach out beyond death as a beautiful corpse, laid out like Snow White, thereby forcing the others to "repent at the graveside" (Kind 1992).

As different as these patients may have been, they all had one thing in common: when the usual coping system broke down and the menacing sensation of not being seen threatened to overwhelm them, they reacted with suicidal decompensation. "The imprinted childhood trauma, therefore, quite literally retains its 'preverbal nature' and has to be produced either in fantasies or real acts in order to demonstrate itself" (Rohde-Dachser 1986, p. 51).

The spiritual need, evidenced in the suicide attempts, demonstrates that each suicidal act is an acting out, as the unconscious conflict is not experienced but acted out. Due to the dominating feelings of desperation and uselessness, I interpret these female patients' suicidality in this context in the sense of an appealing object-searching function and as a "struggle toward empathy," which is combined with a wish to be seen by the other person and to be present in another person.

Suicidality as an Expression of Unsolved Separation and Individuation Conflicts

My following hypotheses are based on a very special group of fifteen women. The patients were between 32 and 40 years of age and were single with no children. At the beginning of their treatment they differed greatly from other female suicide patients because of their successful careers on the one hand, and the absence of heterosexual or homosexual partnerships on the other (Gerisch 1993a). The motivating causes given by thirteen of the patients were somewhat unspecific, such as minor insults at work or in their private lives. The suicidal crises in two of the patients appeared to have been triggered by separation from their partner. All of the patients shared the fear of no longer being able to work, a reaction they had never experienced before. Before continuing with my theoretical conclusions I wish to present a representative case study.

Case Study

The 39-year-old Ms. K., who was the head secretary to the chief editor of a large regional radio station, appeared at the center for therapy of suicidal behavior after having made an appointment by telephone. She was a tall, blonde, well-built woman who appeared to be self-confident and was very carefully made up and dressed. Her initial self-confidence and controlled manner was emphasized by a clear, deep voice. I spontaneously noticed the contrast between her dark facial makeup and her very red, powerful neck; it was as if there was no connection between the head and the neck, or body. (I later learned that, when she had been born, the umbilical cord wrapped around her neck twice, and that she had only survived thanks to a midwife and her father.) One could sense that the patient was under enormous pressure that she could control only with great effort.

Ms. K. gave a very structured report of her responsible position, which had always been her one support and where she worked up to 60 hours per week. She enjoyed her secretarial work but was afraid of not making intellectual headway. However, for some time—as in previous years—she had been feeling permanently depressed and suicidal and was afraid that she would no longer be able to work. Apart from work, she was a member of a sports club where she exercised excessively up to four times a week. Other than that she did nothing, lived alone, and was extremely isolated. Apart from the depressive phases with latent suicidality, which she had experienced in irregular episodes since childhood, she reported phobic anxieties when driving and extensive psychosomatic symptoms such as attacks of choking and extreme hunger. Ms. K.'s main grievance was that she had never felt herself perceived as "the way I am," aside from her beauty and achievement.

Ms. K. grew up with her parents and a two-and-a-half-years older brother in her paternal grandparent's house. The maternal grandmother also lived with the family. The mother had been a dental assistant, but was later a housewife. The father was a managing director. The mother had always been depressive and had attempted suicide several times, as well as suffered from many illnesses. The mother had often lost consciousness, and it was always the daughter who had to deal with the emergency. As soon as the mother had regained consciousness, she showered her daughter with endless complaints about her husband and son. According to the patient, life at home was always a matter of "life and death." Superficially everything ran smoothly for the patient; she was well-behaved, well-adapted, and was good at school. It had always been the mother's wish that her daughter should be independent and successful in her work. When she was 10, sleeping problems and school anxieties began, but the parents obtained only medication for her. Until she was 25 she continually took benzodiazepine but then underwent inpatient withdrawal.

Conflictual and aggressive arguments had been impossible with the mother. The daughter's reproaches were always met with a diffuse flood of words. She still felt defenseless in the face of a "maternal deluge." Ms. K. repeatedly emphasized that she hated her mother and wished she were dead, but was terrified of just that. She described her father, whom she greatly idealized, as a quiet and introverted man. She had, however, never felt really sure of his affection as he often escaped into his work to avoid the tension at home. The patient remembered that she had sometimes caused small accidents to receive the father's attention. However, as the result of a repeated dream, she now believed that she had been sexually abused by her father. She had always had a good and close relationship with her older brother, and there had been several sexual contacts between them; they were always seen as a "perfect couple." As a result of her efforts at separation from home, she had attempted suicide twice, at the ages of 18 and 20.

When she was 25, she had become engaged to a fellow student who led a double life as a transvestite, and whom she described as "spiritually related." One year later he died as a result of a car accident. All further relationships were purely of a sexual nature, and for the past four years she had rejected all relationships as she could not bear the splitting of "sex and spirit."

If one looks for possible explanations from conventional suicide theories, one is somewhat at a loss. In the case of this patient, and in most of the others there were — with two exceptions — no obvious partnership problems; nor was a real conflict evident. The patients did not appear to be bound by any suicidally predisposing traditional role behavior; also their careers were not — as is often assumed — experienced as burdensome, but supportive. Briefly, one can conclude that these patients' problems elude traditional suicide theories. Observed psychodynamically, the suspicion grew in me that these patients' cases also dealt with an aggression conflict (Freud 1917) and with a narcissistic problem (Henseler 1974), but that the suicidality was especially based on an unsolved separation and individuation process. The separation and individuation process described by Mahler and her colleagues (1968, 1975) is the phase of infant development between the age of 4 and 36 months. During this time, the child gradually develops from an undifferentiated, symbiotic fusion with the mother, to a differentiated and separated individual, with a separate physical and psychological identity of its own. The assumption of an unsolved separation process, resulting from biographical facts and defense mechanisms, proved to be of central importance in the psychodynamics of all fifteen patients.

An early traumatization (e.g., depressive mother; death of the maternal grandmother shortly after the daughter's birth) and the resulting preambivalent mother–daughter fixation caused the establishment of a "bad" and persecuting mother-imago with defended regressive fusion anxieties on the one hand, and a strong yearning for the mother on the other. These patients' fundamental feeling of not having been seen corresponded with their experience as a daughter of having served as a projection surface for the mother's wishes. Early pseudoautonomy contrasted with inadequate separation and individuation from the mother.

In addition to suicidality, the unsolved separation conflict manifested itself in obvious eating disorders with phases of bulimia and anorexia in twelve of the patients during puberty — in some, however, permanently. In spite of their differing concepts, the numerous explanatory patterns of eating disorders are relatively unanimous in judging the mother–daughter relationship, including the unsolved attempts at separation and division, to be the central conflict (Berger 1989b, Steiner-Adair 1992). This core problem was later demonstrated in a conflictive cathexis of the "pregnancy-motherhood" complex. More recent theoretically based attempts at explaining female eating disorders see the core conflict to be that women, in opposition to their relationship orientation, feel an obligation to a false (i.e., male) autonomy ideal (Steiner-Adair 1992). In this connection, attention should also be drawn to an interesting anorexia interpretation by von Braun (1992), who sees not an attempt at separation from the mother, but rather a solidarity act in an attempt to make the egoless, powerless mother visible.

The relationship with the father—who was degraded by the mother as a failure and a weakling—provided further disappointment, either because he was not physically present or was not emotionally available and did not deal with the daughter's needs adequately. This disappointment in the father was permanently warded off by means of his persistent idealization. Turning to and identifying with the idealized father helped to stabilize the achievement area but it could not contribute to the development of a mature, female identity. Although idealization of the father had a stabilizing effect, there were equally serious consequences because idealization was not only bound to the condition that it should never break down, it also proved to be a fragile basis for autonomy (Gerisch 1993a). So as not to be suspected of wishing to further the hypertrophia of the "bad" and "guilty" mother, I emphasize that I am describing the patient's internal experience—her mother-imago—which is not identical with the real mother, although some overlapping cannot be excluded. If the father does not appear in the discussion, it is not because he is of no significance, but because the absence of a third person also seems to be symptomatic for suicidal development (Stork 1986).

From this constellation a female identity problem, in identification with the mother, developed, in the sense of an incomplete development step from identification to identity. Instead of a successful integration of maternal and paternal identification, "two layers of identity" were achieved (Reich 1992), that is, introjection of the degraded mother and partial identification with the idealized father. The important difference between identification and introjection is that identification with the object is selective and partial and normally enhances the ego, whereas introjections are undifferentiated, global, and constricting, and, above all, also include the conflictive and frustrating aspects of the object.

A significant difference between the development of male and female gender identity seems to be that traumatization of any type during the boy's primary relationship with the mother can, if all goes well, be compensated by turning to the father and identifying with him, whereas a girl always identifies with her mother in favor of her female development, regardless of how disappointing she has experienced this to be.

With this background knowledge, I interpret the patients' suicidality as an expression of an unsolved separation and individuation process. Even if the attempted suicide is apparently caused by very different motives, it contains the repeated attempt to create an individual female identity from the mother's on the one hand and, on the other, the desire to maintain the dual union with the mother. The psychodynamics briefly described here can also be observed in the life and work of a variety of female writers, such as Virginia Woolf (1976), Sylvia Plath (1963, 1965, 1975; also see Stevenson 1989, Wagner-Martin 1987), Anne Sexton (1979), Marina Zwetejawa (1979), and Unica Zürn (1969). All of these women committed suicide.

It is generally a difficult and complicated gender-specified development process for a girl to identify with the mother's femininity and, at the same time, to achieve a separate identity from the mother (Bell 1991, Berger 1989a,b, Fast 1984). Berger (1989b), therefore, comes to the conclusion that "female development is linked to an almost continual separation-individuation work-process in the relationship with her own mother, including progressive separation attempts, as well as regressive approach maneuvres" (p. 255).

Sylvia Plath's poetic threat to her mother "Mother, stay out of my yard, I'm becoming another person" (Stevenson 1989, p. 298), expresses an impression frequently mentioned by my patients, that the development of an individual identity can only be achieved by obliterating the mother or the mother identifications. Hatred of the mother is, however, not an ubiquitous and naturally anchored factor in female development but is, as in the case of Ms. K., the result of complex interwoven processes. In that case, it had become a structured conviction, which supported her like a corset.

I propose that the greater the hatred of the mother, that is, the less ability there is of integrating ambivalent feelings, the stronger the self-hatred will be and suicidality all the more of a threat. This aspect is allowed for in Freud's (1917) suicide theory, in which the extermination of an introjected object is preceded by serious ambivalent conflict. The important difference seems to be that a boy's hatred of his mother during the process of dis-identification (Greenson 1978) can mean a temporary psychic relief—at the price, however, that he fears his mother, or women, for the rest of his life—whereas hatred of the mother always affects the girl herself because of the female development identification.

It can be assumed that Ms. K. experienced a depressive mother at an early age, one who was absorbed with herself and her own family conflicts. This early emotional deprivation seemed to have added to her inability to cope with her own depressive position, and to an ego weakness, in the sense of the lability in controlling archaic anger and feelings of hate and, especially, to have encouraged the persistence of splitting processes. All of the good images were applied to the father, and all of the bad and frightening ones to the mother, or to an "inner image of femininity" and, therefore, to herself. She described her condition in a poem as "the divided self." The doubling and splitting of a female identity experienced as damaged was a central moment in this patient's psychodynamics, and manifested itself in double-personality fantasies and depersonalization phenomena.

The untiring efforts of this patient to achieve her own identity was made more difficult from her viewpoint by the fact that she had been functionalized not only by the mother to satisfy her needs, but also as the mother's narcissistic self object. It seems as if the mother always demanded that the daughter achieve the second development step before the first. Pressed into early pseudoautonomy as a caring child-mother, the daughter was prevented from experiencing a period of exclusivity with the mother, to be like her for a time. On investigating the latent content of this hatred of the mother, it appears that she did not initially want divergence but unity with her mother, in the sense of "identification love" (Benjamin 1988, 1993). Her fearful entreaty — "I don't want to be like her" — conceals an anger about the fact that she was not permitted to be like her.

According to the patient's portrayal, the mother appeared to be caught in a traditional web, dependent on her husband's subjectivity with no space to develop her own subjectivity. All of the mother's unlived wishes and potential were, therefore, delegated to the daughter (Dührssen 1967). The mother's wish seemed to indicate that her daughter should have a better life and be independent and successful. Because of this self-degradation the mother's message to her daughter was, Do not be like me, be someone else. This wish, however, also permitted no space for the development of individual self-images but seemed already preformulated by the mother. In contrast to the mother's imagined male femininity ideal, feelings such as anger, envy, fear, and aggression dominated, and these, being explicitly unfeminine and non-ego, had to be warded off. In her identification with the mother's nonautonomous identity, the tortuous splitting she experienced and the feelings of impending doom were continued on two levels. She was not permitted to be herself, nor like her mother, but only allowed to fulfill her mother's fantasies of an ideal. She reported that merely feeling herself as a person meant having no identity and, therefore, no justifiable existence.

In the context of depersonalization, Wurmser (1993) speaks of the "double nature of alienation": to meet the ideals demanded means receiving recognition but not being oneself; not meeting the demands means being oneself but not being seen.

Due to the central feeling of not being acknowledged in her subjectivity, and the feelings of uselessness and hopelessness — which remind one of a "false self" (Winnicott 1990a) — I interpret the patient's first two attempted suicides as an expression of a death-feigning reflex, in the sense of an object-directed function that is connected with the existential hope to be seen by, and to be present in, another person.

The splitting of my patient's female identity, which was marked by incestuous encroachments, manifested itself as a contrast between her ego-ideal reminiscent of a small girl and an externally represented facade of female identity created with effort, in which the attempt and the anxiety of being a woman was equally expressed. On the one hand, she attempted an exaggerated adaption of current fashion and beauty ideals, and, on the other, she presented herself in a muscular body, of which her mother disapproved, as a career woman and a man-hungry "femme fatale."

In the relationship with her transvestite fiancé in which the gender difference appeared erased, sexuality could and should not be experienced, but only the "soul relationship," which she had vainly searched for with her mother, could be. After he died she was no longer able to differentiate "where she began and where he ended," and there had been a strong impulse to follow her friend, the "soul relation," to the grave. On this level I interpret the patient's third suicide attempt to be a result of her early identification with maternal self-destruction, supporting the removal of separation and individuation, and combined with the goal of reintroduction of the dual union with the mother, in the sense of "double suicide" fantasy.

All of my patients lead a futile battle against identification with the degraded mother as they are, indeed, identified with her and irrevocably welded to her idealized image of femininity. They do not want to be like her, but cannot renounce her; they cannot imagine a self-determined life of their own, and have no femininity image of their own. In this double existence there is a gap, which is experienced as insurmountable, between the mother-self and the mother-ideal, that of individuation. In this confusion they would have needed the father to confirm to them — "You are and may be a person other than your mother" — in the sense of acknowledging their autonomy.

For the female child, however, it is of central significance that, even with successful identification with the father, female identity conflicts are created if the girl is confronted with the mother's lack of subjectivity. In other words, it is questionable whether the intervention of a third person or, as for instance Dinnerstein (1976) demands, whether solely a change of the social arrangement during primary socialization can present a way out of the projected unclear mother–child dual union (Benjamin 1993). In agreement with Benjamin I assume that the mother's stable ego identity is a necessary prerequisite for disidentification from her own child. Only the maintenance of the mother's own subjectivity, that is, the defense of her own wishes and her own autonomy, while acknowledging the child at the same time, can prevent the child — entangled in projective processes — from having to remain attached to her as a self object. In the following hypotheses I discuss the unsolved separation and individuation conflicts in detail, using the pregnancy-motherhood complex as an example.

Suicidality as an Expression of the Conflictual Experience of Pregnancy and Potential Motherhood

> *"I should have murdered this, that murders me."*
> Sylvia Plath, "Three Women"

There are numerous epidemiological studies of the rare phenomenon of suicidal acts during or after pregnancy. The studies discuss at which point during pregnancy more or less violent suicide attempts or achieved suicides occur (Schmidke 1988). Triggering factors are generally considered to be hormone changes, including pregnancy psychoses, which are interpreted as hormone dependent. Social reasons or partnership problems are only considered peripherally. It is stated unanimously, however, that pregnancy provides a quasi-natural protection against suicide and attempted suicide. And whenever nature fails to do its duty there is an obstinate denial of the psychic significance of pregnancy, even to the curious premise that suicide during pregnancy is not related to the pregnancy itself (Gerisch 1994).

The following discussion illustrates that, under certain conditions, the suicide's predisposing experience of menstruation, pregnancy, birth, and motherhood is not solely the result of hormone changes, but that the adoption of a stable, mature femininity including motherhood and the "putting oneself at someone's disposal" is, to a great extent, determined by the fate of the primary identification with one's own mother (Berger 1987, 1988, 1989a,b, Bergmann 1991, Besch-Cornelius 1987, Blos 1962, Blum 1978, Bouchart-Godard 1987, Gambaroff 1984, Halberstadt-Freud 1987, 1993, Hardach-Pinke 1982, Jacobsen 1936, Kestenberg 1977, Schilling and Scheer 1993, Wiese 1993).

My deliberations, however—in continuation of Berger (1989b)—are based on the premise "that neither the lack of children nor the existence of a child is an indicator of female and maternal identity stability and the ability of accepting the realities of one's body" (p. 267).

In some of the above-mentioned patients the suicidal crisis or attempted suicide was closely connected with an abortion or the pregnancy-motherhood complex, which was experienced with highly ambivalent feelings or was warded off, so that it frequently did not play a role during initial treatment; only a few patients spoke explicitly of their desire to have a child, but it was mostly a diffuse wish. The important fact was that the patients themselves were not aware of a connection between the suicidal crisis and the pregnancy-motherhood complex, including the unsolved separation conflict. Observed psychodynamically, the patients demonstrated a noticeable mutuality with the so-called split mother described in the literature (Berger 1989a, Bergmann 1991), that is, with those women who, after having had a successful career, decide to have a child shortly before menopause.

The following points, which have already been presented in detail, describe certain conformities observed in all of my patients' psychodynamics and biographies:

1. Identification with the degraded mother and the idealization of the mostly absent or seductive father was of central significance.
2. The fundamental feeling of not being seen and recognized.
3. A relatively successful career, on the one hand, and the predominant lack of a partnership relationship on the other.
4. Due to the experience of having adopted maternal functions, in the sense of parenting the own needy, helpless mother, it appeared impossible for the patients to be able to care for a child as a result of their own defended regressive wishes.
5. Six of the fifteen patients had been unwanted children themselves, and a further five fantasized that they had not been wanted.

The development of a female identity separate from the mother is made additionally complicated for the woman because nature forces the daughter to be similar and to identify with her; that is, the development of specifically female functions, such as menstruation, pregnancy, birth, and menopause, not only repeatedly actualize the early mother–daughter relationship, but also always threaten to endanger the internal separation-individuation process anew (Berger 1989b). According to Blos (1962) a postambivalent relationship to one's own mother is an essential condition for motherhood. The daughter must allow the fantasy of having been the mother's child, and to become the mother of a child. She must develop the fantasies that "good" can come out of her, and she must be allowed to remember having been in the mother's uterus without feeling anxiety. One patient, for instance, reported having read that everyone, and particularly suicidal people, have the wish to return to the womb. She asked me fearfully and with uncertainty whether it were normal if one did not have that wish.

Berger (1989a) summarizes the necessary conditions for motherhood as follows:

> These important conditions refer, first of all, to a relatively stable inner separation from the early infantile and oedipal parent representatives, from which the relationship ability to non-mother and non-father objects, and to mature couple relationships can grow. Secondly, maternal development depends on stable feelings of female identity as well as, thirdly, the transformation of infantile fantasies of wanting a child which lead to a far-reaching renouncement of the imagined aspects of a child for a more mature, maternal adaption to the needs of a child. [p. 23]

Pregnancy fantasies, the wish for a child, real pregnancy, and motherhood not only actualize highly conflictive unconscious aspects, these wishes and fantasies can also be utilized by quite different functions:

1. Collapse of the "symbiotic illusion" with one's own mother and actualization of ambivalent feeling toward her (Gambaroff 1984, Halberstadt-Freud 1993, Wiese 1993). Halberstadt-Freud (1987) describes a symbiotic illusion as a fantasy mother–daughter relationship where, because of the shared gender, awareness is primarily centered on the unseparated similarity rather than on the differences. For this reason, it is more difficult for girls to create a separated, individual female ego.

2. Regressive approach or regressive desires toward one's own mother, on the one hand, and fear of being consumed, on the other (Berger 1987, Bergmann 1991). At the same time, however, the wish to have a child can also express that one's own mother would be forgiven (Bergmann 1991).

3. Actualization of one's own unsolved separation and individuation conflict, including the conviction of only then being able to separate from the mother when one has offered her a "substitute" for oneself in the form of a child (Berger 1989a, Bouchart-Godard 1987).

4. If a high degree of identification with the mother's delegation exists in the daughter, for example, after a successful career and independent life (as with Ms. K.), the wish for a child, including the traditional role division, cannot be fulfilled simply because the daughter would experience this as a breach of loyalty. Furthermore, realization of the wish for a child would require separation from the mother and the maternal identification, which may be desired but can also be combined with separation anxieties.

5. Anxiety-cathected feelings of rivalry can also be kindled when the daughter begins to extricate herself from the "mummy's little girl" position and claims female identity of her own, intruding upon the mother's pregnancy and motherhood domain (Wiese 1993).

6. Pregnancy fantasies and pregnancy can lead to actualization of destructive mother aspects and, therefore, to suicidality. Paranoid fantasies of being both consumed and destroyed by a bad introjection could be created in this way (Berger 1987, p. 113).

In her forensic psychoanalytical study, Wiese (1993) speaks of a mother–daughter–child melting pot, and the closely related involvement of suicide and murder of one's own child. The child is experienced as a part of the self and also as a part of the mother. The aggressive impulse is directed against the child, but equally against the mother as well as against the self. As many as 25 percent of the mothers who have killed their child committed suicide afterward.

Kleiner (1984) also established a conflictive and ambivalent relationship between the woman and her mother as an uninterrupted leading motive. While one half of the ambivalence longed to love and be loved, producing the wish for a child, the other half of the ambivalence caused hatred so that the aggression was not only directed against the mother and one's own child but, by means of double identification, also against the self.

These aspects will now be illustrated by means of short case studies.

The more conflictive and threatening the mother–daughter relationship was experienced, the more anxiety cathected were the pregnancy fantasies, up to the point that these had to be totally warded off. Becoming pregnant then takes place unconsciously.

One patient described her pregnancy at 17 "as if I had conceived a child like the Virgin." After the delivery she handed her daughter over to her mother, whom she hated, in order to cope with her, as yet unresolved, separation conflict; the patient went to another city to complete her education and only dared to take this separation step after she had offered the mother, who had had five children of her own, a substitute for herself. The serious feelings of guilt to have left her own child were rationalized by saying that the "bad" mother had taken the child away from her. Shortly afterward the patient developed serious anorexia and was treated as an inpatient for six months after attempting suicide. Two further suicide attempts followed shortly after the respective abortions.

This same patient often used the term *take away*. I should, for instance, "take away" her mother problem. Or she reported destructive aggressive dreams, which frightened her extremely; she presented me her dreams without any of her own fantasies or ideas, like a foreign body with the implied demand that I should "take them away" or, explained and interpreted — in analogy, fed and diapered — I should give them back to her.

A 30-year-old patient had the fantasy that she should not separate from her mother until she had offered her a child of her own as an adequate substitute. The curious aspect here was that the wish to have a child always developed independent of a father. The man's/father's significance was reduced solely to his reproductive ability. "I must have a child" seemed to be the implied battle cry; not, however, to form a family, but to achieve her separation from the mother with whom she still lived.

A 33-year-old patient experienced a suicidal crisis that appeared superficially to have been caused by the separation from her male partner. The patient was referred to me by a gynecologist with the laconic remark that the patient had "heartache," and that there was a possibility of pregnancy, which was later disproved. The gynecologist had frequently made it plain in the past that the patient should hurry if she wanted a child as her "biological time" was running out.

It became clear that the suicidal crisis was less a question of narcissistic insult because of having been deserted, but more a fear of pregnancy that had actualized the entire complex of the ambivalent mother–daughter relationship. On the one hand, the anxiety consisted of identifying with the mother and of being like her, and, on the other, of becoming a mother herself, which meant a forced separation from the mother, to whom her wishes were still totally oriented.

One patient, who had been placed in an infants home at birth, had herself sterilized when she was 28.

A 40-year-old patient took the pill continuously although she had not had sexual contacts with men for years. In her pregnancy fantasies, which she never actually wanted to realize, there was always a little girl who supported her in her battle for life, just as she had supported her depressive, suicidal mother. Her menstruation was always accompanied by severe pain, suicide impulses, and depersonalization feelings. The identification moment with the mother seemed to move threateningly near, especially during this time, and a warding off of this regressive maelstrom was attempted with this depersonalization.

She wrote: "During my period I am not myself, I feel like a shattered mirror, metallic and as if I am in a trance."

In this context, the following recommendation by a physician appears to be more than questionable in dealing with premenstrual tension, in which the "solution becomes a problem":

> If girls could clearly and consciously connect their emotional fluctuations with menstruation, they could perhaps view the feelings that result from premenstrual tension as not belonging to the self. They could say, At this time I am not myself because I will soon have my period and am affected as a result, affected by changes within my body; this is not really my behavior. [Douvan 1970, quoted in Steiner-Adair 1992, p. 244]

In addition, it became apparent that patients felt bound to the ideal of a "superwoman," that is, they had the impression that they had to cope with, and integrate all areas of life, such as career, partnership, children, family, and friends, without problems. Almost all of the patients also fantasized that as a woman with a child they would automatically have to become like their own mother, which meant having to renounce their career and independence in favor of financial and emotional dependency on the man. Along with a mother's real social conflict, which should not be belittled, this fantasy illustrates the deficient separation from one's own mother, which prevented the daughter from developing her own individual femininity image, in the sense of a "non-mother."

Suicidality as an Expression of the Wish for Individuation and Autonomy

In some of the above-mentioned fifteen patients, the suicidal crisis was caused by a breakdown of the existence-stabilizing, achievement-oriented defense mechanism in the sense of sublimation. According to Freud, sublimation describes a process in which instinctual wishes can be converted into artistic or intellectual productivity, which can bind them. The breakdown did not result from a lack of authenticity of this premature sublimation but, according to Green (1993) "sublimations soon reveal their inability to play a harmonising role in the psychic economy. The subject remains vulnerable in one specific area; in her love life" (p. 217).

Along with the classical role division, the following peculiarities could be observed in the patients described here: The mother's ego-ideal (and later that of the daughter) was not directed exclusively by the image of the "perfect mother" (Chodorow 1978) but included definite "male" wishes. The central point, therefore, in which these patients' fates clearly differed from other women's and from that of their mothers' was that they had received early signals that they should not make themselves dependent on men. For this reason the daughter was acknowledged predominantly in the achievement area, in the sense of mother's loyal substitute or "bound delegate" (Stierlin 1978), and the mother developed precise career plans for the daughter, with financial security as the goal. This decision was, however, also not the daughter's original wish but was the "inheritance from her mother," because the mother's delegation implied the daughter's identification with the idealized father and his principles reserved for the male, such as ambition and the striving for a successful career. While the mother intended the daughter's autonomy, she, in turn, saw a career as a way of being independent not of a man but, initially, of the mother. With this background description the discrepancy between the consciously perceived conflict, which motivated the suicide attempt, and the unconscious conflict becomes clear (Henseler 1981). It was decisive that comparable experiences in the past could be coped with by means of compensatory achievement, whereas during the actual crisis the proven defense mechanism threatened to collapse. Career stability was needed for defense and for securing identity. On the one hand, it was a guarantee of independence from the mother and combined a certain narcissistic gratification. In fulfilling the maternal wishes, on the other hand, the fantasy of unseparated duality with the mother could at the same time be maintained, at the price that necessary steps toward individuation were again avoided.

Furthermore, career achievements represented the bond with the idealized father, who also functioned as a guarantee of independency from the mother. Maintaining efficiency meant, in short, that the involved and warded-off relationship difficulties and anxieties remained concealed. That means that not the conscious conflict but only its subsequent reaction implied by the defense breakdown revealed the fundamental conflict and caused the suicidal conflict. The "two layers of identity" (Reich 1992) solidified to a rigid "either-or pattern" with success and career on the one hand, and anxieties of being consumed and identity loss on the other. All of the patients expressed threatening and hardly realistic prognoses regarding the fantasy that they could stop functioning perfectly and fail in their work. Along with the battle to maintain their functional ability there was, at the same time, a strong urge to fail in order to frustrate the mother's plans.

Ms. K. reported, "This hatred of the parents who never loved me as I am but only as they intended me to be. I never found myself in that. I always had the feeling that if I did something that was not within their expectations a great destruction would overcome me. It is not the desired heroine who has come out of this but a ruined suicide-hungry creature."

Ms. K.'s words provide a graphic background for my final hypothesis—in agreement with von Braun (1992)—that the creation of epoch-related female symptoms such as hysteria, anorexia, bulimia, and suicidality has always been expressed by paradoxes of affirmation and denial, autonomy and dependence, rebellion and betrayal of loyalty, and the wish to live and the wish to die. In this sense I understand the attempted suicide as an act of "autonomous self-authorship" (Bronfen 1987) in which not the refusal "to be a woman" is expressed but the refusal to identify with an identity model, traditionally defined heteronomously as well as by the mother. The female body, which Artemidoros likened to a writing slate, should be withheld from foreign inscriptions and inscribed with its own wordlessly enacted conflict. Only in this sense can Schmidt's (1938) metaphor of "theatrical suicide" be maintained as a physical production of hidden suffering and the desire to produce a self-defined life. The wish to fail and die in order to liberate oneself from the various identifications in favor of the so-far failed individuation and autonomy justifies understanding suicide/attempted suicide in the sense of a self-healing attempt, or, as Tilmann Moser (1985)—referring to Winnicott (1990a)—states "the last act to save the real or true self from the unbearable, permanently and agonisingly experienced destruction of the real from false self, forced upon it externally or by identifications" (p. 165).

REFERENCES

Adorno, T. W., and Horkheimer, M. (1947). *Dialektik der Aufklärung*. Frankfurt a.M.: Fischer.

Akashe-Böhme, F., ed. (1992). Frau/Spiegel—Frau und Spiegel. In *Reflexionen vor dem Spiegel, Gender Studies*, pp. 9–11. Frankfurt a.M.: Suhrkamp.

Balint, E. (1963). On being empty of oneself. *International Journal of Psycho-Analysis* 44:470–480.

Balint, M. (1968). *Therapeutische Aspekte der Regression: Die Theorie der Grundstörung*. Stuttgart: Klett.

Beauvoir, S. de. (1951). *Das andere Geschlecht*. Reinbek bei Hamburg: Rowohlt.

Bell, K. (1991). Aspekte weiblicher Entwicklung. *Forum der Psychoanalyse* 7:111-126.

Benedetti, G. (1983). *Todeslandschaften der Seele*. Göttingen: Vandenhoeck & Ruprecht.

Benjamin, J. (1986). Die Entfremdung des Verlangens: Der Masochismus der Frauen und die ideale Liebe. In *Psychoanalyse der Frau jenseits von Freud*, ed. J. Alpert, pp. 123-149. Berlin: Springer.

———— (1988). *The Bonds of Love: Psychoanalysis, Feminism and the Problem of Domination*. New York: Pantheon.

———— (1993). *Phantasie und Geschlecht: Studien über Idealisierung, Anerkennung und Differenz*. Basel: Stroemfeld.

Berger, M. (1987). Das verstörte Kind mit seiner Puppe—Zur Schwangerschaft in der frühen Adoleszenz. *Praxis der Kinderpsychologie und Kinderpsychiatrie* 36:107-117.

———— (1988). Die Mutter unter der Maske: Zur Entwicklungsproblematik von Kindern adoleszenter Eltern. *Praxis der Kinderpsychologie und Kinderpsychiatrie* 37:333-345.

———— (1989a). Klinische Erfahrungen mit späten Müttern und ihrem Wunschkind. *Praxis der Kinderpsychologie und Kinderpsychiatrie* 38:16-24.

———— (1989b). Zur Bedeutung des "Anna-selbdritt"—Motivs für die Beziehung der Frau zum eigenen Körper und zu ihrem Kind. In *Der eigene Körper als Objekt*, ed. M. Hirsch, pp. 241-277. Berlin: Springer.

Bergmann, M. V. (1991). "Rollenumkehr," verspätete Ehe und Mutterschaft. *Psyche* 45:17-37.

Besch-Cornelius, J. (1987). *Psychoanalyse und Mutterschaft*. Göttingen: Vandenhoeck & Ruprecht.

Blos, P. (1962). *On Adolescence: A Psychoanalytic Interpretation*. New York: Free Press.

Blum, H. P. (1978). Reconstruction in postpartum depression. *Psychoanalytic Study of the Child* 33:335-362. New Haven, CT: Yale University Press.

Bouchart-Godard, A. (1987). Entwicklungsweg einer Tochter. In *Die übertragene Mutter: Psychoanalytische Beiträge*, ed. U. Konnertz, pp. 19-28. Tübingen: Edition diskord.

Bovenschen, S. (1979). *Die imaginierte Weiblichkeit: Exemplarische Untersuchungen zu kulturgeschichtlichen und literarischen Präsentationsformen des Weiblichen*. Frankfurt a.M.: Suhrkamp.

Braun, C. von (1985). *Nicht ich: Logik, Lüge, Libido*. Frankfurt a.M.: Verlag Neue Kritik.

———— (1989). *Die schamlose Schönheit des Vergangenen: Zum Verhältnis von Geschlecht und Geschichte*. Frankfurt a.M.: Verlag Neue Kritik.

———— (1992). Das Kloster im Kopf: Weibliches Fasten von mittelalterlicher Askese zu moderner Anorexie. In *Weibliche Adoleszenz: Zur Sozialisation junger Frauen*, ed. K. Flaake, and V. King, pp. 213-239. Frankfurt a.M.: Campus.

Bronfen, E. (1987). Die schöne Leiche. Weiblicher Tod als motivische Konstante von der Mitte des 18. Jahrhunderts bis in die Moderne. In *Weiblichkeit und Tod in der Literatur*, ed. R. Berger, and I. Stephan, pp. S87-115. Köln: Böhlau.

———— (1994). *Nur über ihre Leiche: Tod, Weiblichkeit und Ästhetik*. München: Kunstmann.

Canetto, S. (1992). She died for love and he for glory: gender myths of suicidal behavior. *Omega* 26:1-17.

Chasseguet-Smirgel, J., ed. (1964). *Psychoanalyse der weiblichen Sexualität*. Frankfurt a.M.: Suhrkamp, 1974.

———— (1986). *Zwei Bäume im Garten: Zur psychischen Bedeutung der Vater- und Mutterbilder*. München: Verlag Internationale Psychoanalyse.

Chodorow, N. (1978). *The Reproduction of Mothering: Psychoanalysis and the Sociology of Gender*. Berkeley, CA: University of California.

Diggory, J. C., and Rothman, D. Z. (1961). Values destroyed by death. *Journal of Abnormal and Social Psychology* 63:205-210.

Dinnerstein, D. (1976). *The Mermaid and the Minotaur: Sexual Arrangements and Human Malaise*. New York: Harper & Row.

Dührssen, A. (1967). *Zum Problem des Selbstmords bei jungen Mädchen*. Göttingen: Verlag für medizinische Psychologie.

Durkheim, E. (1987). *Der Selbstmord*. Frankfurt a.M.: Suhrkamp.

Eagle, M. N. (1984). *Recent Developments in Psychoanalysis: A Critical Evaluation.* New York: McGraw-Hill.

Fast, I. (1984). *Gender Identity.* Hillsdale, NJ: Analytic Press.

Federn, P. (1929). Selbstmordprophylaxe in der Analyse. *Zeitschrift für Psychoanalytische Pädagogik* 3:379-389.

Fliess, R. (1961). *Ego and Body Ego: Contributions to their Psychoanalytic Psychology.* New York: International Universities Press.

Foucault, M. (1976). *Sexualität und Wahrheit.* Frankfurt a.M.: Suhrkamp.

Freud, S. (1896). Zur Ätiologie der Hysterie. *Standard Edition* 3:187-221.

_____ (1900). The interpretations of dreams. *Standard Edition* 4/5:1-626.

_____ (1905). Drei Abhandlungen zur Sexualtheorie. *Standard Edition* 7:123-243.

_____ (1917). Mourning and melancholia. *Standard Edition* 14:237-258.

_____ (1920). The psychogenesis of a case of homosexuality in a woman. *Standard Edition* 18:145-172.

_____ (1933a). Femininity. In New Introductory Lectures on Psychoanalysis. *Standard Edition* 22:112-135.

_____ (1933b). Die Zerlegung der psychischen Persönlichkeit. In New Introductory Lectures on Psychoanalysis. *Standard Edition* 22:57-80.

Gambaroff, M. (1984). *Utopie der Treue.* Reinbek bei Hamburg: Rowohlt.

Gaupp, R. (1905). *Über den Selbstmord.* München: Gmelin.

Gerisch, B. (1993a). Aspekte zum psychodynamischen Verständnis der Suizidalität bei Frauen. *Forum der Psychoanalyse* 9:198-213.

_____ (1993b). Übertragung und Gegenübertragung aus einer geschlechterdifferenten Perspektive. In *Suizidalität: Deutungsmuster und Praxisansätze,* ed. T. Giernalczyk, and E. Frick, pp. 107-110. Regensburg: Roderer Verlag.

_____ (1994). *"Auf den Leib geschrieben": Der weibliche Körper als Projektionsfläche männlicher Phantasien zum Suizidverhalten von Frauen.* Paper presented at the Hamburg Symposium: "Kurzpsychotherapie mit Suizidgefährdeten?" (Short-term psychotherapy with suicidal patients?), Hamburg, March.

Gerisch, B., and Köhler, T. (1993). Freuds Aufgabe der "Verführungstheorie": Eine quellenkritische Sichtung zweier Rezeptionsversuche. *Psychologie und Geschichte* 4:229-246.

Gilligan, C. (1982). *In a Different Voice.* Cambridge: Harvard University Press.

Goldner, V. (1992). Liebe und Gewalt: geschlechtsspezifische Paradoxe in instabilen Beziehungen. *Familiendynamik* 17:109-140.

Grande, T., Wilke, S., and Nübling, R. (1992). Symptomschilderungen und initiale Beziehungsangebote. *Zeitschrift für Psychosomatische Medizin und Psychoanalyse* 38:31-48.

Green, A. (1993). Die tote Mutter. *Psyche* 47:205-240.

Greenson, R. R. (1978). *Explorations in Psychoanalysis.* New York: International Universities Press.

Habermas, J. (1971). Der Universalitätsanspruch der Hermeneutik. In *Theorie-Diskussion: Hermeneutik und Ideologiekritik,* ed. K. O. Apel, et al., pp. 120-159. Frankfurt a.M.: Suhrkamp.

Halberstadt-Freud, H. C. (1987). Die symbiotische Illusion in der Mutter-Tochter-Beziehung. In *Bei Lichte betrachtet wird es finster,* ed. Psychoanalytisches Seminar Zürich, pp. 139-165. Frankfurt a.M.: FrauenSichten, Athenäum.

_____ (1993). Postpartale Depression. *Psyche* 47:1041-1062.

Hammer, S. (1978). *Töchter und Mütter.* Frankfurt a.M.: Fischer.

Hardach-Pinke, I. (1982). Schwangerschaft und Identität. In *Die Wiederkehr des Körpers,* ed. D. Kamper, and C. Wulf, pp. 193-208. Frankfurt a.M.: Suhrkamp.

Hausen, K., and Nowotny, H., eds. (1986). *Wie männlich ist die Wissenschaft?* Frankfurt a.M.: Suhrkamp.

Henseler, H. (1974). *Narzisstische Krisen: Zur Psychodynamik des Selbstmords.* Opladen: Westdeutscher Verlag.

———— (1981). Krisenintervention — Vom bewussten zum unbewussten Konflikt des Suizidanten. In *Selbstmordgefährdung: Zur Psychodynamik und Psychotherapie*, ed. H. Henseler, and C. Reimer, pp. 136–156. Stuttgart: Frommann-holzboog.

Henseler, H., and Reimer, C., eds. (1981). *Selbstmordgefährdung: Zur Psychodynamik und Psychotherapie*. Stuttgart: Frommann-holzboog.

Hirsch, M., ed. (1989). *Der eigene Körper als Objekt*, pp. 1–32. Berlin: Springer.

Jacobsen, E. (1936). Beitrag zur Entwicklung des weiblichen Kind-Wunsches. *Internationale Zeitschrift für Psychoanalyse* 22:371–379.

Jordan, J. V., and Surrey, J. L. (1986). The self-in-relation: empathy and the mother–daughter relationship. In *The Psychology of Today's Woman*, ed. T. Bernay, and D. W. Cantor, pp. 81–100. Hillsdale, NJ: Analytic Press.

Kestenberg, J. (1977). Regression and reintegration in pregnancy. In *Female Psychology: Contemporary Psychoanalytic Views*, ed. H. Blum, pp. 213–250. New York: International Universities Press.

———— (1988). Der komplexe Charakter der weiblichen Identität: Betrachtungen zum Entwicklungsverlauf. *Psyche* 42:349–364.

Kind, J. (1992). *Suizidal: Psychoökonomie einer Suche*. Göttingen: Vandenhoeck & Ruprecht.

Kleiner, G. J. (1984). *Suicide in Pregnancy*. Boston: John Wright.

Klemann, M. (1983). *Zur frühkindlichen Erfahrung suizidaler Patienten*. Frankfurt a.M.: Peter Lang.

Kneissl, M. (1984). *Suizidversuche bei Frauen*. Dissertation am Fachbereich Erziehungswissenschaften.

———— (1985). Geschlechtsspezifisches Verhalten und Suizidversuche bei Frauen. *Suizidprophylaxe* 12:280–293.

Kohut, H. (1967). Die psychoanalytische Behandlung narzisstischer Persönlichkeitsstörungen. In *Die Zukunft der Psychoanalyse*, pp. 173–204. Frankfurt a.M.: Suhrkamp.

Konnertz, U. ed. (1987). *Die übertragene Mutter: Psychoanalytische Beiträge*. Tübingen: Edition diskord.

Krebs, W. (1982). *Zukunftserleben und Selbsttötung* (Dissertation). Frankfurt a.M.: Verlag Peter Lang.

Kuhn, T. S. (1962). *The Structure of Scientific Revolutions*. Chicago: University of Chicago Press.

Laqueur, T. (1990). *Making Sex: Body and Gender from the Greeks to Freud*. Cambridge: Harvard University Press.

Lester, D. (1979). Sex differences in suicidal behavior. In *Gender and Disordered Behavior: Sex Differences in Psychopathology*, ed. E. S. Gomberg, and V. Franks, pp. 287–300. New York: Brunner/Mazel.

Linden, K. (1969). *Der Suizidversuch*. Stuttgart: Enke.

Lindner-Braun, C. (1990). *Soziologie des Selbstmords*. Opladen: Westdeutscher Verlag.

Mahler, N. (1968). *Symbiose und Individuation, Bd. 1: Psychosen im frühen Kindesalter*. Stuttgart: Klett-Cotta.

Mahler, M., Pine, F., and Bergmann, A. (1975). *Die psychische Geburt des Menschen*. Frankfurt a.M.: Fischer.

McDougall, J. (1978). *Plädoyer für eine gewisse Anormalität*. Frankfurt a.M.: Suhrkamp.

Mitscherlich, M. (1985). *Die friedfertige Frau*. Frankfurt a.M.: Fischer.

Mitscherlich-Nielsen, M. (1978). Zur Psychoanalyse der Weiblichkeit. *Psyche* 32:669–694.

Moser, T. (1985). *Romane als Krankengeschichten*. Frankfurt a.M.: Suhrkamp.

Olivier, C. (1980). *Jokastes Kinder: Die Psyche der Frau im Schatten der Mutter*. Düsseldorf: Claassen.

Plath, S. (1963). *The Bell Jar*. London: William Heinemann.

———— (1965). *Ariel*. London: Faber & Faber.

———— (1968). *Three Women*. London: Turret.

———— (1975). *Sylvia Plath: Letters Home, 1950–1963*. New York: Harper & Row.

Reich, G. (1992). Identitätskonflikte bulimischer Patientinnen. *Forum der Psychoanalyse* 8:121–133.

Rohde-Dachser, C. (1986). Ringen um Empathie. *Forum der Psychoanalyse* 2:44–58.

_____ (1989a). Abschied von der Schuld der Mütter. *Praxis für Psychotherapie und Psychosomatik* 34:250-256.

_____ (1989b). Unbewusste Phantasie und Mythenbildung in psychoanalytischen Theorien über die Differenz der Geschlechter. *Psyche* 43:193-218.

_____ (1990). Weiblichkeitsparadigmen in der Psychoanalyse. *Psyche* 44:30-52.

_____ (1991). *Expedition in den dunklen Kontinent: Weiblichkeit im Diskurs der Psychoanalyse.* Berlin: Springer.

Rousseau-Dujardin, J. (1987). Ausser sich. In *Die übertragene Mutter. Psychoanalytische Beiträge*, ed. U. Konnertz, pp. 53-76. Tübingen: Edition diskord.

Rudolf, G., and Stratmann, H. (1989). Psychogene Störungen bei Männern und Frauen. *Zeitschrift für psychosomatische Medizin und Psychoanalyse* 35:201-219.

Schilling, G., and Scheer, J. F. (1993). Der versagte Kinderwunsch – Zur Bedeutung des Kindes und der Kinderlosigkeit. *Familiendynamik* 18:359-370.

Schmidke, A. (1988). *Verhaltenstheoretisches Erklärungsmodell suizidalen Verhaltens.* Regensburg: Roderer Verlag.

Schmidt, G. (1938). Erfahrungen an 700 Selbstmordversuchen. *Nervenarzt* 11:353-358.

Schuller, M. (1990). *Im Unterschied: Lesen/Korrespondieren/Adressieren.* Frankfurt a.M.: Verlag Neue Kritik.

Schwarz, F. (1946). *Probleme des Selbstmordes.* Bern: Huber.

Sexton, A. (1979). *A Self-Portrait in Letters*, ed. L. G. Sexton, and L. Ames. Boston: Houghton Mifflin.

Spitz, R. A. (1963). Das Leben und der Dialog. *Psyche* 26:149-164.

Steiner-Adair, C. (1992). Körperstrategien: Weibliche Adoleszenz und die Entwicklung von Essstörungen. In *Weibliche Adoleszenz: Zur Sozialisation junger Frauen*, ed. K. Flaake, and V. King, pp. 240-253. Frankfurt a.M.: York Campus.

Stevenson, A. (1989). *Bitter Fame: A Life of Sylvia Plath.* Boston: Houghton Mifflin.

Stierlin, H. (1978). *Delegation und Familie: Beiträge zum Heidelberger familiendynamischen Konzept.* Frankfurt a.M.: Suhrkamp.

Stolorow, R. D. (1975). Die narzisstische Funktion des Masochismus (und Sadismus). In *Leiden am Selbst: Zum Phänomen des Masochismus*, ed. J. Grunert, pp. 94-111. München: Kindler.

Stork, J., ed. (1986). *Das Vaterbild in Kontinuität und Wandel.* Stuttgart: Frommann-holzboog.

Wagner-Martin, L. (1987). *Sylvia Plath: A Biography.* New York: Simon & Schuster.

Weigel, S. (1989). *Die Stimme der Medusa: Schreibweisen in der Gegenwartsliteratur von Frauen.* Reinbek bei Hamburg: Rowohlt.

Weigel, S., and Stephan, I. (1983). *Die verborgene Frau: Literatur im historischen Prozess.* Berlin: Argument Verlag.

Wiese, A. (1993). *Mütter, die töten: Psychoanalytische Erkenntnis und forensische Wahrheit.* München: Wilhelm Fink Verlag.

Winnicott, D. W. (1990a). Ego distortion in terms of true and false self. In *The Maturational Processes and the Facilitating Environment*, pp. 182-199. Frankfurt a.M.: Fischer.

_____ (1990b). Mirror-role of mother and family in child development. In *Playing and Reality*, pp. 128-135. Stüttgart: Klett-Cotta.

Woolf, V. (1976). *Augenblicke: Skizzierte Erinnerungen.* Stuttgart: Deutsche Verlags-Anstalt.

Wurmser, L. (1993). *Die Maske der Scham.* Berlin: Springer.

Zürn, U. (1969). *Der Mann im Jasmin: Dunkler Frühling.* Frankfurt a.M.: Ullstein.

Zwetejawa, M. (1979). *Mutter und die Musik.* Frankfurt a.M.: Suhrkamp.

14: CULTURAL DYNAMICS AND SUICIDE IN JAPAN

Yoshitomo Takahashi and Douglas Berger

An overview of all the intricacies of Japanese behavior and unconscious thought processes discussed in the literature would necessitate a book of its own. For the purposes of this chapter we introduce a few issues related to the Japanese concept of the unconscious. First, there is an overwhelming and intense desire for the establishment of an identity by belonging to a group (Berger 1985, Christopher 1983, Doi 1973, Sugiyama-Lebra 1976). A sense of oneness (*ittaikan*) is generated unconsciously with the group, and there is a social sensitivity to any possible disruptions in the harmony of this relationship. Ostracism from the group is to be avoided at all costs. There are pressures to conform to a limited pattern of behavior and thought and an expectation for a total commitment to the group.

A consequence of this is that both the pride and shame of an individual are shared by the group, and vice versa. Shame, conscious and unconscious, is thus quite powerful and is often an important factor in suicide in Japan. Guilt is involved in relationships of reciprocity where a favor (*on*) is accompanied by the burden of the duty of reciprocity (*giri*), which may be very intense and emotionally uncomfortable. (This is in contrast to the Western sense of guilt that stems from an internal sense that one has done something wrong.) This sense of a never-ending "owing" is quite pervasive in the unconscious of the Japanese especially in relation to those who have taken care of you.

Suicidal Japanese have similar risk factors for suicide to those in other countries, including psychiatric disorders, substance abuse, prior suicide attempts, lack of social support systems, male gender, older age, various kinds of loss, family history of suicide, and accident proneness (Takahashi 1992,

1993a,b). English-language reports on suicide in Japan often overemphasize the cultural differences. With this caveat in mind, this chapter discusses some of the culturally related dynamics and unconscious processes related to suicide in Japan. After a review of the demographics, we present two exemplary kinds of suicide peculiar to the Japanese context—*shinju* and *inseki jisatsu*.

STATISTICS

After World War II, there was a peak in the number and the rate of suicide in Japan in the 1950s, followed by a declining tendency, and then a second peak in the mid-1980s (National Police Agency 1993, Takahashi 1993a). In 1986 there were 25,524 suicides in Japan, the highest number in any year since the war. However, since 1987 both the number and the rate of suicides gradually decreased despite various socioeconomic problems, such as changes in social values and family structure, increases in crime and substance abuse, severe competition in society, and a widening gap between the rich and the poor. All of these factors have been reported by suicidologists to be associated with an increasing suicide rate. In 1992 the declining tendency waned and there were 22,104 suicides, an increase of 4.8 percent. The economic recession might account for this increase, but any meaningful interpretation should be postponed for several more years.

In summary, there have been about 21,000 to 22,000 suicides in Japan annually in recent years, which represents a suicide rate of 17 to 18 per 100,000 per year. Although this number is about twice as many as that of those killed by traffic accidents, attention to suicide prevention in Japan has unfortunately not been adequate.

As for the variation in suicide rates by age, in the 1950s and 1960s the suicide rate showed two peaks, one in young adults and one in the elderly. At that time, Japan had one of the highest suicide rates in the world. For the past three decades, the suicide rate in young people has been decreasing. The suicide rate in the elderly has also decreased, but this decrease has not been very large. Thus, Japanese still exhibit higher suicide rates with increasing age. In 1992, while those over 65 years old accounted for 13 percent of the population, suicides in this age group represented 27 percent of all suicides. While suicide is an especially serious problem for the elderly, it has been mostly ignored by Japanese society (Takahashi et al. 1995).

Although it has been suggested that attitudes toward suicide vary between cultures, there have been few comparative studies between Japan and other cultures. Domino and Takahashi (1991) studied medical students' attitudes toward suicide in Japan and the United States using the Suicide Opinion Questionnaire, and the findings indicated that the Japanese students were more likely to think that suicide is not always an abnormal behavior and that it might be permissible in certain situations. In contrast, the American students were more likely to think that suicide is usually a result of some psychiatric problem with aggression expressed toward oneself, and that suicide should be prevented. Because the sample size was limited in this study, the findings should not be overgeneralized. The study is meaningful, however, because it utilized the same data base in both countries. The results suggest that, in a culture where suicide may be permissible, social factors may need to be taken into consideration. Attitudes toward suicide may differ in these cultures even if the suicide takes place while the person is in a normal mental state.

SHINJU

The word *shinju* in Japanese originally meant a mutual suicide agreement by lovers in order to prove the genuineness of their love to each other. According to the strict and original definition given by Ohara (1985), *shinju* is an act in which more than two people commit suicide voluntarily at the same place, at the same time, and for the same purpose. The definition has become looser and now also includes murder-suicides where some of those involved are killed against their will (Fukushima 1984). The definition of *shinju* now includes both a genuine suicide pact, extended suicide (assisted suicide followed by suicide), and murder-suicide in which the killer and the victim(s) have a strong emotional tie with each other before the act. The feeling of oneness of those involved in *shinju* is important.

Shinju literally means "heart-inside" or "oneness of hearts" (Walsh 1969), and this probably reflects a psychological joining of the participants. (The heart character also means mind or spirit.) The participants may possibly have a conscious awareness of wanting to join or unite with their partner in the afterlife, but unconsciously there may be a wish for infantile symbiosis and an intolerance of separation anxiety. The development of clear ego boundaries is probably impaired in these individuals, although state-related regressions (related to depression or psychosis) may also be at play in some individuals. Uniting with their suicide partner may be a reaction to failure to fit into society or a group.

The Japanese language has diverse words for *shinju*. *Shinju* has been classified into two major categories, *johshi* (mutually consented lovers' suicide) and *oyako-shinju* (parent–child suicide), the latter of which is subclassified further such as *boshi-shinju* (mother–child suicide), *fushi-shinju* (father–child suicide), and *ikka-shinju* (family suicide). The number of *johshi* have been declining in the past three decades. Although the number of *oyako-shinju* has been declining since the 1950s as well, it is still a serious problem.

Most cases of *shinju* are *boshi-shinju* in which the children, who are too young to decide on suicide themselves, are killed by their mothers. Ohara

(1963, 1965) and Inamura (1977, 1993) have both pointed out that *boshi-shinju* and *fushi-shinju* have important differences. In *boshi-shinju*, mothers in their twenties and thirties kill their children and then commit suicide. The children most often victimized in *boshi-shinju* are of preschool age. In *fushi-shinju*, the fathers (who are usually older than the *boshi-shinju* mothers) kill their children (who are older than the victims of *boshi-shinju*), and then commit suicide. The most common reasons for *boshi-shinju* are psychiatric disorder and family conflict, while those of *fushi-shinju* are financial problems and physical illness. Japanese often show considerable sympathy toward parents who are not able to find any other recourse but to commit suicide with their children.

Japanese society as a whole fosters a mutual interdependency in the socialization process, in contrast to the emphasis placed on individuality in the West (Christopher 1983). To promote this mutual dependency there is probably some unconscious muting of the separation-individuation process on the part of caregivers as described by Margaret Mahler (1972). As a consequence, the boundaries, both conscious and unconscious, in one's nuclear family can be more blurred than in Western society, and this may have led to the development of *shinju* as a Japanese cultural phenomenon. Postpartum depression may also be an important factor in *boshi-shinju*.

Marzuk and colleagues (1992) have reviewed research on murder-suicide, but their use of the term has some important differences from *shinju*. Thus, it should be kept in mind that *murder-suicide* and *shinju* are not quite the same, an indication that suicide is often interpreted differently in different cultures, as will be discussed below.

Marzuk and colleagues reviewed the studies on suicide published in the United States over the past 30 years and found that the incidence of murder-suicide was 0.2 to 0.3 per 100,000 per year. The overall suicide rate, which has been fairly stable over this period in the United States, was about 12. They estimated, therefore, that the proportion of murder-suicides among all suicides was about 1.7 to 2.5 percent. They also reviewed seventeen papers published from 1900 to 1979 in various countries in North America and Europe and found that the rates of murder-suicide in those countries were similar, 0.2 to 0.3. While the reason for this similarity is not clear, Marzuk and colleagues point out that, although the incidence of murder-suicide is similar, the type of murder-suicide may differ from country to country. For example, in the United States one-half to three-quarters of murder-suicides are those in which a husband murders his wife and then kills himself. In Britain and Japan, most murder-suicides are those in which a mother kills her children and then commits suicide.

Inamura (1993) reported that *shinju* has accounted for 1.6 percent of recent suicides. Based on this figure, the rate of *shinju* is estimated to be 0.29 per 100,000 per year, which is similar to that reported by Marzuk and colleagues. In Japan, the type of *shinju* has been changing; in 1950s *johshi* was the most prevalent, but since the 1960s the number of *boshi-shinju* has become the most common.

While the incidence of murder-suicide is not all that different in different cultures, each society deals with it differently, as Marzuk and colleagues have noted. Aizawa (1975) states, "The important thing in studying the relationship between *shinju* and Japanese culture is not to focus only on statistical analysis and literature on *shinju* in Japan and other cultures, but to concentrate on the sympathy Japanese have toward *shinju*" (p. 143).

Similar cases may be interpreted differently in different cultures. Most Western cultures would consider *oyako-shinju* to be murder-suicide, and not parent–child suicide, because the children usually do not commit suicide of their own free will, but are killed by their parents. A case in Santa Monica, California was a typical example of this kind of suicide (*Japan Times* 1985). On January 29, 1985, a 32-year-old Japanese immigrant woman tried to drown herself, her infant daughter, and her 4-year-old son by entering the ocean on Santa Monica Beach. Although they were quickly pulled out of the water, only the mother survived. She was tried in California court for child abuse and first-degree murder. When this was reported in Japan, it shocked Japanese society. There was also the added feature for the Japanese of being subjected to foreign censure in this case, something not easily accepted.

This mother had attempted *oyako-shinju* about a week after discovering that her husband had been having a secret extramarital affair for years, leaving her depressed and ruminating about suicide. The reasons for her despair were personal, and, although maladaptive, the method she chose to resolve it was cultural, and very Japanese.

Although she had lived in the United States for fourteen years, she remained Japanese in her thinking and lifestyle, isolated from American culture. She did not drive, spoke little English, knew nothing of her husband's business, and had no hobbies or close friends outside the family. In other words, she was virtually without any kind of support system that might have sustained her in time of emotional distress. Social supports have been found to be important for preventing suicide in Western society (Berger 1993).

In Japan, the mother–child bond and the mother's dedication to the child are very important. Why then, is infanticide committed by the mother relatively common in Japan? Paradoxically, it is this very bond between mother and child that causes *oyako-shinju*. According to Japanese logic, the suicidal mother cannot bear to leave the child to survive alone; she would rather kill the child because she believes that nobody else in the world would take care of the child better than she, and that the child would be better off dying with her.

This feeling of oneness (which may be delusional in nature) and symbiosis between a mother and her children has intensified as a result of the breakdown of the traditional community in which children belonged to a wider circle and where they had fictive as well as substitute parents along with their real parents. Today, because of the development of the close-knit nuclear family, children, particularly those of preschool age, belong to their parents alone. The mother–child bond may also be reinforced in Japanese-society because females do not usually have the emotional and social supports afforded by a career, owing to the male-focused orientation in the workplace, the lack of an outside social support system, and a twenty-four-hour focus on the family.

When *boshi-shinju* takes place, sympathy is usually given to the mother who was not able to think about ways other than *shinju* to solve her problems. Japanese society rarely accuses the mother of infanticide. In Japan, or in other Asian countries where Confucianism is prevalent, conscious and unconscious symbiotic ties between oneself and significant others are very common and these kinds of relationships may be valued highly (Takahashi 1989). In this situation, murdering one's children can be unconsciously regarded as murdering a part of oneself. The mother may not necessarily realize that she is killing another human being separate from herself, but rather feels as though she is killing a part of herself. In the psychology of the mother who commits *boshi-shinju*, killing her own children is equivalent to actually killing herself, and this is interpreted as a kind of "extended suicide." It is impossible for her to imagine a world for her children after her death. Japanese society often gives sympathy to this psychodynamic. In addition, Japanese have a general reluctance to criticize one another, which may be related to a filial piety to the group. However, we should also note the proverb, *"Shinu kiga areba nandemo dekiru,"* which means, "If one has a will to die, one could do anything." This proverb probably reflects Japanese society's ambivalence to *shinju*, both praising and denigrating suicide.

Some *boshi-shinju* may be a way for a wife to get revenge on her husband. She may react to the discovery of her husband's having an extramarital affair, or a demand for divorce by killing her children in order to punish her husband, after which she commits suicide. In most of cases of *boshi-shinju*, however, there is a strong tendency for the mother to consider the children as an essential part of herself. In Japan, this tendency is observed even among parents with much older children. It is believed that children cannot or should not be left alone in the world where parent(s) have killed themselves. The children are killed before the parent commits suicide because they are loved deeply. It may also be that, because children are considered a part of the parent, the parent should take care of them. An alternative interpretation could be that pathological separation-individuation (in the Western sense), or an overly symbiotic oneness (in the Eastern sense) could have caused blurring of unconscious ego boundaries.

The concept of *amae* was popularized by Takeo Doi, a well-known

Japanese psychiatrist (Berger et al. 1994, Doi 1973). *Amae* may be described as a mutual dependency where the assurance of another's goodwill permits a certain degree of self-indulgence. Much of this process is unconscious and partly explains the insularity of Japanese society since foreigners cannot readily fit into this mutual goodwill interaction.

A Western concept that Doi felt was equivalent to *amae* is that of "passive object love" described by Michael Balint (1965). The importance of *amae* is that it is a harmonious state of affairs where one can be relieved of the burden of *on* and *giri*. When the unconscious expectations of *amae* fall apart or, if, for example, the mother feels she cannot provide an *amae* relationship for her children in the face of severe family conflict, this may be a risk factor for *shinju*. Shame and severance of one's connection to the group (family) are important factors as discussed above.

Western society, in contrast, would usually consider a child, even an infant, as having a separate existence from the parent. The concept of *oyako-shinju* could not easily take root in this cultural context. In Western society it would be felt that the suicidal mother chooses to kill her children for selfish motives. The converse is true in Japan, where the concept of children being separate from their parents has not taken root. (Although there is intervention by social agencies, children are rarely taken from their parents in abusive situations.) In the Western cultural context the mother is usually held responsible, and may be tried for murder. In Japan there would also be a court case, but the sentencing would likely be lighter and more sympathy would be given to the mother.

Although there are different unconscious dynamics involved here from those of Western psychology, we must emphasize that the adults involved in *shinju* do not represent the norm of Japanese society. They are usually individuals who become desperate due to a combination of life stressors, concomitant psychiatric illness such as depression or psychosis, and pre-morbid personality vulnerabilities (possibly a personality disorder) that when interact with certain cultural tendencies. The average psychologically healthy Japanese would not consider *shinju* as a solution to his or her problems. (The vast majority of Japanese who experience the family stressors thought to be associated with *shinju* do not engage in this behavior.)

As clinicians practicing in Japan, we have to weigh the risk of *shinju* carefully when we evaluate patients who may be at risk. If the patient has a poor social support system, therapists have to mobilize available resources and solicit as much support from relatives as possible in order to prevent *shinju*.

INSEKI-JISATSU

Throughout the history of Japan, there has been almost no period when suicide was prohibited by law. The exception was in the early eighteenth century when a cluster of *johshi* suicides (lovers' suicide pact) was triggered by melodramas written by Chikamatsu Monzaemon. The government prohibited *johshi* in order to prevent these suicides. If a *johshi* occurred, a funeral was prohibited, and the bodies were left in the public view at Nihonbashi Bridge for three days. If one died and the other survived, the survivor was convicted of murder.

The most widely known form of suicide outside of Japan is *harakiri*, or *seppuku*, which means suicide by stabbing one's abdomen. *Harakiri* was the ritual form of suicide practiced by feudal warriors to show that they accepted responsibility for their actions (Fusé 1985), and had its beginnings about one thousand years ago. Japanese warriors used to respect the abdomen because it was considered to be the seat of the soul, so when they assumed responsibility for some serious action or course of conduct, they would cut open their abdomen to demonstrate their innocence and bravery. Cutting one's abdomen itself was not a very effective way to kill oneself, so another person severed their neck. Since the late nineteenth century, when the Edo era ended, *harakiri* has rarely been practiced either as a form of suicide or as a punishment. The *harakiri* suicide of the famous Japanese novelist Yukio Mishima in 1970 was an extremely exceptional case, and astonished even the Japanese.

While contemporary Japanese do not commit suicide by *harakiri, inseki-jisatsu* is a form of suicide sometimes regarded as a way of taking responsibility. (*Inseki* means taking responsibility, and *jisatsu* means suicide in Japanese.) Fusé (1985), a sociologist and suicidologist, has been conducting suicide research from a cross-cultural perspective and noted that suicide often takes place when political or social scandals occur in Japan. Fusé noted an interesting difference here between Japan and the United States.

> Some of the officials who were found guilty in the Watergate Scandal, when on bail or after release from prison, wrote memoirs, and gave lectures. . . . Almost no one killed themselves suffering from the crime they committed. When scandals occur in Japan, persons who hold important information and feel loyal to the key figures, those who actually control affairs from behind the scenes, often commit suicide. It is rare for the key figures themselves to commit suicide. [p. 208]

The key differences here may relate to the strong bond people have to members of their group in Japan, reminiscent of the bond to the mother. (The other side of the coin is the strong exclusion of those not in the group.)

Japanese individuals feel an intense indebtedness to their group and, as noted above, their unconscious need to relieve this burden can result in their taking responsibility as a way to prevent ostracism from the group. This can be seen in everyday life where workers may work late into the night for fear that their co-workers would resent them if they left earlier than the rest of the group. While superficially it seems that the individual is sacrificing for the group, it is actually the unconscious and preconscious needs of the individual to maintain group acceptance that is expressed in one's self-sacrifice.

Ono (1991), in his discussion of the difference between the Western concept of social phobia and the Japanese concept of social phobia or *taijin kyoufu*, has stressed how Japanese evaluate themselves. The Western social phobics are concerned about their behavior as assessed by their own standards, while the *taijin kyoufu* patients assess this by the standards of others. This is related to two kinds of shame. In Western shame the feeling comes from the discrepancy between the person's own ego ideal and his behavior, resulting in anxiety that this discrepancy will be noticed by others. The Japanese type of shame, on the other hand, is characterized by the feeling that comes from the concern about how others view his/her behavior and from the fear that as others become aware of his/her shortcomings he/she will be excluded from the group of significant others.

The mass media in Japan have not recently reported suicide cases in an exaggerated fashion. This does not hold, however, for cluster suicides in young people or for suicides of those involved in political scandals. The mass media report such cases repeatedly and sensationally. While only the facts are briefly reported for ordinary suicides, great details of the behavior before the suicide and the methods of the suicide are often reported for *inseki-jisatsu*. They usually do not touch upon the psychiatric problems that might have existed in those killing themselves. There is also a trend for the suicide to be viewed as a way of taking responsibility for some wrongdoing.

Often, someone who has important information about the facts of the situation commits suicide and leaves a note saying something like, "I did nothing wrong. However, I have caused a great deal of trouble to my organization. Therefore, for this I will take responsibility by committing suicide." De Vos (1968) called exaggerated self-identification to a role given by others or an organization to which an individual belongs, "role narcissism." De Vos pointed out that suicide may take place because unconscious identification to a group (or its leader) is so strong that it becomes almost impossible to imagine dissolution of the group.

In Western culture, the high value placed on individuality does not lend itself to the type of suicide resulting from overidentification to a group (such as *inseki-jisatsu*); consequently, statistics are not available to compare with *inseki-jisatsu* in Japan.

CONCLUSION

Suicide is a complex human behavior that includes multiple unconscious processes and needs to be interpreted multidimensionally from a biopsychosocial perspective. Suicide should not be interpreted from a psychiatric or a cultural perspective alone but by an integrated view of these variables. We have presented a general overview of those unconscious and cultural factors involved in suicide in contemporary Japan as a way to foster an understanding of this variable, although there are other important aspects involved in any individual suicide.

REFERENCES

(Note: References preceded by an asterisk are written in Japanese.)

*Aizawa, S. (1975). Cultural background of shinju. In *Suicidology: Suicide and Culture*, ed. K. Ohara, pp. 142–182. Tokyo: Shibundo.

Balint, M. (1965). *Primary Love and Psychoanalytic Technique*. New York: Liverwright.

Berger, D. (1985). On the practice of medicine and on the culture and customs in Japan. *Tokai Journal of Experimental and Clinical Medicine* 10:637–645.

———— (1993). Suicide evaluation in medical patients: a pilot study. *General Hospital Psychiatry* 15:75–81.

Berger, D., Ono, Y., Kumano, H., and Suematsu, H. (1994). The Japanese concept of interdependency (letter). *American Journal of Psychiatry* 51:628–629.

Christopher, R. C. (1983). *The Japanese Mind*. Tokyo: Charles E. Tuttle.

De Vos, G. A. (1968). Suicide in cross-cultural perspective. In *Suicidal Behaviors: Diagnosis and Management*, ed. H. L. Resnik, pp. 235–245. Boston: Little, Brown.

Doi, T. (1973). *The Anatomy of Dependence*. Tokyo: Kodansha International.

Domino, J., and Takahashi, Y. (1991). Attitudes towards suicide in Japanese and American medical students. *Suicide and Life-Threatening Behavior* 21:345–359.

*Fukushima, A. (1984). Shinju. In *Kodansha's Comprehensive Dictionary of Psychiatry*, ed. H. Shinfuku, pp. 430–431. Tokyo: Kodansha.

*Fusé, T. (1985). *Suicide and Culture*. Tokyo: Shincho-sha.

*Inamura, H. (1977). *Suicidology: Treatment and Prevention*. Tokyo: Tokyo University Press.

*———— (1993). Recent characteristics, risk estimations and preventive methods of shinju (double suicide) in Japan. *Archives of Psychiatric Diagnostics and Clinical Evaluation* 4:173–184.

Japan Times. (1985). Japanese mother attempts suicide with two children in California, January 31, p. 2.

Mahler, M. (1972). Rapprochement subphase of the separation individuation process. *Psychoanalytic Quarterly* 41:487–506.

Marzuk, P. M., Tardiff, K., and Hirsch, C. S. (1992). The epidemiology of murder-suicide. *Journal of the American Medical Association* 267:3179–3187.

*National Police Agency. (1993). *National Police Agency's 1990 Annual Report*. Tokyo: Printing Section of Ministry of Finance.

Ohara, K. (1963). Characteristics of suicide in Japan: especially on parent–child double suicide. *American Journal of Psychiatry* 120:382–385.

*———— (1965). *Suicide in Japan: Understanding Solitude and Anxiety*. Tokyo: Seishin-shobo.

*———— (1985). Shinju. In *Encyclopedia of Psychiatry*, rev. ed., ed. M. Kato, H. Hozaki, Y. Kasahara, T. et al., pp. 330–331. Tokyo: Kohbundo.

Ono, Y. (1991). Presentation at the 2nd International Congress on the Disorders of the Personality, Oslo.

Sugiyama-Lebra, T. (1976). *Japanese Patterns of Behavior*. Honolulu: University of Hawaii Press.

Takahashi, Y. (1989). Suicidal Asian patients: recommendations for treatment. *Suicide and Life-Threatening Behavior* 19:305–313.

*———— (1992). *Clinical Evaluation of Suicide Risk and Crisis Intervention*. Tokyo: Kongo-shuppan.

———— (1993a). Suicide prevention in Japan. In *Suicidology: Essays in Honor of Edwin S. Shneidman*, ed. A. A. Leenaars, pp. 324–334. Northvale, NJ: Jason Aronson.

———— (1993b). Depression and suicide. In *Affective Disorders: Perspectives on Basic Research and Clinical Practice*, ed. T. Kariya, and M. Nakagawara, pp. 85–98. New York: Brunner/ Mazel.

Takahashi, Y., Hirasawa, H., Koyama, K., et al. (in press). Suicide and aging in Japan: an examination of treated elderly attempters. *International Psychogeriatrics*.

Walsh, L. (1969). *Read Japanese Today*. Tokyo: Charles E. Tuttle.

15: THE HEALING PATH: SUICIDE AND SELF-DESTRUCTIVE BEHAVIOR IN NORTH AMERICAN NATIVE PEOPLE

Edward A. Connors

THE PAST

There is evidence that suicide occurred in native communities in North America prior to contact with nonnative peoples (Barter and Weist 1970). This information demonstrates that at least some native tribes practiced suicide as a method of conflict resolution, in order to reunite with a deceased loved one, as a means of gaining honor and respect from the community, and to exit from life into the next life when one no longer felt oneself to be a productive member of the community. All of these forms of suicide were practiced in many tribes despite belief systems that emphasized a respect and reverence for life. In fact, most tribes embraced beliefs that acknowledged the Creator as the only entity that can determine when one's life was to end. Further, many tribes appear to believe that a person's spirit remains trapped in this world and does not pass onto the next life until the time predetermined by the Creator.

Despite these beliefs, suicide did exist within native communities. It is probable that where suicide occurred it was rationalized by the community as an act that was in compliance with superordinate mores. Generally speaking, the mores that often enabled death to be chosen over life were those of contributing to the healthiness of the tribe by choosing to remove oneself from this life. Since native peoples' worldviews (Ross 1992) tended to be oriented toward construing oneself as a part of the much larger whole, acts such as suicide would have been considered in this context.

This form of thought stands in sharp contrast to the forms of thought promoted by other racial groups that tend to place people at the top of a hierarchical structure of subservient entities. It allows a person to hold a very egocentric image of him- or herself, and thus suicide can be viewed as an act of aggression against society. The traditional native worldview, which is often referred to as holistic, tended to lead the native person to consider his/her movement from life within the context of the functional impact on the entire community and, to a degree, on all of creation. Therefore, suicide through the eyes of a traditional native person was often viewed as an act that would promote the health and survival of the larger group.

In the case of the warrior who forfeited his life when facing certain death, his suicidal act was inspired by the honor he and his relatives received from his promoting the continuance of the tribe. The native person who took her/his life after being treated disrespectfully or not in accordance with tribal custom invoked the tribe to correct the imbalance within the tribe by dealing harshly with the transgressor. Many of the people who violated tribal custom in such a way as to dishonor a person's spirit, such that the person would choose to leave this life, were banished from the tribe. Therefore, the suicide resulted in a reestablishment of balance within the community and the maintenance of a healthy lifestyle.

The suicidal action was not egocentrically motivated but ecocentrically guided, that is, behavior directed by a concern for maintaining health and survival of the group by maintaining balance between all of creation. The native persons who took their lives after a precious loved one died tragically and honorably often did so to further mark the value of their loved one's action in support of the healthy growth and survival of the community. Often the honorable suicide and related honorable events became part of the community folklore through story or song, which continued to promote the value that no greater love hath a person than giving one's life for the healthy continuation of one's people. This was the thinking of those native elders who, when they had decided they had become too much of a burden on their people, chose their time to enter into the next life. However, even this time was considered to be determined by the Creator and was, therefore, a spiritually condoned act.

THE PRESENT

If one understands the form of native thought before its transformation through the process of acculturation, it is possible to recognize that suicide was viewed in a very different light than it is considered today. In fact, suicide in traditional native culture was both rational and adaptive when viewed in the context of survival of the tribe and maintaining equilibrium within all of creation.

Most First Nations tribes of North America have prophecies that predicted the coming of other races to this land, the decline and suffering of native people through the early stages of the acculturation period, and the eventual resurgence of native people to health. It is prophesied that this time of healing among native people will lead to a sharing of native knowledge about healing with all races. This in turn will assist with a worldwide healing that will reestablish balance and harmony among all of creation so that we can survive in peace with one another. At this time the signs identified by native elders and those gifted with the ability to interpret the signs indicate that we are now entering into the period of world transformation and healing.

The period of acculturation on this continent began when the first contact occurred between the First Peoples of this land and Europeans. From that point, the process of acculturation began disconnecting native people form our holistic thinking and introduced the scientific, linear, reductionist thinking. By examining how this shift in thinking has affected the ability of First Nations peoples to maintain health we can begin to see the links between this change and self-destructive behavior.

It is evident from the accumulated anthropological evidence that native people, prior to contact with Europeans, had a sophisticated and effective system of healing that was based on their holistic worldview (Vogel 1970, Weatherford 1988). This healing system accepted that maintaining health and effecting healing required a knowledge of the interaction between the physical, mental, emotional, and spiritual.

It was understood that a healthy lifestyle rests upon one's ability to maintain a balanced commitment to growth and maintenance in all four areas. Failure to attend to growth of any one aspect of self can throw the entire organism into a state of imbalance, resulting in deterioration within the other realms of experience. For example, deterioration of physical well-being simultaneously affects emotional well-being, mental state, and spiritual well-being. This approach to illness offers a holistic systemic perception as opposed to the linear, reductionist form of thought used by European science and medicine. Consequently, native healing employed elements of diagnosis and treatment that addressed aspects of health and healing on all four planes.

For instance, healing within the Sweat Lodge of the Ojibway peoples in Northwestern Ontario offers physical healing through the release of toxins in bodily fluids, the ingestion of herbs, and the inhalation of herbal properties within the smoke of burnt offerings. At the same time the ritualistic ceremonies, combined with the physiological demands, often induce a trance state that promotes properties of psychological healing. During the course of the ceremony, the rituals employed create an atmosphere of trust, safety, and healing. Consequently, many people find this to be a haven of refuge in which they can bare their souls in an emotionally cathartic fashion. Finally, the rituals performed invoke the aid of many spirit guides and the Creator, who assist in the healing of the spirit. Some native people perceive the source of their illness to be related to their loss of spirit and therefore seek healing to restore their spirit. Among the Salish tribe of British Columbia their name for their shaman or "Indian Doctor" translates from Salish to English as "searcher of souls" (Jilek 1982, p. 145).

The above explanation of the Sweat Lodge ceremony is a translation into a reductionistic linear perspective. For the Ojibway people the process of healing is not broken down into its separate properties. Rather, holistic thought permits one to see the entire process as a complex, integrated whole. Therefore, spiritual, physical, psychological, and emotional healing are all the same thing and are inseparable.

HEALING PRACTICES

Within the holistic worldview there are many healing practices that were used by the Ojibway people to maintain health and overcome illness. These were in full use until interference from religious groups and the government occurred. By placing moral and legal restrictions on these practices non-native society limited these practices and forced native healers to go "underground." During this period of time, the prophecy of the decline and devastation of native peoples became reality as attempts were made to assimilate them by disconnecting them from their holistic worldview. In the realm of healing this meant that performing or engaging in traditional healing became punishable by imprisonment. Consequently, many of the important ceremonies, rituals, and practices that had once maintained the healthy balance within individuals, families, and community were no longer readily accessible. The ability to practice these healing ceremonies openly as part of the communities daily activities was removed.

As a consequence, the healing that once enabled native peoples to ward off such experiences as depression and helped people to restore their spirits when they became lost was removed. As the many destructive forces of acculturation took hold, the native communities were virtually defenseless. Self-destructive behavior has risen unabated to the point that the highest rates of suicide in North America are experienced within the native communities. In Canada the suicide rate in First Nations communities averages from three to five times the Canadian rates. One suicidologist who had collected data from a native community in Manitoba concluded,

> If the suicide rate in Winnipeg, a city of 600,000, was the same as that for Treaty Indians, we would have close to 500 documented suicides per year. At the Norway House rate for Treaty women, we would expect doctors in Winnipeg to see about 12,000 overdoses per year! Clearly, if the population of Winnipeg was overdosing at this rate, a major multi-million dollar public health campaign would be launched immediately. [Ross and Davis 1986 p. 331]

In contrast to the holistic worldview, the scientific, linear, reductionistic worldview promotes a form of thought that emphasizes focusing on the parts of the whole as opposed to viewing the entire picture. This way of thinking has promoted specialization of skills in areas of knowledge that are increasingly distant from the whole. In the pursuit of knowledge, this form of thought has fostered a belief that by tracing a continuous abstraction of the parts from the whole, we will eventually know everything we need to know about the whole. In the area of healing and maintenance of health this has meant that specialists have emerged in the areas of physical, mental, and spiritual health. Within each of these disciplines exist further subdisciplines. This approach to understanding appears to have produced an increasing ability to understand an aspect of a phenomenon and a decreasing ability to understand how all aspects of the phenomenon may interact to produce the event under examination.

This major shift of worldviews by First Nations peoples from the holistic to the reductionistic was accompanied by dramatic changes in lifestyle and adjustments in the state of well-being or health. It has produced a change in lifestyle that disrupted the balanced, healthy lifestyles that native peoples had enjoyed for hundreds of years. This imbalance was evidenced in the dramatic rise of self-destructive behaviors within native communities. While suicide had been present during the precontact period, it now was escalating out of control and had taken on a different character.

In the traditional native community, suicide was perceived as an act that maintained and promoted community stability, viability, and health. Now suicide has transformed, along with the changing thought processes of native peoples, into an act of violence against oppressive forces that are often unrecognized and mislabeled. This self-destructive behavior is often seen as the final act of empowerment for native people who have experienced powerless, identityless, meaningless, purposeless, and spiritless lives. As the painful consequences of acculturation and oppression mounts, for some, the only viable escape appears to be suicide.

Suicide is no longer perceived as a functional act that contributes to the survival of the race and the healthy balance of the community. Instead it is now an act of self-annihilation that reflects a society out of balance and unhealthy. The more native society has adopted the current scientific worldview and accompanying lifestyle of the other races, the more unbalanced and unhealthy it has become. Part of this unhealthiness has included self-destructive behavior. However, most First Nations peoples appear to be consciously unaware of how this process of acculturation has led to self-destructive behavior. This knowledge seems to be locked within their unconscious.

This case example demonstrates the healing process that often helps native people shift from a state of self-destruction to life promotion. This shift entails assisting people to become consciously aware of the connection between their anger, sadness, and despair and the disconnection from their cultural identity.

Robin was 13 years old when I was introduced to him by his adoptive parents. He is an Ojibway child who was adopted by a non-native couple when he was 2 years old. His adoptive parents had been asked by his biological mother to raise him because she had lost her husband and was unable to provide for Robin. Up until the time of his adoption Robin had been raised by his mother and her extended family within a remote First Nations community that had maintained some of their traditions and lifestyle. However, upon adoption Robin was moved with his new parents to a large non-native community where he was raised until we met.

At the time of our first contact Robin's parents were desperately searching for a psychotherapist who could help Robin and them. Apparently, from the time Robin joined their family he was demonstrating anger and had difficulty forming healthy emotional attachments. Despite his adoptive parents' efforts to form an emotional connection with him, he remained distant and angry. As a young child he showed his anger by destroying property. For example, he smeared his feces on the walls, destroyed household items, and nearly burned down the family home on a few occasions. He killed a family pet during his preadolescent years, and during his teen years he began lying, stealing, and using drugs. In an effort to correct his destructive behavior, Robin's adoptive parents sought help from numerous psychotherapists and on one occasion placed him in an inpatient treatment center. None of these interventions proved to have any appreciable effect on Robin's destructive behavior.

When we met I quickly recognized that part of Robin's difficulties stemmed from issues of abandonment and separation from his biological family. In part, his self-destructiveness and destructive behavior were related to anger that often results from complications that stem from the adoption process. This part was common to many adoptions regardless of the racial backgrounds of the adoptees. However, this was a cross-cultural adoption in which the adoptive parents had not realized the importance that cultural identity plays in healthy development. Even if they had understood this, they had limited ability to assist this child with the development of his Ojibway identity. In short, Robin was subjected to a complete acculturation process within the period of his short 13 years. While he was not able to articulate the source of his anger and discomfort, he did know that he did not fit in comfortably with his adoptive family or the community in which he had been raised.

The first step in assisting Robin involved reframing for him the reasons for his discomfort and anger. I told him that I did not believe he was crazy but rather that he was angry and frustrated because he had been disconnected from his personal and cultural identity and that those around him did not realize the importance of this information for him. Also, these people were not able to teach him the information that he sought. I then recommended to Robin and his adoptive parents that he be admitted to an Ojibway adolescent treatment program.

Within the treatment program Robin received daily counseling from Ojibway counselors, and for the first time in his life (aside from his first two years) he lived with his people and began to be reintroduced to his cultural ways. While the counseling proved to be helpful, the cultural components of the program seemed to have the greatest impact on Robin's behavior. He began attending daily sessions at the local Friendship Center (an Ojibway cultural center) where he met elders and other teachers who reintroduced him to his culture of birth. By the time he completed the treatment program he had joined an Ojibway drum group, had learned to sing in Ojibway and was learning to dance powwow. In addition, he had begun many other cultural learnings through his involvement with elders and counselors from the program.

Upon leaving the treatment program Robin requested that he be permitted to move to live within his First Nation community. Through counselors associated with the program he was able to contact his extended family who invited him to live with them. After Robin moved I resumed the counseling with him. By that point he had developed good relationships with elders from his community, had joined a drum group in the community, and was attending sweats regularly.

While my counseling with Robin did entail some reflection upon his past experiences of self-destruction and destructive behavior, this was limited. From the time shortly after Robin had entered the treatment program he had discontinued all overt self-destructive behavior and anger directed toward others. Our counseling sessions consisted mainly of Robin recounting his numerous discoveries about his cultural identity as he encountered new teachers and experiences. Metaphorically it was like watching a flower bloom after years of constricted growth. Or from another perspective, as unconscious needs became conscious, Robin was able to free himself from his self-destructive tendencies and turn his energies toward fulfilling his needs—to develop his identity as an Ojibway man. While Robin's healing has involved numerous steps— including reunification with his family—the major theme for his change appears to have been the acknowledgment that he could not live a healthy life unless he resumed his cultural identity. In fact, its denial appears to have been intimately linked with his tendency to direct anger toward himself and others. Since Robin has reconnected himself with his cultural identity and become consciously aware of how his separation from his family, community, and culture had produced anger and resentment within him, he has progressively reduced his destructive behavior.

This case history offers an example of how the disconnection from cultural identity can contribute to the self-destructive tendencies expressed by many First Nations youths today. This is a unique case that has been selected for the purpose of illustration; it is not my intention to imply that all self-destructive behavior expressed by First Nations youths can be understood in this manner. However, I do believe that the disconnection from cultural identity is an element behind most self-destructive behavior within First Nations people.

As stated in the above case history, the forced disconnection from cultural identity has produced anger and sadness, which has been only unconsciously understood. Since the source of this anger has generally not been consciously construed, the tendency has been to direct these feelings at the self. Therefore, a portion of the healing process must entail making the unconscious conscious. In other words, First Nations people must come to understand that much of the anger and sadness that we carry has been produced by the forced disconnection from our cultural identities and that we are not to blame for this process. Further, the identities that we have attempted to form based on the beliefs and practices of the other races who have come to this land may be leading us further down a path of self-destruction and the destruction of all of creation.

THE FUTURE

There is really no scientific or other method by which men can steer safely between the opposite dangers of believing too little or of believing too much. To face such dangers is apparently our duty, and to hit the right channel between them is the measure of our wisdom. [James 1920, p. 226].

What does the future hold for native people, considering our progressive movement into ill-health and self-destruction? Are we destined to destroy ourselves? I think not. Our prophecies tell of a healing time when native people will regain our health and eventually share our refound knowledge to help all races and all of creation restore harmony and balance on Mother Earth.

There is ample evidence that we have already begun our movement into the healing time. Many people of all races are speaking of the emergence of a new paradigm to replace the reductionistic model of the old science (Fosshage 1978, Proctor 1993, Schaef 1992). In fact, for more than thirty years many scientists have openly acknowledged that the reductionistic model is "not necessarily or always valid or that it is too narrowly conceived. It is not able to deal adequately with the experiences of illness in contemporary society" (Proctor 1993, p. 5). As an alternative to the reductionistic model Proctor believes that we are witnessing the emergence of the new environmental paradigm that explains illness and disease in terms of all aspects of our world environment and our bodies.

Interestingly, this new paradigm is remarkably similar to the holistic worldview of the traditional native society. Authors such as Knudston and Suzuki (1992) demonstrate the strong convergence of thought between elder scientists and native elders. Both groups provide their wisdom through a holistic, environmental paradigm. Could this convergence of knowledge, reemergence of native traditional wisdom, and sharing of knowledge between the races be the signs spoken of in the prophecies?

Within native communities there are numerous indicators of a powerful healing movement taking hold. The elders are teaching once again, and the young are beginning to seek this wisdom. Powwows are occurring with increasing frequency year round as native people recapture their identities through our traditions. The numerous healing ceremonies are reemerging from their hidden places and are being practiced openly. Young people are apprenticing in these healing arts, and people of other races are sharing interest in learning these healing ways. All of these changes are connected with a reemergence of holistic thinking among First Nations peoples.

Within the non-native society some researchers have begun to evolve alternative research models that will better match the environmental/holistic paradigms that underlie native healing practices (Fosshage 1978, Young et al. 1989). Their efforts appear to be facilitating the communication of healing knowledge that previously was ruled out by the causation paradigm. In Fosshage (1978), a number of authors begin to open the door to a new understanding of the healing process. They begin to expand our thinking about the possible sources of healing. In particular, they introduce causation thinkers to the greater potential for healing offered through an environmental/holistic paradigm.

Within native communities the healing offered from the medicines produced by the causation model have proven almost ineffective in dealing with the illnesses of native peoples. While the physical healing approaches have had some influence in fighting diseases, their overall impact appears to be dwarfed by the accumulating illnesses that are associated with the cures. For example, the warehousing of various unused medications within native homes has contributed to addictive behavior and serves as a method for many native persons' suicides. This model of healing often does not address the sources of the illness and may also produce illness.

Many native communities are beginning to recognize the limitations of non-native healing practices in addressing the healing needs within our communities. Consequently, many communities are reviving the traditional native healing practices and are seeking ways to integrate this knowledge with non-native healing within the new environmental paradigm. For native people this transition is a relatively easy one since traditional holistic thought is the source of the environmental paradigm.

Traditional native healing practices often assist native people to reconnect with the holistic worldview. This development, along with the emergence of the environmental paradigm, will lead to our healing and the healing of our communities and eventually the world community.

It could be argued that some of the recent cluster suicides of Canadian native youths can be viewed as representations of these youths' unconscious desires to contribute to the ultimate survival of their people. Perhaps this is the only meaningful action that they believed they could take that would draw attention to the illness of all of society and our struggle for survival. In effect their suicides could have been construed as their giving their lives for the survival of the community. From a traditional native viewpoint, these youths may be acting consistently with our traditional ways. They may be leaving messages and insights that will lead us back to the knowledge that we need to survive as native peoples and for the survival of all of creation.

Native people who engage in native healing practices appear to regain the knowledge they require to reestablish a balanced life. The Ojibway call this *Meno Bemadiziwin*—loosely translated this means the good life or healthy life. When referred to, it leads one to reflect on the knowledge or life ways that lead one to maintain balance and live a healthy, good life. The knowledge that comes through these healing ways consists of a sophisticated holistic perception that leads one increasingly to perceive health as a product of endless balanced relationships between all facets of creation. Certainly, this is a knowledge that all races require if peace, harmony, and survival are important goals.

The signs that our prophecies are unfolding provide hope that the future for all creation on our Mother Earth will be brighter. However, much hard work remains if we are to continue on the path of healing and not get sidetracked again on another self-destructive path. Native people have a knowledge of healing that will lead us out of this time of despair and will help all of creation to find the way to world health.

REFERENCES

Barter, J. T., and Weist, K. M. (1970). *Historical and Contemporary Patterns of Northern Cheyenne Suicide*. Unpublished manuscript.

Fosshage, O. (1978). *Healing*. New York: Human Sciences Press.

James, H. (1920). *Edited Letters of William James*, vol. 2. Boston: Atlantic Monthly.

Jilek, W. G. (1982). *Indian Healing*. Surrey, BC: Hancock House.

Knudston, P., and Suzuki, D. (1992). *Wisdom of the Elders*. Toronto: Stoddart.

Proctor, R. (1993). *Changing the way we think about health*. Paper presented at Royal Commission on aboriginal peoples: Roundtable on health and social issues, Vancouver, B.C., March.

Ross, C. A., and Davis, B. (1986). Suicide and parasuicide in a northern Canadian native community. *Canadian Journal of Psychiatry* 31:331–334.

Ross, R. (1992). *Dancing with a Ghost: Exploring Indian Reality*. Markham, Ont.: Octopus.

Schaef, A. W. (1992). *Beyond Therapy, Beyond Science*. San Francisco: Harper.

Vogel, V. (1970). *American Indian Medicine*. Norman, OK: University of Oklahoma Press.

Weatherford, J. (1991). *Native Roots: How the Indians Enriched America*. New York: Crown.

Young, D., Ingram, G., and Swartz, L. (1989). *Cry of the Eagle*. Toronto: University of Toronto Press.

Part VI
APPLICATIONS
FOR TREATMENT

Therapy with a suicidal patient is difficult. Yet, sound understanding should lead to better praxis. As a rule, suicidal people need to be aware of more than conscious processes of the suicidal mind. The suicidal solution, in fact, is chosen because of the lethal constriction — what one knows about one's own suicide is only a fragment. The clinician can be guided by his/her knowledge of the unconscious. Without this, it is likely that treatment will stagnate and/or be partial. Although the topic of treatment requires at least its own volume, Part VI outlines a few directions on the application of the unconscious to the treatment of suicidal people. It consists of two chapters: a perspective that working with the highly lethal person requires a different involvement, namely lowering the immediate risk, than traditional psychotherapy that would emphasize unconscious meaning, and a case discussion of the psychotherapy of a suicidal patient.

16: PSYCHOTHERAPY WITH SUICIDAL PATIENTS

Edwin Shneidman

It seems logical that before we consider what the psychotherapy of a suicidal person ought to be, we have some common understanding of the suicidal state itself. Of course, everybody agrees that suicide is an enormously complicated term, encompassing a wide variety (and different ranges) of dysphoria, disturbance, self-abnegation, resignation, terror-cum-pain — to mention but a few inner states that are involved. But perhaps nowhere is there as insightful a description of suicide in as few words as that found in the opening paragraph of Melville's *Moby Dick*: "a damp and drizzly November in my soul." For that is what, metaphorically, most suicide is: a dreary and dismal wintry gale within the mind, where the vital issue that is being debated is whether to try to stay afloat in a stormy life or willfully to go under to nothingness.

Suicide is the human act of self-inflicted, self-intended cessation (i.e., the permanent stopping of consciousness). It is best understood as a bio-socio-psychologico-existential state of malaise. It is obviously not a disease, and just as obviously a number of kinds of trained individuals other than physicians can help individuals who are in a suicidal state.

If we are to escape many of the current somewhat simplistic notions of suicide (especially those which totally equate a disease called suicide with a disease called depression), then we need to explicate what the suicidal state of mind is like. Our key source in this can be the ordinary dictionary — eschewing any nomenclature of technical and, especially, technically diagnostic terms. In the dictionary there are words, for example, angered, anguished, cornered, dependent, frustrated, guilty, helpless, hopeless, hostile, rageful, shamed, that will help us in our understanding. For us, in this chapter, two less common (but ordinary) dictionary words—*perturbation* and *lethality*—will be the keystone words of our understanding.

Perturbation refers to how upset (disturbed, agitated, sane–insane, discomposed) the individual is—rated, let's say, on a 1 to 9 scale. Lethality refers to how lethal the individual is, that is, how likely it is that he will take his own life—also rated on a 1 to 9 scale.

At the outset, I need to indicate what kinds of suicidal states I am talking about in order to indicate what kinds of psychotherapy are appropriate for them. We can arbitrarily divide the seriousness (or risk, or lethality, or suicidality) of all suicidal efforts (actions, deeds, events, episodes)—whether verbalizations (ordinarily called threats) or behaviors (ordinarily called attempts)—into three rough commonsense groupings: low, medium, and high. In this chapter, I shall focus on the suicidal events or deeds of *high* lethality, where the danger of self-inflicted death is realistically large and imminent; what one might ordinarily call high suicide risks. Of course, a suicide act (deed, occurrence, event, threat, attempt) *of whatever lethality* is always a genuine psychiatric situation and should be treated without any iatrogenic elements. Thus, in the treatment of the suicidal person there is almost never any place for the therapist's hostility, anger, sardonic attitudes, daring the patient, or pseudo-democratic indifference.

By focusing solely on the *psycho*therapeutic approaches to high suicide risks, it should be obvious at the beginning that this chapter is a moiety—omitting entirely (and advertently) the lively areas of treatment suicidal individuals receive by means of chemical, electrical, or institutional modalities.

Theoretically, the treatment of an acutely highly suicidal person is quite simple: It consists, almost by definition, of lowering his lethality level; in practice, this is usually done by decreasing or mollifying his level of perturbation. In short, we defuse the situation (like getting the gun), we create activity of support and care around the person, and we make that person's temporarily unbearable life just enough better so that he or she can stop to think and reconsider. The way to decrease lethality is by dramatically decreasing the felt perturbation.

Working intensively with a highly suicidal person—someone who might be assessed as 7, 8, or 9 on a 1 to 9 scale of lethality—as distinguished from someone of moderate or low lethality, is different from almost any other human encounter, with the possible exception of that of working intensively with a dying person—but that is another story. Psychotherapy with an intensely suicidal person is a special task; it demands a different kind of involvement. The goal is different—not that of increasing comfort, which is the goal of most ordinary psychotherapy, but the more primitive goal of simply keeping the person alive. The rules are therefore different, and it follows (or rather precedes) that the theoretical rationale is different.

At this juncture, I wish to make a distinction among *four* psychologically different kinds of human encounters: conversation (or "ordinary talk"); a hierarchical exchange; psychotherapy or a "professional exchange"; and, finally, clinical suicidology or working psychologically with a highly lethal person.

1. In ordinary talk or conversation, the focus is on the surface content (concrete events, specific dates, culinary details); on what is actually being said; on the obviously stated meanings; on the ordinary interesting (or uninteresting) details of life. Further, the social role between the two speakers is one in which the two participants are essentially equal. Each participant has the social right to ask the other the same questions which he or she has been asked by the other. The best example of ordinary talk is two friends conversing with one another.

2. In a hierarchical verbal exchange the two participants are socially, and hence psychologically, unequal. This difference may be imposed by the situation, such as the exchange between a military officer and an enlisted person, or it may be agreed to by the two involved parties, such as between a physician and a patient. In either instance, the two are not psychologically equal. For example, an officer or a physician can ask an enlisted person or a patient, respectively, certain personal questions to which a rational response is expected, that the person of "lower status" could not ask the other person in return without appearing impertinent or aberrant. Yet most of the talk is still on the surface, concerning the real details of everyday life.

3. In a professional psychotherapeutic exchange the focus is on feelings, emotional content, and unconscious meanings, rather than on what is apparently being said. The emphasis is on the latent (between-the-lines) significance of what is being said more than on the manifest and obvious content; on the unconscious meanings, including double-entendres, puns, and slips of the tongue; on themes that run as common threads through the content, rather than on the concrete details for their own sake. Perhaps the most distinguishing aspect of the professional exchange (as opposed to ordinary talk) is the occurrence of transference, wherein the patient projects onto the therapist certain deep expectations and feelings. These transference reactions often stem from the patient's childhood and reflect neurotic patterns of reaction (of love, hate, dependency, suspicion, etc.) to whatever the therapist may or may not be doing. The therapist is often invested by the patient with almost magical healing powers, which, in fact, can serve as a self-fulfilling prophecy and thus help the interaction become therapeutic for the patient. In this paragraph, the use of the words therapist and patient already implies that, of the two parties, one has tacitly agreed to seek assistance and the other has agreed to try to give it. The roles of the two participants, unlike those in a conversation, are, in this respect, not coequal. A therapist and a patient could not simply exchange roles.

4. In working as a clinical suicidologist with an individual who is highly suicidal, the focus is again different. In this situation, the attention is primarily on the lethality. Most importantly, what differentiates this modality of therapy from any other psychotherapy is the handling of the transference feelings. Specifically, the transference (from the patient to the therapist) and the countertransference (from the therapist to the patient)—especially those positive feelings of affection and concern—can legitimately be much more intense and more deep than would be seemly or appropriate (or even ethical) in ordinary psychotherapy where time is assumed to be endless and where it is taken for granted that the patient will continue functioning in life.

Working with a highly suicidal person demands a different kind of involvement. There may be as important a conceptual difference between ordinary psychotherapy with individuals where dying or living is not *the* issue and psychotherapy with acutely suicidal persons as there is between ordinary psychotherapy and ordinary talk.

The main point of working with a lethally oriented person—in the give and take of talk, the advice, the interpretations, the listening—is to increase that individual's psychological sense of possible choices and sense of being emotionally supported. Relatives, friends, and colleagues should, after they are assessed to be on the life-side of the individual's ambivalence, be closely involved in the total treatment process. Suicide prevention is not best done as a solo practice. A combination of consultation, ancillary therapists, and the use of all the interpersonal and community resources that one can involve is, in general, the best way of proceeding.

Recall that we are talking about psychotherapy with the highly suicidal persons—not one of low or even medium lethality. With this in mind—and keeping in mind also the four psychological components of the suicidal state of mind (heightened inimicality, elevated perturbation, conspicuous constriction of intellectual focus, and the idea of cessation as a solution)—then a relatively simple formula for treatment can be stated. That formulation concentrates on two of the four psychological components, specifically on the constriction and the perturbation. Simply put, the way to save a highly suicidal person is to decrease the constriction, that is, to widen the range of possible thoughts and fantasies (*from* the dichotomous two—either one specific outcome or death—*to* at least three or more possibilities for an admittedly less-than-perfect solution), and, most importantly—without which the attempt to broaden the constriction will not work—to decrease the individual's perturbation.

How does a psychotherapist decrease the elevated perturbation of a highly suicidal person? Answer: by doing anything and almost everything possible to cater to the infantile idiosyncrasies, the dependency needs, the sense of pressure and futility, the feelings of hopelessness and helplessness that the individual is experiencing. In order to help a highly lethal person, one should involve others; create activity around the person; do what he or she wants done — and, if that cannot be accomplished, at least move in the direction of the desired goals to some substitute goals that approximate those which have been lost. Remember that life — and remind the patient of this fact (in a kindly but oracular way) — is often the choice among terrible alternatives. The key to functioning, to wisdom, and to life itself is often to choose the least terrible alternative that is practicably attainable.

Taken down to its bare roots, the principle is: To decrease lethality one puts a hook on perturbation and, doing what needs to be done, pulls the level of perturbation down — and with that action brings down the active level of lethality. Then, when the person is no longer highly suicidal — the usual methods of psychotherapy can be usefully employed.

As to how to help a suicidal individual, it is best to look upon any suicidal act, whatever its lethality, as an effort by an individual to stop unbearable anguish or intolerable pain by "doing something." Knowing this usually guides us as to what the treatment should be. In the same sense, the way to save a person's life is also to "do something." Those "somethings" include putting that information (that the person is in trouble with himself) into the stream of communication, letting others know about it, breaking what could be a fatal secret, talking to the person, talking to others, proferring help, getting loved ones interested and responsive, creating action around the person, showing response, indicating concern, and, if possible, offering love.

I conclude with an example — actually a composite of several actual highly suicidal persons I have known.

CASE STUDY

A young woman in her twenties, a nurse at the hospital where I worked, asked me pleadingly if I would see her teenage sister whom she considered to be highly suicidal. The attractive, younger woman — agitated and tearful but coherent — told me, in the privacy of my office, that she was single, pregnant, and determined to kill herself. She showed me a small automatic pistol she had in her purse. Her being pregnant was such a mortal shame to her, combined with strong feelings of rage and guilt, that she simply could not "bear to live" (or live to bear?). Suicide was the *only* alternative, and shooting herself was the *only* way to do it. Either she had to be unpregnant (the way she was before she conceived) or she had to be dead.

I did several things. For one, I took out a sheet of paper and — to begin to "widen her blinders" — said something like, "Now, let's see: You could have an abortion here locally." ("I couldn't do that.") It is precisely the "can'ts" and the "won'ts" and "have to's" and "nevers" and "always" and "onlys" that are to be negotiated in psychotherapy. "You could go away and have an abortion." ("I couldn't do that.") "You could bring the baby to term and keep the baby." ("I couldn't do that.") "You could have the baby and adopt it out." ("I couldn't do that.") "We could get in touch with the young man involved." ("I couldn't do that.") "We could involve the help of your parents." ("I couldn't do that.") and "You can always commit suicide, but there is obviously no need to do that today." (No response.) "Now first, let me take that gun, and then let's look at this list and rank them in order and see what their advantages, disadvantages and implications are, remembering that none of them is perfect."

The very making of this list, my fairly calm and nonhortatory and nonjudgmental approach already had a calming influence on her. Within 15 minutes her lethality had begun to deescalate. She actually rank-ordered the list, commenting negatively on each item, but what was of critical importance was that suicide, which I included in the total realistic list, was now ranked third—no longer first or second.

She decided that she would, reluctantly, want to talk to the father of her child. Not only had they never discussed the "issue," he did not even known about it. But there was a formidable obstacle: He lived in another city, almost across the country and that involved (what seemed to be a big item in the patient's mind) a long distance call. It was a matter of literally seconds to ascertain the area code from the long distance operator, to obtain his telephone number from information, and then—obviously with some trepidation and keen ambivalence for her—to dial his number (at university expense), and with the support of my presence to speak to him directly.

The point is not how the issue was practically resolved, without an excessive number of deep or shallow interpretations as to why she permitted herself to become pregnant and other aspects of her relationships with men, and so forth. What is important is that it was possible to achieve the assignment of that day: to lower her lethality.

In general, any suicidal state is characterized by its transient quality, its pervasive ambivalence, and its dyadic nature. Psychiatrists and other health professionals are well advised to minimize, if not totally to disregard, those probably well-intentioned but shrill writings in this field which naively speak of an individual's right to commit suicide—a right which, in actuality, cannot be denied—as though the suicidal person were a chronic univalently self-destructive hermit.

A number of special features in the management of a highly lethal patient can be mentioned. Some of these special therapeutic stratagems or orientations with a highly lethal patient attend to or reflect the *transient, ambivalent,* and *dyadic* aspects of almost all suicidal acts.

1. A continuous, preferably daily, monitoring of the patient's lethality rating.

2. An active outreach; being willing to deal with some of the reality problems of the patient openly, where advisable; giving direction (sans exhortation) to the patient; actively taking the side of life. It relates to befriending and caring.

3. Use of community resources including employment, Veterans Administration (when applicable), social agencies, and psychiatric social work assistance.

4. Consultation. There is almost no instance in a psychiatrist's professional life when consultation with a peer is as important as when he is dealing with a highly suicidal patient. The items to be discussed might include the therapist's treatment of the case; his own feelings of frustration, helplessness, or even anger; his countertransference reactions generally; the advisability of hospitalization for the patient, and the like.

5. Hospitalization. Hospitalization is always a complicating event in the treatment of a suicidal patient but it should not, on those grounds, be eschewed. Obviously, the quality of care—from doctors, nurses, and attendants—is crucial.

6. Transference. As in almost no other situation and at almost no other time, the successful treatment of a highly suicidal person depends heavily on the transference. The therapist can be active, show his personal concern, increase the frequency of the sessions, invoke the magic of the unique therapist–patient relationship, be less of a *tabula rasa*, give transfusions of (realistic) hope and succorance. In a figurative sense, I believe that Eros can work wonders against Thanatos.

7. The involvement of significant others. Suicide is most often a highly charged dyadic crisis. It follows from this that the therapist, unlike his usual practice of dealing almost exclusively with his patient (and even fending off the spouse, the lover, parents, grown children), should consider the advisability of working directly with the significant other. For example, if the individual is male and married, it is important to meet his wife. The therapist must assess whether, in fact, she is suicidogenic; whether they ought to be separated; whether there are misunderstandings which the therapist can help resolve; or whether she is insightful and concerned and can be used by the therapist as his ally and cotherapist. The same is true for homosexual lovers, for patient and parent, and so forth. It is not suggested that the significant other be seen as often as the patient is seen, but that other real people in the suicidal patient's life be directly involved and, at the minimum, their role as hinderer or helper in the treatment process be assessed.

8. Careful modification of the usual canons of confidentiality. Admittedly, this is a touchy and complicated point, but the therapist should not ally

himself with death. Statements given during the therapy session relating to the patient's overt suicidal (or homicidal) plans obviously cannot be treated as a "secret" between two collusive partners. In the previous example of the patient who opened her purse and showed me a small automatic pistol with which she said she was going, that day, to kill herself, two obvious interpretations would be that she obviously wanted me to take the weapon from her, or that she was threatening me. In any event, I told her that she could not leave my office with the gun and insisted that she hand her purse to me. She countered by saying that I had abrogated the basic rule of therapy, namely that she could tell me anything. I pointed out that "anything" did not mean committing suicide and that she must know that I could not be a partner in that kind of enterprise. For a moment she seemed angered and then relieved; she gave me the gun. The rule is to defuse the potentially lethal situation. To have left her with a loaded gun would also leave her with a latent message.

9. Limitation of one's own practice to a very few highly lethal patients. It is possible to see a fairly large number of moderate and low-rated lethal patients in one's patient load, but one or two *highly* lethal patients seem to be the superhuman limit for most therapists at any given time. Such patients demand a great deal of investment of psychic energy and one must beware of spreading oneself too thin in his or her own professional life.

Working with highly suicidal persons borrows from the goals of crisis intervention: not to take on and ameliorate the individual's entire personality structure and to cure all the neuroses, but simply to keep him or her alive. That is the *sine qua non* of the therapeutic encounter with a suicidal person.

17: PSYCHOTHERAPY OF A
SUICIDAL PATIENT

Frank Auld

I was the supervisor of a recent graduate of the clinical psychology program at the university where I was then teaching when he saw the patient described in this chapter. His work provided me an opportunity to learn a great deal about the dynamics of suicide.

Mrs. A., a married woman in her late fifties, worked as an accounting clerk for a small business. Her two children (a boy and a girl) had grown up and were no longer living at home. Mrs. A. took an overdose of sleeping pills, was discovered by her husband when she was almost comatose, and was taken by the emergency medical service to the emergency room of a general hospital. There, they admitted her to the psychiatric ward. She stayed in the psychiatric ward for about ten days, then was discharged and referred for follow-up outpatient therapy.

When they first met, Mrs. A. told the therapist that she didn't know why she had overdosed herself. She should not have done that, she said; she believed that she had been wrong and thoughtless to cause others so much trouble. Her husband, she reported, was very upset with her for trying to kill herself, although she was not sure that she really wanted to die. Others would be better off, though, not to be burdened by her, she thought. She did not have much interest in anything.

Mrs. A. had little interest in therapy either. She came to therapy because she felt an obligation to come—as a good wife and dutiful mother, she should cooperate with the doctors who were trying to help her. She felt that she did not deserve to feel better or to live a more rewarding life.

Mrs. A.'s depression interfered with her effectiveness in her work. Because she felt so discouraged about achieving anything, she took for granted that she could not learn the new, computerized accounting system that her company was adopting, would be overwhelmed by the work load, could not protest the shifting of responsibilities to her from others, and could not object to the deficiencies in data used in her work, which she was given by others in the company. She felt unable to ask for instruction or help when she needed it; she would be simply paralyzed, unable to get started on her work.

At the same time, she believed that her work was so poor that she was in imminent danger of being fired. She could not judge whether this was a realistic concern because in fact her depression so immobilized her that she was not working as effectively as she should be. Although her boss expressed concern about her and tried to reassure her that he wanted her to succeed, she did not take much comfort from these reassurances.

Mrs. A.'s family life seemed rather bleak. She said that she thought her marriage was an average one, no better or worse than most. She acknowledged that her husband drank too much, and had for years, and that his drinking concerned her greatly. She believed, too, that he smoked far too much (about two packs a day) and was concerned about the effects of his smoking on his health. When she had told him she was worried about his drinking, he brushed her concerns aside, saying that he had no drinking problem.

Mrs. A. and her husband spent little time together, shared few interests, and seemed not to provide much emotional support for each other. He was absorbed in his work and in his own pastimes — golfing and his home workshop — and spent little time with her.

At the same time, Mrs. A. could not have been much fun to be with. She could hardly drag herself out of bed each day; she did not feel like cooking, cleaning the house, or shopping for groceries. She was gloomy, and she blamed herself for dragging other people down.

A psychiatrist had prescribed antidepressant medication, but she so despaired of anything helping her that she neglected to take it.

ATTEMPTS TO ESTABLISH A WORKING ALLIANCE

For therapy to be effective, the patient and the therapist must arrive at a common understanding of the goals of the therapy and commit themselves to achieving those goals. Thus a patient like Mrs. A., who anticipates that nothing good can come of her efforts, in therapy or in any other endeavor, will find it hard to ally herself with her therapist.

Mrs. A. had great difficulty in talking at all. Invited to speak her thoughts as they came to her, she would remain silent for long stretches.

Asked about the events of her daily life, or about what she felt about her experiences in her life (for example, what satisfactions and what frustrations she had in her marriage), she found little to say.

As the therapist prodded Mrs. A. to talk, and as he tried to encourage her to adopt as a goal for the therapy that she would feel less defeated by life and less hopeless about ever feeling satisfaction in living, a theme emerged: Mrs. A. regarded herself as a thoroughly bad person who deserved to suffer because she had not pleased others and had, instead, caused them a great deal of trouble by making an attempt at suicide.

To make matters worse, Mrs. A. came late to the therapy sessions more often than not. Sometimes she failed to show up at all. After Mrs. A. had missed a couple of sessions and had been late for half a dozen other sessions, on the next occasion when she had not appeared within ten minutes of the appointed time the therapist called her to find out whether she was coming. It turned out that Mrs. A. was at home, was not sick or otherwise prevented from coming, but had just not started out for the therapy session. The therapist urged her to come for whatever time would remain after she got to the clinic. (It took her about twenty minutes to travel from her house to the clinic.) On several subsequent occasions, as well, the therapist called the patient when she had not appeared within five to ten minutes after the appointed time, and urged her to come. He reasoned that her deep discouragement, with therapy and with everything else, was interfering with her ability to take any action; accordingly, demonstrating that he believed that the therapy was worthwhile and that she ought to come might help her to develop the conviction that therapy offered some hope.

ATTEMPTS AT INTERPRETATION

When a person is as deeply discouraged as this patient, urging action and offering support are not likely to be sufficient to overcome the patient's inertia. Recognizing this, the therapist attempted to interpret the patient's inner conflicts (Auld and Hyman 1991). First he had to formulate to himself what these conflicts were.

When a person expects that life will not be rewarding, one naturally wonders what has gone wrong with the most important interpersonal relationships of this person. When the person is married, one wonders what satisfactions are missing in the marriage.

Mrs. A.'s marriage seemed quite barren of reward. More than that, she hinted that her husband generally ignored her and that, when he did pay any attention to her, he tried to dominate her, disregarding her needs. Her husband drank more than his wife thought was good for him. He was unpleasant to others when he had been drinking. For example, when they (very rarely) had guests at the house, he often insulted the guests.

The therapist suggested that Mrs. A.'s marriage could not be very satisfying to her. He proposed that she must find her husband's failure to meet her needs very frustrating. He proposed, further, that inwardly she must feel a good deal of resentment at her husband for this.

Although Mrs. A. acknowledged that her marriage was not terribly satisfying, she denied that she harbored any resentment about it. That was just the way it was, and she could not do anything about it anyway. She really did love her husband—or, at least, wish him well—even though they had little in common, particularly now that their children were grown and gone. She did feel some bitterness at his having drunk so much in the past; but now he was drinking a good deal less.

The therapist also made interpretations of Mrs. A.'s tendency to blame and disparage herself. He pointed out, for instance, her guilt over having caused trouble to others through the suicide attempt. He probed for object representations toward whom Mrs. A. unconsciously felt anger, which had been displaced toward herself. He asked about her relationships, earlier, with her mother and with her father, and tried to figure out the identifications she had with them. In pursuing these inquiries the therapist was guided by Freud's (1917) hypotheses in *Mourning and Melancholia* about how object attachments, ambivalences, identifications, and object losses are related to depression.

In responding to these inquiries, Mrs. A. provided scant material. The therapist got the impression that her relationship with her father had provided her with very little satisfaction; he seemed a distant and unsupportive figure. She did not speak of her mother with any great warmth. She felt as much closeness to her sister as to anyone.

About these relationships and about her experiences in general Mrs. A. could speak in only the most general terms. Was this because she had always been that way—hardly aware of her feelings—or was it a *result* of her depression? If she had always had difficulty in knowing what her feelings were, she would fit the description that Krystal (1988) has given of persons who have trouble coming up with words to describe their feelings. Krystal called this difficulty *alexithymia*. This word, coined from the Greek, means "not having words for feelings." According to Krystal, those who are traumatized early in their lives—who suffer important object losses—frequently develop alexithymia.

It is clear that Mrs. A.'s lack of hope that therapy could be helpful—which may have been the main reason for her frequently coming late for therapy sessions and for her failing to show up for about half of the scheduled appointments—presented a major obstacle to effective therapy. Therefore the therapist tried to overcome Mrs. A.'s mistrust of therapy through interpreting this lack of hope, through interpreting her disappointments in the therapist (some of these perhaps provoked by the therapist's actual disappointing actions, some provoked by transferences), and through interpreting other aspects of the transference. He pointed out, for instance, that she believed herself to be unworthy of having anyone give her undivided attention, much as she longed for it, and therefore found it necessary to avoid the intense guilt she would feel if she relaxed and enjoyed communicating to the therapist. It seems that none of these interpretations was very effective, because Mrs. A. continued to have great difficulty talking when she came to therapy, usually late, and more often than not did not come at all.

COUNTERTRANSFERENCES TO THIS RESISTANCE

The reader should have the impression by now that Mrs. A. was a very difficult, even infuriating, patient. The reader would be right. The therapist struggled with intense feelings of anger at the patient for her frequently standing him up, with feelings of inadequacy and helplessness at the ineffectiveness of his interventions, and with anxiety that she would try suicide again for which he would be blamed. The therapist felt intense dislike for Mrs. A.'s husband, whom she had described as almost totally insensitive to her needs. The therapist felt strong impulses to rescue this hapless person, to mother her.

In dealing with the countertransference, the therapist first had to become aware of his feelings that had been preconscious or unconscious. Then he had to examine the interaction between him and Mrs. A. to try to understand what had provoked the countertransference feelings. For instance, he asked himself whether she intended to infuriate him — and why — and if so, how he could interpret this. He had to remind himself that the best way for him to prevent her succeeding in killing herself was to stick to his task of understanding her inner life and of enabling her, too, to acquire some understanding of it. He reasoned that if this approach did not work, probably nothing would.

To keep from acting inappropriately on these reactions to his patient (some of them being conscious, and therefore not countertransference, strictly speaking), the therapist had to examine them and decide what actions of his would be adaptive. The therapist had to remind himself that he saw the patient's husband through her eyes, probably not as the husband in fact was. In any event, Mrs. A. in describing him as such a monster was trying to evoke pity and mothering from the therapist. Would it not be better to recognize this process, to point it out to Mrs. A. when there seemed to be some chance that she could accept that kind of interpretation, and to abandon his belief that he was more loving and more virtuous than others, especially her husband?

The therapist did, of course, urge Mrs. A. to take the antidepressant medication that had been prescribed for her. And he did, in the manner of Klerman and colleagues (1984), challenge the self-defeating interpersonal strategies that Mrs. A. often enacted—for example, her blaming herself, her withdrawing from others, and her becoming immobilized when she became angry at her husband, rather than challenging her husband about what he did that had angered her.

LATER DEVELOPMENTS IN THE THERAPY

With the best efforts of the therapist, Mrs. A. seemed to get only slightly better and slightly less depressed. She became even more irregular in attending therapy sessions, and at length she stopped coming altogether. The therapist telephoned her to find out whether she wanted to come at all, and she told him that she did not. He agreed that they would discontinue the therapy. He said that he thought she could benefit from more therapy and that he stood ready to continue the therapy when she wanted to pick it up again. He made clear that if she felt very depressed or felt suicidal, he wanted her to call him. If she should feel suicidal again, he pointed out, checking into a hospital would offer some protection from her acting on the suicidal thoughts.

Several months later, Mrs. A.'s husband discovered that he was suffering from prostate cancer. He was operated on, and it was necessary for Mrs. A. to offer a great deal of care and support to him throughout his medical crisis and his recovery. She did this with rather good grace, although she found it a strain to provide so much nurturance to a person who had not been as nurturing to her, earlier, as she had wanted him to be.

Mrs. A. called the therapist and asked for a therapy appointment. The therapy resumed and continued for some months. Throughout this period, the therapy focused on Mrs. A.'s quite ambivalent feelings toward her husband. Then she dropped out of therapy again.

Some months after this, the therapist received a call from Mrs. A.'s sister, who reported that Mrs. A. was deeply depressed and was expressing suicidal thoughts. The therapist asked to talk with Mrs. A. on the telephone. He discussed with her the advantages to her of going into the psychiatric ward of a general hospital or into a psychiatric hospital, and urged her to go to one or the other until she had better control of her suicidal impulses. He pointed out that her suicidal intent would probably subside, if she stayed alive, but it could not diminish if she killed herself; she would have no chance for second thoughts. He interpreted some of the hostility toward others lying behind her suicidal intent.

She did in fact decide to check herself into the hospital, and she did so that night. The therapist did not continue his psychotherapy with Mrs. A. after this second hospitalization; she did not ask to meet with him.

A QUICK BOW TO SYSTEMATIC RESEARCH

Before writing up this case history I canvassed the literature on psychodynamic explanations of suicide, looking especially for systematic research (rather than case-history material) that would support or refute psychoanalytic formulations. I know that case histories have some value for science (Dollard 1935). Allport (1942) also argued that case studies can contribute to knowledge.

Still, we have to ask how case studies contribute to knowledge. Are they useful only for giving us hunches about what may be true, for helping us to generate hypotheses, but not for verification, not for distinguishing between what is true and what is not? Grünbaum (1993) has argued that case studies are heuristic but cannot, without help from other observations made systematically and in the framework of better control of variables and better replicability of observations, bear the burden of verifying or refuting psychoanalytic hypotheses. I find his argument persuasive.

Therefore, I looked for systematic, empirical studies that would bear on various psychoanalytic hypotheses about the dynamics of suicide. I found good summaries of psychoanalytic hunches about why people kill themselves and about research bearing generally on the dynamics of suicide. Among the more useful summaries of this literature are reviews by Hendin (1991, 1992), Buie and Maltsberger (1989), Furst and Ostow (1979), and Lester (1992).

Some of the research summarized in these reviews relies on impressions developed while the researcher was doing clinical work with suicidal persons, whereas other research relies on case studies. Other papers included in these surveys, or included in the PsychINFO data base, make use of comparisons between those who seem more prone to suicide (for example, those in a college-student sample who say they have seriously considered suicide) with those presumably less prone to suicide (who do not report such thoughts). Very few of the more systematic studies, however, were pertinent to psychoanalytic hypotheses.

Research in Windsor

The research on suicide done in Windsor constitutes a little-known body of systematic research (that is, research not relying on impressions or on case studies) on the psychodynamics of suicide. The work done includes studies by Leenaars (1988), Cohen (1990), and Szabo (1992).

Leenaars (1988), an independent researcher in Windsor, developed an ingenious way to generate implications of a theory of suicide and to test whether such implications matched what one observes in the suicide notes of persons who killed themselves. If we find that these expected characteristics of the notes indeed occur more strongly in real suicide notes than in notes produced by persons, not suicidal, who have been instructed to write "suicide notes," we have evidence for the validity of the hypotheses. (The device of comparing genuine and made-up suicide notes was invented by Shneidman and Farberow [1957].) Leenaars derived ten descriptive statements from each of ten theories of suicide, then checked whether these descriptions matched the observed differences between genuine and simulated suicide notes. For the statements derived from Freud's writings, five of the ten statements were congruent, to a statistically significant degree, with raters' judgments about the content of the notes; this was a better match of theory with observation than Leenaars obtained for any of the other theories.

Cohen (1990), a graduate student at the University of Windsor, comparing adolescents who had considered suicide, adolescents who came to a psychiatric clinic but did not have suicidal ideation, and adolescents who were neither suicide ideators nor clinic attenders, found that a lack of gratification of the person's need for maternal empathy was most character-istic of the suicidal-ideation group. Finally, Szabo (1992), a graduate student at the University of Windsor, took up the hypothesis that turning of anger against the self is a prime mechanism leading to suicide, and found substantial support for this proposition.

These studies show that it is possible to design and carry out studies testing psychodynamic hypotheses about suicide. It is to be hoped that others, too, will do research on psychodynamic hypotheses, thereby changing our uncertainties about these hypotheses into confirmation or disconfirmation. We would expect that some psychoanalytic hypotheses will be confirmed, while others will be refuted.

PRINCIPLES DEMONSTRATED IN THIS CASE

The most obvious lesson of the therapy case presented here is that the therapy of a suicidal patient is difficult. The patient's motivation for therapy is marginal, the patient's feelings toward important persons in her/his life are ambivalent, and the hopelessness that the patient feels about everything in his or her life applies also to the therapy.

All of the principles of psychotherapy in general apply to work with the suicidal person. The therapist will meet resistances and have to interpret them. The therapist will see transferences and have to deal with them. Countertransferences are generated within the therapist, who will have to become aware of them and decide on an appropriate way to manage them. The therapist will have the task of defining with the patient the goals of the therapy and of building a working alliance.

There is no simple formula explaining suicide that will provide a royal path to understanding the patient's suicide attempt and to enabling the patient to overcome the suicidal impulses. It seems often to be true that the patient feels anger toward some important person in her life (as Mrs. A. did toward her husband); but interpreting that does not take care of the whole problem; it is more complicated than that. It often seems that the patient has a deep problem with self-esteem, a pervasive sense of helplessness, as Bibring (1953) pointed out. Closing the gap between the patient's aspirations and his actual achievements (as Bibring suggested) is a worthy goal. The therapist's experience in this case shows that such a goal is not easy to attain.

Exploring the patient's fantasies about the meaning of death—for example, death as a suitable punishment for one's hostile thoughts toward others, or as a way to put an end to a chronically unsatisfying life situation— also does not, by itself, clear up all difficulties.

It seems that we have to resign ourselves to therapeutic work that is frustrating most of the time. We are often not able to be sure, if the patient does not later kill herself (or himself), that what we have done made the difference. Yet from all of this uncertainty, we come away with the impression that the therapist's relationship to the patient plays a decisive role in the outcome. In this case the therapist was able to persuade Mrs. A. that she should check into the hospital. If he had not been previously involved with her in psychotherapy for almost a year, he could not have had this impact on her.

Thus, despite his feelings about the effectiveness of the psychotherapy, he had been successful!

REFERENCES

Allport, G. W. (1942). *The Use of Personal Documents in Psychological Science*. New York: Social Science Research Council.

Auld, F., and Hyman, M. (1991). *Resolution of Inner Conflict: An Introduction to Psychoanalytic Therapy*. Washington, DC: American Psychological Association.

Bibring, E. (1953). The mechanism of depression. In *Affective Disorders: Psychoanalytic Contribution to their Study*, ed. P. Greenacre, pp. 13–48. New York: International Universities Press.

Buie, D. H., and Maltsberger, J. T. (1989). The psychological vulnerability to suicide. In *Suicide: Understanding and Responding*, ed. D. Jacobs, and H. N. Brown, pp. 59–71. Madison, CT: International Universities Press.

Cohen, D. R. (1990). *A Multidimensional Study of Adolescent Suicidal Ideation*. Unpublished doctoral dissertation, University of Windsor, Windsor, Canada.

Dollard, J. (1935). *Criteria for the Life History—with Analysis of Six Notable Documents*. New Haven: Yale University Press.

Freud, S. (1917). Mourning and melancholia. *Standard Edition* 14:237–258.

Furst, S. S., and Ostow, M. (1979). The psychodynamics of suicide. In *Suicide: Theory and Clinical Aspects*, ed. L. D. Hankoff, and B. Einsidler, pp. 165–178. Littleton, MA: PSG.

Grünbaum, A. (1993). *Validation in the Clinical Theory of Psychoanalysis*. Madison, CT: International Universities Press.

Hendin, H. (1991). Psychodynamics of suicide, with particular reference to the young. *American Journal of Psychiatry* 148:1150–1158.

———— (1992). The psychodynamics of suicide. *International Review of Psychiatry* 4:157–167.

Klerman, G. L., Weissman, M. M., Rounsaville, B. J., and Chevron, E. S. (1984). *Interpersonal Psychotherapy of Depression*. New York: Basic Books.

Krystal, H. (1988). *Integration and Self-Healing: Affect—Trauma—Alexithymia*. Hillsdale, NJ: Analytic Press.

Leenaars, A. A. (1988). *Suicide Notes: Predictive Clues and Patterns*. New York: Human Sciences Press.

Lester, D. (1992). *Why People Kill Themselves*, 3rd ed. Springfield, IL: Charles C Thomas.

Shneidman, E., and Farberow, N. (1957). *Clues to Suicide*. New York: McGraw-Hill.

Szabo, P. (1992). *The Role of Hostility Against Self in Suicide Attempt*. Unpublished doctoral dissertation, University of Windsor, Windsor, Canada.

APPENDIX: SUICIDE
AND THE UNCONSCIOUS:
A BIBLIOGRAPHY

We conducted a search using PsycINFO and Medline for publications whose titles and abstracts contained the words "suicide" and "unconscious" during the period 1967 to 1993. The list of publications identified is shown below.

Asch, S. S. (1980). Suicide, and the hidden executioner. *International Review of Psycho-Analysis* 7(1):51-60.

Brandwin, M. A., and Blunt, L. W. (1968). Suicidal emergencies in a university medical center: a five- and ten-year comparison. *Comprehensive Psychiatry* 9(6):551-562.

Deikel, S. M. (1974). The life and death of Lenny Bruce: a psychological history. *Life-Threatening Behavior* 4(3):176-192.

Dolan, Y. (1989). "Only once if I really mean it": brief treatment of a previously dissociated incest case. *Journal of Strategic and Systemic Therapies* 8(4):3-8.

Faber, M. D. (1978-1979). Seneca, self-destruction, and the creative act. *Omega* 9(2):149-165.

Fish, W. C., and Waldhart-Letzel, E. (1981). Suicide and children. *Death Education* 5(3):215-222.

Fortuna, J. W., and Podvoll, E. M. (1980). The psychotic journey: II. Paradise lost: a case study. *Naropa Institute Journal of Psychology* 1(1):32-44.

Frances, R. J., Wikstrom, T., and Alcena, V. (1985). Contracting AIDS as a means of committing suicide. *American Journal of Psychiatry* 142(5):656.

Frederick, C. J. (1971). The present suicide taboo in the United States. *Mental Hygiene* 55(2):178-183.

Hendin, H. (1991). Psychodynamics of suicide, with particular reference to the young. *American Journal of Psychiatry* 148(9):1150-1158.

——— (1992). The psychodynamics of suicide. *International Review of Psychiatry* 4(2):157-167.

Janov, A. (1974). Further implications of "levels of consciousness": on suicide. *Journal of Primal Therapy* 1(3):197-200.

Johnson, W. D. (1991). Predisposition to emotional distress and psychiatric illness amongst doctors: the role of unconscious and experiential factors. *British Journal of Medical Psychology* 64(4):317-329.

Kaplan, H. B., and Pokorny, A. D. (1976). Self-derogation and suicide: II. Suicidal responses, self-derogation and accidents. *Social Science and Medicine* 10(2):119-121.

Kincel, R. L. (1981). Suicide and its archetypal themes in Rorschach record study of a male attempter. *British Journal of Projective Psychology and Personality Study* 26(2):3-11.

Leenaars, A. A. (1986). Brief note on latent content in suicide notes. *Psychological Reports* 59(2, Pt. 1):640-642.

——— (1992). Suicide notes of the older adult. *Suicide and Life-Threatening Behavior* 22(1):62-79.

Lester, D. (1971). Ellen West's suicide as a case of psychic homicide. *Psychoanalytic Review* 58(2):251-263.

Martin, W. T. (1984). Religiosity and United States suicide rates, 1972-1978. *Journal of Clinical Psychology* 40(5):1166-1169.

McLister, B., and Leenaars, A. A. (1988). An empirical investigation of the latent content of suicide notes. *Psychological Reports* 63(1):238.

Meyer, W. S. (1985). The Oedipus complex: a reminder of its clinical import. *Clinical Social Work Journal* 13(3):234-245.

Pfeffer, C. R. (1979). Clinical observations of play of hospitalized suicidal children. *Suicide and Life-Threatening Behavior* 9(4):235-244.

Rice, E. (1973). Fantasy, masturbation, and suicide. *International Journal of Psychoanalytic Psychotherapy* 2(2):194-220.

Rosenberg, M. (1967). On accidents and incidents: a study of self-destruction. *Comprehensive Psychiatry* 8(2):108-118.

Sabbath, J. C. (1971). The role of the parents in adolescent suicidal behavior. *Acta Paedopsychiatrica* 38(7-8):211-220.

Winnik, H. Z. (1976). On suicide. *Mental Health and Society* 3(3-4):175-177.